JOURNAL FOR THE STUDY OF THE NEW TESTAMENT
SUPPLEMENT SERIES
84

Executive Editor
Stanley E. Porter

JSOT Press
Sheffield

Marinus de Jonge

From Jesus to John

Essays on Jesus and New Testament Christology in Honour of Marinus de Jonge

edited by
Martinus C. De Boer

Journal for the Study of the New Testament
Supplement Series 84

Published by JSOT Press
JSOT Press is an imprint of
Sheffield Academic Press Ltd
343 Fulwood Road
Sheffield S10 3BP
England

Typeset by Sheffield Academic Press
and
Printed on acid-free paper in Great Britain
by Biddles Ltd
Guildford

British Library Cataloguing in Publication Data

From Jesus to John:
Essays on Jesus and New Testament Christology
in Honour of Marinus de Jonge.—
(JSNT Supplement Series, ISSN 0143-5108;
no. 84)
I. Boer, Martinus C. De II. Series
232

ISBN 1-85075-422-5

CONTENTS

PREFACE

The essays in this volume are offered to Marinus de Jonge, Professor
of New Testament and Early Christian Literature at the University of
Leiden from 1966 until his retirement at the end of 1990. He is perhaps best known outside his native land for his provocative and foun-
dational work on the *Testaments of the Twelve Patriarchs*, about
which he has published numerous books and articles, beginning with
his doctoral dissertation in 1953. However, he is also much admired
for his New Testament scholarship, especially in the area of
Christology, and for that reason the present volume of essays in his
honour is devoted to this theme.[1]

Particularly in his work as a New Testament scholar, de Jonge has
consistently regarded himself not only as a historian but also as a
theologian. In his inaugural lecture at Leiden in 1966, *De Nieuwtesta-
menticus als Historicus en Theoloog*,[2] he eloquently maintained that
the New Testament scholar must be both, if justice is to be done to the
nature of the documents themselves and to the humanity of those who
wrote them and now interpret them. To allow biblical authors to
speak their own minds in their own language, de Jonge here argued,
the New Testament interpreter has to acknowledge the cultural and
linguistic 'distance' between people living today and the biblical
writers. The very particular situations in which the documents were
composed can also not be ignored. For such reasons, the New
Testament scholar must be a historian making rigorous, scientific use
of the historical-critical tools requisite to historical reconstruction and

1. A full bibliography of his writings has been compiled by his close associate
and successor, H.J. de Jonge (no relation). This bibliography, containing 286
items (!) and still counting, is appended to a collection of M. de Jonge's scholarly
articles, *Jewish Eschatology, Early Christian Christology and the Testaments of the
Twelve Patriarchs: Collected Essays of Marinus de Jonge* (ed. H.J. de Jonge;
NovTSup, 63; Leiden: Brill, 1991), pp. 314-26.
2. Leiden: Brill, 1966.

understanding. But the New Testament scholar must also be a theologian
who recognizes that genuine 'listening' to the New Testament authors
and what they have to say inevitably leads to 'engagement' with the
theological subject matter. It cannot be overlooked that the various
New Testament documents were written to elicit, strengthen, defend
and correct faith in Jesus as God's final emissary and representative.
Furthermore, the New Testament authors and their audiences were
living, breathing human beings, and the New Testament scholar is no
different. He or she is no mere cataloguer of interesting bits of
historical information. For such reasons, the claims of contemporary
relevance cannot finally be evaded or suppressed. In de Jonge's eyes, a
New Testament scholar claiming to be either a historian or a theologian
brings sure distortion to both historical and theological understanding
of the New Testament.[1]

De Jonge's stance is exhibited not only in his writings on the New
Testament, but also in his professional career. Prior to taking up an
academic appointment at Groningen in 1962, he was for many years a
full-time preacher and pastor within the Reformed Church of the
Netherlands. De Jonge pursued his scholarly interests while still a full-
time pastor and continued to serve the church throughout his full-time
academic career. His work as a historian and a theologian converged
most visibly in his efforts as a translator with the Dutch Bible Society
from 1962 to 1973, a task that took advantage of his considerable
philological skills as well.

Indeed, de Jonge evidently regards all his activity as an exercise in
appropriate 'translation'. He has described himself as someone 'who is
occupied in scholarly work on the Bible, especially the New
Testament, and who constantly tries to ask how he must now put into
words and can translate into deeds what is found in the Bible'.[2]
Regrettably if understandably, apart from the volume just quoted, his
written efforts at 'translation' are mostly available only in Dutch.[3]

---

1.   More recently, de Jonge has written that 'research in early Christianity
requires the tools and abilities of the philologist, the literary critic, the historian and
the theologian' (*Collected Essays*, p. xvii).

2.   *Jesus, Inspiring and Disturbing Presence* (Nashville: Abingdon Press,
1974).

3.   Here we may highlight two brief volumes: *Taal en Teken: Ontmoetingen met
Jezus in het evangelie van Johannes*, with H.M.J. van Duyne (Nijkerk: Callenbach,
1978) and *Van tekst tot uitleg: Luisteroefeningen in het Nieuwe Testament*, with

There are, however, numerous people in many lands speaking diverse languages who can testify from personal experience to his successful 'translation' in word and in deed of 'what is found in the Bible'. I myself first met Rien de Jonge in the autumn of 1986, at the beginning of six months of research in Leiden. Rien became my proverbial Dutch uncle, dispensing sage and frank, even blunt, advice in his characteristically open and friendly manner. My wife, Paula, and I shall always be grateful to him and his lovely wife, Vera, for the generous hospitality extended to us during our stay.

Beyond the boundaries of his native land, de Jonge has had particularly close contacts with scholars in England and the United States. With two exceptions, the contributors to this Festschrift reflect that fact. When I began work on it a few years ago, I did not know that in 1991 I would be leaving the United States and taking up a post at Manchester University where forty years earlier, 'during an inspiring year' (1951–1952), de Jonge wrote his doctoral dissertation under the supervision of J. de Zwaan and T.W. Manson.[1] De Jonge's connection to Manson and Manchester, as well as to the United States, has been visible more recently as well. His Shaffer Lectures at Yale University in 1989 took place exactly fifty years after Manson's. The title of de Jonge's Shaffer Lectures, *Jesus, The Servant-Messiah*,[2] is a clear evocation of the title of Manson's, *The Servant-Messiah: A Study of the Public Ministry of Jesus*.[3] Furthermore, de Jonge's Shaffer Lectures provided the theme for a farewell symposium in his honour at Leiden University on 25 January 1991 and were the basis for a series of lectures at English universities, including Manchester, in March 1991. It thus seems fitting that this Festschrift, devoted to the christological issues that have recently engaged de Jonge's erudite attention in public forums in the United States, England and the Netherlands, should also be edited at Manchester University by someone who is both a native of the Netherlands and an American!

The scope of these essays, epitomized in the volume's title, *From Jesus to John*, reflects what Martin Dibelius regarded as the crucial

H.M.J. van Duyne (The Hague: Boekencentrum, 1982).

1. De Jonge, *Collected Essays*, p. xi.
2. New Haven: Yale University, 1991. Also available in Dutch under the title *Jezus als Messias: Hoe Hij zijn zending zag* (Boxtel: Katholieke Bijbelstichting; Bruges: Tabor, 1990).
3. Not published until 1953 by Cambridge University Press, Cambridge.

question of New Testament Christology: 'How did knowledge of the historical Jesus change so quickly into faith in the heavenly Son of God?'[1] But the title also reflects Rien de Jonge's abiding interest in the full range of christological issues presented by the New Testament—the self-understanding of the historical Jesus (what de Jonge calls 'Jesus' own Christology'),[2] the earliest responses to Jesus both before and after Easter,[3] and the astonishing portrait of Jesus as the heavenly Son of God in the Gospel of John.[4] De Jonge's work in these areas has been marked by an insistence on the importance of contemporary Jewish eschatology as the matrix within which the work of Jesus himself and the various responses to him are to be understood.[5] Furthermore, de Jonge is convinced that the various responses to Jesus, and thus the diverse Christologies found in the New Testament, cannot really be understood, historically or theologically, apart from an account of Jesus himself, of his own teaching and his own understanding of his mission.[6] In many ways, de Jonge has sought to highlight the recoverable continuity between the responses to Jesus, both

1. As quoted by J. Ashton, *Understanding the Fourth Gospel* (Oxford: Clarendon Press, 1991), p. 51.

2. De Jonge's first scholarly publication after the completion of his dissertation in 1953 was a survey article on the historical Jesus, 'Enige recente studies over het leven van Jezus', *Theologie en Practijk* 15 (1955), pp. 97-11. See further 'Nieuwe bijdragen tot de Leben–Jesu Forschung in Duitsland', *Vox Theologica* 29 (1958–59), pp. 129-44 and other articles collected in *Jesus: Inspiring and Disturbing Presence*. De Jonge returned to this subject in his 1989 Shaffer Lectures (see above).

3. *Christology in Context: The Earliest Christian Response to Jesus* (Philadelphia: Westminster Press, 1988).

4. *Jesus: Stranger from Heaven and Son of God: Jesus Christ and the Christians in Johannine Perspective* (SBLSBS, 11; Missoula, MT: Scholars Press, 1977). See also the item mentioned in the following note.

5. See the essays collected under the heading 'Eschatology and Christology', in *Collected Essays*, pp. 1-144. Also *Jezus en het Koninkrijk van God* (Leiden: Leiden Press, 1991), de Jonge's farewell lecture at his retirement symposium on 25 January 1991; *Jesus' Message About the Kingdom of God in Light of Contemporary Ideas* (Ethel M. Wood Lecture; London: London University, 1991), a lecture delivered on 12 March 1991; and 'Christology and Theology in the Context of Early Christian Eschatology, particularly in the Fourth Gospel', in *The Four Gospels* (Festschrift F. Neirynck; BETL, 100; Leuven: Peeters, 1992), III, pp. 1835-53.

6. See his concluding chapter in *Christology in Context*, entitled 'The One with Whom it All Began', pp. 203-11. His Shaffer Lectures represent an elaboration of the argument put forth here.

before and after Easter, and Jesus' self-understanding and teaching.

These provocative claims, made with special force in his Shaffer Lectures, are put to the test in the first three contributions to this volume—those of H.J. de Jonge, Wayne A. Meeks and Dieter Lührmann. These three essays were initially presented as public lectures at his farewell symposium. They have previously been published in a Dutch volume emerging from that symposium[1] and appear here in slightly altered form, though they still happily bear the stamp of oral presentations. They also exhibit the widespread respect and admiration for de Jonge and his work among New Testament scholars.

Two essays devoted to Qumran messianic texts follow. John J. Collins contributes a fresh appraisal of the famous 'Son of God' text (4Q 246), relating it to the 'Son of Man' passage in Daniel 7 and to expectations surrounding a Davidic messiah. George J. Brooke gives a detailed discussion of two Qumran fragments that concern a priestly messianic figure and that have been linked to the Greek *Testament of Levi*, one of the *Testaments of the Twelve Patriarchs* to which de Jonge has devoted so much of his scholarly attention.[2] Both Collins and Brooke briefly outline the implications of their investigations for understanding the Christology of the New Testament.

Several essays on Paul then follow. J.W. van Henten investigates background texts, both Jewish and pagan, in order to illuminate Rom. 3.25 from a tradition-critical angle. J. Louis Martyn follows with a redaction-critical analysis of Gal. 2.16 in which Rom. 3.25 also plays a prominent role. J.D.G. Dunn then considers the extent to which Paul's Christology was a source of controversy with his opponents. E. Earle Ellis investigates 1 Cor. 10.4, 9, while J. Christiaan Beker probes the relationship between Christology and anthropology in Paul, Luke–Acts and Marcion.

Also extending his reach beyond that of the New Testament is Graham N. Stanton in the first of four essays on the Synoptic Gospels. Stanton investigates the theme of the two parousias of Christ in the

1. H.E. Wevers *et al.* (eds.), *Jezus' visie op Zichzelf: In discussie met de Jonge's christologie* (Leidse Lezingen; Nijkerk: Callenbach, 1991), pp. 19-64. The translations are published here with the kind permission of the editors and publisher of the Dutch volume.
2. So much so that at his retirement symposium he was celebrated as the Thirteenth Patriarch.

works of Justin Martyr in order to shed light on the Gospel of
Matthew. Christopher M. Tuckett then takes on the Son of Man in
Q. Morna D. Hooker probes Luke's use of Scripture as a clue to his
Christology, while David Catchpole ponders the threads of continuity
between the historical Jesus of Nazareth and the Lukan episode of
Jesus reading and interpreting scripture in a Nazareth synagogue
(Lk. 4.16-30).

D. Moody Smith follows with an essay on the possible value of the
Gospel of John as an independent witness alongside the Synoptics to
reliable historical information about Jesus. Peder Borgen investigates
how John 6 seems to develop themes adumbrated in Jn 5.36-40.
Maarten J.J. Menken finishes the series of essays on John with a
survey of recent studies on Johannine Christology, in the Netherlands
as well as elsewhere.[1]

Leander E. Keck concludes the volume with his programmatic essay
on the renewal of New Testament Christology.[2] Keck read this essay
at the 40th General Meeting of Studiorum Novi Testamenti Societas in
Trondheim on 20 August 1985 in the presence of Rien de Jonge who
was President of the Society that year.[3]

All the essays in this volume are in honour of a scholar who is both
a historian and a theologian and who has fostered renewed
investigations into the full range of New Testament christological
issues, from Jesus to John.

Martin de Boer
Manchester, March 1993

1.   This is a considerably expanded form of an article that appeared under the
title 'Die christologie van het vierde evangelie', *NTT* 45 (1991), pp. 16-33. The
editorial staff and the publisher of *NTT* have kindly granted permission for the
translation and use of this article in the present volume.

2.   First published in *NTS* 32 (1986), pp. 362-67. Published here with permission of Cambridge University Press.

3.   De Jonge's presidential address was 'The Earliest Christian Use of
Christos', subsequently published in *NTS* 32 (1986), pp. 321-43 (also in *Collected
Essays*, pp. 102-24).

ACKNOWLEDGMENTS

I would like to thank David Orton, formerly of Sheffield Academic Press and now with E.J. Brill in Leiden (of all places), for his initial and continuing support of this project. Similar thanks must be extended to Alison Bogle, Desk Editor at Sheffield Academic Press. I owe a special debt of gratitude to Henk Jan de Jonge and Christopher Tuckett for their invaluable and generous assistance at numerous points.

ABBREVIATIONS

AB	Anchor Bible
ABR	*Australian Biblical Review*
AGJU	Arbeiten zur Geschichte des antiken Judentums und des Urchristentums
AnBib	Analecta biblica
Anton	*Antonianum*
AOAT	Alter Orient und Altes Testament
ATANT	Abhandlungen zur Theologie des Alten und Neuen Testaments
BASOR	*Bulletin of the American Schools of Oriental Research*
BBB	Bonner biblische Beiträge
BDF	F. Blass, A. Debrunner and R.W. Funk, *A Greek Grammar of the New Testament*
BDR	F. Blass, A. Debrunner and F. Rehkopf, *Grammatik des neutestamenlichen Griechisch*
BETL	Bibliotheca ephemeridum theologicarum lovaniensium
BJRL	*Bulletin of the John Rylands University Library of Manchester*
BZ	*Biblische Zeitschrift*
BZAW	Beihefte zur *ZAW*
BZNW	Beihefte zur *ZNW*
CBQ	*Catholic Biblical Quarterly*
CBQMS	*Catholic Biblical Quarterly*, Monograph Series
CRAIBL	*Comptes rendus de l'Académie des inscriptions et belles-lettres*
CRHPR	Cahiers de la revue d'histoire et de philosophie religieuses
CTSRR	College Theology Society Resources in Religion
DJD	Discoveries in the Judaean Desert
EHPR	Etudes d'histoire et de philosophie religieuses
EvT	*Evangelische Theologie*
ExpTim	*Expository Times*
FRLANT	Forschungen zur Religion und Literatur des Alten und Neuen Testaments
FFNT	*Foundations and Facets: New Testament*
HDR	Harvard Dissertations in Religion
HSM	Harvard Semitic Monographs
HTKNT	Herders theologischer Kommentar zum Neuen Testament
HTR	*Harvard Theological Review*
ICC	International Critical Commentary
Int	*Interpretation*
JBL	*Journal of Biblical Literature*
JJS	*Journal of Jewish Studies*

JSJ	*Journal for the Study of Judaism in the Persian, Hellenistic and Roman Period*
JSNTSup	*Journal for the Study of the New Testament*, Supplement Series
JSPSup	*Journal for the Study of the Pseudepigrapha*, Supplement Series
JTC	*Journal for Theology and the Church*
LCL	Loeb Classical Library
LSJ	Liddell–Scott–Jones, *Greek–English Lexicon*
MeyerK	H.A.W. Meyer (ed.), Kritisch-exegetischer Kommentar über das Neue Testament
NCB	New Century Bible
NICNT	New International Commentary on the New Testament
NIGTC	The New International Greek Testament Commentary
NovT	*Novum Testamentum*
NovTSup	*Novum Testamentum* Supplements
NTA	*New Testament Abstracts*
NTD	Das Neue Testament Deutsch
NTS	*New Testament Studies*
OTKNT	Ökumenischer Taschenbuch—Kommentar zum Neuen Testament
OTS	*Oudtestamentische Studiën*
RB	*Revue biblique*
RHPR	*Revue d'historie et de philosophie religieuses*
SBFLA	*Studii biblici franciscani liber annuus*
SBLMS	SBL Monograph Series
SBLSBS	SBL Sources for Biblical Study
SBLSP	SBL Seminar Papers
SBS	Stuttgarter Bibelstudien
SBT	Studies in Biblical Theology
SCHNT	Studia ad corpus hellenisticum novi testamenti
Sem	*Semitica*
SJLA	Studies in Judaism in Late Antiquity
SJT	*Scottish Journal of Theology*
SNTSMS	Society for New Testament Studies Monograph Series
SNTU	Studien zum Neuen Testament und seiner Umwelt
SPB	Studia postbiblica
SVTP	Studia in Veteris Testamenti pseudepigrapha
TDNT	G. Kittel and G. Friedrich (eds.), *Theological Dictionary of the New Testament*
TLZ	*Theologischer Literaturzeitung*
TNTC	Tyndale New Testament Commentaries
TU	Texte und Untersuchungen
TWNT	G. Kittel and G. Friedrich (eds.), *Theologisches Wörterbuch zum Neuen Testament*
TZ	*Theologische Zeitschrift*
VC	*Vigiliae christianae*
WBC	Word Biblical Commentary

WMANT	Wissenschaftliche Monographien zum Alten und Neuen Testament
WUNT	Wissenschaftliche Untersuchungen zum Neuen Testament
ZNW	*Zeitschrift für die neutestamentliche Wissenschaft*
ZTK	*Zeitschrift für Theologie und Kirche*

LIST OF CONTRIBUTORS

J. Christiaan Beker
Richard J. Dearborn Professor of New Testament Theology, Princeton Theological Seminary, New Jersey.

Peder Borgen
Professor of New Testament, Department of Religious Studies, University of Trondheim, Norway.

George J. Brooke
Lecturer in Intertestamental Literature, Department of Religions and Theology, University of Manchester, England.

David R. Catchpole
St Luke's Foundation Professor of Theological Studies, Department of Theology, University of Exeter, England.

John J. Collins
Professor of Hebrew Bible and Intertestamental Judaism, the Divinity School, University of Chicago, Illinois.

M.C. de Boer
Lecturer in Biblical Studies, Department of Religions and Theology, University of Manchester, England.

H.J. de Jonge
Professor of New Testament and Early Christian Literature, Faculty of Theology, University of Leiden, The Netherlands.

James D.G. Dunn
Lightfoot Professor of Divinity, Department of Theology, University of Durham, England.

E. Earle Ellis
Research Professor of Theology, Southwestern Baptist Theological Seminary, Fort Worth, Texas.

Morna D. Hooker
The Lady Margaret's Professor, Faculty of Divinity, University of Cambridge, England.

Leander E. Keck
Winkley Professor of Biblical Theology, Divinity School, Yale University, New Haven, Connecticut.

Dieter Lührmann
Professor of New Testament, Faculty of Theology, University of Marburg, Germany.

J. Louis Martyn
Edward Robinson Professor Emeritus of Biblical Theology, Union Theological Seminary, New York.

Wayne A. Meeks
Woolsey Professor of Biblical Studies, Department of Religious Studies, Yale University, New Haven, Connecticut.

Maarten J.J. Menken
Professor of New Testament Exegesis, Faculty of Theology, Catholic University of Nijmegen, The Netherlands.

D. Moody Smith
George Washington Ivey Professor of New Testament, Divinity School, Duke University, Durham, North Carolina.

Graham N. Stanton
Professor of New Testament Studies, Department of Theology and Religious Studies, King's College London, University of London, England.

Christopher M. Tuckett
Rylands Professor of Biblical Criticism and Exegesis, Department of Religions and Theology, University of Manchester, England.

Jan Willem van Henten
Lecturer in New Testament and Early Judaism, Faculty of Theology, University of Utrecht, The Netherlands.

THE HISTORICAL JESUS' VIEW OF HIMSELF AND OF HIS MISSION[*]

H.J. de Jonge

Introduction

In 1991 Marinus de Jonge published his book, *Jesus, The Servant-Messiah*.[1] This work examines what opinion the historical person Jesus of Nazareth had of himself and his mission. In this article I wish to examine some of de Jonge's most important conclusions in more detail. In particular, I wish to reconsider the question whether Jesus spoke of himself as the 'Messiah' and as the 'Son of Man'.

1. *The Views of M. de Jonge*

For clarity, let me first briefly restate the conclusions of de Jonge. (His arguments will be discussed in sections 2 and 3 of this contribution in which I will go into two main themes more fully.)

To begin with, de Jonge considers it highly probable that Jesus saw himself as a prophet in the line of the prophets of Israel. If Jesus regarded himself as a prophet, he must also have expected that his message and person would be rejected and that he would meet a violent death.[2]

It can also be assumed that Jesus regarded himself as a suffering

---

[*] A somewhat longer Dutch version of this essay was read as a paper at a symposium held in Leiden, 25 January 1991, honouring M. de Jonge on the occasion of his retirement from the Faculty of Theology at Leiden. The Dutch version was published in the proceedings of that symposium in H.E. Wevers *et al.* (eds.), *Jezus' visie op Zichzelf: in discussie met de Jonge's Christologie* (Nijkerk: Callenbach, 1991), pp. 48-64.

[1] M. de Jonge, *Jesus, The Servant-Messiah* (New Haven: Yale University Press, 1991), also published in Dutch as *Jezus als Messias: Hoe Hij zijn zending Zag* (Boxtel: Katholieke Bijbelstichting; Brugge: Uitgeverij Tabor, 1990).

[2] De Jonge, *Jesus*, p. 37.

righteous man.[1] He must therefore also have reckoned not only with resistance, suffering and a violent death, but also with his early rehabilitation or vindication by God in the form of an exaltation to heaven. Jesus probably expected to be resurrected soon after his death.

It is not excluded, though it cannot be proven, that Jesus reckoned with the possibility of dying a martyr's death. In other words, it is uncertain whether Jesus felt that he would die as the representative of a group of like-minded people, for their sake and in their place. It also remains uncertain whether Jesus expected that, thanks to his death, God would be reconciled to those others and grant them his favour.

At this point, de Jonge's argument enters a stage of critical importance. He states that the earliest traditions we can discover already do not represent Jesus as one prophet among many, or just another martyr who remained true to God until his death. From the beginning they present Jesus as the last prophet sent by God, as God's suffering and righteous servant *par excellence*, as the man in whom the history of Israel and the world had reached a point of no return and had definitively taken a new turn. The person and the work of Jesus, the earthly Jesus included, were already regarded as unique in history by Christians soon after Jesus' death.

De Jonge's viewpoint can be summarized as follows. First, he argues that the recognition of Jesus as a unique emissary of God by the Christians in the time soon after his death must go back to the same recognition of Jesus by his followers in the time before his death.

Secondly, he explains (and this is the most important part of his argument) that the view of Jesus as a unique intermediary authorised by God, the view that must already have been held by his followers during his activity in Galilee and Judea, goes back to pronouncements of the historical Jesus himself. In those pronouncements Jesus must have communicated his vision of himself and his special task in God's plan to his disciples. The question which especially concerns de Jonge is therefore in what terms did Jesus speak of himself and his task, and what did these terms mean for him.

According to de Jonge there is nothing to show that Jesus understood himself and spoke of himself as the suffering servant of the Lord in Isaiah 52–55. But it may be assumed that Jesus spoke of himself as the 'Son of Man'.[2] This term, according to de Jonge, is absent from

1.   De Jonge, *Jesus*, pp. 38-39.
2.   De Jonge, *Jesus*, pp. 53-54.

contemporary Judaism and both Mark and Q show little enthusiasm for this epithet. Indeed, both exhibit a certain resistance to it.[1] On the grounds of the so-called criterion of dissimilarity, the use of the title 'Son of Man' can be ascribed to Jesus himself. The term indicated a rejected and humiliated person, yet one with authority, even if this authority was contested. The 'Son of Man' was also someone who would be vindicated by God, that is, justified and rehabilitated. All in all, the term 'Son of Man' denoted the suffering righteous man *par excellence.*

De Jonge also takes the view that Jesus not only taught that God's reign was at hand, but also that God's reign was in a way already a reality in his (Jesus') own deeds, and it was therefore not only Mark and Q who placed the beginning of God's reign on earth in the activities of Jesus—Jesus himself did so.

The historical Jesus, in de Jonge's view, claimed to act by virtue of a special mandate granted him by God.[2] Thus Jesus himself already had a Christology, so to speak, and indeed not merely an implicit but an explicit one. De Jonge writes that in the lifetime of the historical Jesus 'an incipient explicit Christology' already existed both for Jesus' disciples and for himself.[3]

Apart from the term 'Son of Man', de Jonge claims that Jesus also applied the designation 'the anointed of the Lord' or, for short, the term 'anointed' (Messiah, Christ) to himself. This was because of his realization that he was a prophetic son of David.

We do not know whether Jesus also called himself the 'Son of God'. But Jesus addressed God as father in a way which betrays his awareness of a unique relationship to this father.

Thus far I have summarized the thesis of de Jonge. I wish now to examine in more detail two important points of this thesis. First, the question whether Jesus spoke of himself as 'the anointed one' and then whether he spoke of himself as the 'Son of Man'.

2. Did Jesus Speak of Himself as 'The Anointed One'?

Did Jesus speak of himself as 'the anointed one', or did others give him this name? And if the latter is the case, did it happen during Jesus' lifetime or after his death?

1. De Jonge, *Jesus*, p. 53.
2. De Jonge, *Jesus*, p. 65.
3. De Jonge, *Jesus*, p. 68.

De Jonge's initial assumption is that the name of *Christos* cannot only have become attached to his person after his death. Formulaic expressions such as 'Christ has died' and 'Christ died and rose again' were, to judge by their frequency in traditional material in the epistles of Paul, disseminated too early for the designation *Christos* to have only become attached to him after his death. I emphatically agree with de Jonge on this point and add an argument of my own. After the death of Jesus there was no special historical motive to apply the title 'anointed' to Jesus, as something new, if it had not already been bestowed on him. Consequently he must already have borne that title before his death, during his earthly activity.

The rest of de Jonge's argument runs as follows.[1] The term 'the anointed one' occurs surprisingly rarely in Jewish sources around the beginning of the Christian era, as a title of an expected eschatological person. In these sources, the term can indicate a king, a priest and a prophet. But when the disciples of Jesus applied the term 'anointed' to *him*, they clearly used this word to indicate a king. This usage fits in well with certain Jewish sources of about the same date. To be sure, as I have just noted, the term 'the anointed one' rarely occurs in them as the title of one who will play a role in God's decisive intervention, but when it does occur it is mostly with reference to a future ideal Davidic king of Israel.

At this point I begin my discussion with de Jonge. Would Jesus have wished to present himself as a future earthly king of Israel? The historical Jesus had no ordinary political ambitions or pretensions. Must one therefore conclude that Jesus did not refer to himself as the 'anointed' one, but that only others, his followers, gave him this name? De Jonge is unwilling to draw this conclusion, because he deems it very unlikely that in early Christianity the word *Christos*, 'anointed one', could have become the central term to be used for Jesus if Jesus himself had always avoided it and advised his disciples not to use it in connection with him.[2] Consequently, de Jonge argues that Jesus himself must already have spoken of himself as the 'anointed one'.

The problem then arises that Jesus can hardly have proclaimed himself a future ruler in a national-political sense, but de Jonge offers an attractive solution. It is an important and truly innovative contribution to historical research into the origins of Christology. He

1. De Jonge, *Jesus*, pp. 69-72.
2. De Jonge, *Jesus*, pp. 68-70.

points out that in *Psalm of Solomon* 17, the anointed one on whom the poet has fixed all his hopes for the future of Israel is not only an earthly and national ruler, but is also characterized as 'strong in the holy spirit, wise in prudent counsel, with power and righteousness' (v. 37) in the style of the king described in Isa. 11.2-5. De Jonge recalls that in the Old Testament, David was not only a king but also a poet, prophet and exorcist, and that Josephus, Pseudo-Philo and the Psalms Scroll from Qumran describe David as an exorcist, poet and prophet. De Jonge has thus established that in the literature of Judaism up to the time of Jesus the image of a prophetic David, who was a prophet, a wise man and an exorcist, occurs alongside the image of a royal David.

And now de Jonge can reap the fruit of his argument—the historical Jesus can have seen himself as a second prophetic David, as a prophetic son of David. Because Jesus regarded himself as a prophet, teacher and exorcist in the style of David, he could already regard himself both as a 'son of David' during his ministry in Galilee and therefore also as 'the anointed of the Lord'.[1] Jesus also communicated this vision of himself to the disciples, who acknowledged him as 'the anointed of the Lord'.[2] So—according to de Jonge—Jesus came to be known as the anointed one/Messiah/Christ, and, most importantly, he did so on his own initiative.

This, then, is de Jonge's creative attempt to answer the question whether Jesus already described himself as the 'anointed one'. Of course de Jonge is cautious enough to observe that he cannot produce conclusive proof of his theory. But he considers it 'probable'.[3]

For clarity, I will summarize the constituent parts of de Jonge's answer. There are three stages: (1) The historical Jesus was a prophet, teacher and exorcist, and saw himself this way. (2) On the basis of his self-perception he could call himself a second David or a son of David, for David too had been a prophet, wise man and exorcist. (3) Once Jesus called himself 'son of David', he could also call himself 'the anointed of the Lord' for the titles come down to the same thing.

Let me now proceed to formulate some objections. A vulnerable point in the argument of de Jonge appears to be the idea that because of his self-awareness as a prophet, teacher and exorcist, Jesus could

1. De Jonge, *Jesus*, p. 72.
2. De Jonge, *Jesus*, p. 72.
3. De Jonge, *Jesus*, p. 72.

have called himself the son of David. I do not deny that Jesus acted as prophet, teacher and exorcist. But I wonder if it is really probable that a Jewish teacher around the year 30 CE could have found the fact that he acted as prophet, teacher and exorcist, sufficient grounds to apply to himself the designation of son of David, let alone 'the anointed of the Lord'. It is true that in the literature of Israel and Judaism, David has the characteristics of a prophet, wise man and exorcist. But would a preacher ever have called himself a second David or 'son of David' because of his prophetic, didactic and exorcising gifts? Is not the title 'son of David', in spite of all the evidence de Jonge deploys to bring out its nuances, too much a reference to a ruler, however great his spiritual gifts, who will in the first place rule over Israel as its true king?

Psalm of Solomon 17 appears to me to argue against, rather than for, the view of de Jonge. He cites this psalm as a witness to the existence of the ideal of the son of David who, in the image of the messianic king of Isa. 11.2-5, will excel in his spiritual qualities. Now it is true that the son of David to whom the poet of *Psalm of Solomon* 17 looks forward exercises power by his word and not by force. Wisdom, justice and trust in God are his attributes. But this son of David must first acquire and exercise the kingship of Israel, much as David had been the political king of Israel (v. 4c). He must take the place of the hated and illegitimate kings of the house of the Hasmoneans. He must have the strength to break the power of the lawless leaders (v. 22a). He must cleanse Jerusalem of the heathens (that is the Romans) who are crushing and ruining it (v. 22b). The dominion of this king must be recognised far beyond Israel (v. 31), but his greatness will rest on his political function as king of the people of Israel (v. 42). Heathen peoples will serve under his yoke (v. 30), and the charismatic gifts which he will enjoy are not so much those of a prophetic son of David as they are the lawful attributes of someone who is primarily a true political king of Israel, albeit much more than an ordinary king.

This raises the question whether Jesus could have called himself 'son of David' in the sense of the figure depicted in *Psalm of Solomon* 17 without implying at the very least that he aspired to political kingship. I think not.

And if, as most researchers accept, Jesus did not have such ambitions, then in my opinion it is difficult to assume that he called himself the son of David. And if he did not call himself the son of David, then the grounds on which de Jonge assumed that he spoke of himself as 'the anointed one' fall away.

I therefore come to suspect that it was not Jesus who applied the title of 'anointed one' to himself but some of his followers. My argument is that I find it hard to imagine that Jesus the prophet, teacher and exorcist characterised himself as the 'son of David'. That was too plain a reference to a ruler in the political sense.

For clarity I add a further remark. De Jonge can assume that Jesus called himself the 'son of David' because de Jonge on the one hand gives the concept the broad 'spiritual' content of a *prophetic* 'son of David', and on the other hand allows the traditional political meaning of the term to fade into the background. It was this broad and less political image of the son of David, according to de Jonge, which Jesus then applied to himself. I feel that, on the contrary, the political and royal element in the term was so inalienable and dominant, that it cannot be admitted that Jesus ever applied it to himself.

At this stage it is appropriate to ask whether any support can be found for my point of view in the fact that, as is known, the source Q does not use the term 'Christ' for Jesus at all. The reason for this may be that only some of Jesus' followers used the term 'anointed one' for him. If Jesus had proclaimed himself the anointed of the Lord, then this title would probably not have been missing from any of the early streams of tradition.

Now de Jonge will probably counter with the following questions, which I shall attempt to answer.

1. Does not Mark also make a connection between Jesus' functions as prophet, teacher and exorcist on the one hand, and the reference to Jesus as son of David and Christ on the other hand? For in 10.47 and 10.48 Mark notes Bartimaeus's call to Jesus as 'son of David', after not much more has been said of Jesus than that he acted as preacher, prophet, healer and exorcist. And if Mark does so, why could not Jesus already have made this connection himself?

My answer is that the title given to Jesus by Bartimaeus in Mk 10.47 and 10.48 must, in my view, be strictly understood on the literary level of Mark, in relation to the pericope which directly follows it, that of Jesus' entry into Jerusalem. In the account of the entry, those who accompanied Jesus called out 'Blessed be the coming kingdom of...David' (11.10). Now Bartimaeus's call in 10.47-48 seems to be above all Mark's preparation for the call on Palm Sunday in 11.10. It remains to account for that call in the scene of the entry.

In the entry, it is true that Jesus is not honoured literally as the son of David, but as the one with whom the kingdom of David comes. But that comes down to practically the same thing. I should explain the presentation of Jesus as a Davidic king in the entry to Jerusalem as follows: the account of the entry described, possibly before Mark had incorporated it (cf. Jn 12.12-19), a royal entry of Jesus into Jerusalem. What Mark keeps implicit is made explicit by Matthew (21.5) and John (12.13, 15); Jesus entered Jerusalem as king of Israel in agreement with Zech. 9.9. Matthew even says 'so that the word of the prophet was fulfilled' (21.4). The account may well not have originated until after Jesus' death. In any case the origin of the account can in my opinion be adequately explained by the wish of some of Jesus' followers to provide 'legitimation' in 'historical events' for the recognition of Jesus as Messiah/Christ. The account of the entry offers that legitimation because it presents Jesus' actions as the fulfilment of Zech. 9.9. In this explanation, neither Mark nor Jesus need have seen a specific relationship between the prophetic-exorcist activity of Jesus and his being given the title of a future Davidic king. It is sufficient to assume that in Jesus' day, some of his followers saw in him (contrary to his intention) a potential political leader and liberator of Israel. They therefore spoke of him as 'son of David' and Messiah/Christ. They legitimated these functions, which they ascribed to Jesus, after a certain time, by the account of his royal entry into Jerusalem. And Mark in his turn could hardly place that account, perhaps with other subsequent material, at any other point in his narrative than that where he too related the arrival of Jesus in Jerusalem.

The reconstruction of the state of affairs which is here offered makes it uncertain whether Mark in fact saw a connection between Jesus as prophet, teacher and exorcist on the one hand, and his title as 'son of David' on the other hand. And if it is uncertain whether Mark saw this connection, it is *a fortiori* uncertain whether Jesus could have been able to style himself 'son of David' on the grounds of his awareness of himself as a prophet.

2. The second question which de Jonge will raise will, I expect, be this: although it may be difficult to accept that Jesus came to see himself as 'son of David' and 'anointed of the Lord' *solely* on the grounds of his self-image as a prophet, teacher and exorcist, is it not possible

that the impulse to do so may have originated in an already existing concept of himself as the 'Son of Man'?

My answer would be that this only shifts the problem to another plane, that is, did Jesus speak of himself as the 'Son of Man'? I shall discuss this question in section 3, but I state right away that my answer is in the negative, and that because he did not regard himself as the 'Son of Man', he cannot have come to see himself as the 'son of David'.

3. In the third place, de Jonge will no doubt ask whether the absence of the title 'Christ' for Jesus in Q does in fact point to the use of that title by only a part of Christ's following. Was Q, in any case, a theologically finished, complete work? Did it have an identifiable function and place in the life of an early Christian community? Was it ever more than a torso?

Although I cannot go into these questions here, I observe that Q has in fact been regarded by many researchers as theologically complete in itself and functional in the context of the community in which and for which it originated. But I should like to answer with a further question. Would one wish to call the whole of the extant epistles of Paul incomplete from a theological point of view and doubt that they were really functional either as a whole or individually, in certain contexts in the early church, *for the reason* that they never refer to Jesus as the 'Son of Man'?

Clearly certain titles were given to Jesus in some streams of tradition and not in others. And that may have been caused by the fact that these designations were used from the beginning in certain circles of Jesus' followers, and not in others. The absence of the title *Christos* for Jesus in Q may be the result of the fact that only a part of Jesus' following regarded him and referred to him as *Christos*, that is as the future ideal king of Israel, and Jesus did not do so himself.

3. Did Jesus Ever Speak of Himself as the 'Son of Man'?

This question is one of the most complicated and most often discussed puzzles of New Testament scholarship. It concerns the origin of the title given to Jesus, 'Son of Man'. The question can of course only be dealt with briefly and in outline here.

I agree with de Jonge that by reasoning back from Mark and Q one may assume that the historical Jesus spoke of the 'Son of Man', and

not only in the sense of 'one' or 'someone' as Aramaic usage permits.
Jesus also referred to an eschatological person who would play a
leading role in the coming judgment.

I differ, however, from de Jonge on the reasons for which it can be
assumed that Jesus spoke of a 'Son of Man'. De Jonge states first that
the term 'Son of Man' is highly unusual in Greek and must derive
from a Semitic idiom and, secondly, that early Christians did not use
the term in their own preaching except when they quoted Jesus' own
words.[1] Early Christian preachers would not have introduced the term
'Son of Man'; consequently, it must have come from Jesus himself.

The second alleged reason appears less strong to me. If early
Christians shaped or reshaped the words of Jesus in such a way that
the term 'Son of Man' appeared in them, as in fact happened to a certain extent, then they used the term *eo ipso* in their own preaching as
well, even if they only gave the term a place in the direct speech of
Jesus. And then the term could indeed have been introduced by
Christians, that is, by others than Christ.

The first reason cited by de Jonge, the linguistic argument, I too
consider to be valid. But it only traces the term 'Son of Man' into
Aramaic, and not back to the lips of Jesus. I should wish to urge
another argument, which de Jonge prefers not to use. Besides Mark
and Q, the 'Son of Man' as a future eschatological judge and saviour is
also mentioned by *1 Enoch* 37–71 and *4 Ezra* 13, at least by *4 Ezra* 13
in an earlier textual form, underlying the Latin translation which has
been preserved. Naturally, de Jonge knows of, and mentions the
passages in *1 Enoch* and *4 Ezra* in which the 'Son of Man' appears, yet
he appears to prefer to treat Mark and Q separately from *1 Enoch* and
4 Ezra. Discussing the incomprehensibility of the term 'Son of Man'
for a Greek-speaking audience, and pointing to the fact that Mark and
Q clearly did not regard 'Son of Man' as a title readily understood, de
Jonge observes: '(contrary to what is often thought) we do not find a
proper titular use of the expression anywhere in contemporary
Judaism'.[2] Now it is true that *4 Ezra* and perhaps *1 Enoch* 37–71 only
originated at the end of the first century of our era, but they speak of
the 'Son of Man' in a way which has so much in common with Mk
13.26 and 14.62 that the Christian use of the term and that in *1 Enoch*
and *4 Ezra* 13 must, in my opinion, go back to common pre-Christian,

1.   De Jonge, *Jesus*, p. 53.
2.   De Jonge, *Jesus*, p. 53.

Jewish tradition. What they have in common is located not only in the explicit reminiscences of Dan. 7.13-14, but also in the picture of the 'Son of Man' as an individual[1] and not as a collective. In that common, older, Jewish tradition there must have been reference, building on Dan. 7.13-14, to the 'Son of Man' as a heavenly adjutant of God who would appear in the future dawning of the eschaton to punish the godless and to save the righteous.

One must therefore, I believe, assume that there was a pre-Christian, Jewish tradition, expressed in Aramaic, in which the Son of Man was spoken of as an individual, eschatological, heavenly intervener who will come forward at the last judgment, pronounce justice and rule thereafter.

I say 'individual' because this is the point at which the view of the 'Son of Man' in the common tradition behind Mark/Q, *1 Enoch* and *4 Ezra* differs from that in Dan. 7.13-14, from which it was nonetheless derived. In the vision of Dan 7.13-14, the Aramaic *kebar enash* means nothing more than 'someone like a man'. But this man in the vision proves, in the exposition in Dan. 7.22, to be the symbol of the 'saints of the Most High', who will be rehabilitated and saved in the future, and will rule. The 'someone like a man' of Dan. 7.13 is thus a collective. The 'Son of Man' in Mark/Q, *1 Enoch* 4 and *Ezra* on the other hand is an individual.

In sum, I maintain that three stages can certainly be distinguished in speaking of the 'Son of Man'. The first is that of Daniel 7, in which the term is a symbol for the righteous ones of Israel who will be

---

1. I wrote this in January 1991. In July 1991, at the Bethel Meeting of the Studiorum Novi Testamenti Societas, John J. Collins gave his lecture 'The Son of Man in First Century Judaism'. In it he enumerated the following four features which the 'son of man' concept of the *Similitudes of Enoch* and that of *4 Ezra* have in common: (1) both assume that the 'one like a son of man' in Daniel refers to an individual and is not a collective symbol; (2) this figure is identified in both works as the messiah; (3) he is pre-existent; (4) he takes a more active role in the destruction of the wicked than was explicit in Daniel. Collins did not go into the relationship between the 'son of man' concept in first-century Judaism and that in the Gospels. It is clear, however, that *1 Enoch* and *4 Ezra* share the first of their common features mentioned by Collins with Mark and Q, the second also with Mark, and possibly the fourth with Q. In my opinion the correspondences at issue between *1 Enoch* and *4 Ezra* and the Gospels are best accounted for by assuming common pre-Christian tradition. I wish to thank Dr Collins for sending me the text of his Bethel lecture before it was published in *NTS* 38 (1992), pp. 448-66.

vindicated in the coming judgment, and endowed with royal dominion. The second stage is the common tradition behind both the early Christian use of the 'Son of Man' in Mark and Q and the presentation of the 'Son of Man' in *1 Enoch* and *4 Ezra*. In this stage, which is still pre-Christian, the 'Son of Man' is already an individual, someone who will act as judge and saviour in the coming judgment. The third stage is that in which this eschatological individual judge and saviour is identified with the person of Jesus. It follows from this that the title 'Son of Man', originally attached to a future person and to Jesus as a future eschatological intervener, was gradually extended to descriptions of the life of the earthly Jesus. The title is attached to the Jesus who suffered, died and rose again, to the Jesus who preached with authority, and to the Jesus who experienced resistance and rejection.

It should be clear that the history of tradition which is briefly sketched here proceeds from the assumption that the presentation of the 'Son of Man' in *1 Enoch* and *4 Ezra* is related to that found in the oldest Christian witnesses to the title in question, Mark and Q. On this point, it appears to me, there is a difference between my appraisal and that of de Jonge. The relationship does not consist in the fact that the Christian witnesses, on the one hand, and *1 Enoch* and *4 Ezra*, on the other, go back separately to Daniel 7. Then one would have to assume that both groups, independently of each other, came to see the 'Son of Man' of Daniel 7 as an individual. But that is improbable. The common tradition in the two groups must, in my opinion, be explained by a common earlier tradition, and to be specific, by that identified above as the second, pre-Christian stage of tradition.

It appears to me that in terms of the history of tradition, it has now been made acceptable that in the two centuries between 165 BCE and 35 CE, that is from the book of Daniel to the death of Jesus, there existed in Jewish apocalyptic circles a concept of the future 'Son of Man' who would take part in the judgment and who was regarded as an individual. It is therefore not impossible that Jesus himself also spoke in this way of the coming of the 'Son of Man'. But for the moment that is only saying that he spoke of the 'Son of Man' as of someone other than himself, someone who would appear in the future, much as he does in Lk. 12.8-9; 12.40; Mk 8.38 (although here the evangelists will have meant that Jesus and the 'Son of Man' are one and the same person). We can also establish that at least some of Jesus' followers went so far as to identify him with the eschatological 'Son of Man'.

Now it is not probable that followers of Jesus thought that the 'Son of Man' had already come in the earthly Jesus, whose ministry they experienced. That earthly activity would have borne too little resemblance to that of one who exercised God-given royal dominion (Daniel 7), condemned sinners as a heavenly judge (*1 Enoch* 69), crushed the heathen and saved the 'remnant' of Israel (*4 Ezra* 13).

But the followers of Jesus could have thought, and even said, during his activity on earth, that if the 'Son of Man' were to appear shortly, he would prove to be their leader Jesus. For there is continuity and identity between earthly persons and the future Son of Man in Daniel 7 and *1 Enoch* 71. According to Daniel 7, God's saints, and according to *1 Enoch* 71, Enoch himself acts as 'Son of Man' (although in Daniel 7 'Son of Man' is not yet a title). But they would have reached this conclusion before the death of Jesus, rather than after that disappointing end to his life.

The great question is, did Jesus himself say that he saw himself as the future 'Son of Man'? This difficult question has received various answers. Certainty on this point is, of course, unattainable. De Jonge's answer is positive. Both in his *Christology in Context*[1] and in his *Jesus, The Servant-Messiah*[2], he considers it probable that Jesus used the term 'Son of Man' of himself.

His arguments are (1) that the available sources all show the term being used exclusively by Jesus himself, that is, in direct speech, and (2) that in discussion with a non-Jewish audience 'Son of Man' was not a suitable designation to explain Jesus' dignity and his relationship to God and man.

But are these reasons strong enough to make it unlikely that the identification of Jesus with the 'Son of Man' was only brought about by his admirers? That the term 'Son of Man' only occurs in the Gospels in the direct speech of Jesus may also be due to narrators and redactors and, logically considered, need not have been caused by Jesus' use of the term 'Son of Man' to designate himself. Other explanations are possible. The term may well have been unsuitable for

---

1. M. De Jonge, *Christology in Context: The Earliest Christian Response to Jesus* (Philadelphia: Westminster Press, 1988), p. 207.

2. De Jonge, *Jesus*, p. 53.

clarifying the authority of Jesus to a non-Jewish audience but, on the other hand, the evangelists repeatedly introduce the term 'Son of Man' where their source has 'I' or 'me' (for example in Mt. 16.13, cf. Mk 8.27). The term was certainly productive as a title of Jesus. I would incline to a negative answer for four reasons.

1. I think that the attention paid in the preaching of Jesus to the imminence of God's kingdom and to the consequent radical demand for obedience to God's will is so strong that, in comparison with it, the identity of the person of the 'Son of Man' will have been of little or no importance for Jesus. For the preaching of the kingdom the identity of the 'Son of Man' was irrelevant and the identification of the 'Son of Man' with Jesus was therefore superfluous. This identification would only have distracted attention from what really mattered to Jesus—the imminent coming of the kingdom of God and the conversion of humankind which it called for.

2. If one assumes that Jesus did identify himself with the 'Son of Man', why is no trace of this preserved in the epistles of Paul? Cannot one of the reasons for the complete absence of the term 'Son of Man' in Paul be that the identification of Jesus as the 'Son of Man' was only familiar to *part* of Jesus' following and therefore probably did not derive from Jesus himself?

3. There is also an argument of a more theoretical nature. Reasoning back from Mark and Q, one may assume that the followers of Jesus saw him as the coming 'Son of Man'. We can form a good historical picture of how they came to do so. Followers of Jesus must have been so impressed by his activities that they came to believe that Jesus would soon reveal himself as the eschatological 'Son of Man'. In this way the origin of the identification of Jesus with the 'Son of Man' can be satisfactorily explained. It is easy to imagine a *Sitz im Leben* for the origin of this identification, but to build a second hypothesis on top of this hypothesis, namely, that Jesus himself already spoke of himself as the 'Son of Man' is undesirable in principle. The explanation based on the fewest assumptions is the best. Occam's razor has to be wielded here. In other words, the question is not whether Jesus could have spoken of himself as the 'Son of Man', but whether it is necessary to assume that he did so. In my opinion the answer is no.

4. Finally, a traditional argument used for the same purpose by,

among others, Bultmann.[1] It is precisely in the synoptic sayings where he speaks of the 'Son of Man' and his parousia (e.g. Mk 8.38; Lk. 12.8-9 par. Mt. 10.23, 19.28) that Jesus does not identify himself with the 'Son of Man', although the evangelists in the context of their gospels and on their redactional level will have had this identification in view. But contrary to what happens in the sayings concerning the actions of the 'Son of Man' on earth and those concerning his passion, in which the identification of Jesus and the 'Son of Man' is abundantly clear, Jesus speaks in the first group of sayings of the 'Son of Man' as if of someone else. Now transmitters and redactors of Christian tradition will also have tended to make the identification more explicit in the parousia sayings. That these sayings have resisted this tendency could indicate that there was nothing in this group of words of Jesus to point to an identification of him with the 'Son of Man'.

My conclusion is that the historical Jesus probably did *not* call himself the 'Son of Man'. At the end of this section, however, it is necessary to observe that when I refer to Jesus' view of himself and of his mission I am speaking exclusively of the vision that Jesus explicitly made known. What silent thoughts he had of himself, what calling or responsibility, perhaps also what ambition he felt but did not express (and who expresses all his motives?) cannot be the object of historical study.

4. Jesus' View of Himself and of his Mission

The way is now to some extent clear to answer the question how the historical Jesus regarded himself and his mission. There can be no doubt that Jesus primarily saw his task as proclaiming that God's kingdom was at hand and, as the immediate consequence of this, calling his audience to turn away from wrong conduct, to change their lives, and to obey God's will without compromise. Jesus thus saw himself as a prophet more or less in the style of earlier prophets of Israel who had called for repentance and conversion and who had threatened those who did not obey God's will. Certainly Jesus regarded his prophetic work as being imposed upon him by God.

But Jesus thought that God's kingdom was so imminent that he saw his own prophetic preaching, accompanied by his exorcisms and

---

1. R. Bultmann, *Theologie des Neuen Testaments* (Tübingen: Mohr [Paul Siebeck], 5th edn, 1965), pp. 31-32.

healing, as the approach or the first beginning of the coming dominion of God and described it in these terms. Lk. 11.20 par. Mt. 12.28 and Lk. 16.16 par. Mt. 11.12 rightly preserve, as do other passages, the recollection that Jesus saw his own actions as the beginning of the kingdom of God.

If, as one may assume, Jesus did not see himself as just another prophet, then it was not because he regarded himself as 'the anointed of the Lord' or as 'the Son of Man', but simply because he thought God's kingdom was so close at hand that there was no more time left for further prophets. The time was 'full'; Jesus regarded himself as God's definitive prophet only because the time was 'up'.

When he was confronted by scorn and rejection and finally had to take into account his violent death, Jesus trusted that after his death he would be vindicated and rehabilitated; he counted on his speedy exaltation to heaven. Jesus viewed that exaltation or resurrection as the vindication of a suffering, righteous individual and not as part of the eschatological resurrection.

Jesus himself, I believe, did not think that he would be playing a leading part, as the 'Son of Man' for example, in the imminent acute coming-to-pass of God's dominion. Since his aspirations did not run in the direction of kingship over Israel, he did not call himself 'the anointed of the Lord' (Messiah/Christ). Under the influence of the authority and charisma with which he acted, some followers saw in him a future ideal king of Israel and therefore called him son of David and Christ. Others saw in him the future Son of Man, who according to Jewish apocalyptic traditions, would appear as judge and saviour as this aeon turned to the future aeon.

In separate parts of later tradition these terms for Jesus established themselves, but after Jesus' death they soon lost their original meaning. They became names for Jesus or, if they were still used functionally, they acquired a different significance.

Finally a few words which go beyond the bounds of historical writing. For faith, church and theology, the historical reconstruction offered here is not only harmless but even salutary, even more salutary than that in which the titles Messiah/Christ and Son of Man were applied by Jesus to himself.

It is harmless because it does not make any difference whether the question of a positive reaction to Jesus' message derived from the historical Jesus himself or from his followers. The good reaction, in both cases, can only be expressed in trust and self-surrender. The 'leap' is the same in both cases.

It is salutary for the following reason. It is more natural to recognise the special significance of Jesus on the grounds of the judgment and witness of those who knew him than on the grounds of claims Jesus made of himself. Even if contemporaries of Jesus characterised him inadequately with such titles as 'the anointed one' and 'Son of Man', it says a great deal that Jesus could have provoked these reactions. It makes him more worthy of belief if others recognised, from their own observation and experience, that he was worthy of those titles, than if he had applied them to himself.

Let me conclude with a question, which also includes a suggestion. Would theology and the church not do better, when putting into words the meaning of Jesus for a present-day audience, to refrain from using such unclear, misleading functional terms as 'Christ', 'Messiah' and 'Son of Man'? Jesus' message and the message about Jesus could be well communicated without those obscure and ambiguous terms. He himself had no need of them to describe his own role. That at least is what I have argued here.

ASKING BACK TO JESUS' IDENTITY*

Wayne A. Meeks

When I began graduate study of the New Testament, not quite three decades ago, the topic of the moment was the 'New Quest of the Historical Jesus'. I was privileged that year to hear lectures by Nils Dahl on the Christology of the New Testament as well as Dahl's Shaffer Lectures, and to participate in a seminar on the history of Christology with Hans Frei. In the same year I read an impressive book by a young Dutch scholar of whom I had never heard, a form-critical analysis of the *Testaments of the Twelve Patriarchs*. I did not see any significant connection between old or new quests for the historical Jesus and the enigmas of that pseudepigraphon, and I never dreamed then that I and the master of the latter would become collaborators and close friends. I also could not have foreseen that Marinus de Jonge would become one of the most interesting and reliable writers on the subject of early Christology. Yet the reason why his work on Christology requires our earnest attention is just the same meticulous care, the respect for the ancient texts, and the soberness of historical inquiry that de Jonge demonstrated already in his dissertation. Those qualities are evident in his book, *Jesus, The Servant-Messiah*.[1]

---

* A slightly longer version of this essay was read as a paper at a symposium held in Leiden, 25 January 1991, honoring M. de Jonge on the occasion of his retirement from the Faculty of Theology at Leiden. I have largely retained the form of the oral presentation. The paper has also been published in Dutch translation in the proceedings of that symposium in H.E. Wevers *et al.* (eds.), *Jezus' visie op Zichzelf: in discussie met de Jonge's christologie* (Nijkerk: Callenbach, 1991), pp. 34-47.

1. New Haven: Yale University Press, 1991; also published in Dutch as *Jezus als Messias: Hoe Hij zijn zending zag* (Boxtel: Katholieke Bijbelstichting; Brugge: Uitgeverij Tabor, 1990).

In Quest of Continuity

It is important to keep in mind that this book on 'the historical Jesus' is the sequel to another book that, in reverse chronological order, treats 'The Earliest Christian Response to Jesus'.[1] De Jonge thus reminds us of a lesson that New Testament scholars have learned only very slowly and imperfectly—the beginning point for understanding as much as we can about Jesus' identity is not with some supposed 'bare facts' of his life, as if these could be extracted by some antiseptic science untainted by human interactions. On the contrary, the beginning point is with the responses (I always thought the subtitle of the former book should have been in the plural!) of those people near to Jesus who first tried to understand him. The way to proceed, as de Jonge explains in the new book, borrowing a word from Ferdinand Hahn, is by a *Rückfrage*, a process of 'asking back' from the responses to the one who evoked them. I believe, as I said in the foreword to *Christology in Context*, that this focus upon the interaction between Jesus and those who responded, as the point from which to explore his identity, has profound implications for the task of historical and theological under-standing. If we followed out some of those implications, we might arrive at some conclusions different from some of those that de Jonge reached in *Jesus, The Servant-Messiah*. I shall return to this question later; at the outset I only want to underline how much confusion and obscurity de Jonge has cleared away by locating the starting point so simply and directly where—we now see, thanks to him—it obviously must be.

The method to be employed in the Rückfrage toward Jesus is succinctly stated by de Jonge: 'We must view Jesus in the context of the Palestinian Judaism of his days and at the same time work back-ward from the various formulations of primitive Christianity toward the man who is at their center'.[2] The inquiry is thus doubly contextual and thus thoroughly historical. In a series of important articles, de Jonge has proved himself master of the earlier context, the shape of eschatological expectations in Second Temple Judaism. The results of those essays as well as the rigor of their method are apparent

1. *Christology in Context: The Earliest Christian Response to Jesus* (Philadelphia: Westminster Press, 1988).
2. De Jonge, *Servant-Messiah*, p. 11

throughout the present book and its predecessor. Three characteristics of that research deserve to be singled out. First, de Jonge has shown us good reason to be skeptical about the existence of 'eschatological titles' as the semantic carriers of Jewish beliefs about the future, and he is correspondingly chary about organizing the quest for Jesus' identity around such titles. Secondly, he fully recognizes the variety and fluidity of Jewish movements and factions contemporary with the rise of Christianity, and he acknowledges a related variety in the emerging Christian movement. Thirdly, he exercises admirable caution in historical questions about the putative sources and causes for that variety. The second context, the evolution of early Christian beliefs about Jesus, has been equally central to the projects of de Jonge's career as an exegete and historian. What has impressed me most about his christological essays has been his freedom from the need to define his work in terms of prevailing schools, whether in allegiance or in opposition. A striking example of his independence is his earnest dialogue with the work of the late T.W. Manson, who has been largely ignored by most recent European scholars and by most Americans of my generation and later. At the same time, de Jonge fully recognizes the limitations of Manson's position. Not least of those limitations was Manson's hearty skepticism about form criticism—de Jonge is a practicing form critic. Yet he has his own well-grounded skepticism about many of the results that seemed assured to an earlier generation of form critics. In his freedom to go his own way, taking what is best from all schools, de Jonge reminds me very much of my own teacher, Nils Dahl. De Jonge expressly adopts a good part of Dahl's proposed method for inquiry about Jesus, the combination of a 'cross-sectional' analysis of christological formulations found in several different early witnesses to the Jesus traditions with a 'longitudinal' unraveling of those traditions back toward their origins. In de Jonge's work we see the power not of some clever new method, but of clear, common sense thinking and sober, hard work. He continues in the main stream of scholarship in a way that could be called in the strict sense 'conservative', yet at the same time he remains continuously open to new discoveries and to the uncovering of gaps and faults in the scholarly tradition. I will reiterate the main conclusions that emerge from this admirable method, then introduce some questions about some of those conclusions from my own, more skeptical, perspective.

There are three crucial dimensions of continuity, de Jonge concludes, between what Jesus taught his disciples before his death and what the followers later proclaimed about him. First, the focus of the kerygma upon Jesus himself was a way of continuing Jesus' own sense of having the decisive, eschatological mission to establish the sovereign reign of God. Secondly, the proclamation of Jesus' exaltation and/or resurrection was rooted in Jesus' own reflection on the likelihood of his death and his confidence that God would not allow the mission to fail. Thirdly, the variety of ways the early Christians named Jesus was founded on the sense he had communicated to his disciples a unique relation with God.

Some Questions

The 'central issue', as de Jonge says, is the first of these, for in his analysis he undertakes to escape from the dilemma that has so narrowly constrained most discussion of the historical Jesus since the beginning of this century—as Bultmann formulated the question all too simply, 'How did the proclaimer become the proclaimed?'[1] This formulation assumes that Jesus is to be understood quintessentially as a prophet who announced the imminent arrival of the kingdom of God, and that the post-Easter kerygma, on the contrary, announces Jesus, the crucified and risen messiah. De Jonge's reformulation is less succinct but more judicious, and it avoids the sharp dichotomy between before and after the events at Passover:

> Already during his earthly ministry Jesus' disciples must have been firmly convinced that he was not just a prophet, but the final prophet, and that he not only announced the coming of God's Kingdom like a second John the Baptist, but had inaugurated it through his own words and actions. Given the multiple attestation of Jesus' message concerning the Kingdom, we may assume that he himself did, in fact, claim to bring the Kingdom onto earth, modestly present now but soon to be realized in full power and glory.[2]

The way in which de Jonge arrives at this reformulation is one of the most significant interpretive moves in the book. His beginning point is not, as one might have expected from the way the debate has

1. See R. Bultmann, *Theology of the New Testament* (trans. K. Grobel; New York: Charles Scribner's Sons, 1951), I, p. 33: '*The proclaimer became the proclaimed*—but the central question is: in what sense?' (italics original).

2. De Jonge, *Servant-Messiah*, p. 78.

traditionally been conducted, a ranking of Jesus-sayings on a scale of probable authenticity followed by a deduction of Jesus' intention from the critical minimum. Rather, de Jonge begins with the kerygmatic interpretation of Jesus' death. The 'opalescent' notion of resurrection, whatever one might speculate about the origins of the belief that Jesus was raised, was not in itself sufficient to explain the centering of the kerygma. The interpretive models applied to Jesus' death did not in themselves imply a decisive, 'eschatological' change in the relation between God and humanity. The fact that the followers did see Jesus' death as the 'final', decisive event can best be understood on the assumption that they had already believed that Jesus had inaugurated God's sovereign reign among humans. Again, de Jonge's own words make the point better than my paraphrase:

> The post-Easter belief that God's vindication of Jesus had ushered in a new era (a new era that was already manifesting itself in the lives of his followers and that would culminate in their resurrection at the end of time) would never have received such prominence if the dynamic presence of the Kingdom of God had not been recognized in Jesus even before Easter, and if this had not led to the expectation that its complete realization was at hand.[1]

This argument, while not altogether unprecedented, in its full context here is quite novel. It seems to me, moreover, quite convincing. It could be regarded as a way of putting some flesh onto Bultmann's rather grudging concession that Jesus' teaching implied a Christology. About the other two conclusions, continuity of the early church's proclamation with Jesus' interpretation of his own death and with his sense of his relation with God, I have more questions, four of which I will address briefly here.

a. *Models for Interpreting Jesus' Death.*
De Jonge, in his second chapter, reminds us of Bultmann's response to the 'New Quest'. It remains impossible, Bultmann believed, to say anything about Jesus' understanding of his own death. Furthermore, he believed that theologically the question was unimportant. De Jonge disagrees on both counts. On the theological side, he says:

---

1.   De Jonge, *Servant-Messiah*, p. 58.

> Had Jesus not stood in a unique relationship with God and had he not
> been fully aware of everything this involved, the crucifixion would have
> been robbed of its dignity and its depth of meaning.[1]

On the historical side, he argues that it is at least plausible that Jesus could have used for himself each of the three main models that his followers later used to interpret his death. It is here that de Jonge comes closest to the concerns and approach represented by Manson. In both the theological and the historical side of the question, I find myself unpersuaded. I am rather inclined to believe that in this instance Bultmann was more nearly right.

The theological issue that disturbs me here is raised by the telltale phrase in the sentence I quoted, 'fully aware'. Unless Jesus was 'fully aware' both of his relationship with God and of the meaning of his impending death, then that death could not have full meaning for others. This claim presupposes a conception of human identity wholly determined by individual self-consciousness. That conception underlay much of the discussion of the historical Jesus, especially in English, in the first half of this century, for the key question was often put in terms of 'Jesus' messianic self-consciousness'. T.W. Manson is a prime representative of that tradition. Yet why should we equate the historic identity of a person with that person's self-awareness? All of what I significantly am can surely not be limited to what I am 'fully aware' of being. Moreover, what I really am is not identical with what I think myself to be in the privacy of my introspection—I have become what I am through a process of interaction with others, and I am what I am in the context of others, both in memory and in presence. Let us take an example of our own time, one about whom we know a great deal more than we know of Jesus. From the writings and recorded speeches of Martin Luther King, Jr, it is clear that he thought of himself as a prophet. It is also clear that he anticipated the likelihood of his own violent death, and that he reflected on the meaning of that eventuality in the light of scripture, the Christian tradition about Jesus' Passion, the history of African Americans' suffering, the life of Gandhi, and other models. Nevertheless, it was not his thoughts about himself alone that made him a prophet and a martyr for millions of people. Were it not for the responses of his followers and of his opponents and of a variety of public figures and institutions to him

---

1. De Jonge, *Servant-Messiah*, p. 32.

and his movement, his thoughts about himself might have been a delusion. But because of those responses, and equally because of his responses to those responses, he became indeed and remains a prophet and a martyr. It is only in retrospect that historic identity becomes apparent. Even those people close enough to Mikhail Gorbachev to know what images he has of himself could not tell us what his historic identity will turn out to be; we shall have to wait some years to know that. So, too, the 'dignity and depth of meaning' of the crucifixion could only become apparent as Jesus' followers responded to it and reflected on it. I see no theological reason why we should imagine that Jesus was fully aware of all that it would come to mean. We might go so far as to say that what Jesus may have thought about his death is of relatively little importance either to his first followers or to us. What is important is what God thought about it and did about it. It seems to me that the early church's reflection on just this point is visible in the Gethsemane tradition in the Synoptics, in which Jesus prays God to 'take this cup away from me' (Mk 14.36), its development in the Epistle to the Hebrews ('Even though he was the son, he learned obedience from what he suffered' [4.8]), and its rejection in the Fourth Gospel (12.27-33). We find very little in the New Testament about Jesus' intentions. Rather, the leitmotiv that we find 'cross-sectionally' in the New Testament's reflections on Jesus' death is Jesus' obedience. Hence de Jonge's formulation that we find later in the same chapter of *Jesus, The Servant-Messiah* is much to be preferred to the statement I quoted earlier: '[Jesus'] death could not have served God's purpose had his life not been dedicated to the service of God and humankind all along'.[1]

I have argued so far that, even if we could know in some detail what images Jesus used to make sense of his own identity and his mission and of the possibility that he might die violently, that knowledge would not make much difference theologically. That is not the same as saying that such knowledge would be completely irrelevant or uninteresting theologically. But how much can we in fact know? Historically, the key question is this: was Jesus' understanding of his mission organized around the same three models that, according to de Jonge, shaped the earliest post-Easter tradition? These are the traditions of an envoy of God rejected by Israel, of a suffering, righteous servant

1. De Jonge, *Servant-Messiah*, p. 44.

vindicated by God and of one who suffers and dies for others. I am not sure just how strong a claim de Jonge is really making here. It is certainly plausible that Jesus and his followers would have understood the dangers of his provocative mission and, at some point, would at least have considered the possibility that it might lead to his death. It is also certainly plausible that Jesus himself would have reflected on biblical images that would help to make sense of that contingency. What seems to me to be lacking is sufficient positive evidence to convert this plausibility into probability. What evidence is there in the earliest tradition that Jesus understood his whole mission under the central category of suffering and violent death? Precisely because de Jonge operates with such high standards for historical evidence, the support he adduces for this claim is really quite small.

b. *A Suffering Son of Man?*
A surprising amount of weight in de Jonge's argument rests on certain claims that have been made about the meaning of the 'son of man' figure in Daniel 7. Now it is important to recognize that de Jonge parts company sharply with Cullmann, Manson and many others who have argued that 'Son of Man' was an eschatological *title* carrying a whole, relatively fixed constellation of beliefs. He does argue that Jesus used the phrase for himself, and that his doing so implies that he had reflected upon the text in Daniel and the tradition of its interpretation as a means of understanding his own mission. That is, again, altogether plausible, though it is far from certain. Following C.K. Barrett, Morna Hooker and Graham Stanton, de Jonge then goes a step further, arguing that the way in which the 'son of man' is depicted in Daniel and the subsequent tradition already entails a mission of vicarious suffering. This is a curious notion, and I am unable to see how the relevant texts support it. Now it is certainly the case that Daniel was written in the context of grave suffering on the part of those citizens of Israel who regarded themselves as faithful to the covenant. It is further true that the interpretation of the vision in Dan. 7.18 equates the human figure with 'the holy ones of the Most High', who are probably the faithful of Israel (rather than, say, the angels representing Israel). Thus we can argue that the vision implies that the very ones presently suffering will later obtain power. But that is very far from saying that it is *by means of their suffering* that they achieve vindication, or that the mission of the human-like figure is to suffer. In the

idiom of the vision itself, the human-like figure does not in fact suffer. For the reader to draw the conclusion that 'he' *must* suffer is thus an interpretive leap that is not justified in the text. There is, of course, no guarantee that Jesus and his contemporaries would have read the text in a way that we would regard as legitimate. They may very well have misread it in just the way that Barrett and company have done. In order to see whether that was likely, however, we need to find an example of an interpretation of the text near to Jesus' time that contains the required viewpoint. Barrett, Hooker, Stanton and de Jonge find this in *1 Enoch* and *4 Ezra*. As far as I can see, however, in both cases the situation is very nearly the same as with Daniel 7. That is, the *Similitudes of 1 Enoch* allude to the suffering of Israel, and *4 Ezra* dwells on the problem of these sufferings, and both show the results of reflecting on the human-like figure of Daniel 7—but they do not connect the two in such a way that suffering is conceived of as part of the mission of the human figure. If indeed Jesus did call himself 'the son of man', and if his earliest followers were correct in assuming that it was Dan. 7.13 to which he alluded, rather than the more commonplace senses of the Aramaic phrase, then it would surely betray a very high sense of his own importance in God's eschatological actions. Nevertheless, I do not believe it would tell us anything about the way Jesus may have thought about his potential death.

c. *A Prophetic Son of David*?

The older debates about the historical Jesus focused almost obsessively on the question whether Jesus called himself 'the Messiah' or whether he acted in a way congruent with the ideology of messiahship that was supposed to exist in the Judaism of the time. Now we have come to understand that there was no such monolithic 'doctrine' of what must happen at the end of days. De Jonge himself has played a large role in the revisionist research that has opened our eyes to the variety of Jewish belief and practice both in and outside the land of Israel in Roman times. His studies of the fluidity with which the adjective 'anointed' was used in the Qumran texts and in other extant documents of the period are particularly important, and they show us that 'Messiah' (like 'son of man') was not a 'title' or 'office' entailing a fixed role to be played by an eschatological figure.[1] The question the

1. 'The Use of the Term "Anointed" in the Time of Jesus', *NovT* 8 (1966), pp. 132-48; 'The Role of Intermediaries in God's Final Intervention in the Future

historian has to answer is therefore, why did the followers of Jesus after his death so quickly treat the adjective as if it were a title, so intimately linked with the story of Jesus' death and resurrection that in a short time it becomes virtually a cognomen for Jesus? That is rather more complicated than the question posed by an older generation of scholars, such as Wrede, who asked why the messianic *title* was applied to someone whose life looked unmessianic, the latter meaning 'not royal' and 'not military'. De Jonge approaches this question from an unusual direction. He observes that biblical and postbiblical traditions about David often emphasize what we might call 'charismatic' attributes— possession of the Spirit, prophecy, composition of psalms. It is therefore possible, de Jonge suggests, not only that the author of the Gospel of Mark may have had such traits in mind in portraying Jesus as 'the Christ, son of David', but that Jesus may actually have thought of himself in this way. If 'anointed' did not mean exclusively 'royal' even when applied to David or his descendant, then absence of royal traits from the early Jesus-tradition does not preclude his having understood himself as a *prophetic* son of David and therefore 'anointed'. Perhaps it is possible, but if Jesus had said any such thing to his disciples, would we not expect to find much clearer evidence in the Gospels than in fact de Jonge is able to adduce? Further, while the Davidic tradition does include attribution of prophetic and 'wisdom' traits to David and the Davidides, are these traits not always subsumed under the general umbrella of kingship? One of the clearest examples is one on which de Jonge's argument depends heavily, *Psalm of Solomon* 17. Certainly the longed-for savior for whom the psalmist prays will be 'powerful in the holy spirit and wise in the counsel of understanding with strength and righteousness'.[1] But he displays these virtues precisely as 'their king, son of David' (v. 21), and he is throughout the relevant verses of the psalm pre-eminently a royal figure. The prophetic, wisdom, and, we may add, priestly features of

according to the Qumran Scrolls', in O. Michel (ed.), *Studies on the Jewish Background of the New Testament* (Assen: Van Gorcum, 1969), pp. 44-63; 'The Earliest Christian Use of *Christos*: Some Suggestions', *NTS* 32 (1986), pp. 321-43; among other essays. All are now conveniently reprinted in M. de Jonge, *Jewish Eschatology, Early Christian Christology and the Testaments of the Twelve Patriarchs: Collected Essays* (NovTSup, 63; Leiden: Brill, 1991).

1. *Ps. Sol.* 17.37, trans. R.B. Wright in J.H. Charlesworth (ed.), *The Old Testament Pseudepigrapha* (Garden City, NY: Doubleday, 1985), II, p. 668.

the Davidic (and Solomonic) traditions go back after all to courtly
encomia that attribute to the king all the virtues of the institutions
over which he presides. Thus I remain skeptical whether there was
any distinct tradition of a 'prophetic son of David', and even more
skeptical that Jesus identified himself with such a tradition.

d. *An Exclusively Religious Identity?*

My final question is a more general one. What I miss most in this
book is the sort of attention to the political and social situation of
Roman Palestine that we see, although briefly, in ch. 10 of
Christology in Context. The people who were reading Daniel 7 in
Jesus' day, those who were speculating about a king like David who
might arise, those who listened for the voice of a new prophet, an
Elijah or a Moses did so not as a 'theological' exercise, but because
they were desperately hoping for a change in the world in which they
lived. In other writings, de Jonge has shown his sensitivity to that
context. In the present book, however, we learn a great deal about the
ways Jesus may have responded to some contemporary ways of interpreting scriptural texts, but we do not hear very much about the ways
Jesus may have responded to the resentments and anxieties engendered
by Rome's power and the opportunism of Rome's local clients. I can
imagine that de Jonge has avoided those questions here in order to
distance himself from the anachronisms and the modernizing agendas
that too often control our attempts to understand the social and economic context of Jesus. I only wish that, precisely because he knows
how to avoid those pitfalls, he had given us more of his insight into
the real world that Jesus saw and to which he responded.

Identity and Interaction

I have ventured these peripheral criticisms of the work of our
honored colleague and friend, because his work characteristically
invites and welcomes critical response. Moreover, the metaphor of
'response', as I noted at the beginning of my remarks, is central to the
design of the earlier book and fundamental to the later one. Now in
conclusion I want to pose a question—or rather to suggest that
de Jonge's understanding of Christology as response to Jesus poses a
question about the way in which we ought to think about the identity
of any historic figure, above all of Jesus. The question, put as simply

as possible, is this: is the identity of Jesus something that can intelligibly be separated from the sum of all knowable responses to him? I will not try to answer the question, not only because an adequate argument would require far more space than this essay allows, but also because it needs a philosophical and theological competence that I do not possess. I raise it because I hope others will take up the task of working it out.

In many fields of human science over several decades of this century we have seen a gradual abandonment of essentialist definitions of human identity. In psychology, in philosophy and in literary theory, strong voices have suggested that it is only in processes of interaction with others that a human self is shaped. Indeed, some would say that the self *is* a process, a relationship. Perhaps some will insist with Kierkegaard that the self is centrally 'a relation that relates itself to itself'.[1] But even so, the relationship to itself is possible only because first it is related to others. There is no self apart from community. Hence we often say of someone, 'he's a different person when he's with her'. The self exists pre-eminently in social space; even that private self that is present in our inward reflection has been shaped by and depends upon the social transactions that it has experienced or imagined. There is, I think, a similar trend in the discussion of the concept of 'charisma' since Max Weber first borrowed that term from theologians, who had borrowed it from Paul. Charisma is not a 'stuff' to be found in the makeup of the leader; it is not what the leader thinks about himself or herself. Charisma is located somewhere in the intersection of many processes: a tradition in the process of transformation and reappropriation, a situation tense with need and possibility, a people ready to be led—and some figure who, to use de Jonge's metaphor, 'sparks it off'. All of this suggests to me that we ought to understand de Jonge's method of 'asking back' from the recorded responses to Jesus not as a preliminary to knowing the 'real' Jesus but as the *only* way we may know Jesus. There is no Jesus we can know apart from responses to him. Perhaps we can dare to go even further and to say that Jesus, like every human person, became who he 'really is' in that process of interaction with others. I do not mean by this formulation to deny the critical function of history and biography. Is it not the job of historians, not only biblical historians, to pry behind the public visage of notable people, to discover ways in which their

1. S. Kierkegaard, 'The Sickness unto Death', in *Fear and Trembling and The Sickness unto Death* (trans. W. Lowrie; Garden City, NY: Doubleday, 1954), p. 146.

contemporaries were misled or mistaken about them? Yes, but that is
not the same as discovering some inner self, the real person. Even
where we have direct statements from the subject that enable us to
know something of the way the subject thought about himself or herself, our experience with ourselves and our contemporaries does not
suggest that we can assume that the self-images are 'correct' while
those of others are 'false'. The historian who tries to discover the real
John F. Kennedy or the real Martin Luther King is still exploring
processes of interaction and perception between that person and
others. Yes, but what about the sense that each of us has, as we reflect
upon our own lives, that something of our identity remains uncap-
tured by all that even our closest friends see in us, a mysterious,
incommunicable continuity of our person? I think it is important that
we recognize this experience, and that we acknowledge this ineffable
center in others. It would be a mistake, however, to suppose that this
mysterious self-awareness is more fully 'myself' than the self that is
formed by and exists in relationship. Without dialogue, without
response, without transactions there is no self, no identity. The real
Jesus is the figure who appears, in de Jonge's phrase, 'at the cross-
roads of traditions'. Of course there is more, there is an ineffable
center we cannot grasp. The very peculiar rhetoric invented by the
Gospel of Mark seems to me the paradigmatic acknowledgment of the
limits to our knowledge. The ineffable must be left unsaid.

MARINUS DE JONGE'S SHAFFER LECTURES:
WHERE DOES JESUS RESEARCH NOW STAND?*

Dieter Lührmann

Professor de Jonge's Shaffer Lectures were given in Yale University
in February 1989. The title of those Lectures, *Jesus, The Servant-
Messiah*, goes back 50 years to the Shaffer Lectures of 1939 given by
his English teacher T.W. Manson (1893–1958). The central point of
Manson's argument was that Jesus had understood his own work as
that of the 'servant of God' of Isaiah 53. This theory had great
influence also in the German-speaking world where Joachim Jeremias
and Oscar Cullmann came to very similar conclusions.

However, subsequent research has rightly insisted that the
significance of Isaiah 53 for early Christian Christology has been
considerably overrated here, especially in relation to the possible
significance of that chapter for Jesus' own self-understanding. De
Jonge therefore chooses his methodological starting point much more
carefully. He takes seriously the insight of form criticism, that the
sources which we have available reflect primarily the influence of
Jesus and provide no immediate access to the historical Jesus himself.
In the case of Paul, we have texts from his own hand; in the case of
Jesus we do not—we do not even have texts in Aramaic, the language
that he spoke. Further, we only have texts which are positive about
Jesus' preaching. Statements from Jewish or Roman sources are much

* A somewhat longer German version of this was read as a paper at a
symposium held in Leiden, 25 January 1991, in the presence of Professor de Jonge
to mark his retirement from the Faculty of Theology at Leiden. A Dutch version
appeared in the proceedings of that symposium in H.E. Wevers *et al.* (eds.), *Jezus'
visie op Zichzelf: in discussie met de Jonge's christologie* (Nijkerk: Callenbach,
1991), pp. 19-33. This translation is by Christopher Tuckett. Professor de Jonge's
Shaffer Lectures have been published under the title *Jesus, The Servant-Messiah*
(New Haven: Yale University Press, 1991).

later and in turn also reflect what had happened as a result of Jesus' preaching.

We thus encounter primarily the influence which was generated by Jesus; we do not encounter Jesus' own activity directly. De Jonge rightly emphasizes three early ideas in which this influence found expression; all three arise not from the theological reflections of individuals but are more widely based:

1. The interpretation of Jesus' death as the death of one of God's messengers rejected by Israel. This occurs above all in the Sayings Source Q, but also in Mark and Paul. It goes back to the deuteronomistic tradition as Odil Hannes Steck has shown.[1]

2. The idea of Jesus as a suffering, righteous servant who will be justified by God. This idea is above all central for the Christology of the Gospel of Mark and is linked there with the Son of Man title. It too goes back to Old Testament traditions.

3. The view of Jesus' death as vicarious. This is linked with the Christ title, and is determinative not only for Paul but also for the tradition used by Paul. The location of this in terms of its tradition-history is more difficult; de Jonge is probably correct in tracing it back to Hellenistic Judaism, though he acknowledges that a sharp distinction between Palestinian and Hellenistic Judaism has been shown to be more and more questionable.

At the end of his third chapter, de Jonge leaves open the possibility in relation to all three ideas whether Jesus himself could have interpreted his own activity and his coming death in such a way, without any one of these ideas necessarily excluding any of the others. For me too these seem to be the most important interpretative categories which emerge from the earliest sources, that is, Mark, Q and Paul.

The book of Acts on the other hand reflects the beginnings of the Christian movement from a distance of two or three generations, and John's Gospel has Jesus himself as the guarantor of a Christology which proceeds along a route from pre-existence, via the incarnation to exaltation. However gnostic, docetic, naively docetic or incarnational this may be, it is clearly a later development in the early Christian history of theology which allows scarcely any conclusions to be drawn about the historical Jesus.

Martin Luther had preferred John's Gospel to the Synoptics for

1. O.H. Steck, *Israel und das gewaltsame Geschick der Propheten* (Neukirchen–Vluyn: Neukirchener Verlag, 1967).

precisely this reason; there is much more here to be learnt about Jesus' relationship to his Father than in the other Gospels. Schleiermacher too wanted to ground the Christology of his *Glaubenslehre* (*The Christian Faith*) on the sayings of the Johannine Jesus, even though Schleiermacher himself has his place in the history of the two source theory. However, ever since the quest for the historical Jesus in the nineteenth century, it has been agreed that Mark and Q are the two sources which enable a reconstruction of the 'picture of our Redeemer that is genuine and true to life with the only reliable means of historical criticism', as Heinrich Julius Holtzmann put it in his book *Die synoptischen Evangelien* of 1863 which put forward in summary form the two-source theory. Ever since then it has been Mark and Q, perhaps with some of the special material peculiar to Matthew and Luke, which have been the sources used for trying to discover who Jesus was.

Form criticism however focused primarily on the Christian proclamation. The recollection of Jesus' words and actions had its *Sitz im Leben* in early Christian preaching—so Dibelius; but the essence of the preaching was that Jesus was present as Lord of the Church.[1] According to Bultmann, the Jesus tradition was handed on by the Hellenistic community which consistently restricted Jesus' influence to the saving significance of his death and saw this as encompassing Jesus' significance for their present.[2] For form criticism the basis of Christianity was the preaching *about* Jesus, not his own preaching.

Nevertheless both Dibelius and Bultmann could write books about Jesus, though it was unclear what they were thereby trying to do. Bultmann's book was the start of a series 'The Immortals',[3] which continued with volumes on Buddha, Confucius, Friedrich Nietzsche, Giordano Bruno and Zarathustra. In Bultmann's book itself there is nothing discernible of his later antithesis between the historical Jesus and the proclaimed Christ, if indeed Bultmann had developed the idea at this time. One could in fact read the book at the time of its publication in 1926 as a presentation (admittedly a very strange one) of the founding of Christianity in the preaching of Jesus.

1.   M. Dibelius, *From Tradition to Gospel* (London: Nicholson, 1934 [1919]).

2.   R. Bultmann, *The History of the Synoptic Tradition* (Oxford: Basil Blackwell, 1963 [1921]).

3.   R. Bultmann, *Jesus and the Word* (London: Charles Scribner's Sons, 1934 [1926]).

However, form criticism did not aim to find the basis of Christianity in the historical Jesus. Christianity was based on the early Christian kerygma; and Jesus himself belonged within Judaism. Form criticism was linked with dialectical theology and thereby became in the German-speaking world a highly theological way of interpretation. It found its classic form in Bultmann's *Theology of the New Testament* with the sharp distinction there between kerygma and theology.[1] Only with Paul and John does a theology arise, according to Bultmann's definition of 1925: 'Theology means the conceptual description of man's existence as determined by God'[2]. The kerygma on the other hand is the proclamation of Jesus as the eschatological saving event, where such a conceptual description of man's existence as determined by God is still lacking.

From this developed the search for the so-called 'pre-Pauline formulae'. In his *Theology*, Bultmann had ascribed practically all the christological statements in Paul's letters to the kerygma of the earliest Hellenistic or Palestinian communities. They were therefore pre-Pauline. There is no Christology in the strict sense in Paul, but a soteriology, namely the concept of justification as the 'description of man's existence determined by God'.

This was followed by the well-known compendia of Ferdinand Hahn, Klaus Wengst and others[3]. Already in 1951, in a short article on Rom. 3.24-26, Ernst Käsemann had developed criteria for determining such pre-Pauline traditions—un-Pauline vocabulary, formal unity, and relative independence in relation to the context.[4] This has in the meantime been widely accepted. There are often sufficient indications in the texts themselves. Paul himself describes what he writes in 1 Cor. 15.3ff. as words he has taken over and is now handing on to

1. R. Bultmann, *Theology of the New Testament* (2 vols.; London: SCM Press, 1955 [1948]).

2. R. Bultmann, 'Das Problem einer theologischen Exegese des Neuen Testaments', *Zwischen den Zeiten* 3 (1925), pp. 334-57, repr. in G. Strecker (ed.), *Das Problem der Theologie des Neuen Testaments* (Darmstadt: Wissenschaftliche Buchgesellschaft, 1975), pp. 249-77, on p. 272.

3. F. Hahn, *The Titles of Jesus in Christology* (London: Lutterworth, 1969 [1963]); K. Wengst, *Christologische Formeln und Lieder des Urchristentums* (Gütersloh: Gütersloher Verlagshaus, 1972).

4. E. Käsemann, 'Zum Verständnis von Röm 3.24-26', *ZNW* 43 (1950–51), pp. 150-54, repr. in *Exegetische Versuche und Besinnungen*, I (Göttingen: Vandenhoeck & Ruprecht, 1964), pp. 96-100.

the Corinthians, and he points to preaching as the context for this process. So too he describes the eucharistic tradition in 1 Cor. 11.23-25 as a piece of tradition; the *Sitz im Leben* of this will no doubt have been the celebration of the Eucharist by the community.

Similar observations had of course been made before Bultmann. What was new with him and with subsequent work was that the 'kerygma', in distinction from theology, became a category of its own, and indeed far more than the examples mentioned show. It was my church history teacher, Hans Freiherr von Campenhausen, who forcefully exorcized me of the *Formelitis* which I too indulged in. He thought in larger epochs than the couple of decades which have left their deposit in the New Testament. There was no confession going back as far as the earliest community, far less any baptismal confession before the third, if not the fourth, century. And that was confirmed for me in my further work. There was thus a yawning gap between the early Christian confessions assumed by New Testament scholars and what was actually formulated as a confession in the early church.

Bultmann and the Bultmann school had, however, achieved a methodologically workable model—theology as interpretation of the kerygma. This was understandable especially against the background of the German Confessing Church which had provided the life situation of New Testament scholars, particularly from Bultmann's circle—these included my New Testament teachers Günther Bornkamm and Hans Conzelmann together with Ernst Fuchs, Ernst Käsemann and Herbert Braun as well as Heinrich Schlier who then went his own way by converting to Catholicism. They all reached their positions in German Universities only after 1945, and they saw themselves engaged as teachers of the church, interpreters of the confession, but as a result of the debate about demythologizing coming under the suspicion of heresy—some more, some less.

A generation after Bultmann and indeed already after his pupils, the questions are posed differently, not only in terms of exegesis and methodology, but also in terms of systematic theology. Bultmann and his pupils had started the discussion about the theological significance of the historical Jesus themselves, but in the meantime this has become an issue independent of the restriction by the kerygma.

What is important above all for me is the fourth chapter of Professor de Jonge's Shaffer Lectures: 'Jesus as Inaugurator of the

Kingdom: Eschatology and Christology'. In response I will pose a few questions that are in no way intended to be rhetorical but are rather intended to promote dialogue.

In this fourth chapter we can see more of de Jonge's skill in his exegetical overview, in his clear presentation and in his concentration on key issues. He starts from the observation that already the earliest sources understand Jesus' death as the final, eschatological turning point. They do not understand it simply as a further example of the fate of prophets or of righteous ones who are always persecuted and whose death could even effect atonement. Where then did this insistence on the final eschatological nature of the turning point which had occurred with Jesus' death and his justification by God come from?

De Jonge's first answer is that the early witnesses believed that God's unlimited sovereign rule had already begun during Jesus' earthly activity. That is carefully stated; it is still about the faith of those who followed Jesus, not of Jesus' own self-understanding. The claim does however lead back correctly from Jesus' death to the influence of Jesus on people during his lifetime. It raises the question of the continuity of Christian faith over, or behind, the cross. This continuity is the central theme of de Jonge's fourth chapter and it will provide the central theme of my dialogue with him too.

I would like straightaway to raise the key question of whether this continuity has a basis in the activity of Jesus himself, or even in his own understanding of his work, or whether it is only formulated by the faith of his disciples.

Form-critical interpretation of the Gospels has had to engage in debate with William Wrede's book on the messianic secret which destroyed a number of illusions. According to Wrede, Jesus had not regarded himself as Messiah, nor had his activity been in any way spectacularly messianic.[1] All messianic elements in the Gospels and in the traditions behind them owed more to the 'messianic dogma' of the early Christian community. Traditional Protestant dogmatics had based the messiahship of Jesus on the proof from prophecy and on his miracle-working activity. Neither, according to Wrede, could any longer be established in the activity of the historical Jesus. Out of this necessity, form criticism—and with it dialectical theology—made a virtue: the terminology of the 'messianic dogma' was replaced by

1. W. Wrede, *The Messianic Secret* (London: James Clarke, 1971 [1901]).

Christology; Christology, however, was understood first of all as soteriology, subsequently also by the means of traditional dogmatics as the application of attributes to the Messiah, be it miracles which were ascribed to him, or the christological proof 'from the Scriptures'.

In Wrede one can see not only the conflict between exegesis and dogmatic tradition, but also the abiding dogmatic context of exegetical work. In our own time this relationship can perhaps be most clearly seen in the conflict which Catholic colleagues have with the papal teaching authorities, where there is historical criticism of the dogma that has been handed down. They still have a dogma which can be criticized. In the Protestant domain, historical criticism has long won the victory over dogma and there is no longer any binding church teaching, or at least hardly any. Within the Protestant tradition, therefore, the difficulty arises in trying to formulate historical statements that are universally valid, since they are so much at the mercy of historical criticism.

Perhaps the reason why the 'rule of God' has been so consistently stressed as the centre of Jesus' preaching in the Catholic sphere is because this theme seems from a historical-critical angle to be useful over against ecclesiastical understanding. This, however, goes back to Wrede's generation. Wrede's contemporary Johannes Weiss wrote his book on *The Kingdom of God in the Teaching of Jesus*, a book which amounted to a critique of German Protestant theology at the end of the nineteenth century in general.[1] The 'Kingdom [German *Reich*] of God' could no longer indicate anything comparable to the 'German Empire [*Reich*]' founded in 1871; what Jesus had proclaimed was rather the 'Kingdom *of God*' as an alternative to all earthly rule—it was apocalyptic, looking forward to the end of existing power relationships.

Within German Protestantism, New Testament exegesis in the period that followed was led as a result to look at the difference between what Jesus had preached and what the early Christian community believed, especially when Albert Schweitzer had made exegetes aware that all portraits of Jesus which aimed either to establish or to criticize contemporary Christianity were simply reflecting contemporary questions. In the German-speaking milieu, after the collapse of the Wilhelmian Reich in 1918, the terminology of

1.   J. Weiss, *Jesus' Proclamation of the Kingdom of God* (London: SCM Press, 1971 [1892]).

the 'Kingdom [*Reich*] of God' was replaced in dialectical theology by 'Reign [German *Herrschaft*] of God', but still as before regarded as central in the preaching of Jesus.[1] This replacement by 'Reign of God' led to criticism from the anti-authoritarian movement, and afterwards from the feminist movement.[2] It is therefore significant that more and more German Catholic literature prefers the simple transliteration of the Greek *basileia tou theou* which begs no questions.

Ever since Alfred Loisy (1857–1940) said 'Jesus preached the Kingdom of God; it was the church that came', this critique of the church has remained within the memory of *all* theology and *all* exegesis. Ever since, the alternatives have seemed clear—either the church, in whatever form, is to be criticized on the basis of what Jesus himself wanted, or the church, renewed in whatever form, is based on early Christian Christology. Is there a third possibility under the cipher of continuity?

The question about the continuity between Jesus and Christology appears to be above all a modern problem arising on the basis of the historical critical method itself. John's Gospel, for example, offers such a continuity, since Jesus presents himself there as the Son of God sent by the Father. The 'Kingdom of God' does not constitute the content of Jesus' preaching, apart from a few marginal references (Jn 3.3,5; 18.36). John's Gospel does however provide a hermeneutical model for the difference between the earthly Jesus and the exalted Christ, when for example it says that the disciples did not yet understand what Jesus' entry into Jerusalem involved, but only after he was glorified (12.16, cf. 2.22). Thus it was John's Gospel that was central for Wrede's theory of the 'messianic secret' in the Gospels in general.

Historical criticism has rightly rejected John's Gospel as a primary source for Jesus. But even in the Synoptic tradition it can be shown that the question of continuity has already shaped the oldest layers of the Jesus tradition. In the Sayings Source, those sent out by Jesus are to proclaim, 'The Kingdom of God has drawn near' (Lk. 10.9/ Mt. 10.7), and these messengers stand under the promise 'Whoever hears you hears me, and whoever rejects you rejects me; and whoever rejects me rejects him who sent me' (so Lk. 10.16 as opposed to the version in

1.   A. Schweitzer, *The Quest of the Historical Jesus* (London: A. & C. Black, 1925 [1906]).

2.   Since the German term *Herrschaft* carries both authoritarian and patriarchal overtones, as verbally it calls for obedience and asserts the rule of men.

Mt. 10.40 which replaces 'hear' by 'accept', cf. Mt. 25.31-46). For Q there is thus a continuity between Jesus as the one in whose activity the Kingdom of God is near (cf. Lk. 11.20/Mt. 12.28) and those who are sent out by him; they represent the one who has sent them, and not only him but God himself who in turn has sent Jesus.

In the Gospel of Mark on the other hand there is no such description of the content of the missionaries' preaching in the parallel account of the sending out of the Twelve in Mk 6.7-13, 30. Rather, the imminence of the Kingdom of God is exclusively the content of Jesus' preaching in Galilee (Mk 1.15); after Jesus' resurrection, the gospel to be preached is not simply a continuation of Jesus' preaching. One could not have in Mark 'whoever hears you hears me'; rather, 'whoever hears you hears the gospel which had its beginning with Jesus'. But its definitive form is only to be found just as it appears in the Gospel of Mark itself.

This idea of the difference between Jesus and the gospel as the preaching of the church reflects the historical circumstances of the time of Mark. There is an even greater distance from the events concerned in Matthew and Luke. In Paul, however, earlier than Mark, we find as in John marginal references to Jesus' theme of the Kingdom of God; but his theology has provoked in its sharpest form the antithesis between the historical Jesus and the proclaimed Christ, however 2 Cor. 5.16 is to be understood.

Paul does not draw out the theological consequences, for example with regard to the relationship between Jews and Gentiles, by referring to Jesus' behaviour; rather he refers to a new teaching about God which he sees as based on the claims about Jesus' death on the cross and about Jesus' justification by God in the resurrection. Modern historical criticism develops out of this the alternative 'Jesus or Paul?' This can be in very varied forms depending on the circumstances, but usually presents Jesus as the means of rescuing a Pauline Christianity that has been swamped by dogma. Only in the era of dialectical theology, with Barth's commentary of Romans and Bultmann's commentary on John, has the interpretation of the preaching about Jesus, rather than Jesus' own preaching, been central. Indeed for Bultmann, the latter belongs to the presuppositions of New Testament theology and is not itself a part of it. So too for Barth, it is what Paul said that is valid for the present.

Continuity between the content of the preaching of Jesus and the

early Christian preaching is thus a problem which was already posed
by our earliest sources, most pointedly perhaps in the Sayings Source
Q which we can only reconstruct—here Jesus' claim about the imminence of the Kingdom of God is re-presented by those who follow in
his footsteps. De Jonge, along with many others, therefore tries to go
in the opposite way, from the early Christian preaching back to Jesus,
when he asks whether the christological titles applied to Jesus can be
traced back to Jesus' own activity.

He firmly separates off the title 'Son of Man' and concentrates on
'Christos = Messiah' and 'Son of God'. He starts with Nils Astrup
Dahl's views on the specifically Pauline usage 'crucified Messiah'[1];
with this he refers to the well-known criterion of dissimilarity in
relation to Jewish tradition, for there the Messiah is never a suffering
figure, let alone crucified. According to Dahl, it was in fact really
Jesus' opponents who finally forced Jesus to accept the Messiah title
for himself. Caiaphas was, so to speak, the father of Christology. De
Jonge thus tries to show that Jesus regarded himself as Messiah of his
own accord. He is aware of the methodological problems, since the
title Christ is missing in the Sayings Source Q and occurs in Mark
only seven times.

The crucial passages in this context are Peter's confession that Jesus
is the Christ, the Messiah (Mk 8.29), Jesus own confession before the
Sanhedrin, that he is the Christ, the Son of the Blessed (Mk 14.61-62),
the address as Son of David (Mk 10.46-52) and the debate which ends
negatively about whether the Messiah has to be the Son of David
(Mk 12.35-37). In the light of Jewish messianic expectations, de Jonge
is led to the theory that Jesus' crucifixion as 'King of the Jews' is only
intelligible if the Christ/Messiah title had already been applied to Jesus
earlier and had indeed corresponded with Jesus' own self-
understanding.

De Jonge argues very carefully, yet it seems to me that doubts
remain. I agree with him that the inscription 'King of the Jews' over
the cross gives the historical reason for Jesus' death sentence. But I do
not think that this provides us with convincing evidence for drawing
conclusions about Jesus' self-understanding. It is true that the Gospels
themselves do suggest a correlation, at times more clearly, at times
less so. But is 'King of the Jews' really to be connected with the

    1.   N.A. Dahl, 'The Crucified Messiah', in *The Crucified Messiah and Other
Essays* (Minneapolis: Augsburg, 1974), pp. 10-36.

Christ/Messiah title? The question remains—was it necessarily the case that the basis for Jesus' conviction was formulated appropriately?

There are also questions for me in relation to de Jonge's observations about the title 'Son of God'. On the basis of Nathan's prophecy in the Old Testament, he sees a close connection between Christ/Messiah and Son of God to be found in various layers of early Christian Christology. Both Mark and Q show that Jesus himself addressed God as Father. In Mark this occurs in the Gethsemane scene in Mk 14.36 where Mark gives the Aramaic address *abba* and then explains it in Greek as 'father'. In Q such an address occurs in the Lord's prayer, and above all in Jesus' thanksgiving to his father for the unique relationship he has with him (Lk. 10.21/Mt. 11.25-27). But is this connection really 'unique' when it is clear that all of God's children may address him as father? In Paul, *abba* is the way in which all children of God address him (Gal. 4.6; Rom. 8.15), something made possible by the Son of God. Can one then deduce from the address of God as father the exclusive description of Jesus as 'Son of God' in early Christology? In terms of the history of the tradition, is this title to be traced back to messianic ideas or to the divine sonship of the righteous one?

I can, however, agree with de Jonge's starting point in his summarizing conclusion—Jesus not only preached the Kingdom of God, but also made it present in his own activity. The conclusions which he draws from this have raised for me the question why I really baulk so much at the idea of continuity. De Jonge, who throughout expresses himself very cautiously, regards it as possible that Jesus saw himself as the Son of David promised by God, as the Messiah. And, according to de Jonge, Jesus spoke of God as father, which led to the title Son of God, whether Jesus himself used it or whether it was first used in early Christian confessions.

Why do I hesitate to accept this conclusion? I could give reasons based on my historical-critical work on the texts, and I have in any case already brought these reasons to bear in the guise of questions. The footnotes would refer almost exclusively to secondary literature in German, while there is an amazing calmness in literature of other languages in relation to this question. But wherever continuity is asserted in the German-speaking milieu, this occurs with a great deal more passion and also a claim to orthodoxy.

Historical criticism of the Christian tradition began with the Enlightenment in England, Holland and France; the German-speaking world at first took over only what had been first thought of there. In the nineteenth century, however, German theological study brought itself up to date to a great extent, from which we are all profiting right up to the present. The two-source theory was developed in this context as everywhere work on historical sources in the whole of Europe received a great boost. It was against such historical theology that the fundamental protest of dialectical theology developed which, in terms of methodology, took up form criticism. Form criticism as a method, however, postulated a fundamental discontinuity—it sought to discover not what Jesus had said but what the early Christian community had proclaimed who Jesus really had been. This was initially adopted with great scepticism, especially in Western Europe, but has in the meantime been widely accepted in moderate form. In the German-speaking world too, form criticism has in the meantime become one method alongside others, and no longer signifies *the* means for understanding the Gospels.

What then makes me hesitate to ask about continuity, and indeed makes me rather stress discontinuity? The history of theology is a part of history generally; and so the presuppositions of the history of theology have been historically determined. However, history is not a cabinet of curios in which one can assure oneself how much more modern the present is; nor is it a discipline dealing with hard facts. Rather, it has attained its best achievements when it has destroyed critically the dogmatically asserted claims of legitimation of each present era; it has achieved even more when it has been able to offer to each present era convincing models of legitimation that have not simply elevated by historical means what seemed to be self-evident.

The situation in theology is no different. In the history of theology, the acceptance of models to be used has been clearly dependent on the measure of their appropriateness to the times they were proposed. Now German history, from which I come, is not a history for which continuity should be asserted. Our German present can only be claimed as legitimate if 1945, 1933 and 1918, and also 1871, are emphasized as dates of discontinuity. Connected with this too is the fact that the significance of personalities who have determined history must also decline. Jesus cannot simply be one of the men who have made history.

It is therefore the context of historical experience that makes me, as a New Testament scholar in the German-speaking world, hesitate to look for some basic continuity. In Yale in February 1989, when de Jonge gave his Shaffer Lectures, I was very often asked—to my surprise—whether Germany should ever be reunited again. Very soon I had a stereotyped answer ready—from 1871–1945, for just over 70 years, only what could be reunited had lasted; the division, however, has already lasted for more than 40 years! I could not suspect what would happen in the same year 1989—but that is how history goes!

German history was defined for us, and also legitimated, by the discontinuity of the dates 1871, 1918, 1933, 1945. These dates also mark turning points in the history of theology in Germany. After 1871 the history-of-religions school arose, after 1918 form criticism, which in turn proved in 1933 to be the exegetical method for dialectical theology, and after 1945 redaction criticism appeared reflecting the experiences of the confessing church, seeking to actualize the confession in the present. The legitimation of what has happened now in Germany has still to be found. I only hope that any fear that there might be a continuity between 1871, or even 1933, and 1989/91 will be shown to be unfounded.

Certainly the work of exegesis should not be simply a naive reflection of general historical presuppositions; it must make its own critical contribution to defining the present. But as historical criticism, the work of exegesis is also a reflection on the present and contributes to the modernization of the present. The history of theology, and with it the history of New Testament exegesis, has shared in the particular aspects of European history in the nineteenth and twentieth centuries. The common origins in the Enlightenment in Western Europe, together with its often underestimated branches on the east coast of North America, have been developed in quite varied directions since the nineteenth century. That is due to many factors, not least to the demands of national cultures, to which the various disciplines have also been reckoned.

The history of theology had to follow after, and subsequently leave behind, the impulses which had started with the Enlightenment for the mutual understanding of the varied Christian churches. The question of the nature of Christianity obviously was determined by the special historical circumstances of the European nations that developed separately. The Studiorum Novi Testamenti Societas is one of the best results of the ecumenical movement; it reminded the European churches very early of their common gospel. Its founding was indeed delayed by the event which devastated Europe and determined its shape for decades, an event once again started by Germany—the war which was already the 'second' world war.

The common tradition of early Christianity can make us aware of all that. I have therefore no fundamental disagreement with Marinus de Jonge. I simply offer my thanks to him for the questions he poses and for the solutions he offers. These thanks come from Marburg, the city of Rudolph Bultmann, the city also in which in 1529 the question of a theological agreement between Luther and Zwingli on how Christianity was to be made concrete in the fellowship of the Eucharist came to grief, the city finally also of that Elizabeth who for Protestants will not be a saint,[1] yet who can remind us of the *caritas*, the love, which according to Paul can surpass even faith and hope.

---

1.   St Elizabeth (1207–1231), daughter of the King of Hungary, widow of an Earl of Thüringen. She is known for her fervent piety and compassion for the poor, the hungry and the sick. After the death of her husband, she lived in great deprivation near Marburg. A church bearing her name was erected above her grave. She was declared a saint in 1235.

THE *SON OF GOD* TEXT FROM QUMRAN

John J. Collins

Among the previously unknown texts that have come to light in the Dead Sea Scrolls, none is more fascinating, at least from a Christian point of view, than the fragment designated as 4Q246, better known as the 'Son of God' text. The interest in this text has been heightened by the delay in publication. It was acquired in 1958, and entrusted to J.T. Milik. Fourteen years later, in December 1972, Milik presented it in a lecture at Harvard University, and promised to publish it in the *Harvard Theological Review*. The publication did not follow. Part of the text was published by Joseph Fitzmyer in an article on 'Qumran Aramaic and the New Testament' in 1974.[1] Since then, there have been, to my knowledge, two articles on the document, by David Flusser[2] and F. García Martínez,[3] and numerous passing references in other studies. It has now finally been published by Emil Puech in the centenary volume of *Revue Biblique*.[4]

---

1.   J.A. Fitzmyer, 'The Contribution of Qumran Aramaic to the Study of the New Testament', *NTS* 20 (1973–74), pp. 382-407; reprinted in his *A Wandering Aramean: Collected Aramaic Essays* (SBLMS, 25; Chico, CA: Scholars Press, 1979), pp. 85-113. See also his comments in *The Gospel according to Luke I-IX* (AB 28; Garden City, NY: Doubleday, 1981), pp. 205-206, 347-48.

2.   D. Flusser, 'The Hubris of the Antichrist in a Fragment from Qumran', *Immanuel* 10 (1980), pp. 31-37; reprinted in his *Judaism and the Origins of Christianity* (Jerusalem: Magnes, 1988), pp. 207-13.

3.   F. García Martínez, '4Q 246: Tipo del Anticristo o Libertador Escatologico?', in *El Misterio de la Palabra* (Festschrift L. Alonso Schökel; Valencia: Madrid, 1983) pp. 229-44, reprinted as 'The Eschatological Figure of 4Q246', in his *Qumran and Apocalyptic: Studies on the Aramaic Texts from Qumran* (Leiden: Brill, 1992), pp. 162-79.

4.   E. Puech, 'Fragment d'une apocalypse en Araméen (4Q246=ps Dan[d]) et le "Royaume de Dieu"', *RB* 99 (1992), pp. 98-131.

The fragment was dated by Milik to the last third of the first century BCE.[1] It consists of two columns, of nine lines each. Column 1 is torn vertically, so that one third to a half of each line is missing, but col. 2 is substantially intact. Since col. 2 ends with a construct form (תהומי, depths), there was apparently a third column. There may also have been another column before col. 1. The fragmentary opening verse says that someone 'fell before the throne'. The following verses are apparently addressed to a king, and refer to 'your vision'. The passage goes on to say that 'affliction will come on earth...and great carnage among the cities'. There is reference to kings of Asshur and Egypt. Then the second half of v. 7 reads 'will be great on earth'. This could possibly continue the affliction described in the previous verses. It could also refer forward, to the figure who is the subject of the following lines. Line 8 says that 'all will serve...' and l. 9 that 'by his name he will be named'. Then col. 2 continues as follows:

> 'Son of God' he shall be called, and they will name him 'son of the Most High'. Like sparks which you saw [or: of the vision], so will be their kingdom. For years they will rule the earth, and they will trample all. People will trample on people and city on city [VACAT] until the people of God arises [or: until he raises up the people of God],[2] and all rest from the sword. His [or its] kingdom is an everlasting kingdom and all his [or its] ways truth. He [or it] will judge the earth with truth and all will make peace. The sword will cease from the earth, and all cities will pay him [or it] homage. The great God will be his [or its] strength.[3] He will make[4] war on his [or its] behalf; give nations into his [or its] hand and cast them all down before him [it]. His [or its] sovereignty is everlasting sovereignty and all the depths...

The interest of the fragment clearly centers on the figure who will be called 'Son of God'. The correspondences with the infancy narrative in Luke are astonishing. Three phrases correspond exactly: 'will be great', 'he will be called son of the Most High' (both in Lk. 1.32) and 'he will be called Son of God' (Lk. 1.35). Luke also speaks of an unending reign. It is difficult to avoid the conclusion that Luke is dependent in some way, whether directly or indirectly, on this long lost text from Qumran.

---

1. Puech, 'Fragment', p. 105.
2. See Puech, 'Fragment', p. 117, on the alternative readings.
3. Puech, 'Fragment', p. 121. Cf. Ps. 88.5. Alternatively 'help, succour'.
4. Puech, 'Fragment', p. 121, reads as participle.

Proposed Interpretations

The correspondence with Luke might be taken as *prima facie* evidence for a messianic interpretation, but the fragmentary state of the text leaves many points of uncertainty. At least five distinct interpretations have already been proposed.

Milik, in his presentation at Harvard, argues that the figure was an historical king, Alexander Balas, son of Antiochus Epiphanes.[1] He could be called 'Son of God' because he is identified on coins as *theopator,* or *Deo patre natus.* Milik suggests that the name by which he was called was that of Alexander the Great. Ingenious though this interpretation is, it has found no followers to date, although Puech now allows the possibility of a reference to a Seleucid king, whether Alexander Balas or Antiochus Epiphanes.[2]

As early as 1961 Arthur Darby Nock reported the opinion of Frank Moore Cross that 'there is further evidence forthcoming from Qumran for the use of royal ideology, expressing the Messiah's relation to God in terms of sonship'.[3] Apparently, the reference was to this text.[4] A messianic interpretation is also allowed by Puech.[5] Fitzmyer's interpretation would also be classified as messianic by most scholars, although he resists this terminology, since such terms as Messiah or anointed one are not used. He sees the text as 'properly apocalyptic', and takes the enthroned king who is addressed as 'someone on the Jewish side rather than on the Seleucid side'. He then takes the 'Son of God' figure as 'a "son" or descendant of the enthroned king who will be supported by the "Great God", possibly an heir to the throne of David'.[6] Seyoon Kim, in his book *The 'Son of Man' as the Son of God,*

---

1. Milik's interpretation is reported by Fitzmyer, *A Wandering Aramean*, p. 92.
2. Puech, 'Fragment', p. 127. Puech contends (p. 115) that the terminology could be drawn from the 'reformed' Jerusalem cult in the time of Antiochus Epiphanes, but there is no evidence that such titles were ever used with reference to a Seleucid king in a Jewish context.
3. A.D. Nock, review of H.-J. Schoeps, *Die Theologie des Apostels im Lichte der jüdischen Religionsgeschichte,* in *Gnomon* 33 (1961), p. 584.
4. Cross continues to defend a messianic interpretation in private correspondence.
5. Puech, 'Fragment', p. 127.
6. Fitzmyer, *A Wandering Aramean*, pp. 92-93. It is not clear to me how Fitzmyer can simultaneously take the text to refer to an heir to the Davidic throne, in an apocalyptic context, and yet say that 'there is no indication that he was regarded as

follows Fitzmyer's interpretation, but has no reservations about calling it 'messianic'.[1]

David Flusser countered Fitzmyer's comments by observing that there is a blank space immediately before the rise of the people of God in col. 2, l. 4. He argues that this is the turning point in the eschatological drama, and that everything preceding it pertains to the afflictions and tribulations. Unlike Milik, however, Flusser refers these titles not to a historical figure, but to the Antichrist. He points out that in Christian tradition the Antichrist lays claim to such titles, and he argues that the idea of an Antichrist is surely Jewish and pre-Christian. He claims to find a close, Jewish, parallel in the little-studied *Oracle of Hystaspes*, referring to a future king who will be 'a prophet of lies, and he will constitute, and call himself God and will order himself to be worshipped as the Son of God'.[2] The *Oracle of Hystaspes*, however, is only known in so far as it is cited by Lactantius, and the extent of the citations and their ultimate provenance is in dispute. Many scholars think that Hystaspes was in fact a Persian-Hellenistic oracle, but in any case this passage about the Antichrist is very probably Christian.[3] There are plenty of Jewish texts, at Qumran and elsewhere, that refer to an eschatological adversary of some sort, but the figure in question is always described in negative terms in the Jewish texts.[4] (One of the paradigmatic texts in this regard is found in Daniel 11, where 'the king shall act as he pleases. He shall exalt himself and consider himself greater than any god and shall speak horrendous things against the God of gods' [Dan 11.36]. We are left in no doubt about the negative character of the king in question.) The idea of an Antichrist, however, who mimics the titles and power of Christ, the

an anointed agent of Yahweh. Hence this text supplies no evidence for the alleged messianic use of the title "Son of God" in pre-Christian Palestinian Judaism' (p. 106).

1. S. Kim, *The 'Son of Man' as the Son of God* (WUNT, 30; Tübingen: Mohr [Paul Siebeck], 1983), p. 22.

2. Flusser, *Judaism and the Origins of Christianity*, p. 212; Lactantius, *Divinae Institutiones* 7.17.2-4.

3. See J.R. Hinnells, 'The Zoroastrian Doctrine of Salvation in the Roman World: A Study of the Oracle of Hystaspes', in E.J. Sharpe and J.R. Hinnells (eds.), *Man and his Salvation: Studies in Memory of S.G.F. Brandon* (Manchester: Manchester University Press, 1973), pp. 125-48. Hinnells defends the Persian origin of the oracle, but does not include this passage among the fragments.

4. This point is made well by García Martínez, '4Q246', p. 242.

Messiah, is only found in Christian texts, and cannot safely be inferred from this Qumran fragment.[1]

García Martínez agrees with Fitzmyer on the eschatological character of the text, and on the positive character of the nomenclature, but he seeks to interpret the text primarily in the light of other Qumran documents. He draws his parallels primarily from 11QMelch and the War Scroll, and concludes that the mysterious 'Son of God' is the figure designated elsewhere as Melchizedek, Michael or the Prince of Light.[2] This conclusion, however, is asserted rather than argued, and requires critical examination.

Finally, the possibility of a collective interpretation in terms of the Jewish people has been noted by Martin Hengel.[3] To my knowledge, no one has actually argued for such an interpretation, but Hengel is correct that it cannot be ruled out in principle.

The Literary Context

Fundamental to any interpretation of the 'Son of God' figure is an analysis of the structure of the text and his place therein. It is apparent that most of the fragment is the interpretation of a vision, apparently the vision of a king, interpreted by someone else, who falls before the throne in the opening verse. We do not know whether the vision was described in an earlier part of the document. The general situation of an interpreter before a king suggests a relationship to the Daniel literature. The content of the interpretation also has some points of contact with Daniel. The clearest points are at 2.5, 'its kingdom is an everlasting kingdom', compare Dan. 4.3; 7.27, and at 2.9, 'his sovereignty will be an everlasting sovereignty', (compare Dan. 4.31; 7.14). The conflict between the nations in col. 1 is reminiscent in a general way of Daniel 2, but such conflict is a commonplace in apocalyptic literature. (See, for example, Mk 13.8: 'nation will rise against nation and kingdom against kingdom'; also *Sib. Or.* 3.635-36; 4 *Ezra* 13.31.) Another possible allusion to Daniel in the use of the word to trample (דוש) at 2.3. The same verb is used with reference to the

---

1. See the recent review of the evidence in G.C. Jenks, *The Origin and Early Development of the Antichrist Myth* (BZAW, 59; Berlin: de Gruyter, 1991).
2. García Martínez, 'The Eschatological Figure', p. 178.
3. M. Hengel, *The Son of God* (Philadelphia: Fortress Press, 1976), p. 44.

fourth beast in Daniel 7.[1] These verbal contacts are most simply explained by positing influence of the book of Daniel on the Qumran document. Puech, however, speaks only of proximity of theme and language, and suggests that 4Q246 was roughly contemporary with Daniel.[2]

The reminiscences of Daniel may provide clues to some of the problems presented by the text. The kings for whom Daniel provided interpretations were, of course, Gentile kings, not kings 'on the Jewish side'. There is no necessary relationship, however, between the enthroned king and the figure mentioned later.[3] A more important issue concerns the relationship between the 'Son of God' figure and the people of God. As we have seen, the introduction of this figure is followed by a reference to the transience of human kingdoms and the conflict between peoples. Milik and Flusser inferred that the 'Son of God' figure belonged to this era of tumult, whether as a historical king or as an eschatological Antichrist. We have also seen that the honorific language is hard to reconcile with such an interpretation. Some light may be thrown on the sequence of events by analogy with Daniel 7. There the sequence of tribulation followed by deliverance is fully laid out in Daniel's vision. Then the interpretation gives a brief summary of the same sequence in other terms (vv. 17-18) and finally the tribulation and deliverance are reviewed again, with more emphasis on the fourth beast. The conferral of the kingdom is repeated three times: first it is given to the 'one like a son of man', then to the holy ones of the Most High, finally to the people of the holy ones of the Most High. The chapter does not proceed in simple chronological sequence. Rather it goes over the same ground in slightly different ways, and this, in fact, is a well-known feature of apocalyptic writing.[4] I suggest that the 'Son of God' text can be understood in much the same way. The description of the conflict between the

1. Two other verbal reminiscences of Daniel may be noted. The word שנוֹי at 1.2 recalls the expression זיוהי שנוֹהי (his expression changed) at Dan. 5.6 (I owe this observation to F.M. Cross). The verb ישמשון (will serve) at 1.8 also occurs at Dan. 7.10, where the service is rendered to God ('a thousand thousands served him').
2. Puech, 'Fragment', p. 129. This suggestion is consonant with his suggestion that the 'Son of God' figure may refer to Antiochus Epiphanes.
3. *Pace* Fitzmyer, *A Wandering Aramean*, p. 92.
4. See further J.J. Collins, *The Apocalyptic Vision of the Book of Daniel* (HSM, 16; Missoula, MT: Scholars Press, 1977), pp. 116-17.

peoples in col. 2 is redundant, but such redundancy is a feature of apocalyptic style. If this is correct, then the mutual trampling of the nations in col. 2 is simply an alternative formulation, or another aspect, of the carnage between the nations in col. 1, and the rise of the people of God is parallel to the advent of the 'Son of God' or 'Son of the Most High'.

Another major problem of interpretation is presented by the use of the third person masculine suffix in the lines that follow the rise of the people of God. The suffix could in principle refer back either to an individual (the Son of God, so 'his kingdom is an everlasting kingdom') or to the people (so 'its kingdom is an everlasting kingdom'). The immediate antecedent is certainly the people. Yet the people is an unlikely antecedent for the statement 'he will judge the earth with truth'. In the Hebrew Bible, it is the Lord himself who is judge of the earth (Gen. 18.25; 1 Sam. 2.10; Pss. 7.9; 9.9). Judgment is a royal function, and the Davidic king transmits the divine justice to the people Israel (Ps. 72.1-2). The ideal king of the future has a wider role. He will 'judge the poor with righteousness, and decide with equity for the meek of the earth' (Isa. 11.4). In the pesher on Isaiah at Qumran, his sword will judge all the peoples.[1] Again in the *Psalms of Solomon*, the eschatological king will 'judge peoples and nations in the wisdom of his righteousness' (*Ps. Sol.* 17.29). In no case, however, is the function of judgment given to the people collectively.

Here again the analogy of Daniel 7 may be helpful. There the four beasts from the sea are interpreted as 'four kings' (v. 17), yet the fourth is 'a fourth kingdom' (v. 23). The eternal kingdom is explicitly given both to the 'one like a son of man', and to the people of the holy ones. A king can stand for a kingdom, and a representative individual can stand for a people. The ambiguity of the third person suffixes in col. 2 of our Qumran fragment can be explained most satisfactorily if the one who is called 'Son of God' is understood as the ruler or representative of the people of God. The everlasting kingdom, then, belongs to both, and the 'Son of God' exercises universal judgment on behalf of his people.

In light of these analogies, it is tempting to suggest that the 'Son of God' represents an early interpretation of the 'one like a son of man'

---

1.   4QpIs[a] 7 iii 26. See M.P. Horgan, *Pesharim, Qumran Interpretations of Biblical Books* (CBQMS, 8; Washington: Catholic Biblical Association, 1979), p. 76.

in Daniel 7, who also stands in parallelism to the people.[1] This is, indeed, a possibility, but a word of caution is in order. The 'Son of God' text is not simply an exposition of Daniel 7. While some words and phrases are drawn from that source, most elements of the biblical vision are ignored (the sea, the beasts, the clouds, the judgment, for example). The vision interpreted here is a vision of a king, not Daniel's vision, and it is presented as an original revelation.

Moreover, Daniel is not the only book of which we find reminiscences here. There are at least two echoes of the Qumran War Scroll: the reference to the kings of Asshur and Egypt (1.6; cf. 1QM 1.2, 4, where there is reference to the Kittim of Asshur and the Kittim of Egypt) and the rare word נחשיר/נחשירון, carnage (a Persian loan word found in 1QM 1.9). As is well known, the War Scroll itself makes extensive use of Daniel, which was apparently understood to refer to the eschatological war.[2] The echoes of the War Scroll here suggest that the 'Son of God' text makes use of Daniel in a similar context. We cannot assume that it reproduces the message of Daniel in any essential way, but comparison with Daniel is nonetheless a promising key to the text.

The parallels with the War Scroll raise the question whether the 'Son of God' text comes from a sectarian milieu. There is no reference in the extant text to a separate community such as the יחד of the Community Rule, or even to distinctively sectarian terminology such as 'Sons of Light'. Most scholars, however, would grant that the War Scroll is sectarian, whether it was originally composed at Qumran or not.[3] The terminological echoes of the War Scroll here suggest that the 'Son of God' text also comes from a sectarian milieu. The evidence is not clear cut, and does not warrant any sweeping assumptions that the text is in conformity with other sectarian compositions. Comparison with other scrolls, however, is not only valid but necessary, if it is pursued as a heuristic exercise. In short, the text must be viewed not only against the backdrop of Daniel, but also against the backdrop

---

1. So Kim, 'The Son of Man', p. 21.

2. See A. Mertens, *Das Buch Daniel im Lichte der Texte vom Toten Meer* (Stuttgart: Echter Verlag, 1971), p. 79.

3. See, however, C. Newsom (' "Sectually Explicit" Literature from Qumran', in W.H. Propp, B. Halpern and D.N. Freedman [eds.], *The Hebrew Bible and its Interpreters* [Winona Lake, IN: Eisenbrauns, 1990], pp. 176-77) who questions whether the dualistic terminology of the War Scroll is necessarily sectarian.

of other eschatological scenarios, especially those attested in the Scrolls.

The analogy with Daniel 7 suggests that there is a parallelism between the 'Son of God' and the people. Parallelism, however, admits of different relationships. In the case of Daniel 7, everyone agrees that there is parallelism between the 'one like a son of man' and the people of the holy ones, but scholars are sharply divided as to what that parallelism entails. Some argue for simple identity, taking the 'son of man' as a collective figure,[1] others for an individual figure who is representative of the people. The latter group again is split between those who take the 'son of man' as the archangel Michael,[2] who is explicitly identified as the prince of Israel in Daniel 10–12, and those who hold to the messianic interpretation, which was standard for many centuries but has fallen into disfavor in recent times.[3] A similar range of possibilities is present in the relationship between the Son of God and the people of God in the fragmentary text from Qumran.

The Collective Interpretation

In fact, these three interpretations, communal, angelic and messianic, are all well attested for the expression 'Son of God' in the Hebrew Bible.[4] The prophet Hosea speaks of Israel as the Son of God in the famous passage: 'When Israel was a child, I loved him, and out of Egypt I called my son'. Already in Exod. 4.22b-23, Moses is instructed to say to Pharaoh: 'Thus says the Lord: Israel is my firstborn son. I said to you, "let my son go that he may worship me" '. Closer to the period of the Scrolls, Sirach prays: 'Have mercy, O Lord, on the people called by your name, on Israel, whom you have named your firstborn' (36.17). This latter instance is especially interesting here because of the element of being called by name.

1. So e.g. L.F. Hartman and A.A. DiLella, *The Book of Daniel* (AB 23; Garden City, NY: Doubleday, 1978), pp. 85-102.

2. E.g. Collins, *The Apocalyptic Vision*, pp. 144-46; A. LaCocque, *The Book of Daniel* (Atlanta: John Knox, 1979), p. 133; C. Rowland, *The Open Heaven* (New York: Crossroad, 1982), p. 182.

3. On the traditional interpretation, see A.J. Ferch, *The Son of Man in Daniel 7* (Berrien Springs, MI: Andrews University Press, 1979), pp. 4-12; for a recent defence of a messianic interpretation see G.R. Beasley-Murray, 'The Interpretation of Daniel 7', *CBQ* 45 (1983), pp. 44-58.

4. P.A.H. de Boer, 'The Son of God in the Old Testament', *OTS* 18 (1973), pp. 188-201; Fitzmyer, *A Wandering Aramean*, p. 104.

A collective interpretation is not impossible in the text from Qumran, but nonetheless it seems unlikely. As we have noted already, there is no parallel for the notion that the people, collectively, will judge the earth. Moreover, although Israel is often said to be God's son, 'Son of God' is scarcely used as a title with reference to the people. The eschatological kingdom of Israel, which is well attested, is usually associated with an eschatological ruler under God, whether an angel, such as Michael in Daniel and the War Scroll, or a messianic figure. While certainty is not possible because of the fragmentary state of col. 1, an interpretation that allows for such an individual ruler here should be preferred.

The Angelic Interpretation

The sons of El, in the plural, are most often heavenly beings in the Hebrew Bible. Examples include Genesis 6 and Psalm 82; also Deut. 32.8-9, where the Greek reading, according to which the Most High fixed the boundaries of the people according to the number of the sons of God (not of Israel), is supported now by a manuscript from Qumran.[1] In Daniel 3, when the king sees a fourth man in the fiery furnace, who looks like 'a son of gods', this is evidently an angelic being. It must be admitted, however, that the use of the singular in this sense is rather unusual. Despite the proliferation of names and titles for 'principal angels' in the Hellenistic period (Michael, Melchizedek, Prince of Light, son of man in the *Similitudes of Enoch*) in no case is one of them called 'the Son of God'.

García Martínez has proposed that the 'Son of God' in the Qumran fragment should be identified with the figure known in other texts as Michael, Melchizedek or Prince of Light.[2] While his argument is not developed, it would seem to rest on the assumption that the document is sectarian and that its eschatology is coherent with that of such compositions as the War Scroll and 11QMelch. While that assumption is open to question, I am prepared to grant it, in view of points of contact already noted between the 'Son of God' text and the War Scroll. The great carnage involving the kings of Asshur and Egypt can plausibly be identified with the great battle described in the War Scroll. In

---

1. P.W. Skehan, 'A Fragment of the "Song of Moses" (Deuteronomy 32) from Qumran', *BASOR* 136 (1954), pp. 12-15.
2. García Martínez, 'The Eschatological Figure', p. 178.

that battle, God himself fights for Israel from heaven (1QM 11.17). He has also appointed a Prince of Light to come to its support (1QM 13.10). In the final phase of the battle 'he will send eternal succour to the company of His redeemed by the might of the princely Angel of the princedom of Michael' (17.6) and 'raise up the princedom of Michael in the midst of the gods and the dominion of Israel among all flesh'. It is evidently possible to read the 'Son of God' text in the light of this scenario. It is still God who comes to the aid of Israel, but there is also a role for another heavenly figure under God in the defeat of the nations.

11QMelch is more directly midrashic than either the 'Son of God' text or the War Scroll. Its starting point is not the eschatological battle, but the year of Jubilee, as proclaimed in Leviticus 25. The description of Melchizedek is of interest here, however. The document applies to him Ps. 82.1: ' "Elohim stands in the assembly [of El], in the midst of Elohim he judges." And concerning it, he sa[id], "Above it to the heights, return! El judges the nations" '.

It goes on to say that 'Melchizedek will exact the ven[geance] of E[l's] judgments'. We have seen that the 'Son of God' is said to judge the earth, a function usually reserved for God in the Hebrew Bible. 11QMelch provides an instance where the divine judgment is executed by a figure other than the Most High, the heavenly *elohim*, Melchizedek.

One other text should be considered in support of the angelic interpretation of the 'Son of God'. The *Similitudes of Enoch* are not found at Qumran, and are probably the product of a different sect, although their apocalyptic world-view is similar in many respects to that of the community. A central role in this document is filled by a figure called 'that son of man', who is patently meant to recall the 'one like a son of man' of Daniel 7. This figure is enthroned on 'the throne of glory' and the kings of the earth fall down and worship before him, and entreat him for mercy.[1] It is reasonable to infer that he shares in the divine function of judge. The fact that the kings of the earth worship before him deserves special notice, since such homage is seldom given to anyone under God in Jewish texts.

These parallels lend substance to the angelic interpretation of the 'Son of God' text, but they are not decisive. At least two aspects of the

---

1. *1 En.* 62.5, 9, compare 48.5, where all those who dwell on the earth fall down and worship before him.

text continue to give pause. First, although the principal angel is known by many names at Qumran, the title 'Son of God' is not attested for him. Secondly, it is surprising that God should be said to be the strength of an angelic figure and to fight on his behalf. Usually, the angel is the agent through whom God gives support to his people on earth. If the third person suffix in col. 2 refers back to the 'Son of God', this presents a problem for the angelic interpretation.

The Messianic Interpretation

The individual most often designated as 'the Son of God' in the Hebrew Bible is undoubtedly the Davidic king, or his eschatological counterpart. The adoption of David as God's son is clearly stated in 2 Sam. 7.14 ('I will be a father to him and he will be a son to me') and in Ps. 89.26-27 ('He shall cry to me: "you are my father"...I will make him the firstborn, the highest of the kings of the earth'). The relationship is expressed in more mythological terms in Ps. 2.7-8 ('I will tell of the decree of the Lord: he said to me, "You are my son; today I have begotten you" '). The statements in the 'Son of God' text, that the great God will be his strength and will give peoples into his hand, can apply equally well to the king in the Psalm. God is also said to sustain the 'shoot of David' in 4QpIsa[a] 7iii 23.

The notion that the Messiah or Christ is the Son of God is obviously of crucial importance in the New Testament, notably the Lukan infancy narrative cited earlier. The attestation of this notion in Jewish texts of the Hellenistic and Roman periods is not extensive, but an important instance is found in *4 Ezra*. The Latin and Syriac texts of this pseudepigraphon refer to the Messiah as 'my son' in a number of passages, in ch. 7, ch. 13 and finally in 14.9. The originality of this reading has been disputed. Some versions use words that mean 'servant' in a few instances, and there are other textual variations.[1] Michael Stone has argued that the Greek version, which has not been preserved, read *pais*, and reflected an original Hebrew 'servant' rather than 'son'.[2] Yet the scene in ch. 13, where the messianic figure takes his stand on a mountain and repulses the attack of the nations, is clearly dependent on Psalm 2, where God sets his anointed king on

1. The evidence is laid out clearly in M.E. Stone, *Fourth Ezra* (Hermeneia; Minneapolis: Fortress Press, 1990), p. 208.
2. Stone, *Fourth Ezra*, p. 207.

Zion, his holy mountain, and terrifies the nations, and where the king is also told 'you are my son, today I have begotten you'. Even if the Greek read *pais*, as the versions that read 'servant' require, this term too could be used for 'son' as is evident from Wisdom of Solomon, where the righteous man calls himself a child of God (*pais theou*, 2.13) and boasts that God is his father (2.16). The Latin and Syriac reading, 'my son', should be accepted as a faithful rendering of the original, at least in ch. 13.

4 Ezra 13 is of considerable interest for the interpretation of the 'Son of God' text from Qumran. Ezra's vision of a man coming up out of the heart of the sea and flying with the clouds is evidently inspired by Daniel 7. In the preceding chapter, *4 Ezra* 12, Ezra has seen an eagle coming up from the sea, and was told that this was 'the fourth kingdom that appeared in a vision to your brother Daniel, but it was not explained to him as I now explain to you or have explained it' (*4 Ezra* 12.11-12). A similar comment might be made about the man from the sea in ch. 13, who must equally be identified with the 'one like a son of man' from Daniel's vision, but is also interpreted in a new way. As in the Qumran text, the advent of this figure is preceded by conflict between the nations: 'They shall plan to make war against one another, city against city, place against place, people against people and kingdom against kingdom' (13.31).

In *4 Ezra* 13, the Messiah repulses the attack of the Gentiles with a fiery breath (cf. Isa. 11.4) and gathers the dispersed of Israel. He is also said to reprove the assembled nations for their ungodliness (13.37). In the preceding vision of the eagle, the Messiah has a more prominent judicial function: 'First he will bring them alive before his judgment seat, and when he has reproved them he will destroy them' (12.33). It is clear then that the Messiah has taken over some of the function of judging the nations, which was usually reserved for God in the Hebrew Bible. There is no place here, however, for worship of this figure by the nations, since they are destroyed after the judgment, like the fourth beast in Daniel.

The eschatology of *4 Ezra* is considerably different from that of a document like the Qumran War Scroll. It has no place for an angelic deliverer, although the Messiah has a transcendent character (he rises from the heart of the sea and flies with the clouds). The scrolls, however, have a place for the Davidic Messiah. He is presumably the 'Messiah of Israel' in the well-known allusions to 'the Messiahs of

Aaron and Israel' in the Damascus Document and the Community Rule. A more explicit reference is found in the so-called 'blessings of Jacob', which are part of a longer text based on Genesis. This text offers the following interpretation of Gen. 49.10:

> Whenever Israel rules there shall [not] fail to be a descendant of David upon the throne. For the staff is the covenant of the kingdom [and the clans] of Israel are the feet, until the Messiah of righteousness comes, the Branch of David. For to him and to his seed was granted the Covenant of kingship over his people for everlasting generations...[1]

Another, more clearly sectarian, reference to the Davidic Messiah is found in the Florilegium, apropos of 2 Samuel 7:

> The Lord declares to you that He will build you a House. I will raise up your seed after you. I will establish the throne of his kingdom [for ever]. I [will be] his father and he shall be my son. He is the Branch of David who shall arise with the Interpreter of the Law [to rule] in Zion [at the end] of time.

The association of the Messiah with the 'Interpreter of the Law' provides a link with specifically sectarian terminology.[2] The citation from 2 Samuel 7 provides an explicit basis for identifying the branch of David as the 'Son of God'. Since the branch is explicitly called the Messiah of righteousness in the patriarchal blessings, it is surely justified to speak of him as a Davidic Messiah.[3]

Two other texts may be cited in connection with the view that the Davidic Messiah was regarded as 'Son of God' at Qumran, but both are fragmentary and problematic. The first, and better known, is in 1QSa, the so-called messianic rule. This passage describes the session of the council of the community at the end of days, when the Messiah comes. The words before the mention of the Messiah are damaged. The late Patrick Skehan claimed that the word יוליד (causes to be born) could be made out 'on the testimony of half a dozen witnesses, including Allegro, Cross, Strugnell and the writer [Skehan], as of the

---

1.   An English translation of this passage is found in G. Vermes, *The Dead Sea Scrolls in English* (Harmondsworth: Penguin Books, 1975), p. 224.

2.   On the relation of this passage to other eschatological passages in the Scrolls, such as CD 6.2-11 see J.J. Collins, *The Apocalyptic Imagination* (New York: Crossroad, 1984), pp. 125-26.

3.   *Pace* Fitzmyer, *The Gospel According to Luke*, I, p. 206.

summer of 1955'.[1] The following word would then be restored as אל,
God, so 'when God causes the Messiah to be born...' Cross, however,
later accepted Milik's reading, יוליך (brings),[2] and other restorations
have also been proposed,[3] so the text remains uncertain.

The second passage is found in an obscure fragment from Cave 4
(4Q369) which says 'you made him a first-born son to you' and goes
on to speak of someone 'like him for a prince and ruler in all your
earthly land'. This passage is extremely fragmentary, and the context
is quite uncertain, but a prince and ruler who is treated as a first-born
son must surely be related to the Davidic line, whether past or future.

We are now well aware that texts found at Qumran do not all necessarily pertain to one coherent system. The one Qumran document with
which the 'Son of God' text has demonstrable affinities is the War
Scroll. As we have seen, in the War Scroll, the agent of God's deliverance is the archangel Michael rather than the Messiah. Yet there
may also be a place for messianic figures in the War Scroll. In the
rule for the standards of the congregation, mention is made of 'the
prince of the whole congregation' (1QM 5.1) and in 1QM col. 11,
Balaam's oracle is cited: 'A star shall come out of Jacob and a sceptre
shall rise out of Israel'. No interpretation is given in the War Scroll,
but the same passage is cited in the Damascus Document (CD 7.18-21):

> The star is the Interpreter of the Law who shall come to Damascus; as it is
> written. A star shall come forth out of Jacob and a sceptre shall rise out of
> Israel. The sceptre is the Prince of the whole congregation, and when he
> comes he shall smite all the children of Seth.

By analogy with the Florilegium, we might infer that the Prince of the
Congregation is none other than the Branch of David. In the Scroll of
the Blessings (1QSb) there is a blessing for the Prince of the Congregation, 'that he may establish the kingdom of his people for ever', and a
fragmentary text, 4Q285, juxtaposes the titles, 'Prince of the
Congregation' and 'Branch of David' in such a way that their identity
seems assured.[4] This latter text seems to describe an eschatological

1. P. Skehan, 'Two Books on Qumran Studies', *CBQ* 21 (1959), p. 74.
2. F.M. Cross, *The Ancient Library of Qumran* (Garden City, NY: Doubleday,
1961), p. 87.
3. See L.H. Schiffman, *The Eschatological Community of the Dead Sea Scrolls*
(SBLMS, 38; Atlanta: Scholars Press, 1989), p. 54.
4. See G. Vermes, 'The Oxford Forum for Qumran Research Seminar on the
Rule of War from Cave 4 (4Q285)', *JJS* 43 (1992), pp. 85-90.

battle in which the Davidic prince is involved in killing some other
party, presumably in an eschatological conflict. We know that there
were considerable differences between different recensions of the War
Scroll. It is not yet clear how the conflict mentioned in 4Q285 should
be related to that literary tradition. Even the familiar recension
preserved in 1QM, however, has some place for the Prince of the
Congregation/Branch of David in its eschatological scenario. The
analogies between the War Scroll and the 'Son of God' text do not,
then require us to identify the 'Son of God' figure with Michael or the
Prince of Light. They can be equally well accounted for by a
messianic interpretation. Since Michael or the Prince of Light are
never called "Son of God", and since there is a clear basis for
applying this title to the Davidic king, whether past or future, the
messianic interpretation should be preferred. Indeed the parallel in
Luke points strongly in this direction: 'He will be great and will be
hailed as Son of the Most High, and the Lord God will bestow on him
the throne of his father David'.[1] Fitzmyer's insistence that 'There is
nothing in the Old Testament or Palestine Jewish tradition that we know
of to show that "Son of God" had a messianic nuance'[2] cannot be
maintained unless 'messianic nuance' is equated with explicit use of the
word 'Messiah'.

It is difficult to say whether the 'Son of God' figure should be
regarded as an interpretation of the 'one like a son of man' in Daniel 7.
If so, it would probably be the oldest surviving interpretation. No other
adaptation or interpretation of that chapter has yet been identified in
the Qumran corpus. The two earliest Jewish interpretations of Daniel 7
are found in the *Similitudes of Enoch* and *4 Ezra* 13.[3] Both these passages assume that Daniel's 'one like a son of man' is an individual, and
both use the term 'Messiah' with reference to him. In both these
documents, the 'son of man' figure is pre-existent, and therefore tran-

---

1. On the relation between the titles 'Son of David' and 'Son of God' (with
reference to Rom. 1.3-4), see M. de Jonge, 'Jesus, Son of David and Son of God',
in *Jewish Eschatology, Early Christian Christology and the Testaments of the
Twelve Patriarchs: Collected Essays of Marinus de Jonge* (NovTSup, 63; Leiden:
Brill, 1991), pp. 135-44.

2. *The Gospel According to Luke*, I, p. 206. Consequently, Fitzmyer's argument that the identification of Jesus as God's son goes beyond his identification as
Davidic Messiah (p. 339) is very dubious.

3. See my essay, 'The "Son of Man" in First Century Judaism', *NTS* 38
(1992), pp. 448-66.

scendent in some sense. In *4 Ezra*, however, he also had a Davidic ancestry. The *Similitudes of Enoch* also apply some traditional messianic language to the 'son of man', for example, 'the spirit of righteousness was poured out on him and the word of his mouth kills all the sinners' (*1 En*. 62.2, cf. Isa. 11.2, 4), but he functions as a heavenly judge, higher than the angels, rather than as a Messiah on earth. In both the *Similitudes* and *4 Ezra*, the 'son of man' figure is to some degree assimilated to the deity. This is more prominent in the *Similitudes*, where he sits on the throne of glory and becomes an object of worship.

The 'Son of God' in the Qumran text is not identical with either of these figures, but he has much in common with them. While he is not called Messiah, the titles he is given have messianic overtones. His role in the eschatological battle is closer to *4 Ezra*, but he is worshipped by the nations like the Enochic 'son of man'. It should be emphasized that the extant fragment from Qumran lacks clear allusions to Daniel's 'one like a son of man' such as we find in the *Similitudes* and in *4 Ezra*. Nonetheless, it is difficult to avoid the impression that the author had Daniel's figure in mind.

If this Qumran fragment is indeed the earliest interpretation of Daniel 7, and takes the 'one like a son of man' as the Davidic Messiah, it may also have implications for the understanding of the text of Daniel itself. The messianic interpretation of Daniel 7 has, in fact, been the predominant one in both Jewish and Christian tradition. It was not without basis. The 'one like a son of man' in Daniel stands in contrast to four beasts, who represent kings or kingdoms. The portrayal of this figure with an entourage of clouds, in the presence of an Ancient of Days, and the contrast with the chaotic sea, all point to a complex of imagery that can be traced back ultimately to Canaanite mythology, but which was associated in Israel with the Davidic kingship.[1]

The messianic interpretation of Daniel 7 has fallen out of favor in this century, and with good reason. There is no clear reference to a Davidic Messiah in Daniel (or, for that matter, in the other literature of the Maccabean period).[2] The only agent of salvation acknowledged

1. See further my essay, 'Stirring up the Great Sea: The Religio-Historical Background of Daniel 7', forthcoming in the proceedings of the Colloquium Biblicum Lovaniense, 1991, under the editorship of A.S. van der Woude.
2. See my essay 'Messianism in the Maccabean Period', in J. Neusner, W.S.

under God is Michael, the 'Prince of Israel'. The 'Son of God' text,
the *Similitudes* and *4 Ezra* all go beyond the text of Daniel in significant ways. None of them can be presumed to have retained the
original understanding of the 'son of man'. The royal, Davidic,
associations of the imagery were important, however, and come to the
fore in different ways in each of these texts.

The fusion of the heavenly 'son of man' figure envisaged in Daniel,
with the traditional hope for a Davidic Messiah was of fundamental
importance for early Christianity.[1] The 'Son of God' text from
Qumran shows that this fusion did not originate in Christianity, but
was already at home in sectarian Jewish circles at the turn of the era.
The implications of the title 'Son of God' would be greatly expanded
in Christian theology in the following centuries. The Qumran text,
however, provides a welcome illustration of the usage of the title in the
matrix from which Christianity emerged: the eschatologically oriented
Judaism of the early Roman empire.[2]

Green and E. Frerichs (eds.), *Judaisms and their Messiahs* (Cambridge: Cambridge
University Press, 1987), pp. 97-109.

1.   On this fusion, see U.B. Müller, *Messias und Menschensohn in jüdischen
Apokalypsen und in der Offenbarung des Johannes* (Gütersloh: Gerd Mohn, 1972).

2.   See the comments of M. de Jonge, *Christology in Context, the Earliest
Christian Response to Jesus* (Philadelphia: Westminster Press, 1988), pp. 167-69. It
is a pleasure to offer this essay to Professor de Jonge. No one in this generation has
labored more fruitfully to illuminate the Jewish context of Christian origins.

4QTESTAMENT OF LEVI^d(?) AND THE MESSIANIC SERVANT HIGH PRIEST

George J. Brooke

The texts from Qumran associated with the title *'Testament of Levi'* are numerous and complex and much detailed study has yet to be done before their relationships to each other and to the whole variegated history of the traditions of the *Testament of Levi* can be adequately described.[1] The purpose of this paper is to offer a translation in English of the two principal fragments of what has recently been tentatively labelled 4QTLevi^d. These passages seem to introduce some significant new evidence into the debate about the extent of the influence of the suffering servant (Isa. 52.13–53.12) on some passages in the NT.

Though there is no agreed list, there are now seven, or possibly eight, manuscripts from Qumran which have been designated *'Testament of Levi'*. In his paper for the 1976 Louvain Qumran congress, J.T. Milik spoke of numerous fragments of five scrolls 'provenant du scriptorium qumranien' of which two, each represented by a single fragment are of recent identification.[2] The three manuscripts that are not so recent presumably correspond with 1QTLevi, 4QTLevi^a and 4QTLevi^b; as yet there is no further information on the two manuscripts attested in single fragments, nor any

---

1. It is a privilege to offer this short study in honour of Professor M. de Jonge who has contributed so much to the study both of the *Testaments of the Twelve Patriarchs* and of NT Christology. As will become clear, this study is heavily dependent on the editorial and interpretative work of E. Puech, 'Fragments d'un apocryphe de Lévi et le personnage eschatologique: 4QTLevi^c-d(?) et 4QAJa', in J. Trebolle and L. Vegas Montaner (eds.), *The Madrid Qumran Congress* (STDJ, 11; Leiden: Brill; Madrid: Editorial Complutense, 1992), pp. 449-501; any reference to Puech in the text is to this study by him.

2. J.T.Milik, 'Ecrits préésséniens de Qumrân: d'Hénoch à Amram', in M. Delcor (ed.), *Qumrân: sa piété, sa théologie et son milieu* (BETL, 46; Gembloux: Duculot; Leuven: Leuven University Press, 1978), p. 95.

technical designation for them. The sixth and seventh manuscripts associated with the *Testament of Levi* have now been tentatively labelled 4QTLevi[c] and 4QLevi[d] by E. Puech who has become responsible for them since the death of J. Starcky. Puech has also proposed that the siglum 4QTLevi[e] be reserved for the manuscript from Starcky's lot published by Milik as a *Testament of Amram* but which he has since identified as a *Testament of Levi* with correspondences with *T. Levi* 19.1.[1]

The date and provenance of the *Testaments of the Twelve Patriarchs* as a whole is still under debate, but the pre-Christian date for the composition of some form of the Aramaic *Testament of Levi* is

---

1.   The following list of Qumran materials results:

1QTLevi (1Q21): J.T. Milik, *Qumran I* (DJD, 1; Oxford: Clarendon Press, 1955), pp. 87-91.

4QTLevi[a] (4Q213; *olim* 4QTLev[b]): J.T.Milik, 'Le Testament de Lévi en araméen: fragment de la grotte 4 de Qumrân', *RB 62* (1955), pp. 398-406; *The Books of Enoch: Aramaic Fragments of Qumrân Cave 4* (Oxford: Clarendon Press, 1976), pp. 23-24. Cf. R.H. Eisenman and M. Wise, *The Dead Sea Scrolls Uncovered* (Shaftesbury: Element, 1992), pp. 136-42.

4QTLevi[b] (4Q214): As yet unedited. Cf. Eisenman and Wise, *The Dead Sea Scrolls Uncovered*, pp. 136-42.

4QTLevi[c] (42540; *olim* 4QAhA bis): E. Puech, 'Fragments d'un apocryphe de Lévi et le personnage eschatologique: 4QTLevi[c-d](?) et 4QAJa', in J. Trebolle Barrera and L. Vegas Montaner (eds.), *The Madrid Qumran Congress*, pp. 479-85. Cf. Eisenman and Wise, *The Dead Sea Scrolls Uncovered*, pp. 142-45.

4QTLevi[d] (42541, *olim* 4QAhA): E. Puech, 'Fragments d'un apocryphe de Lévi'.

4QTLevi[e] (42548, *olim* 4QVisAmram[f]): J.T. Milik, '4QVisions de [c]Amram et une citation d'Origène', *RB* 70 (1972), pp. 77-97.

4QTLevi[f](?), 4QTLevi[g](?): 'chacun représenté par un fragment isolé': J.T. Milik, 'Ecrits prééséniens de Qumrân', p. 95.

Some further detail is available in M.E. Stone and J.C. Greenfield, 'Remarks on the Aramaic Testament of Levi', *RB* 86 (1979), pp. 214-30; H.W. Hollander and M. de Jonge, *The Testaments of the Twelve Patriarchs: A Commentary* (SVTP, 8; Leiden: Brill, 1985), pp. 17-25; E. Schürer, *The History of the Jewish People in the Age of Jesus Christ* (rev. and ed. G. Vermes, F. Millar and M. Goodman; Edinburgh: T. & T. Clark, 1987), III.2, pp. 767-81; J.A. Fitzmyer, *The Dead Sea Scrolls: Major Publications and Tools for Study* (SBLSBS, 20; Atlanta: Scholars Press, 1990), pp. 17, 60. None of these texts are narrowly sectarian, but there is a clear affinity with several tenets of the community; for early discussions of that affinity see J. Daniélou, *The Dead Sea Scrolls and Primitive Christianity* (New York: New American Library, 1958), pp. 114-17, and M. Philonenko, *Les interpolations chrétiennes des testaments des douze patriarches et les manuscrits de Qumrân* (CRHPR, 35; Paris: Presses Universitaires de France, 1960).

confirmed by the direct parallels between 1QTLevi (1Q21) frgs. 3 and
4 and the Bodleian frg., col. a, ll. 2-9, 14-15.[1] These few lines
correspond in part with Greek *T. Levi* 8.18-19, the end of the
narration of the vision of the seven men who make promises about
Levi's descendants. 4QTLevi[a] (4Q213) has only been partially
published so far but it is important for demonstrating the antiquity of
the prayer of Levi which is extant in the Greek tradition only in Ms e
(10th C, Mt Athos), following *T. Levi* 2.3;[2] other fragments of
4QTLevi[a] apparently correspond with both the Bodleian and
Cambridge *T. Levi* materials.[3] For 4QTLevi[b] (4Q214) Milik mentions
that col. 4 of frg. 1, a tiny Aramaic fragment, is in some way parallel
with Cambridge *T. Levi*, cols. c and d which, in turn, is parallel to Gk
T. Levi 11.5–12.5.[4]

As mentioned, 4QTLevi[c] and 4QTLevi[d] have been tentatively designated as such by E. Puech. These manuscripts had previously been
labelled by J. Starcky as 4QAharoniqueA bis (4QAhA bis) and
4QAharoniqueA (4QAhA) respectively. Starcky had made some brief
remarks about these texts in 1963 in his well-known article on
Qumran messianism, but without the actual Aramaic texts it has been
difficult for scholars to know what to make of them.[5] To 4QTLevi[c]
are assigned three fragments of which only one is extensive; the
manuscript is dated palaeographically to the end of the second century
BCE or about 100 BCE. The principal fragment speaks of a little one

1. See the highlighted translation by J.C. Greenfield and M.E. Stone in
Hollander and de Jonge, *The Testaments of the Twelve Patriarchs*, pp. 460-62. For
further interpretative detail, see M.E. Stone, 'Enoch, Aramaic Levi and Sectarian
Origins', *JSJ* 19 (1988), pp. 159-70; J.C. Greenfield and M.E. Stone, 'Two Notes
on the Aramaic Levi Document', in *Of Scribes and Scrolls* (ed. H.W. Attridge, J.J.
Collins and T.H. Tobin; CTSRR, 5; Lanham: University Press of America, 1990),
pp. 153-61.
2. See Hollander and de Jonge, *The Testaments of the Twelve Patriarchs*,
pp. 10-17, 458.
3. An unpublished fragment of 4QTLevi[a] is said to correspond with Bodleian
frg. d, 1-15 and a further two col. frg. apparently matches in col. 1 Cambridge fragment. e 4-f 19, and at the beginning of col. 2 has the last two words of col. f of the
Cambridge fragment.
4. Milik, *The Books of Enoch*, p. 214.
5. J. Starcky, 'Les quatre étapes du messianisme à Qumrân', *RB* 70 (1963),
p. 492.

(זעירא) who seems to have endured some kind of distress (עקא)[1] and of whom it is predicted that he will suffer further hardship. He will leave the home of his birth and reside somewhere else, possibly at the sanctuary, whose building or rebuilding he will instigate. Puech comments that he cannot help but think of Levi and his tribe whose inheritance was not territorial but the cult. The genre of the text is virtually impossible to define, despite several phrases which have their parallels in other testamentary and apocalyptic literature, but the numerical cipher (52?) in frg. 1, l. 2 together with the hardships described may reflect a similar chronology of priesthood and what must be endured until the house of the Lord is restored anew as is depicted in Gk *T. Levi* 17.8-10.

The principal text which Puech has now described in detail is what he tentatively designates 4QTLevi[d]. This consists of 24 fragments, some of which are very small. In only two fragments are there complete or almost complete lines; five fragments preserve the bottom margin. It seems as if the manuscript was made up of columns with eight or nine lines each and the preservation of margins in the fragments allows the conclusion that the manuscript probably had at least eight or nine columns. There is a long vacat at the end of frg. 24 which may correspond with the end of a major section or even of the whole manuscript. On palaeographic grounds Puech dates the manuscript to the end of the second century BCE or about 100 BCE; its writing is akin to that of 1QS, 1QIsa[a], and 4Q175 (4QTest). The Aramaic is replete with Hebraisms— notably the divine name is regularly אל, and in frg. 6, l.3 מכאוביכה appears to have been formed under the influence of מכאב which features in both Isa. 53.3 and 4.

Since Puech has given a fully annotated version of his readings of the text, it is not necessary to repeat all his detailed work. Although there is nothing in 4QTLevi[d] that can be clearly identified as a quotation from what is later represented by the text of Gk *T. Levi*, it is apparent from the two principal fragments of the text as well as from other extant phrases that the text concerns a leading priest who has particular roles and who endures much, possibly being put to death. The association with the *T. Levi* seems thoroughly appropriate, as this brief study of the two principal fragments will reveal.[2]

1. A term used in *Targ. Isa.* 49.8; 50.10.
2. Other links with *T. Levi* include the following. In 4QTLevi[d] frg. 1 ii 2 the word מטעאך, 'error', appears as in 4QHen[c] 4 8 and in frgs. 31 and 52 of 1QTestLevi;

4QTLevi^d (4QAhA) frg. 9, i 2-7, ii 4-7 (Puech, pp. 466-70)

2 [ ]-[   ]-[ח]כמחה ויכפר על כל בני דרה וישתלח לכל בנ[י]

3 [ע]למה מאמרה כמאמר שמין ואלפונה כרעוה   אל שמש עלמה תניר

4 ויחזה נורהא בכול קצוי ארעא ועל חשוכא[|] תניר אדין יעדה חשוכא

5 [מ]ן ארעא וערפלא מן יבישתא שגיאן מלין עלוהי יאמרון ושגה

6 [כדב]ין ובדיאן עלוהי יבדון וכול גנואין עלוהי ימללון דרה באיש יאפיך

7 [ ]לדוה ורי שקר וחמס מקמה [ו]יסעה עמא ביומהי וישתבשון

bottom margin

2]his [wi]sdom.

And he will make expiation for all the sons of his generation;
and he will be sent to all the sons of ^3his [peop]le(?).

His word is like a word of the heavens,
and his teaching conforms to the will of God.

His eternal sun will shine,
^4and its fire will burn in all the corners of the earth.

And on the darkness it will shine;
then the darkness will disappear ^5[fr]om the earth
and the cloud from the dry land.

They will speak many words against him,
and a number of ^6[fiction]s(?).

And they will invent fables against him,
and they will speak all manner of infamies against him.

His generation evil will destroy,
^7[   ] will be;

And because falsehood and violence will be its setting,
[and] the people will stray in his days;
and they will be confounded.

4	be]cause he saw a[	ד]י חזה חזה[	4
5	seven rams looking[	דכרין שבעא דוי-]	5
6	some of his sons will go	קצה בנוהי יהכון]	6
7	and they will be added on ... [	ויתוספון על על]	7

bottom margin

The layout of the translation reflects Puech's proposal that the text is

in frg. 3, after a space, the phrase ארו שׂי may match a partially extant phrase of 1QTestLevi 23 1:]שׁ ־אר. For 4QTLevi^d 9 i 7 with the straying of the people compare Gk *T. Levi* 16.1; in addition for the better understanding of line 7 see Gk *T. Levi* 4.2-4; 10.2; 14.1-2; 16.2-3 (See Puech, 'Fragments d'un apocryphe de Lévi', pp. 455, 459, 469-70).

poetic in a way akin to *T. Levi* 18. Indeed, once it is acknowledged that the text seems to describe some future priest ('he will make expiation for all the sons of his generation and he will be sent to all the sons of his people'), then the parallels with *T. Levi* 18 are almost self-evident. In frg. 9 i 3-4, the images of light and fire echo several passages in the various traditions of the *T. Levi* , such as 'You will light up a bright light of knowledge in Jacob, and you will be as the sun to all the seed of Israel' (*T. Levi* 4.3)[1] and 'His star will arise in heaven, as a king, lighting up the light of knowledge as by the sun of the day' (*T. Levi* 18.3, p. 177).[2] Furthermore, the removal of darkness by this figure is matched in *T. Levi* 18.4 (he 'will remove all darkness from under heaven') and during the priesthood of this new priest 'the Gentiles will be multiplied in knowledge upon the earth and will be enlightened through the grace of the Lord, but Israel will be diminished through ignorance and will be darkened in grief' (*T. Levi* 18.9). This seems to be a development of the thought of Isa. 60.2-3.[3]

Of similar substance as these parallels between 4QTLevi[d] 9 i and *T. Levi* 18 is the parallel in 4QTLevi[d] 9 ii 5 with *T. Levi* 8.2 which mentions 'seven men in white clothing' and the Bodleian frg. col. a, l. 9: 'And those seven departed from me'. This Bodleian verse falls between what remains in frgs. 3 and 4 of 1QTLevi. Although 4QTestLevi[d] 9 ii 5 can be translated as 'seven rams', it is equally possible to translate the phrase as 'seven men'. Puech also finds an echo of the phrasing of 9 ii 7 in the Bodleian frg. col. d, ll. 3-5 and 12-14 where what needs to be added to the sacrifice is described. That fits well, if the suitable subject for 4QTLevi[d] 9 ii 5 is seven rams for some kind of whole burnt offering.

---

1. All translations of Gk *T. Levi* in this study are from Hollander and M. de Jonge, *The Testaments of the Twelve Patriarchs*.

2. Cf. also, 'shine] above [the earth. Do you not shine as the sun and as] the moon? [If] your light is darkened [through impiety, what will all] the [peoples do]? Did not Enoch accuse [...]?' (4QTLevi[a] 8 iii 4-6; Milik, *The Books of Enoch*, pp. 23-24) which is not far from Gk *T. Levi* 14.1-3 which also mentions Enoch: 'heaven is purer than the earth and you are the lights of heaven as the sun and moon' (*T. Levi* 14.3).

3. The many parallels in frg. 9 with *T. Levi* materials lead Puech (p. 469) to suggest that it might be possible to restore the fragment with reference to the Cambridge fragment, col. e, ll.15-16. He provides the alternative reading of 'et une/l'erreur[6] [ils répandr]ont' for the end of l. 5 and the broken start of l. 6.

As these parallels imply, this fragment of 4QTLevi[d] speaks of a priest, possibly the eschatological high priest, since his atoning function may be that of a particular Day of Atonement and his teaching and character is so brilliant and far-reaching. Lines 5-7 also imply that he is the main object of vilification by those that detest him. If 4QTLevi[d] 9 ii 4-7 is to be directly associated with the first column of the fragment, then its partial lines may also be understood to speak about the priest who may have had a vision,[1] and be offering a sacrifice of some sort. If the passage does indeed speak of the eschatological high priest, it is possible to construe the fragment as composed as if it is spoken by Levi to his sons concerning the future Levi.

The priestly role of teaching described in this fragment is not remarkable. However, when combined with certain phrases of other fragments, it is likely that it was a major hallmark of this priest's function. In frg. 2 somebody speaks in the first person of receiving a book and speaking in riddles; there is also a vision. Furthermore, if frgs. 2 to 5 belong together (as Puech convincingly proposes) then the theme of wisdom becomes dominant, as also in frg. 7. If taken together these fragments suggest that the wise man knows of books, parabolic speech and riddles, and has a vision in which a secret is revealed; according to frg. 7 the mission of the future wise man will involve wisdom in all her depths and to every extent. In frg. 9 the wise priest comes invested with heavenly words, teaching conformity to the will of God, and although his enemies will try to outdo his wisdom, their own verbal inventions will all be infamous lies and falsehoods. Fragments 10, 14 and 15 probably mention knowledge, a book and divination respectively.

The atoning function of this priest is clearly described in frg. 9. Here are the closest parallels with the Gk *T. Levi*, especially 4.2-6 and 18.2-9, which have been mentioned above. The priest comes resplendent with light to illuminate all the sons of his people. He speaks with authority. It is important to note that this priest and the wise man of other fragments are almost certainly one and the same, as Gk *T. Levi* 2.10 suggests—the angel declares to Levi, 'You will stand near the Lord and will be his minister and will declare his mysteries to men'. The instructive and illuminating imagery of light is also a connecting

---

1. This is a characteristic of Gk *T. Levi* which contains the narration of two visions: 2.3–6.2, 8.

point between this wise priest and the figure of the servant (Isa. 42.9, 49.6), about whom more is said below.

4QTLevi[d] (4QAhA) frg. 24, ii 2-7 (Puech, pp. 475-79)

2	אׄ]ל תתאבל ב[ה]--]	[ואל ח]
3	ו]יתקן אל שגיא[ן	[--] [כ]	[ן שגיאן מגליאן ואן	[ין]	[
4	בקר ובעי ודע מא יונא בעה ואל תמחי להי ביד שחפא ותגליא כ]ול	[
5	וצצא אל [ח]קרוב בה חקים לאבוכה שם הדוא ולכול אוזיכה יסוד מבחן
6	ח{צ}ו<כס>א וחחזא וחחדה בנהיר עלמא ולא חהוה מן שנאא	vacat
7		*vacat*

bottom margin

2	] and do not [mourn because of [him] [ ] and do not [
3	and] God will redress errors/many[ ] errors disclosed and [
4	Search and seek and know what the dove has sought, and do not chastise the one tired with consumption and hanging a[ll]
5	And a diadem/nail/purity do not bring near to him, and you will establish for your father a name of joy and for all your brothers a proven foundation
6	you will desire {establish}. And you will see and rejoice in eternal light and you will not be from the enemy.

To understand this fragment completely satisfactorily is impossible. As with frg. 9 it is appropriate to begin by comparing some of its motifs with what is already known from Gk *T. Levi*. 4QTLevi[d] 24 ii 2, 'do not mourn (or, grieve) because of him', can be compared with *T. Levi* 18.9: 'but Israel will be diminished through ignorance and will be darkened in grief'. With the phrase, 'you will establish for your father a name of joy', can be juxtaposed the conclusion of *T. Levi* 18: 'Then Abraham and Isaac and Jacob will exult, and I, too, shall be glad, and all the saints will put on joy'. Whereas Levi in the Gk *T. Levi* talks of his joy in the first person, in 4QTLevi[d] 24 ii 5 he speaks of himself in the third person. The final phrase of the fragment is difficult to translate. Evidently there is a contrast between light and something else, 'the one who hates', 'the enemy', just as there is a contrast between darkness and light, and the law of the Lord and the works of Beliar in *T. Levi* 19.1; similar contrasts can be seen in *T. Levi* 14.3-4 and 4QTLevi[a] 8 iii 2-4, as Puech has observed.

With these parallels in mind, it is possible to attempt to construe the significance of this remarkable fragment. The speaker addresses someone in the singular, instructing him to follow the example of the dove, a possible allusion to some element in the Noachic covenant, a feature which has also been thought to lie behind the appearance of the Spirit as a dove in the accounts of Jesus' baptism. The exhortation continues with two prohibitions followed by two positive statements. The prohibitions concern the treatment of one who is being punished or put to death. The first word of l. 5 is particularly difficult to interpret: it might be a defectively written ציצא, possibly 'diadem', part of the high priest's headgear, or it might be a term akin to the Syriac *ṣṣ'*, 'nail' or 'point', or it may be related to another cognate root meaning 'to be clean, pure'. Because the orthography in the manuscript is generally full, Puech argues against the first option, and of the remaining two he suggests that the context makes 'nail' preferable, since it could be a matter of crucifixion or torture.[1] There are then two statements about what the addressee will establish— joy for his father and a proven foundation for his brothers. The text ends with a formula that is almost a blessing. Since 4QTLevi[d] 9 i 7 describes how the future priest will suffer falsehood and violence, it is possible to construe frg. 24 as describing the violence done against this priest[2] and

---

1.   If the figure being tortured and hung (crucified?) here is indeed a future high priest, then a term involving the high priest's headgear may be suitable; the implication might then be that while he is suffering, he cannot function as high priest.

2.   Since the publication of 11QT[a] 64.7-13, the literature on Heb. תלה and its Aram. cognate has become extensive: J.M. Baumgarten, 'Does *TLH* in the Temple Scroll Refer to Crucifixion?', *JBL* 91 (1972), pp. 472-81; reprinted in *Studies in Qumran Law* (SJLA, 24; Leiden: Brill, 1977), pp. 172-82; J.M. Baumgarten, 'Hanging and Treason in Qumran and Roman Law', *Eretz–Israel* 16 (1982), pp. 7-16; A. Dupont-Sommer, 'Observations nouvelles sur l'expression "suspendu vivant sur le bois" dans le Commentaire de Nahum (4QpNah II 8) à la lumière du Rouleau de Temple (11Q Temple Scroll LXIV 6–13)', *CRAIBL* (1972), pp. 709-20; J.A. Fitzmyer, 'Crucifixion in Ancient Palestine, Qumran Literature, and the New Testament', *CBQ* 40 (1978), pp. 493-513; J.M. Ford, '"Crucify him, Crucify him" and the Temple Scroll', *ExpTim* 87 (1975–76), pp. 275-78; D.J. Halperin, 'Crucifixion, the Nahum Pesher and the Rabbinic Penalty of Strangulation', *JJS* 32 (1981), pp. 32-46; M. Hengel, *Crucifixion*, pp. 84-85; L. Merino Diez, 'La crucifixíon en la antigua literatura judía (Período Intertestamental)', *Estudios Eclesíasticos* 51 (1976), pp. 5-27; L. Merino Díez, 'El suplicio de la cruz en la literatura judía intertestamental', *SBFLA* 26 (1976), pp. 31-120; L. Rosso, 'Deuteronomio 21, 22: contributo del rotolo del tempio alla valutazione di una variante medievale dei settanta', *RevQ* 9 (1977–78), pp. 231-36; R. Vincent Saera,

the addressee of the speech as the heir to what will happen afterwards.

Much needs to be said about the detailed interpretation of this fragment, but the following comments, based on many of Puech's excellent observations, focus especially on the way in which allusions to Isaiah may help our understanding of the passage. 4QTLevi[d] frg. 24 ii 4 contains the difficult phrase 'and do not chastise the one tired with consumption and hanging a[ll the day]'. In Hebrew שחפת is associated with נכה 'to strike' (Deut. 28.22) which is rendered in *Targ. Deut.* 28.22 with a form of the verb מחי, 'to smite, wound, chastise'. Hebrew נכה is used of God's activity towards the servant in Isa. 53.4, 'struck down by God', which is rendered in *Targ. Isa.* 53.4 by the aphel passive participle מחן from מחי, the same verb as in this fragment. This verbal association with the suffering servant is enhanced in the use of לחי, 'tired'; the Aramaic homophone לאי is used to render the Hebrew לא ירוץ in Isa. 42.4, the servant will not 'be broken, bruised, crushed' until he has established justice in the earth. There is also the large question of how תליא is best understood. Quite suitably, Puech prefers to see it as a noun from the root תלא, 'to hang', but it may be equally possible to understand it as another form of the verb לאי confirming the link with Isa 42.4.[1] The other link with Isa. in this fragment is in l. 6, 'and you will see light'; this corresponds with Isa. 53.11a in 1QIsa[a] and 1QIsa[b] as well as the *Vorlage* of the LXX, adopted by the NRSV: 'Out of his anguish he shall see light'.[2]

The use of Isaiah is confirmed in other fragments of the manuscript. We have already noted that in frg. 6, l. 3, the occurrence of מכאוביכה seems to be a Hebraism reflecting the use of the same term in Isa. 53.3-4: 'a man of sorrows' (איש מכאבות), 'and he has carried our diseases' (ומכאבינו סבלם). All this is addressed to someone in the second person singular; perhaps this is Levi recounting to his son(s) what someone else had told him at some point. In frg. 10, l. 3, the presence of כור,

---

'La halaká de Dt. 21, 22-23 y su interpretación en Qumrán y en Jn 19, 31-42', in *Salvación en la palabra: targum-derash-berith: homenaje al prof. A. Díez Macho* (ed. D. Munoz Léon; Madrid: Ediciones Cristianidad, 1986), pp. 699-709; M. Wilcox, '"Upon the Tree"—Deut 21: 22-23 in the New Testament', *JBL* 96 (1977), pp. 85-99.

1. To be counted as 2nd s. or 3rd fem. s. impf.
2. Even in 1963 Starcky rightly resisted associating the violence endured by this eschatological high priest with that supposedly suffered by the Teacher of Righteousness ('Les quatre étapes', p. 492).

'furnace', may be related to its use in Isa. 48.10 where it is used to refer to the exile as a 'furnace of affliction' (עני), whereas the metaphor is usually applied to the trials of Israel in Egypt. The text is so fragmentary it is difficult to know what is being described.

In the more substantial frg. 9, it may be possible to see something of the influence of Isaiah in ll. 4 and 5. The first word of l. 4, יחזה, is probably best derived from אזי, 'to kindle, heat, burn', but it may be possible to read it as a Hebraism from נזה which regularly in Aramaic is נדא, 'to sprinkle', though of course for Isa. 52.15 the verb is an old chestnut, commonly understood from an Arabic cognate meaning 'to leap'. If Isa. 52.15 lies behind the phrase here, then the implication would be that as the servant causes many to leap, that is startles them, so the priest's fire will leap in all the corners of the earth. Some support for seeing Isaianic influence behind this phrase comes from 'all the corners of the earth'. The actual parallel Hebrew phrase occurs only in Ps. 65.6, a thanksgiving for harvest in which God is described as the hope of all the ends of the earth, and Isa. 26.15, part of an eschatological psalm expressing the eventual vindication of the righteous. However, a similar Hebrew phrase (קצות הארץ) occurs in Isa. 40.28 (God is 'the Creator of the ends of the earth'), 41.5 ('the ends of the earth tremble'), and 41.9 (Israel 'my servant' is declared to have been taken 'from the ends of the earth').[1] The similarity between frg. 9, ll. 4-5 and Isa. 60.2-3 has already been mentioned.

Puech's study has allowed us to see that something of these verbal associations with the servant texts of Isaiah can also be seen in 4QTLevi[c]. The term in frg. 1, l. 1 used of the distress that will come upon 'the little one' is עקא which is used in *Targ. Isa.* 49.8 and 50.10: 'Who obeys the voice of his servant the prophet? Who does the Law in affliction?' If l. 5 in the same fragment is to be construed as signifying that the servant will rebuild the sanctuary, then this not only corresponds with Gk *T. Levi* 17.10, when in the fifth jubilee the priesthood will renew the house of the Lord, but also with *Targ. Isa.* 53.5 which announces that the messiah will build the sanctuary.

All in all, this priest's activities are not only referred to with some of the phraseology associated with the servant of Isaiah, but his career seems to mirror that of the servant—a universal mission, light against darkness, vilification, violent suffering, sacrifice, benefits for others.

---

1. The phrase occurs elsewhere in the MT only in Job 28.24.

The association of the priest's mission with light and the scattering of darkness mirrors the role of the servant in Isa. 42.6 and 49.6 (also in LXX Isa. 51.4 and 5). In addition the preferred reading of Isa. 53.11 declares how after his trials the servant will see light. The image of light associated with the servant's mission is grounded in his role as illuminator— his teaching needs to be obeyed (Isa. 50.10), reaches the coastlands (Isa. 42.4), is from God (Isa. 50.4). The *Targ. Isa.* brings out the teaching role also in 53.5b and 11b. As in Isa. 50.10 the servant's addressees remain in darkness, so do the contemporaries of the priest figure of 4QTLevi^d 9 i 6-7. Both figures are the subject of ridicule, abuse and infamy (Isa. 50.6-8; 53.2-12); in 4QTLevi^d this may be reflected in frgs. 6 and 10 as well as in frg. 9. In the *Targ. Isa.* 53.11-12 the role of the servant as one who prays for sinners is underlined: 'he will pray concerning their sins', 'and he will pray concerning many sins and for him it will be forgiven the rebellious'. Although the targum makes Isaiah 53 unambiguous so that it cannot speak of the death of the servant, it retains the cultic vocation of the servant which the Hebrew itself suggests in 53.10 with the very difficult אשם. Lastly, it may be possible to construe 4QTLevi^d frg. 24 as speaking of the death of this eschatological figure as Isaiah 53 could itself be construed, possibly even a death by crucifixion.

To appreciate the significance of all this for the NT it is necessary to underline the cultic role of this eschatological figure. This priest will make expiation for all the sons of his generation. Though the reference could be to any of several different kinds of sacrifice, perhaps the allusion is most likely to refer to the eschatological Day of Atonement. Gk *T. Levi* 3.5 acknowledges (as also the Sabbath Songs declare) that along-side the earthly service, there is a heavenly service—'there are angels in the presence of the Lord, those who minister and make expiation to the Lord for all the sins of ignorance of the righteous'. With that in mind and with the possibility that 4QTLevi^d 9 refers to a Day of Atonement, perhaps the text speaks of the earthly counterpart to the heavenly Day of Atonement at which Melchizedek presides according to 11QMelch 7-8: 'And the Day of Atonement is the end of the tenth jubilee'.[1] Priestly

---

1. Again, see the pioneering work of M. de Jonge: M. de Jonge and A.S. van der Woude, '11Q Melchizedek and the New Testament', *NTS* 12 (1965-66), pp. 301-26. But see now E. Puech, 'Notes sur le manuscrit de XIQMelkîsédeq', *RevQ* 12 (1985–87), pp. 483-513.

language can also be seen at 4QTLevi[d] 2 ii 4 where 'and I will bless you' is corrected to 'and I will bless the burnt offering of', perhaps also in 4 ii 4 if 'your blood' is the correct understanding of the remaining letters in the line, in 4 ii 6, if 'the temple' is a correct restoration, in 9 ii 5 when understood as 'seven rams' and l. 7 if 'burnt offering' should be restored there. Priestly activity also seems to be described in the rebuilding of the temple (4QTLevi[c] 1, l. 5).

All this may already be to say too much by way of interpretation, reconstruction and reading between the lines. Yet, if 4QTLevi[d] is indeed speaking of an eschatological high priest servant, we may have in this text the earliest individualistic interpretation of the Isaianic servant songs in a particularly cultic direction. The stance of the *Targ. Isa.* in its particular phraseology and messianism may be directed as much against this kind of interpretation of the servant material in Isaiah as it might be directed against any particularly Christian reading of the biblical text. At this point it is appropriate to turn to the NT itself.

Though some scholars have argued forcefully for the widespread use of the suffering servant model either as part of Jesus' self-understanding or as part of the reflection of the earliest Christian communities or both,[1] it is now commonly argued that the servant of Isaiah, especially 52.13–53.12, was barely of any significance to how either Jesus or his first followers understood his death. As M. de Jonge has concluded:

> 'On close inspection there is little unequivocal evidence for either a close connection between Isaiah 53 and the Markan passages [Mk 10.45;

---

1. See especially C.H. Dodd, *According to the Scriptures* (London: Nisbet, 1952), pp. 92-96; T.W. Manson, *The Servant–Messiah: A Study of the Public Ministry of Jesus* (Cambridge: University Press, 1953; repr. Grand Rapids: Baker, 1977); J. Jeremias, 'Παῖς θεοῦ', *TDNT* 5 (1968), pp. 677-717; *idem, New Testament Theology* (London: SCM Press, 1971), I, pp. 286-99; M. Hengel, *The Atonement: A Study of the Origins of the Doctrine in the New Testament* (London: SCM Press, 1981), pp. 57-60 (significantly and appropriately Hengel's work is dedicated to the memory of J. Jeremias). The analysis of B.D. Chilton is more subtle and relevant: whilst acknowledging the relative lack of material in the NT concerning the identification of Jesus as a suffering servant, he allows for the influence of Isaianic servant material on the NT authors and he posits (now apparently with some vindication) that there was a pre-Christian messianic servant (*The Glory of Israel: The Theology and Provenience of the Isaiah Targum* [JSOTSup, 23; Sheffield: JSOT Press, 1983], pp. 86-96).

14.24] or the theory of Jesus' inspiration by this aspect of Deutero-Isaiah's teaching. More likely is the influence of the Greek translation of 53.12 on the use of the verb "to deliver up" (*paradidonai*) in ancient formulas, and elsewhere, in connection with Jesus' death'.[1]

Or again, more recently: 'Notwithstanding J. Jeremias's careful listing of all the possible references and allusions to the texts, words, phrases and ideas found in Isa. 52.13–53.12 in the writings of the New Testament, the evidence for the use of this passage in early Christianity is slight'.[2] Enter 4QTLevi[d].

4QTLevi[d] must now be taken into account by all future generations of scholars who wish to consider the issue. On the one hand it now seems that there is a Jewish text whose author used the servant passages of Isaiah to support the understanding that there was to be an eschatological priest who would suffer, possibly even that the suffering involved death, death that would lead to joyous benefits for others. M. Hengel's declaration that 'we have no clear text from pre-Christian Judaism which speaks of the vicarious suffering of the Messiah in connection with Isaiah 53'[3] may need to be qualified, as may de Jonge's own statement that 'Isaiah 52.13–53.12 is the only "suffering righteous" passage ... and it seems not to have had much influence in Jewish circles'.[4] On the other hand there are several texts in the NT which try to describe the death of Jesus, even Jesus himself, in cultic and priestly terms. If it was known within early Christian circles that the dominant individualistic understanding of the servant texts linked them to an eschatological Levi, then, for all their suitability in many respects, the servant passages of Isaiah, because Jesus was not a levitical priest, may only have been of limited use to early Christian writers, or even to Jesus himself.

Despite the possibility that the servant passages play only a limited role in the NT because of their dominant association in certain Jewish eschatology with the eschatological priest, nevertheless some NT

---

1.   M. de Jonge, *Christology in Context: The Earliest Christian Response to Jesus* (Philadelphia: Westminster Press, 1988), pp. 180-81.

2.   M. de Jonge, *Jesus, The Servant–Messiah* (New Haven: Yale University Press, 1991), p. 49.

3.   Hengel, *The Atonement*, p. 59. Hengel dares to say without any evidence, 'At all events, a suffering Messiah did not belong to the widespread popular Messianic hope in the time of Jesus and a crucified Messiah was a real blasphemy'.

4.   De Jonge, *Christology in Context*, p. 180.

writings reflect a concern amongst some authors either to use the servant materials and redirect them to enhance the picture of Jesus, the Davidic messiah, or to adjust other aspects of some forms of Jewish cultic practice and expectation to describe the character and effect of Jesus, especially his death. Four authors or schools of thought immediately come to mind.

First, it is clear that the letter to the Hebrews offers an elaborate description of the priesthood of Jesus. Although this is explicitly stated to be different from that of both Levi and of the angels, it is nevertheless resonant with items from earlier Jewish tradition. Jesus' high priesthood is replete with the characteristics of Aaron's priesthood—he is chosen from among mortals, he offers up prayers and supplications with loud cries and tears, he is the source of eternal salvation for all who obey him, but, above all, he is able to deal gently with the ignorant and wayward since he can 'sympathize with our weaknesses' (4.15). The background of this description is that of the Aaronic high priest on the Day of Atonement when he fulfilled his role as no other priest could (cf. Heb. 9.11-14).

Yet Jesus was not of levitical descent, so the author of Hebrews aligns his priesthood with that of Melchizedek. Despite the protestations of some scholars,[1] it is impossible to read this without reference to texts from Qumran.[2] Hebrews insists that Jesus is not an angel, but his priesthood is nevertheless true to what Melchizedek performs in heaven on that momentous Day of Atonement at the end of the tenth jubilee. In 4QTLevi[d] it is the eschatological Levi who completes on earth what Melchizedek acts out in heaven; true to the order of Melchizedek, for the author of Hebrews Jesus's activity is effective on earth and in heaven at the same time, once for all. Furthermore, the language of the cultic servant is adequate for the climax of the

1. For example, F.L. Horton, *The Melchizedek Tradition: A Critical Examination of the Sources to the Fifth Century AD and in the Epistle to the Hebrews* (SNTSMS, 30; Cambridge: Cambridge University Press, 1976), p. 168: 'I have no reason to believe that Hebrews is related to the speculation about Melchizedek demonstrated in the 11Q Melchizedek'.

2. As suitably collected and analysed by P.J. Kobelski, *Melchizedek and Melchireša^c* (CBQMS, 10; Washington: Catholic Biblical Association of America, 1981); as acknowledged most recently by M.M. Bourke, 'The Epistle to the Hebrews', *NJBC*, p. 932, and J.C. VanderKam, 'The Dead Sea Scrolls and Christianity', *Bible Review* 7/6 (1991), p. 46.

description in Heb. 9.28: 'Christ, having been offered once to bear the sins of many' (cf. Isa. 53.12 LXX).[1]

In the Fourth Gospel certain cultic and priestly elements are obvious. Jesus is the lamb of God who takes away the sin of the world. In the Gospel Jesus' ministry is planned around the great festivals which he effectively replaces. In light of this cultic interest and in consideration of 4QTLevi[d] perhaps it is also time to reintroduce a cultic element into some other aspects of the Fourth Gospel's portrayal of Jesus. It might be suitable to begin in ch. 12 where there is an explicit quotation of Isa. 53.1: 'Lord, who has believed our message, and to whom has the arm of the Lord been revealed?' Connected with Isa. 6.9-10 (used in the Synoptic tradition to justify or explain why Jesus spoke in riddles; cf. 4QTLevi[d] 3-4 i 3-4) the Fourth Gospel explains that Isaiah had seen 'his glory' and offers as a last determined public utterance of Jesus: 'I have come as light into the world, so that everyone who believes in me should not remain in darkness... The one who rejects me and does not receive my word has a judge; on the last day the word that I have spoken will serve as judge' (Jn 12.46, 48). An element in the themes of glory and light, so dominant in the Gospel, may be derived from the cultic figure of the servant priest who is glorified (Isa. 52.13 LXX). Might 4QTestLevi[c] frg. 1, when understood as refering to the rebuilding of the temple by the future priest, help explain, together with Psalm 69, the verbal play in Jn 2.19 where at the cleansing of the temple Jesus declares, 'Destroy this temple, and in three days I will raise it up/rebuild it'?[2] To these matters could be added the Johannine concern with Jesus as wisdom.

In addition to these items it is possible to understand one incident in the passion narrative of the Fourth Gospel as hinting at the high priestly status of Jesus. In the incident of the soldiers casting lots for Jesus' tunic (Jn 19.23-24) it is clear that the fact that it is seamless, of one piece from top to bottom, is significant for some reason.

---

1.   4QTLevi[d] frg. 10 (ואמלא רוחא לכור), with רוחא read as 'Spirit', might help in understanding why Heb. 9.14 says that it was through the eternal Spirit that Christ offered himself without blemish to God.

2.   It is possible to understand ἐγείρω as 'rebuild'; cf. 1 Esd. 5.44: 'Some of the heads of families, when they came to the temple of God that is in Jerusalem, vowed that, to the best of their ability, they would erect (ἐγεῖραι) the house on its site'. Cf. 4QTLevi[c] 1, l. 5.

R.E. Brown has collected the relevant evidence.[1] χιτών, 'tunic', is used of one of the garments of the high priest in Exod. 28.4 and Lev. 16.4; though the word ἄρραφος, 'seamless', is not found in the LXX, Josephus (*Ant.* 3.161) describes the ankle-length tunic of the high priest as 'not composed of two pieces, to be stitched at the shoulders and at the sides: it is one long woven cloth'.[2] In addition Brown recalls Philo's interpretation of why the high priest does not rend his clothes (ἱμάτια): this is because the priest's garments are a visual reminder of the clothing that the logos makes for itself in reflecting nature's unbroken mutual harmony and oneness.[3] Such motifs of unity may help explain why the soldiers in the narrative do not tear the tunic. In sum, it seems likely that the Jesus of the Fourth Gospel dies as both high priest and king.

The third NT work to consider is Luke–Acts. Here is a work full of cultic material. This is obvious in Luke's portrayal of Jesus as a man of prayer and in his use of the canticles, as well as his frequent setting of scenes in the temple. In the canticles the theme of light and darkness occurs (Lk. 1.79; 2.32), whilst the whole Nunc Dimittis is a play on Isaiah passages: 42.6; 49.6; 52.10. According to Acts the servant passages feature in the preaching of the early church—in Solomon's Portico Peter in 3.13 speaks of how God has glorified his servant, in 8.32-33, Isa. 53.7-8 is the passage that Philip explains to the Ethiopian eunuch, in 13.47 Paul and Barnabas use Isa. 49.6 to justify their preaching to Gentiles. More particularly it is Lk. 22.37 alone of the Gospels which cites Isa. 53.12 as from Jesus' lips. All this is not especially extensive, as de Jonge and others have noted,[4] but it is intriguing to note also that in Luke's genealogy of Jesus which is constructed in jubilee periods the name Levi occurs twice.[5] It seems as if Luke's

1. R.E. Brown, *The Gospel according to John XIII–XXI* (AB 29A; Garden City: Doubleday, 1970), pp. 920-21.

2. *Josephus* (trans. H. St J. Thackeray; LCL; London: W. Heinemann, 1930), IV, p. 393. Rev. 1.13 may also be relevant: the Greek term ποδήρης used there occurs adjectivally with χιτών in the description of the high priest's robe in LXX Exod. 29.5.

3. R.E. Brown, *The Gospel according to John XIII–XXI*, p. 921, citing Philo, *De Fuga et Inventione*, 108-12.

4. See p. 96 n. 2 and 3.

5. On Luke's genealogy, see the incisive and detailed study of R. Bauckham, *Jude and the Relatives of Jesus in the Early Church* (Edinburgh: T.&T. Clark, 1990), pp. 315-73.

presentation of Jesus is mildly infected with a Palestinian tradition
which associated the priestly messiah with the servant of Isaiah.

In Mark's Gospel too there are some intriguing possibilities for
supporting some earlier interpretations. At Jesus' baptism Mark's
vocabulary of having the heavens rent apart is a deliberate anticipation
of the rending of the veil of the temple at the moment of Jesus's death
(15.38; cf. Gk *T. Levi* 10.3). Thus, according to Mark, Jesus's
vocation of servanthood (Isa. 42.1; Mk 1.11) confirmed at his baptism
is his vocation to die, a death which will grant access to the temple or
rather, to the holy of holies, where only the high priest goes once a
year. This vocation is ratified on two counts. First the Spirit descends
on Jesus as a dove; what this same bird has sought seems to be the
object of a holy quest in 4QTLevi^d 24 ii 4. It may be that what the
dove knows about concerns the chastisement and suffering of the
eschatological high priest. Secondly Jesus's vocation is ratified by a
heavenly voice who appears to cite Ps. 2.7 and then alludes to several
other passages amongst which are Isa. 42.1, 4; 44.2; and Gen. 22.2.
When the *locus classicus*, Mk 10.45, is put alongside these nuances in
narratives which point to something of the significance of the death of
Jesus according to Mark, then we may be glimpsing an understanding of
Jesus not just as a prophetic martyr servant, but as one who fulfils some
cultic role as well.

It seems that very early in Palestinian Jewish Christianity there was
an attempt to use traditions about the suffering of the eschatological
priest (-messiah) to explain something of Jesus' purpose and mission.
Because Jesus was not a levitical priest, the use of this material was
either strongly tempered with appeal to traditions which could be
construed more overtly in relation to the Davidic messiah, such as
Psalm 2, or it was used by those who had a concern to handle the
cultic identity of some forms of Judaism in such a way as to show how
this was continued, absorbed and replaced by what God had done in
the death of Jesus. The earliness of this use of servant high priest ideology may explain why Paul can also, seemingly independently, but
equally reticently, use the same Isaianic texts;[1] its persistence in a
variety of forms through the first century shows that it was the tena-
cious expression of an aspiration worth negotiating with and refining.

---

1.   Isa. 52.15 (Rom. 15.21); Isa. 53.12 (Rom. 4.25); Isa. 53.12 (Rom. 8.34).

THE TRADITION-HISTORICAL BACKGROUND OF ROMANS 3.25:
A SEARCH FOR PAGAN AND JEWISH PARALLELS

Jan Willem van Henten

One of the creative combinations of Marinus de Jonge was the insight that the beneficiary death of the Jewish martyrs and their vindication immediately after death are closely connected. The vindication is only conferred upon someone who died an exceptional death. De Jonge elaborated this insight in his publications on early Christian Christology and the historical Jesus. In this contribution I will argue for a third element which belongs in principle to this martyrological conception—only the death of a special, or, as the case may be, a unique person, can have positive consequences for others. This seems self-evident in connection with christological passages, but nevertheless, one should ask whether this element can be considered as a traditional one which was also applied to persons before and beside Jesus. If so, we would have a traditional connection between (1) the exceptional quality and/or behaviour of someone, (2) the saving meaning of his death (that is, vicarious suffering, redemption of sin, or foundation of a community) and (3) his vindication (postmortem resurrection). I take the close link between elements 2 and 3 as an established fact and will concentrate on the connection between elements 1 and 2. The focal point for our investigation will be the traditional background of the phrase ἱλαστήριον διὰ πίστεως ἐν τῷ αὐτοῦ αἵματι in Rom. 3.25, especially the possible link between ἱλαστήριον and διὰ πίστεως. First a short *status quaestionis* of the research into Rom. 3.25 will be offered. Next the results of an extensive search for parallels of the combination of words in the formula will be discussed. Finally the texts which show the strongest affinity with Rom. 3.25 will be analysed in detail (several passages in *4 Maccabees*, 2 Macc. 7.37–8.5 and LXX Dan. 3.39-40). De Jonge thereby becomes confronted again with a thesis which he once rejected, but which actually is an elaboration of his own conclusions in his article on the death of the Maccabean martyrs.[1]

1. *Romans 3.25*

Rom. 3.25 belongs to a very condensed passage (3.21-26), in which Paul points to the double evidence of God's righteousness to his people (3.25-26).[2] The fact that God regarded Jesus' death as a propitiating

---

1. M. de Jonge, 'Jesus' Death for Others and the Death of the Maccabean Martyrs', in T. Baarda *et al.* (eds.), *Text and Testimony* (Festschrift A.F.J. Klijn; Kampen: Kok, 1988), pp. 142-51; reprinted in M. de Jonge, *Jewish Eschatology, Early Christian Christology and the Testaments of the Twelve Patriarchs: Collected Essays* (NovTSup, 63; Leiden: Brill, 1991), pp. 125-34.

2. See E. Käsemann, 'Zum Verständnis von Römer 3.24-26', *ZNW* 43 (1950-51), pp. 150-54. Reprinted in *Exegetische Versuche und Besinnungen*, I (Göttingen: Vandenhoeck & Ruprecht, 1967), pp. 96-100; S. Lyonnet, 'Le sens de πάρεσις en Rom 3, 25', *Bib* 38 (1957), pp. 40-61; E. Käsemann, 'Gottesgerechtigkeit bei Paulus', *ZTK* 58 (1961), pp. 367-78; J. Barr, *The Semantics of Biblical Language* (Oxford: Oxford University Press, 1961), pp. 187-205; E. Lohse, *Märtyrer und Gottesknecht: Untersuchungen zur urchristlichen Verkündigung vom Sühntod Jesu Christi* (FRLANT, 64; Göttingen: Vandenhoeck & Ruprecht, 1963); U. Wilckens, 'Zu Röm. 3, 21–4, 25', *EvT* 24 (1964), pp. 586-610; G. Klein, 'Exegetische Probleme in Röm 3, 21–4, 25 (Antwort an U. Wilckens)', *EvT* 24 (1964), pp. 676-83; P. Stuhlmacher, *Gerechtigkeit Gottes bei Paulus* (FRLANT, 87; Göttingen: Vandenhoeck & Ruprecht, 1965); J.R. Renschaw, 'A Study of Romans III.21-31', *ABR* 14 (1967), pp. 21-28; K. Kertelge, *'Rechtfertigung' bei Paulus: Studien zur Struktur und zum Bedeutungsgehalt des paulinischen Rechtfertigungsbegriffs* (NTA NS, 3; Münster: Aschendorff, 1972); G. Howard, 'Romans 3: 21-31 and the Inclusion of the Gentiles', *HTR* 63 (1970), pp. 223-33. S.K. Williams, *Jesus' Death as Saving Event: The Background and Origin of a Concept* (HDR, 2; Missoula, MT: Scholars Press, 1975). P. Stuhlmacher, 'Zur neueren Exegese von Röm 3, 24-26', in E.E. Ellis and E. Grässer (eds.), *Jesus und Paulus* (Festschrift W.G. Kümmel zum 70. Geburtstag; Göttingen: Vandenhoeck & Ruprecht, 1975), pp. 315-33; R.B. Hays, 'Psalm 143 and the Logic of Romans 3', *JBL* 99 (1980), pp. 107-15; S.K. Williams, 'The "Righteousness of God" in Romans', *JBL* 99 (1980), pp. 241-90; J.S. Piper, 'The Demonstration of the Righteousness of God in Romans 3: 25, 26', *JSNT* 7 (1980), pp. 2-32; L.T. Johnson, 'Rom. 3: 21-26 and the Faith of Jesus', *CBQ* 44 (1982), pp. 77-90; B.F. Meyer, 'The Pre-Pauline Formula in Rom. 3.25-26a', *NTS* 29 (1983), pp. 198-208; Z.I. Herman, 'Giustificazione e perdono in Romani 3, 21-26', *Anton* 60 (1985), pp. 240-78; J.S. Pobee, *Persecution and Martyrdom in the Theology of Paul* (JSNTSup, 6; Sheffield: JSOT Press, 1985); C. Breytenbach, *Versöhnung: Eine Studie zur paulinischen Soteriologie* (WMANT, 60; Neukirchen–Vluyn: Neukirchener Verlag, 1989), pp. 166-69; L. Keck, '"Jesus"

expiation (3.25) forms the first part of this evidence. Some scholars consider 3.24-26 (partly) as a pre-Pauline formula,[1] others as a later interpolation.[2] Neither the transition in vv. 23-24 nor the vocabulary of 3.24-26 can be considered conclusive evidence for one or the other hypothesis.[3] However, it is probable that Paul made use of traditional imagery and terminology in this soteriological passage. German scholars especially have understood the expression ἱλαστήριον διὰ πίστεως ἐν τῷ αὐτοῦ αἵματι as inspired by the ritual of the Day of Atonement (with the ἱλαστήριον as the golden cover of the Ark). Stuhlmacher writes for instance that the tradition in Rom. 3.25-26a in its original context implied that Jesus was installed as the one who brought atonement in a way which exceeded the ritual of Leviticus 16.[4]

in Romans', *JBL* 108 (1989), pp. 443-60; S.K. Stowers, 'ΕΚ ΠΙΣΤΕΩΣ and ΔΙΑ ΤΗΣ ΠΙΣΤΕΩΣ in Romans 3: 30', *JBL* 108 (1989), pp. 665-74; C.B. Cousar, *A Theology of the Cross: The Death of Jesus in the Pauline Letters* (Minneapolis: Fortress Press, 1990); G.N. Davies, *Faith and Obedience in Romans: A Study of Romans 1–4* (JSNTSup, 39; Sheffield: JSOT Press, 1990); D. Seeley, *The Noble Death: Graeco-Roman Martyrology and Paul's Concept of Salvation* (JSNTSup, 28; Sheffield: JSOT Press, 1990), pp. 19-26 and 105-107. See of the commentaries especially C.E.B. Cranfield, *The Epistle to the Romans* I (ICC; Edinburgh: T. & T. Clark, 1975), pp. 199-218; U. Wilckens, *Der Brief an die Römer* 1 (EKKNT 6.1; Zürich: Benzinger Verlag; Neukirchen–Vluyn: Neukirchener Verlag, 1978), pp. 182-202; J.D.G. Dunn, *Romans 1–8* (WBC 38A; Dallas: Word Books, 1988), pp. 161-83.

1. R. Bultmann, *Theology of the New Testament* (New York: Charles Scribner's Sons, 1951), p. 46; Käsemann, 'Verständnis'; Williams, *Jesus' Death,* pp. 5-19; Meyer , 'Pre-Pauline Formula'.

2. C.H. Talbert, 'A Non-Pauline Fragment at Romans 3.24-26?', *JBL* 85 (1966), pp. 287-96; G. Fitzer, 'Der Ort der Versöhnung nach Paulus', *TZ* 22 (1966), pp. 161-83. This view is convincingly refuted by Williams in *Jesus' Death.*

3. For Pauline coordinations of a participle clause and a clause with a verbum finitum similar to δικαιούμενοι...προέθετο (3.23-24), see J.H. Moulton and N. Turner, *A Grammar of New Testament Greek.* IV. *Style* (Edinburgh: T. & T. Clark, 1980), p. 89. Ἀπολύτρωσις (3.24) also occurs in 8.23 and 1 Cor. 1.30; πάρεσις and προγίνομαι (3.25) are both hapax legomena in NT; ἱλαστήριον occurs further only in Heb. 9.5; but ἀνοχή (3.26, one parallel: Rom. 2.4) and ἔνδειξις (3.25-26, two parallels: 2 Cor. 8.24 and Phil. 1.28) are Pauline words. See G. Delling, *Der Kreuzestod Jesu in der urchristlichen Verkündigung* (Göttingen: Vandenhoeck & Ruprecht, 1972), pp. 12-13; Piper, 'Righteousness of God', pp. 4-10.

4. Stuhlmacher, 'Exegese', p. 329. See also T.W. Manson, 'ΙΛΑΣΤΗΡΙΟΝ', *JTS* 46 (1945), pp. 1-10; C.K. Barrett, *A Commentary on the Epistle to the Romans*

These authors tend to take διὰ πίστεως as a (post-) Pauline addition to the traditional combination of ἱλαστήριον and αἷμα, which would indicate the access to justification for believers.[1] πίστις is a *Fremdkörper* in the cultic passages of the Old Testament.

Williams and other scholars rejected the above-mentioned understanding of Rom. 3.25 and interpret the passage with the Jewish martyr texts as the assumedly traditional background of Rom. 3.25 (especially *4 Maccabees*).[2] There are indeed considerable arguments against the explanation of Jesus as a surpassing *kapporet*.[3] There is friction between the imagery of the mercy-seat and the concept of expiation in Rom. 3.25 in several respects: Jesus would have been sprinkled with his own blood; the mercy-seat was in the forbidden Holy of Holies, whereas Jesus as ἱλαστήριον was revealed (3.21; cf. 1.16-17); all emphasis would lie on God, so that Jesus becomes no more than a passive offering of expiation,[4] and this does not fit Jesus' own role according to other passages (for example, Rom. 5.6, 8-11, 19). That διὰ πίστεως would refer to the faith of Christians, which seems to be the implication of the hypothesis, is not very attractive either. As a matter of fact Paul, or a glossator, could hardly have chosen a worse place for this addition, which breaks the connection between ἱλαστήριον and ἐν τῷ αὐτοῦ αἵματι both referring to Jesus.[5]

The prepositional phrase διὰ πίστεως is put in a different light

---

(Black's NT Commentaries; London: A. & C. Black, 1957), p. 78; F.F. Bruce, *The Epistle of Paul to the Romans* (TNTC; London: Tyndale Press, 1963), p. 106; Dunn, *Romans*, p. 180.

1. See Williams' discussion of this view in *Jesus' Death*, pp. 41-51.

2. Williams, *Jesus' Death*. See also D. Hill, *Greek Words and Hebrew Meanings: Studies in the Semantics of Soteriological Terms* (SNTSMS, 5; Cambridge: Cambridge University Press, 1967), p. 48; L. Morris, *The Apostolic Preaching of the Cross* (London: Tyndale Press, 1972), pp. 159 and 195-98; M. de Jonge, *Christology in Context: The Earliest Christian Response to Jesus* (Philadelphia: Westminster Press, 1988), pp. 182-83 nn. 27 and 35; Seeley, *The Noble Death*.

3. For a summary see Seeley, *The Noble Death*, pp. 20-25. Cf. Lohse, *Märtyrer*, pp. 150-52.

4. Cf. Stuhlmacher, *Gerechtigkeit*, p. 88.

5. Williams, *Jesus' Death*, pp. 43 and 45, notices that ἐν should not be understood as indicating the object of faith. That would be without any parallel in Pauline literature.

because of the recent debate on the expression πίστις 'Ιησοῦ Χριστοῦ (Rom. 3.22)[1] and similar formulations (Gal. 2.16, 20; 3.22; Rom. 3.26; Phil. 3.9; Eph. 3.12).[2] More and more scholars advocate an interpretation which assumes a subjective genitive after πίστεως.[3] If a subjective genitive reading in Rom. 3.22, 26 is the more probable, it is obvious that we should think also of Jesus as subject of διὰ πίστεως[4] in Rom. 3.25.[5] Arguments in favour have included the immediate context with the perfect πεφανέρωται (3.21), which does not fit with an objective genitive, the fact that πίστις usually goes

---

1. G.M. Taylor, 'The Function of ΠΙΣΤΙΣ ΧΡΙΣΤΟΥ in Galatians', *JBL* 85 (1966), pp. 58-76; G. Howard, 'On the "Faith of Christ"', *HTR* 60 (1967), pp. 459-65; G. Howard, 'The "Faith of Christ"', *ExpTim* 85 (1974), pp. 212-15; R.N. Longenecker, 'The Obedience of Christ in the Theology of the Early Church', in R. Banks (ed.), *Reconciliation and Hope* (Exeter: Paternoster Press, 1974), pp. 142-52. A.J. Hultgren, 'The *Pistis Christou* Formulation in Paul', *NovT* 22 (1980), pp. 248-63; Johnson, 'Faith of Jesus'; R.B. Hays, *The Faith of Jesus Christ: An Investigation of the Narrative Substructure of Galatians* 3: 1-9: 11 (SBLDS, 56; Chico, CA: Scholars Press, 1983); S.K. Williams, 'Again *Pistis Christou*', *CBQ* 49 (1987), pp. 431-47; M.D. Hooker, 'ΠΙΣΤΙΣ ΧΡΙΣΤΟΥ', *NTS* 35 (1989), pp. 321-42; reprinted in *From Adam to Christ: Essays on Paul* (Cambridge: Cambridge University Press, 1990), pp. 165-86, Stowers, 'ΕΚ ΠΙΣΤΕΩΣ'; R.B. Hays, 'ΠΙΣΤΙΣ and Pauline Christology: What is at Stake?', in E. Lovering (ed.), *Society of Biblical Literature 1991 Seminar Papers* (SBLSP, 30; Atlanta: Scholars Press, 1991), pp. 714-29; J.G.D. Dunn, 'Once More, ΠΙΣΤΙΣ ΧΡΙΣΤΟΥ', in Lovering (ed.), *SBLS 1991*, pp. 730-44. See for further literature Kertelge, *Rechtfertigung*, pp. 162-66; Hays, 'ΠΙΣΤΙΣ', pp. 714-15; Dunn, 'Once More', pp. 730-31.

2. And Gal. 3.26 according to 𝔓46, Hooker, 'ΠΙΣΤΙΣ ΧΡΙΣΤΟΥ', p.324 n. 3.

3. See Hays, 'ΠΙΣΤΙΣ', p. 714 n. 3; Hooker, 'ΠΙΣΤΙΣ ΧΡΙΣΤΟΥ', p. 321 nn. 2 and 3.

4. The reading of τῆς before πίστεως in 3.25 is doubtful; see B.M. Metzger, *A Textual Commentary on the Greek New Testament* (London: United Bible Societies, 1975), p. 508. If πίστεως refers to the faith of Jesus, the use of the article would not have been necessary (cf. the following αὐτοῦ). Cf. Epiphanius Constantiensis, *Ancoratus* 65,10 (GCS 25, p. 79): δικαιοσύνη μὲν, διὰ πίστεως αὐτοῦ ἁμαρτίαν λύσας..., referring to Jesus and Rom. 3.25.

5. In that case πίστις could mean in Rom. 3.25 beside 'faith', 'faithfulness' or 'obedience'. See for this meaning J. Haussleiter, *Der Glaube Jesu Christi und der christliche Glaube* (Leipzig, 1891); A.G. Hebert, '"Faithfulness" and "Faith"', *Theology* 58 (1955), pp. 373-79; T.F. Torrance, 'One Aspect of the Biblical Concept of Faith', *ExpTim* 68 (1956-57), pp. 111-14 and 221-22; R. Bultmann, 'πιστεύω etc.', *TWNT*, VI, pp. 197-201; Hays, *Faith*, pp. 139-91. Cf. D.M. Hay, '*Pistis* as "Ground for Faith" in Hellenized Judaism and Paul', *JBL* 108 (1989), pp. 461-76.

with a subjective genitive elsewhere in Romans, the parallel ἐκ πίστεως ᾿Αβραάμ in Rom. 4.16 (cf. 4.12), which clearly is a subjective genitive, the redundancy which arises in several of the passages with these formulations when an objective genitive is being assumed, and other Pauline passages expressing the obedience of Jesus (e.g. Rom. 5.15-21). However, there are also serious drawbacks—the absence of the article before πίστεως in 3.22 would indicate an objective genitive (cf. 3.3 gen. subj. with the article), and the expression with the noun has a counterpart in the verb πιστεύω, which always expresses faith in Jesus. According to objectors Paul hardly elaborates the motif of Jesus' faith or faithfulness.[1]

Things being as they are it seems justified to undertake a new tradition-historical analysis of the phrase in Rom. 3.25 as a unity. διὰ πίστεως should not be taken as a foreign element in the traditional material in advance. Most likely the expression should be read sequentially as a staccato formulation which very briefly explains the atonement: 'an atonement—through faith—in (or: by the shedding of; or: at the cost of)[2] his blood'.[3] I investigated the words in this phrase in several combinations, also in relation to similar words. In doing so, extensive use has been made of the *Thesaurus Linguae Graecae* data base.[4]

2. Pagan and Jewish Parallels

1. ἱλαστήριον(-ιος)/ἱλάσκομαιἐξ/ιλάσκομαι/ἱλασμόςἐξ/ιλασμός/ἵλεως + αἷμα

As the advocates of the mercy-seat interpretation of Rom. 3.25 have shown the combination is a very usual one in cultic passages in the Septuagint (with the frequent ἐξιλάσκομαι etc. mostly as translation of כפר pi.), especially in Leviticus 16.[5] Other passages with the

1. See further Dunn, 'Once More'.
2. For ἐν as equivalent of an instrumental dative or a rendering of the *beth pretii*, see Moulton and Turner, *A Grammar of New Testament Greek.* III *Syntax* (Edinburgh: T.&T. Clark, 1963), p. 253; *BDR*, §219.3. Williams, *Jesus' Death*, pp. 46-47 and 50. Cf. Rom. 5.9; Rev. 1.5; 5.9.
3. Dunn, *Romans 1–8*, p. 734 n. 25.
4. L. Berkowitz and K.A. Squitier, *Thesaurus Linguae Graecae: Canon of Greek Authors and Works* (Oxford: Oxford University Press, 1986).
5. Exod. 30.10; Lev. 1.4-5; 4.25-26; 5.9-10; 6.23; 8.15; 10.17-18; 12.7; 14.17-18, 28-29; 16.13-20, 27; 17.10-11; Num. 35.33; Deut. 21.8-9; 2 Chron. 29.24; Ezek.

combination but deviating from a cultic context are 2 Sam. 23.17 and 1 Chron. 11.19 (David refuses to drink the water brought by the three heroes and calls it blood); 2 Kgs 24.4-5 (The Lord did not forgive Manasseh because he had shed innocent blood); Sir. 34.19-22;[1] *4 Macc.* 6.28-29; 17.22. Within the LXX *4 Macc.* 17.22 is by far the closest parallel to Rom. 3.25, because it is the only passage which refers to an expiation by the death of human beings: 'Through the blood (διά τοῦ αἵματος) of these pious ones and their atoning death (τοῦ ἱλαστηρίου θανάτου αὐτῶν) the divine providence rescued Israel' (trans. H. Anderson, slightly altered). Closely connected is another passage from *4 Maccabees*: 'Be merciful (ἵλεως γενοῦ) to Your people and let my (literally: our) punishment be a satisfaction on their behalf. Make my blood their purification (καθάρσιον αὐτῶν ποίησον τὸ ἐμὸν αἷμα) and take my life instead of theirs' (6.28-29, see below).

There are also a few interesting pagan parallels. The combination occurs in Lucian's tragedy on the goddess Podagra (Gout):

ἦν οὔτε λιβάνων ἀτμὸς ἐξιλάσκεται
οὔτε χυθὲν αἷμα βωμίοις παρ' ἐμπύροις,
οὐ ναὸς ὄλβου περικρεμὴς ἀγάλμασιν
(Me [Podagra] no sweet reek of incense can appease
Nor blood of victims burnt in sacrifice
Nor shrine whose walls with idols rich are hung, Lucianus, *Trag.*
140-2).[2]

43.20; 45.18-19. In these passages ἱλαστήριον (-ιος) occurs only in Leviticus 16. See C.H. Dodd, 'ΙΛΑΣΚΕΣΘΑΙ its Cognates, Derivates, and Synonyms, in the Septuagint', *JTS* 32 (1931), pp. 352-60; Manson, 'ΙΛΑΣΤΗΡΙΟΝ'; Lohse, *Märtyrer*, pp. 149-54; Hill, *Greek Words*, pp. 23-48; Morris, *Apostolic Preaching*, pp. 144-213; B. Janowski, *Sühne als Heilsgeschehen: Studien zur Sühnetheologie der Priesterschrift und zur Wurzel KPR im Alten Orient und im Alten Testament* (WMANT, 55; Neukirchen–Vluyn: Neukirchener Verlag, 1982); Breytenbach, *Versöhnung, pp.* 84-100. See for pagan texts: A. Deissmann, 'ΙΛΑΣΤΗΡΙΟΣ und ΙΛΑΣΤΗΡΙΟΝ: Eine lexikalische Studie', *ZNW* 4 (1903), pp. 193-212; H.W. Pleket, 'Religious History as the History of Mentality: The "Believer" as Servant of the Deity in the Greek World', in H.S. Versnel (ed.), *Faith, Hope and Worship: Aspects of Religious Mentality in the Ancient World* (Studies in Greek and Roman Religion, 2; Brill: Leiden, 1981), p. 192 with further references.

1. In this passage there is hardly a connection between the two relevant words, like in Philo, *Vit. Mos.* 1.101.
2. Trans. M.D. Macleod (Loeb). See on Lucian in relation to the New Testament H.D. Betz, *Lukian von Samosata und das Neue Testament: religions-*

The passage shows that the group of words of ἱλάσκομαι in combination with αἷμα occurs in a pagan sacrificial context. In recension ε of the *Historia Alexandri Magni* (17.3) the idea of a vicarious death (ἀρκέσθητι...; cf. *4 Macc.* 6.28) might be expressed. Persian soldiers beg Alexander the Great for mercy, as if he were a god:

> Φωναὶ δὲ αὐτῶν ἱκετηρίαι πρὸς 'Αλέξανδρον ἦσαν· 'Ίλεως ἵλεως ἔσο ἡμῖν, ὦ Διὸς παῖ, μὴ εἰς τέλος καταφάγηται ἡμᾶς ἡ ῥομφαία σου σπλαγχνίσθητι ἐφ' ἡμᾶς καὶ μή δίκην κτηνῶν ἀπολέσῃς, ἀρκέσθητι τοῖς Περσικοῖς αἵμασι τοῖς μέχρι τοῦ νῦν δίκην ὑδάτων ἐκχυθεῖσι...

> (With supplicating voices they said to Alexander: "Be merciful, be merciful to us, child of Zeus. Do not let your sword devour us completely. Feel pity for us, and do not destroy us like beasts. Let the Persian blood which was shed like water until now be enough...")[1]

2. πίστις/πιστός/πιστεύω/πέποιθα[2] + ἱλαστήριον (-ιος)/ἱλάσκο-μαι/ἐξιλάσκομαι/ἱλασμός/ἐξιλασμός/ἵλεως

In pagan literature combinations of these words[3] are sometimes found, but always with a meaning different from Rom. 3.25 (cf. Herodotus, *Hist.* 6.105; Plutarch, *De sera huminis vindicta* [*Mor.* 560 C-D]; and Plotinus, *Enn.* 4.7.15). Not even the passage in Plutarch shows any affinity with Rom. 3.25:[4]

> But ... consider whether in your opinion our own god of this place [Apollo Pythios], knowing that when men die their souls perish immediately, exhaled from the body like vapour or smoke, nevertheless prescribes many appeasements (ἱλασμούς πολλούς) of the dead and

---

geschichtliche und paränetische Parallelen: Ein Beitrag zum Corpus Hellenisticum Novi Testamenti (Texte und Untersuchungen, 76; Berlin: Akademie-Verlag, 1961).

1.   Edition: J. Trumpf, *Vita Alexandri regis Macedonum* (Stuttgart: Teubner, 1974), p. 66. A similar passage occurs in recension γ (2.16). See on the *Vitae Alexandri* H. van Thiel, *Leben und Taten Alexanders von Makedonien: Der griechische Alexanderroman nach der Handschrift L* (Texte zur Forschung, 13; Darmstadt: Wissenschaftliche Buchgesellschaft, 1983), pp. xi-xlviii.

2.   πέποιθα can be considered as synonymous with πίστις/πιστεύω in the meaning trust or faithfulness. Cf. Lk. 18.8-9 and see below.

3.   There is of course a New Testament parallel, Heb. 2.17, also transmitted in quotations of the Church Fathers.

4.   See the commentary by H.D. Betz, P.A. Dirkse, E.W. Smith in H.D. Betz (ed.), *Plutarch's Theological Writings and Early Christian Literature*, I (SCHNT, 3; Leiden: Brill, 1975), pp. 215-16.

demands for them great honours and consideration, deluding and cheating those who put faith in him (τοὺς πιστεύοντας).[1]

The ἱλασμοί are being brought to Apollo on behalf of dead persons. Only two Jewish texts, both from the Septuagint, have the combination: Ps. 48.6-9 and Dan. 3.39-40. In LXX Ps. 48.6-9 after a reference to an attack by those who trust in their power (οἱ πεποιθότες ἐπὶ τῇ δυνάμει αὐτῶν) the idea is expressed that a man cannot pay a ransom for his life.[2] Although some of its details are open to several interpretations, LXX Dan. 3.40 is a much closer parallel to Rom. 3.25: 'Let our sacrifice be as such before You this day. And let Yourself be atoned (from) behind You, because there is no disgrace to those who put their trust in You (καὶ ἐξίλασαι ὄπισθέν σου, ὅτι οὐκ ἔστιν αἰσχύνη τοῖς πεποιθόσιν ἐπὶ σοί)'. The context of the passage expresses the willingness of the three supplicants to sacrifice themselves. In this connection there is a reference to atonement (ἐξίλασαι) and to a group which remains faithful to the Lord, possibly the three men themselves. The passage is important enough to be analyzed in detail. Furthermore it is related to another Jewish passage (2 Macc. 7.37–8.5), which in a somewhat broader context combines ἵλεως (7.37) and πέποιθα (7.40). So this passage too deserves our attention.

3. πίστις/πιστός/πιστεύω/πέποιθα + αἷμα

The results of this search are almost completely negative. The words do occur together in pagan literature, but with a very different meaning from that of Rom. 3.25 (medical or erotic, for example).[3] The same is true of some Jewish passages (e.g. Est. 8.12e; 1 Macc. 7.15-17; Sir. 17.15-16; Philo, *Vit. Mos.* 1.81-82; 284). So there are no pagan or Jewish passages with a close connection of πίστις etc. and αἷμα and a content which is similar to Rom. 3.25. However, if we take a somewhat larger context, 2 Macc. 7.37–8.5 shows affinity with Rom. 3.25: πέποιθα in 2 Macc. 7.40 and αἷμα in 8.3 (see below).

1. Trans. P.H. de Lacy and B. Einarson (Loeb).
2. LXX Ps. 48.8-9: ἀδελφὸς οὐ λυτροῦται· λυθρώσεται ἄνθρωπος; οὐ δώσει τῷ θεῷ ἐξίλασμα αὐτοῦ καὶ τὴν τιμὴν τῆς λυτρώσεως τῆς ψυχῆς αὐτοῦ.
3. Aretaeus Medicus (second cent. CE) uses the expression ἡ πίστις αἵματος, *De causis et signis acutorum morborum* 2.9.9 (ed. Hude p. 77, 24). Herodotus, *Hist.* 3.8. Theognis, *Eleg.* 1.949-50; 2. 1278c-d. Heliodorus, *Aeth.* 2.4.4.

Let me summarize the results. The first combination is surely traditional in Jewish literature, but there are pagan occurrences too. In one of those, although rather late, the combination is possibly used in the context of vicarious suffering. Regarding the content and the terminology (ἱλαστήριον/-ιος) *4 Macc.* 17.22 is the closest parallel. The second combination can be considered as traditional too, but only in Jewish texts. LXX Dan. 3.39-40, which is very similar in content to Jewish martyr texts, shows the greatest similarity with Rom. 3.25. The third combination has no serious pagan parallels either. However, from a broader context 2 Macc. 7.37–8.5 seems to be a very relevant text, because it contains the three words or related terms of the formula in Rom. 3.25. I will therefore look more closely at these texts from the LXX.

3. *Discussion of the Close Parallels*

a. *LXX Dan. 3.39-40*
In Dan. 3.39-40 we find the combination of the verb ἐξιλάσκομαι and πέποιθα. The blood is absent, but there are clear references to the temple cult. The passage is part of the Prayer of Azariah (LXX/Th Dan. 3.24-45),[1] one of the additions to the story of the three companions in the furnace of Nebuchadnezzar.[2] It is a lamentation of the people and a prayer for deliverance at the same time (cf. Neh. 9.6-37).[3] It dates

1.   Unless indicated otherwise we use the edition and numbering of Rahlfs.
2.   C. Kuhl, *Die drei Männer im Feuer: Daniel Kapitel 3 und seine Zusätze* (BZAW, 55; Giessen: Töpelmann, 1930); J. Schüpphaus, 'Das Verhältnis von LXX- und Theodotion-Text in den apokryphen Zusätzen zum Danielbuch', *ZAW* 83 (1971), pp. 49-72; O. Plöger, 'Zusätze zu Daniel', in W.G. Kümmel (ed.), *Jüdische Schriften aus hellenistisch-römischer Zeit I.1* (Gütersloh: Gerd Mohn, 1973), pp. 63-87; C.A. Moore, *Daniel, Esther and Jeremiah: The Additions: A New Translation with Introduction and Commentary* (AB, 44; Garden City, NY: Doubleday, 1977); E. Schürer, *The History of the Jewish People in the Age of Jesus Christ*, III.2 (rev. and ed. G. Vermes, F. Millar and M. Goodman; Edinburgh: T. & T. Clark, 1987), pp. 722-30; K. Koch, *Deuterokanonische Zusätze zum Danielbuch: Entstehung und Textgeschichte* I-II (AOAT, 38; Neukirchen-Vluyn: Neukirchener Verlag/Kevelaer: Butzon & Bercker, 1987); R. Albertz, *Der Gott des Daniel: Untersuchungen zu Daniel 4–6 in der Septuagintafassung sowie zu Komposition und Theologie des aramaeischen Danielbuches* (SBS, 131, Stuttgart: Katholisches Bibelwerk, 1988).
3.   H. Gunkel and J. Begrich, *Einleitung in die Psalmen* (Göttingen: Vandenhoeck & Ruprecht, 1985), p. 117.

probably from the second half of the second century BCE, since the
allusions to historical events in 3.28, 32 can best be explained against
the background of the repression of Antiochus IV in Jerusalem. The
suffering of the people is considered as a just punishment of God,
because of its sins and its disobedience to the law (cf. 3.27-31, 37). In
their appeal to God to save the people Azariah, Mishael and Hananiah
mention three reasons, which are traditional in such prayers:[1] the
name of the Lord which is inextricably bound up with his people
(3.34); the covenant (3.34-35.; cf. Dan. 9.4) and the mercy of the
Lord (3.35; cf. Dan. 9.4, 9, 18 and Nehemiah 9 *passim*). In 3.37-40
the prayer for rescue is coming to a head and can only be understood
in connection with the context of the three young men in the fiery
furnace. First their appeal is being upheld by the conclusion that Israel
suffered more than any other people (v. 37a).[2] Secondly they state in
3.38b-40 that the temple cult does not function any more and hint at a
symbolic or an alternative offering (cf. the double comparative ὡς in
39bc and the beginning of 40a : οὕτω γενέσθω ἡμῶν ἡ θυσία).[3]

The Greek text of Dan. 3.39-40 of Theodotion and that of the
Septuagint differ. There are even variations within the small group of
manuscripts which have the Septuagint version (𝔓967, codex 88 and
Syh). According to the LXX the text reads:

> (39) ἀλλ᾿ ἐν ψυχῇ συντετριμμένῃ καὶ πνεύματι τεταπεινωμένῳ
> προσδεχθείημεν
> ὡς ἐν ὁλοκαυτώμασι κριῶν καὶ ταύρων
> καὶ ὡς ἐν μυριάσιν ἀρνῶν πιόνων·
> (40) οὕτω γενέσθω ἡμῶν ἡ θυσία ἐνώπιόν σου σήμερον
> καὶ ἐξιλάσαι ὄπισθέν σου,
> ὅτι οὐκ ἔστιν αἰσχύνη τοῖς πεποιθόσιν ἐπὶ σοί,
> καὶ τελείωσαι ὄπισθέν σου.[4]

---

1. Esth. 4.17a-z. See further Gunkel and Begrich, *Einleitung*, pp. 117-39.
2. Cf. Neh. 9.32; *Ass. Mos.* 9.3; Josephus, *Apion* 2.225-35.
3. Cf. Isa. 1.11-20 and Mic. 6.6-8.
4. In accordance with Rahlfs with the exception of the accent in ἐξίλασαι (in
Rahlfs: ἐξιλάσαι, interpreted as an infinitive or optative, see below) and τελείωσαι.
In Ziegler's edition the last line is between square brackets. Variations of 𝔓967 are
the absence of ὄπισθέν σου after ἐξίλασαι and of σου after τελείωσαι ὄπισθέν.
See W. Hamm, *Der Septuaginta-Text des Buches Daniel Kap. 3–4 nach dem kölner
Teil des Papyrus 967* (Papyrologische Texte und Abhandlungen, 21; Bonn, Rudolf
Hahelt Verlag, 1977), pp. 294-303. Major differences in the Theodotion-version only
in v. 40:

(Accept us, because we come with broken heart and humbled spirit, as
though we came with burnt-offerings of rams and bullocks and with
thousands of fat lambs. Let our sacrifice be as such before You this day.
And let Yourself be atoned [from] behind You, because there is no
disgrace to those who put their trust in You. And consecrate [from]
behind You)

Dan. 3.39 alludes to the rhetorical question whether God is pleased
by the offering of thousands of rams or ten thousands of rivers of oil
(or: fat lambs) in Mic. 6.7.[1] The verse indicates something which
should function as a replacement of the offerings of the temple cult.
But for two reasons this alternative offering outreaches the merciful
and righteous way of life which is stressed in Micah 6 and Isaiah 1 in
this respect. In the first place there is a connection between v. 39a and
the reference to the suffering of the people in v. 37. The situation
reminds one of Psalm 51(50), where the walls of Jerusalem are
destroyed and God takes no delight in sacrifices (v. 18; cf. Dan. 3.28,
32, 37-38).[2] In Psalm 51(50) God's delight in Zion and the restoration
of the temple cult are invoked by the plea that God consider a broken
spirit as a sacrifice (θυσία τῷ θεῷ πνεῦμα συντετριμμένον) and not
despise a wounded heart (LXX 50.19). Against the background of
Psalm 51(50) the meaning of the reference to the suffering of the
people and the three companions (3.37a, 39a) in LXX Daniel 3
becomes clear. God should take the suffering as an alternative
offering and answer the prayer for rescue.

οὕτως γενέσθω θυσία ἡμῶν ἐνώπιόν σου σήμερον
καὶ ἐκτελέωσαι ὄπισθέν σου
ὅτι οὐκ ἔσται αἰσχύνη τοῖς πεποιθόσιν ἐπὶ σοί.

(Let our sacrifice be as such before You this day. Consider it as perfect behind
You, so that no disgrace shall come to those who put their trust in You).

See C.A. Wahl, *Clavis*, p. 180 s.v. ἐκτελέω. The reading of the Vg *ut placeat tibi*
confirms this interpretation. See for details also in other versions, Koch, *Deuterokanonische Zusätze*, II, pp. 54-59 and 82-84 (for the text I, pp. 88-89) and below.
For the cultic terminology see S. Daniel, *Recherches sur le vocabulaire du culte
dans la Septante* (Etudes et commentaires, 61; Paris: Klincksieck, 1966).

   1.   LXX Mic. 6.7: εἰ προσδέξεται κύριος ἐν χιλιάσιν κριῶν ἢ ἐν μυριάσιν
χειμάρρων πιόνων;Codex A reads ἀρνῶν for χειμάρρων. Χειμάρρων possibly
goes back to the reading χιμάρων ('he-goats'). The terminology of Mic. 6.7 returns
partly in Dan. 3.39: 39a: προσδεχθείημεν; 39b κριῶν; 39c: ἐν μυριάσιν ἀρνῶν
πιόνων.
   2.   Cf. the vocabulary of Dan. 3.39-40 with LXX Ps. 50.18-19.

However, at least in the LXX version there is an extension to the conception in Psalm 51(50). In Dan. 3.39 the prayer no longer focuses on the people but on the role of the three young men (cf. vv. 37-38 with 39-40). Verse 39a refers primarily to the suffering of the three, because their references to the alternative offering can only aim at themselves. The plea 'May *we* be accepted as if *we* came with burnt-offerings...' (3.39a); 'let *our* sacrifice be made before you...' (40a) is backed up with the phrase 'because there is no disgrace to those who put their trust in You' (ὅτι οὐκ ἔστιν αἰσχύνη τοῖς πεποιθόσιν ἐπὶ σοί; LXX 3.40b).[1] This establishment cannot concern the people as a whole, that does not agree with the confession of guilt of 3.27-31, 37. The next phrase confirms that the three are meant: 'and now *we* follow You with whole our heart and fear You' (καὶ νῦν[2] ἐξακολουθοῦμεν ἐν ὅλῃ καρδίᾳ καὶ φοβούμεθά σε; both verbs in the present tense!). So we should read these phrases with the story of the faithfulness of the three until death in MT Daniel 3 in mind. The alternative offering of Dan. 3.39-40 consists of the willingness of the young men to offer themselves rather than obeying Nebuchadnezzar (cf. the reference to burnt-offerings in 39b and the situation in the furnace). This is what Nebuchadnezzar himself says in the conclusion of the story: 'He (God) has sent his angel to save his servants who put their trust in him (Th: ὅτι ἐπεποίθεισαν ἐπ' αὐτῷ; LXX: τοὺς ἐλπίσαντας ἐπ' αὐτόν), who disobeyed the royal command and were willing to yield themselves to the fire...' (3.28 = LXX/Th 3.95).

In LXX Dan. 3.39-40 the young men add to their willingness to offer themselves the appeal to God to atone (ἐξίλασαι). On the ground of internal evidence it is difficult to establish whether ἐξίλασαι in LXX is the preferable reading. Kuhl considered it as a clarification of the problematic ἐκτελέσαι in Theodotion.[3] Taking into consideration the fact that in Daniel Theodotion is often shown to be secondary to LXX by the tendency to solve difficulties by

1. Th reads ἔσται (Codex A like LXX ἔστιν) and has a different meaning (see p. 12 n. 1).
2. καὶ νῦν can indicate an important turn of the prayer, which not necessarily concerns the future. It can introduce an observation concerning acts of individuals, the people or an enemy of Israel unto the moment of the prayer, cf. LXX Neh. 9.32 and LXX Est. 4.17f, 17n, 17o (ed. Rahlfs).
3. Kuhl, *Drei Männer*, pp. 146-47.

abridgement and/or simplification,[1] ἐξίλασαι is probably the more original reading.[2] An appeal for atonement or mercifulness is a common motif in a prayer for deliverance (with ἱλάσκεσθαι in LXX Ps. 24.11 and 78.9; 2 Chron. 6.30; Th Dan. 9.19 and Est. 4.17h; with ἐξιλάσκεσθαι in Th Dan. 9.24). Ἐξίλασαι can here only be a second person singular aorist middle imperative of ἐξιλάσκομαι (normally translated as 'atone for', 'make atonement' or 'propitiate'; the simplex can mean in the passive voice also 'to be merciful').[3] Although ἱλάσκεσθαι/ἐξιλάσκεσθαι usually appears with an object (e.g. Lev. 16.16, 20, 33; Th Dan. 9.24), a prepositional phrase (e.g. περὶ αὐτῶν), or a dative (Est. 4.17h: ἱλάσθητι τῷ κλήρῳ σου; LXX Ps. 78.9: ἱλάσθητι ταῖς ἁμαρτίαις ἡμῶν; cf. LXX Ps. 24.11 and 77.38), there are several occurrences of the verbs used absolutely (LXX Ps. 105.30; Hab. 1.11; 2 Chron. 6.30 and Th Dan. 9.19). The last two occurrences concern, like Dan. 3.40, an appeal for mercy in the context of a prayer.[4]

The words ὄπισθέν σου ('behind you', or 'from behind you')[5] after ἐξίλασαι are considered very problematic. Some scholars interpret them as 'before you' referring to a variant reading ἔμπροσθεν for ὄπισθεν in 2 Kgs 10.29 and 1 Macc. 5.43.[6] Kuhl

---

1. J. Schüpphaus, 'Verhältnis'. Cf. H. Engel, *Die Susanna-Erzählung. Einleitung, Übersetzung und Kommentar zum Septuaginta-Text und zur Theodotion-Bearbeitung* (OBO, 61; Freiburg: Universitätsverlag, 1985), pp. 55-57.
2. ἐκτελέσαι could originate from a simple scribal error, Koch, *Deuterokanonische Zusätze*, II, pp. 56-57.
3. *LSJ*, pp. 594 and 828 s.v. The possibilities of an inf. aor. act. or an opt. aor. act. 3rd sing. are excluded, because ἱλάσκεσθαι is a deponent. The other three occurrences of the form in the LXX are clearly imperatives (Num. 17.11; twice in Lev. 9.7), as the three others in the TLG data base (Athanasius, *Oratio quarta contra Arianos* 31, PG 26. 516B (quotation Lev. 9.7) and Gregory Nazianzus, *In patrem tacentem* (Or. 16), PG 35. 961C.
4. This means that the shorter text of 𝔓967 in v. 40a is not without parallels in LXX. Cf. LXX 2 Chron. 6.30 (part of Solomon's prayer at the dedication of the temple): καὶ σὺ (God) εἰσακούσῃ...καὶ ἱλάσῃ (MT: וסלחת...ותשמע ואתה 'hear and forgive'). Th Dan 9.19: κύριε, ἱλάσθητι; LXX: κύριε, σὺ ἱλάτευσον (MT: אדני שמעה אדני וסלחה 'O Lord, hear; O Lord, forgive'). These imperatives or adhortativus of ἱλάσκομαι are almost synonomous with the appeal ἵλεως γενέσθαι κτλ which occurs in 2 and 4 Maccabees (see below).
5. *LSJ*, p. 1238 s.v.
6. Cf. also Th Dan. 8.4 ἐνώπιον with LXX (codex 88 and sy) 8.4 ὀπίσω.

assumed a confusion of חֲרֹנְךָ and אַחֲרֶיךָ.[1] However, the phrase probably indicates just the location where the atonement takes place, as ἔναντι in LXX Lev. 23.28 (ἐξιλάσασθαι περὶ ὑμῶν ἔναντι κυρίου).[2] The cultic context implies that the sacrifice that should bring atonement is usually offered on the altar before God. This time the location is behind God,[3] maybe because of the idea that God has temporarily withdrawn from the people or the temple. The terminology in the second appeal to God in LXX 3.40d (τελείωσαι; 'consecrate') is also inspired by the temple cult. The verb τελειοῦν is used in LXX for the installation of priests (LXX Exod. 29.9, 29, 33, 35; Lev. 4.5; 8.33; 16.32; Num. 3.3) and the dedication of the temple (2 Chron. 8.16).[4] The combination of τελειοῦν and ἐξιλάσκεσθαι occurs in Lev. 8.33-34 and 16.32-34.

Although the precise meaning of ἐξίλασαι ὄπισθέν σου is hard to establish, the line of thought in LXX Dan. 3.39-40 is clear. Through several cultic references the three companions offer themselves to the Lord as an alternative sacrifice and ask him in this way for atonement, so that the sins of the people are being redeemed. The complete obedience of the three and their willingness to sacrifice themselves make the appeal effective. The additional appeal to God in 3.40d (τελείωσαι) probably means that God is being asked to consider the sacrifice of the young men a definite one, like the installation of the priests and the dedication of the temple, which are in principle definite. After the prayer and the offering God should become merciful again and rescue his people (3.42-45).[5]

1. Kuhl, *Drei Männer*, pp. 146-47. Kuhl's interpretation (see also above) is based on the combination of כלה and חרן in Isa. 10.25; Dan. 11.36 and Ps. 59.14.

2. Cf. LXX Lev. 5.26; 10.17; 14.20, 29, 31; 15.15, 30; 16.10, 30; 19.22; Num. 15.28; 31.50. Cf. also LXX Zach. 8.22 and Mal. 1.9: ἐξιλάσκεσθαι τὸ πρόσωπον κυρίου/τοῦ θεοῦ ὑμῶν.

3. The back of God (אחרי) is referred to in Gen. 16.13 and Exod. 33.23, J. Lindblom, 'Theophanies in Holy Places in Hebrew Religion', *HUCA* 32 (1961), p. 102 n. 21; L. Koehler, W. Baumgartner *et al.*, *Hebräisches und Aramäisches Lexikon zum Alten Testament* I (Leiden: Brill, 1967), p. 34 s.v.

4. The noun τελείωσις can mean a sacrifice of dedication (τὸ ὁλοκαύτωμα τῆς τελειώσεως): LXX Lev. 8.28; cf. LXX Exod. 29.26-27, 31, 34; Lev. 8.22, 28-29; 2 Macc. 2.9-10.

5. Cf. 2 Macc. 1.24-29.

From Jesus to John

b. *2 Macc. 7.37–8.5*
After a few introductory remarks we can concentrate on the
terminology of 2 Macc. 7.37–8.5 which is similar to that of
Rom. 3.25.[1] The martyrdom of Eleazar (6.18-31) and the Maccabean
mother and her seven sons (ch. 7) are in the view of the author
situated in a period of punishment by God, caused by the sins of the
people (2 Macc. 1.7; 4.17; 5.17-20; 6.15-16; 7.18, 32). The structure
of the narrative shows that the sins of the people consist foremost of
the traitorous acts of the Jewish leaders, Simon, Jason, Menelaus and
Lysimachus (4.1–5.10; cf. 3.4-6; 14.1-11), and that the martyrs com-
pensate for the apostasy from the laws (5.8) by their obedience to the
Torah and to the Lord until death (6.23, 28, 30; 7.2, 9, 23, 30, 37).[2]
The historical part of 2 Maccabees should be deemed a history of
liberation,[3] and within this context martyrdom fulfils the conditions
for a successful struggle for liberation. The martyrs restore the
temporary disruption of the covenant, so that God becomes merciful
again and defends the Jewish nation in the military conflict with the
Seleucids (cf. 8.24, 27, 35-36). This description of the broad line of
the narrative is confirmed by the close links in terminology and content
between chs. 7 and 8. There are even one or two cross-references in
ch. 8 to the martyrdoms of ch. 7.

Two passages in 2 Maccabees 7 refer to the effective death of the
martyrs, and the key-phrases therein are part of different semantic
fields: καταλλάσσεσθαι with a dative construction (7.33; cf. 2

1. I dealt with the context and meaning of the chapters on martyrdom in 2
Maccabees extensively in *De martelaren als grondleggers van een nieuwe orde. Een
studie uitgaande van 2 en 4 Makkabeeën* (dissertation, Leiden, 1986). See also
U. Kellermann, *Auferstanden in den Himmel: 2 Makkabäer 7 und die Auferstehung
der Märtyrer* (SBS, 95; Stuttgart: Katholisches Bibelwerk, 1979); M. de Jonge,
'Jesus' Death'; J.W. van Henten, 'Das jüdische Selbstverständnis in den ältesten
Martyrien', in J.W. van Henten, B.A.G.M. Dehandschutter and H.J.W. van der
Klaauw (eds.), *Die Entstehung der jüdischen Martyrologie* (SPB, 38; Leiden: Brill,
1989), pp. 127-61.
2. There is a pattern of six structural elements which returns (partly) several
times in the narrative of chs. 3–15: (1) unfaithfulness of Jewish leaders; (2) threat or
attack by the Seleucids; (3) the faithfulness of individual Jews to the Lord and Jewish
customs; (4) salvation through the Lord; (5) revenge on the enemy; (6) foundation of
a commemoration feast. Van Henten, *Martelaren*, pp. 20-41.
3. Van Henten, *Martelaren*, pp. 51-58. The date of the whole work is
December 124 BCE (2 Macc. 1.9) or shortly afterwards.

Macc. 1.5; 5.20; 8.29);[1] ἵλεως γενέσθαι belonging to the word group of ἱλάσκεσθαι (7.37f.; cf. 2.7, 22; 10.26).[2] Both terms are connected with the wrath of God which has temporarily fallen on the people. In 7.33 the youngest boy says to the king: 'Though our living Lord is angry (ἐπώργισται) for a short time to correct and discipline us, he will again be reconciled to his servants' (καὶ πάλιν καταλλαγήσεται τοῖς ἑαυτοῦ δούλοις; cf. 5.17). The anger of the Lord is caused by the sins of the people (7.18, 32) and the martyrs suffer in solidarity with the people (cf. the inclusive ἡμεῖς in 7.16, 18, 32-33, 38).[3] So the youngest martyr expresses in front of the king his certain expectation that God will soon be atoned again with his people. The only possible means by which this reconciliation could have come about in the context of 2 Maccabees is the death of the martyrs, although the text does not state this explicitly in 7.33. Verses 37-38, however, refer to the appeasement of God through the death of the

1. Cf. Rom. 5.10-11; 2 Cor. 5.18-20. See concerning this vocabulary C. Breytenbach, *Versöhnung*, pp. 40-83. According to M. Wolter, *Rechtfertigung und zukünftiges Heil: Untersuchungen zu Röm 5.1-11* (BZNW, 43; Berlin: De Gruyter, 1978), pp. 41-45, and G. Bader, *Symbolik des Todes Jesu* (Hermenentische Untersuchungen zur Theologie, 25; Tübingen: Mohr, 1988), pp. 70-76, the two semantic fields are connected, which is forcefully rejected with respect to the New Testament passages by Breytenbach, *Versöhnung*, pp. 95-100. In fact, Breytenbach's interpretation of Rom. 3.25-26 (cf. p. 167: ἱλαστήριον as 'Ort der sühnenden Gegenwart Gottes') tallies well with a part of the intercessory prayer of 2 Macc. 7.37-38 (ἐν ἐμοὶ δὲ καὶ τοῖς ἀδελφοῖς μου, see below) and he rightly states (pp. 168-69) that Rom. 3.25-26 should be connected with Rom. 5.9 (cf. καταλλάσσεσθαι in 5.10-11). Concerning the question of the subject of the atonement Paul's conception and that of the martyr texts which have an intercessory prayer differ, but not too much. Through God's acceptance of the prayer atonement is brought and the covenant restored (cf. the imperative ἐξίλασαι in LXX Dan. 3.40).
2. Cf. ἱλασμός in 3.33 and ἐξιλασμός in 12.45. ἵλεως γενέσθαι has in the Septuagint the same meaning as the passive of ἱλάσκεσθαι (be atoned = be merciful): cf. Exod. 32.12 παῦσαι τῆς ὀργῆς τοῦ θυμοῦ σου καὶ ἵλεως γενοῦ ἐπὶ τῇ κακίᾳ τοῦ λαοῦ σου with 32.14 καὶ ἱλάσθη κύριος περὶ τῆς κακίας, ἧς εἶπεν ποιῆσαι τὸν λαὸν αὐτοῦ. Cf. 32.30 ἵνα ἐξιλάσωμαι περὶ τῆς ἁμαρτίας ὑμῶν (subject Moses), see Breytenbach, p. 87. Cf. also Sir. 16.11 where ἔλεος and ἐξιλασμός occur almost as synonyms.
3. Cf. A. O'Hagan, 'The Martyr in the Fourth Book of Maccabees', *SBFLA* 24 (1974), p. 108; U. Kellermann, 'Zum traditionsgeschichtlichen Problem des stellvertretenden Sühnetodes in 2 Makk 7.37-38', *Biblische Notizen* 13 (1980), p. 69; T. Baumeister, *Die Anfänge der Theologie des Martyriums* (Münsterische Beiträge zur Theologie, 45; Münster: Aschendorff, 1980), pp. 41-42.

martyrs. The same boy utters in his final words an intercessory prayer (ἐπικαλούμενος τὸν θεόν, 7.37), which consists of three elements. The martyr (1) appeals to God that he may show mercy speedily to the people (ἵλεως ταχὺ τῷ ἔθνει γενέσθαι), (2) that he may bring Antiochus IV to the confession that he alone is God, and (3) that he[1] in the persons of himself and his brothers[2] may end the anger of the Almighty (ἐν ἐμοὶ δὲ καὶ τοῖς ἀδελφοῖς μου στῆσαι τὴν τοῦ παντοκράτορος ὀργήν). A surrender formula precedes the prayer: ἐγὼ δὲ, καθάπερ οἱ ἀδελφοί, καὶ σῶμα καὶ ψυχὴν προδίδωμι περὶ τῶν πατρίων νόμων[3] ('I, like my brothers, surrender my body and my life for the laws of our fathers', 7.37). This means that we have here, as in Dan. 3.39-40, an invocation which is supported by a pronouncement of the willingness to sacrifice one's own life. So the combination of intercessory prayer and martyrdom should bring about the atonement.[4]

Because he could not persuade the boy, who jeered at him (7.24-25, 39), the king was beside himself with rage and ordered an even worse punishment than his brothers underwent. The concluding v. 40 (καὶ οὗτος οὖν καθαρὸς μετήλλαξεν παντελῶς ἐπὶ τῷ κυρίῳ πεποιθώς) first states that the boy died pure. He did not defile himself with the eating of pork in conformity with the decree of the king (6.18, 21; 7.1). Secondly, the attitude of the boy is characterized as perfect faithfulness to the Lord. This probably forms the motive for his behaviour as it is described in the martyrdom. Likewise in the concluding part of the martyrdom of Eleazar it is stated that he suffered the tortures because of his awe of the Lord (διὰ τὸν αὐτοῦ φόβον ταῦτα πάσχω, 6.30). This indicates that the ancient Jewish martyr texts should be considered as an elaboration of the stories of deliverance of wise and righteous Jews, wherein the faithfulness to the Lord in the face of any adversity is a central motif and ultimately

---

1.   It is tempting to translate 'that the anger may end' or 'that the anger may be ended', but the infinitive στῆσαι is active, so that God should be seen as the subject.

2.   ἐν indicates the location or the mediation of the martyrs, BDR §219.1.

3.   See on οἱ πάτριοι νόμοι H.G. Kippenberg, 'Die jüdischen Überlieferungen als πάτριοι νόμοι', in R. Faber and R. Schlesier, *Die Restauration der Götter: Antike Religion und Neo-Paganismus* (Würzburg: Königshausen & Neumann, 1986), pp. 45-60.

4.   Cf. U. Kellermann, 'Traditiongeschichtlichen Problem', pp. 63-83 (72 and 79).

leads to rescue by the Lord.[1] So Susanna, who did not give in to the two elders, wept and looked up to heaven during their testimony 'because she put her trust in the Lord' (ὅτι ἦν ἡ καρδία αὐτῆς πεποιθυῖα ἐπὶ τῷ κυρίῳ, Th Sus. 35).[2] Th Dan. 6.24 says that Daniel comes out alive and without any injury from the lions' den 'because he trusted in his God' (ὅτι ἐπίστευσεν ἐν τῷ θεῷ αὐτοῦ).[3] Sir. 44.20 explicitly asserts, with respect to Abraham, that this faithfulness is tested in a situation of trial: καὶ ἐν πειρασμῷ εὑρέθη πιστός.[4]

In ch. 8 the struggle for liberation by Judas Maccabee begins. According to 8.1, Judas collected a small army of about 6000 kinsmen and others who remained faithful to Judaism around him. In 8.2-4 these men appeal to God to help his people, to take pity on the profaned temple and the city which was being destroyed, to take action against the blasphemies against his name and the evil that had taken place. This invocation summarizes the terrible events described in chs. 4–7. Some part of it probably refers to the martyrdom of 6.18–7.42, especially to that of the seven brothers and their mother. The Greek text reads: καὶ τῶν καταβοώντων πρὸς αὐτὸν αἱμάτων εἰσακοῦσαι, μνησθῆναι δὲ καὶ τῆς τῶν ἀναμαρτήτων νηπίων παρανόμου ἀπωλείας ('and to give ear to the blood[5] that cried to him for vengeance, and to remember the infamous killing of children without sin', 8.3-4). The blood which cries to God is the blood of innocents who died a violent death (Gen. 4.10; Heb. 12.24; Rev. 6.9-11; cf. *Ass.Mos.* 9.7). The most obvious connection is with the martyrdom of the seven boys in ch. 7. The word νήπιοι (8.4) occurs also in 2 Macc. 5.13, where the slaughtering of different categories of the population of Jerusalem is mentioned. Again, it is very probable that the phrase refers to the martyrdom of the seven boys, of which

1. See J.C.H. Lebram, 'Jüdische Martyrologie und Weisheitsüberlieferung', in J.W. van Henten (ed.), *Martyrologie*, pp. 88-126.

2. LXX Sus. 35: ἡ δὲ καρδία αὐτῆς ἐπεποίθει ἐπὶ κυρίῳ τῷ θεῷ αὐτῆς.

3. MT: די הימן באלהה. Cf. also Th Dan. 6.5: ὅτι πιστὸς ἦν (MT: די מהימן הוא); 1 Macc. 2.59; *4 Macc.* 16.21-22.

4. Probably inspired by the combination of Genesis 15 and 22. See LXX Gen. 15.6; 22.1 and cf. *4 Macc.* 15.28; 16.20, 22 (see below).

5. In the story of the suicide of Razis (2 Macc. 14.37-46), which has a similar function within the unit of chs. 14–15 as 6.18–7.42 within 4.1–10.8, the emphasis on the blood of Razis (14.45-46) reminds one of pagan traditions of a *devotio*; cf. Statius, *Theb.* 10. 756-801 (777); see van Henten, *Martelaren*, pp. 141-44.

the author, in looking back in a somewhat exaggerating way, says that they were only children. The adjective ἀναμάρτητος could very well apply to the martyrs, because it is nowhere stated that they sinned. Their perfect obedience to the Lord implies just the opposite. 7.18, 32 only report that they suffered in solidarity with the people (see above).

Furthermore, 2 Macc. 8.5, 27, 29 should be seen as a fulfilment of the prayer of the youngest martyr, who invoked God to become merciful again. Verse 5 immediately labels Judas Maccabaeus invincible, 'because the Lord's anger had changed to mercy' (τῆς ὀργῆς τοῦ κυρίου εἰς ἔλεον τραπείσης). Judas gains sweeping victories over the Seleucids indeed, because the covenant is restored and the Lord acts again as patron of his people.[1] According to 8.27 the victory over Nicanor is considered as the beginning of God's mercy. In 8.29 Judas and his soldiers appeal to God for a definitive reconciliation (ἠξίουν εἰς τέλος καταλλαγῆναι τοῖς αὐτοῦ δούλοις). These passages show that the prediction of the martyr in 7.33 (cf. καταλλάσσεσθαι in 7.33) has meanwhile been fulfilled and the prayer of 7.37-38 has been answered. Another proof of God's hearing of the martyr's prayer is the confession of Antiochus to become a Jew ('Ιουδαῖον ἔσεσθαι)[2] and proclaim the might of the Lord in every place (9.17; cf. 7.37). An interesting detail in ch. 8 is that according to the author, Judas Maccabaeus and his soldiers show a trust in the Lord similar to that of the martyrs. In 8.18 he opposes Nicanor and his men against Judas and his soldiers: '"They rely on their weapons and their audacity" he (Judas) said, "but we rely on God Almighty, who is able to overthrow with a nod our present assailants and, if need be, the whole world"' (οἱ μὲν γὰρ ὅπλοις πεποίθασιν...ἡμεῖς δὲ ἐπὶ τῷ παντοκράτορι θεῷ...πεποίθαμεν; cf. also 12.14-15 and 15.7).[3] In

1. Concerning this motif, see R. Doran, *Temple Propaganda: The Purpose and Character of 2 Maccabees* (CBQMS, 12; Washington: Catholic Biblical Association of America, 1981).

2. On 'Ιουδαῖος with a religious meaning, see S.J.D. Cohen, 'Religion, Ethnicity, and "Hellenism" in the Emergence of Jewish Identity in Maccabean Palestine', in P. Bilde *et al.* (eds.), *Religion and Religious Practice in the Seleucid Kingdom* (Aarhus: Aarhus University Press, 1990), p. 207.

3. 8.21 expresses the readiness of Judas's soldiers to die for their laws and their fatherland (αὐτοὺς...ἑτοίμους ὑπὲρ τῶν νόμων καὶ τῆς πατρίδος ἀποθνῄσκειν; cf. 13.14 and 14.18). Seeley, *The Noble Death* considers the military context as one of the elements of the noble death.

conclusion we find that the phrases ἵλεως γενέσθαι (7.37), ἐπὶ τῷ κυρίῳ πεποιθώς (7.40) and αἵματα (8.4) form part of a coherent train of thought concerning the effective meaning of the death of the martyrs and their perfect obedience to the Lord.

c. 4 Maccabees

4 Maccabees is a discourse on the autonomy of reason and at the same time a eulogy on the Maccabean martyrs (cf. 1.1 with 1.2, 10).[1] One of the two relevant passages is found in the description of the martyrdom of Eleazar and his *laudatio* (chs. 6–7). The other passage belongs to the *enumeratio* of the glorious acts of all the martyrs (17.2-24).[2]

---

1. The work probably dates from about 100 CE and originated in Cilicia or the northwest of Syria (Antiochia); see J.W. van Henten, 'Datierung und Herkunft des Vierten Makkabäerbuches', in H.J. de Jonge *et al.* (eds.), *Tradition and Re-interpretation in Jewish and Early Christian Literature: Essays in Honour of Jürgen C.H. Lebram* (SPB, 36; Leiden: Brill, 1986), pp. 136-49; H.-J. Klauck, '4. Makkabäerbuch', in W.G. Kümmel and H. Lichtenberger (eds.), *Jüdische Schriften* III.6, 1989, pp. 668-69. See also on *4 Macc.* E. Norden, *Die antike Kunstprosa. Vom 6. Jahrhundert v.Chr. bis in die Zeit der Renaissance*, I (Leipzig: Teubner, 1915), pp. 416-20; A. Dupont-Sommer, *Le quatrième livre des Maccabées: introduction, traduction et notes* (Bibliothèque de l'école des hautes études, 274; Paris: Champion, 1939); E. Bickerman, 'The Date of Fourth Maccabees', in *Louis Ginzberg Jubilee Volume*, English Section (New York: The American Academy for Jewish Research, 1945), pp. 105-12; repr. in *Studies in Jewish and Christian History* I (AGJU, 9; Leiden: Brill, 1976), pp. 275-81; O. Perler, 'Das vierte Makkabäerbuch, Ignatius von Antiochien und die ältesten Martyrerberichte', *Rivista di Archeologia Cristiana* 25 (1949), pp. 47-72; M. Hadas, *The Third and Fourth Books of Maccabees* (New York: Harper & Row, 1953); R. Renehan, 'The Greek Philosophic Background of Fourth Maccabees', *Rheinisches Museum für Philologie* 115 (1972), pp. 223-38; J.C.H. Lebram, 'Die literarische Form des vierten Makkabäerbuches', *VC* 28 (1974), pp. 81-96; O'Hagan, 'The Martyr', pp. 94-120; U. Breitenstein, *Beobachtungen zu Sprache, Stil und Gedankengut des Vierten Makkabäerbuchs* (Basel: Schwabe, 1976); P.L. Redditt, 'The Concept of *Nomos* in Fourth Maccabees', *CBQ* 45 (1983), pp. 249-70; H. Anderson, '4 Maccabees (First Century AD): A New Translation and Introduction', in J.H. Charlesworth (ed.), *The Old Testament Pseudepigrapha*, II (London: Darton, Longman & Todd, 1985), pp. 531-64; van Henten, *Martelaren*, pp. 178-225; H.-J. Klauck, 'Hellenistische Rhetorik im Diasporajudentum: Das Exordium des Vierten Makkabäerbuches (4 Makk. 1.1-12)', *NTS* 35 (1989), pp. 451-65.

2. This *enumeratio* in the second last chapter shows the similarity with the Athenian funeral oration (ἐπιτάφιος λόγος); see Lebram, 'Literalrische Form'; N. Loraux, *L'invention d'Athènes: histoire de l'oraison funèbre dans la 'cité*

The martyrology in *4 Maccabees* has become completely concentrated on the ideal way of life. Neither a struggle for liberation nor the institutions of a Jewish nation matter to the author. The martyrs defeat the tyrant in a moral and spiritual sense by their perseverance (ὑπομονή) until death: 'they became responsible for the downfall of the tyranny which beset our nation, overcoming the tyrant by their fortitude so that through them our fatherland was purified'[1] (1.11). The author clearly used 2 Maccabees as a source for his description of the martyrdom and its historical context (3.20–4.26). As in 2 Maccabees this context is determined by the threat to the Jewish people by Antiochus IV, which the Lord let take place because of the sins of the people (3.21; 4.16-21).

The old priest Eleazar was the first Jew who was brought before Antiochus and forced to eat the flesh of swine and food sacrificed to idols (5.2-4). Although the tyrant goes out of his way to persuade Eleazar, the old man refuses and chooses to die for the law instead (6.27). In his last words before his death (6.30) he invokes the Lord as follows: 'Be merciful to your people and let my (literally: our) punishment be a satisfaction on their behalf. Make my blood their purification and take my life instead of theirs' (ἵλεως γενοῦ τῷ ἔθνει σου ἀρκεσθεὶς τῇ ἡμετέρᾳ ὑπὲρ αὐτῶν δίκῃ. καθάρσιον αὐτῶν ποίησον τὸ ἐμὸν αἷμα καὶ ἀντίψυχον αὐτῶν λαβὲ τὴν ἐμὴν ψυχήν, 6.28-29). Like the martyr in 2 Macc. 7.37-38 Eleazar intercedes[2] in the situation of martyrdom on behalf of the people and invokes God with the formula ἵλεως γενέσθαι τῷ ἔθνει (cf. 9.24 and 12.17). He mentions his own death as foundation of the appeasement of the Lord by asking him to consider his death as sufficient punishment of the people[3] and as vicarious suffering: his life (ψυχή) instead of that of the people, 'life for life' (ἀντίψυχον; see concerning καθάρσιον and αἷμα below).[4]

classique' (Civilisations et Sociétés, 65; The Hague: Mouton, 1981); Klauck, '4. Makkabäerbuch', pp. 660-62 and 750.

1.   Trans. H. Anderson.

2.   Cf. also LXX Exod. 32.11-13, 31-32; Num. 14.13-19; Amos 7.2.

3.   ἀρκέω with this meaning already in tragedies from the classical period: Sophocles, *Oed.Tyr.* 1209; Euripides, *Alc.* 383, *LSJ*, p. 242 s.v. ἀρκέω III. Cf. Williams, *Jesus' Death*, pp. 183-84.

4.   ἀντίψυχον also in 17.21. Cf. Dio Cassius 59.8.3. See on the effective meaning of the death of the martyrs O'Hagan, 'The Martyr', pp. 103-20; Breitenstein, *Beobachtungen zu Sprache*, pp. 171-75; Williams, *Jesus' Death*,

2 Macc. 17.20-22 indicates the honours the martyrs deserve—first their vindication (in connection with a reference to Deut. 33.3 in 17.19),[1] and secondly the honour of their glorious and saving death (cf. also 18.4): '(17.20) And these (the martyrs) were sanctified by God and not only honoured with this distinction, but also by the fact that through them our enemies did not take possession of our people, (17.21) and the tyrant was punished and our fatherland purified (τὴν πατρίδα καθαρισθῆναι; cf. 1.11), since they became, as it were, life for life (ἀντίψυχον) because of the sins of the people (17.22). Through the blood of these pious ones and their atoning death the divine providence rescued Israel, which had been badly treated (διὰ τοῦ αἵματος τῶν εὐσεβῶν ἐκείνων καὶ τοῦ ἱλαστηρίου θανάτου[2] αὐτῶν ἡ θεία πρόνοια τὸν Ισραηλ προκακωθέντα διέωσωσεν)'. The passage expresses at the same time the vicarious, atoning and purifying meaning of the death of the martyrs, as a compensation for the sins of the people (cf. 6.28). Their atoning death restores, as in 2 Maccabees, the covenantal relationship between God and his people and leads to its being saved from the attack of Antiochus IV (17.22; cf. 17.2, 20; 18.5).

The phrase διὰ τοῦ αἵματος...καὶ τοῦ ἱλαστηρίου θανάτου (17.22) shows that the author uses cultic terminology, with the traditional combination of αἷμα and ἱλαστήριον, to express a non-cultic atonement. As in Rom. 3.25 this cultic terminology[3] concerns a non-cultic death of human persons (4 Macc. 17.22). The blood of the martyrs is, however, probably more than a reference to their death, because in 6.29 Eleazar mentions the purifying meaning of his blood.[4]

pp. 165-97; De Jonge, 'Jesus Death'; H.S. Versnel, 'Quid Athenis et Hierosolymis? Bemerkungen über die Herkunft von Aspekten des "effective death"', in van Henten (ed.), *Martyrologie*, pp. 162-96; Klauck, '4. Makkabäerbuch', pp. 670-72.

1. Anderson ('4 Maccabees', p. 563) and Klauck ('4. Makkabäerbuch', p. 752), do not connect this reference ('All the holy ones are under your hands') with 17.20 and translate the verse differently.

2. The reading of MSS A and V (ἱλαστήριον as an adjective, without the article before θανάτου) is the preferable one, see Klauck ('4. Makkabäerbuch', pp. 671 and 753) who assumes a reference to Leviticus 16. Rahlfs takes ἱλαστήριον with MS S as a noun.

3. Cf. σφαγιάζω or ὁλοκαρπόω concerning Isaac (13.12; 16.20; 18.11).

4. In 7.8 αἷμα expresses with other words the reality of the death of Eleazar. According to G. Friedrich (*Die Verkündigung des Todes Jesu im Neuen Testament* [Biblisch-Theologische Studien, 6; Neukirchen–Vluyn: Neukirchener Verlag, 1982],

In 17.20-22 the author refers to the purification of the fatherland (17.21) in connection with the vicarious meaning of the death of the martyrs. So he combines several notions of the effective death. The background of the idea of purification lies probably mainly in Old Testament traditions of a purification of persons or the people as a whole from their sins,[1] but the meaning of καθαρίζω etc. is determined by the sinful situation of the people before the appearance of the martyrs (3.21–4.26) and will therefore hardly differ from that of ὁ ἱλαστήριος θάνατος.[2]

4 Macc. 17.20-22 shows a very close parallel to two of the three key words in the formula of Rom. 3.25 as well as to the conception of an atoning human death. Is there any evidence in *4 Maccabees* that the notion of πίστις is connected with this idea? The central virtue in *4 Maccabees* is εὐσέβεια (piety), as the discourse is on the devout reason (εὐσεβὴς λογισμός, 1.1). In 5.24 Eleazar defines εὐσέβεια as: μόνον τὸν ὄντα θεὸν σέβειν μεγαλοπρεπῶς. In an ideal way the martyrs illustrate how to apply this reason (3.19; 7.9). They keep faithful to the εὐσέβεια or εὐσεβὴς λογισμός until death (μέχρι θανάτου). As is said of Eleazar: 'If, therefore, an old man despised torments unto death on account of his piety (δι᾽ εὐσέβειαν), we must admit that devout reason is leader over our passions' (7.16).[3] Against this background the adjective εὐσεβής in 17.22 (διὰ τοῦ αἵματος τῶν εὐσεβῶν ἐκείνων) probably means that the martyrs remained pious until death. In a passage which is related to 17.20-22 one of the seven boys hints at the appeasement of God because of piety: 'Fight the sacred and noble fight for piety, through it may the just providence that protected our fathers become merciful to our people (στρατεύσασθε περὶ τῆς εὐσεβείας, δι᾽ ἧς ἵλεως ἡ

pp. 78-79), αἷμα in the New Testament does refer to Jesus' violent and not his sacrificial death.

1. Exod. 29.36-37; 30.10; Leviticus 16; LXX Ps. 50.4; Sir. 23.10; 38.10; LXX Jer. 40.8; Ezek. 36.33; 37.23.

2. Cf. the combination of αἷμα, καθαρίζω etc. and ἐξιλάσκομαι in Exod. 30.10; Lev. 8.15; 12.7; 16.15-16, 19-20 καθαρίζω (often translation of כפר in MT) and καθαρισμός are sometimes almost synonymous with ἐξιλάσκομαι and ἐξιλασμός, see Dodd, 'ΙΛΑΣΚΕΣΘΑΙ', pp. 352-53, 360; S. Lyonnet and L. Saborin, *Sin, Redemption, and Sacrifice: A Biblical and Patristic Study* (AnBib, 48; Rome: Biblical Institute Press, 1970), pp. 130, 137, 148.

3. Cf. 6.22, 30-31; 7.1, 18; 8.1; 9.6-7, 24, 29-30; 11.20-21, 23; 12.11, 14; 13.1, 7-8, 27; 14.3, 6; 15.12; 16.1, 13, 17; 17.7; 18.3.

δικαία καὶ πάτριος ἡμῶν πρόνοια τῷ ἔθνει γενηθεῖσα) and take vengeance on the accursed tyrant' (9.24). Because of the combination of ἵλεως with the preposition διά with genitive the phrase reminds one of Rom. 3.25 (ἱλαστήριον διὰ πίστεως).

There is clear evidence that εὐσέβεια in *4 Maccabees* is an alternative word for πίστις, chosen of course in connection with the philosophical character of the work. There are occurrences of εὐσέβεια in *4 Macc.* where other authors would have used πίστις. The author compares the martyrs several times with the three companions of Daniel 3, Daniel in the lions' den and Isaac and/or Abraham.[1] In their encouragements to each other to die in 13.9-12 the martyrs refer to the behaviour of the three young men of Daniel 3 and Isaac during his sacrifice and take this as a demonstration of piety (ἡ τῆς εὐσεβείας ἐπίδειξις, 13.10; cf. 13.12 διὰ τὴν εὐσέβειαν ὑπέμεινεν Ισαακ).[2] In a similar way the mother incites her seven boys to martyrdom by referring to Genesis 22, Daniel 6 and Daniel 3 (16.20-23). They should follow the lead of Abraham, Isaac, Daniel, Hananiah, Azariah and Mishael, who endured their suffering for the sake of God (καὶ ὑπέμειναν διὰ τὸν θεόν, 16.21). In 16.22 the mother continues: 'Therefore, you, having the same faith in God, must not be dismayed' (καὶ ὑμεῖς οὖν τὴν αὐτὴν πίστιν πρὸς τὸν θεὸν ἔχοντες μὴ χαλεπαίνετε). So πίστις functions sometimes as a synonym of the more often used word εὐσέβεια. There are two instances where πίστις or πιστεύω is used of the martyrs themselves (7.21; 17.2). In an intermezzo of the description and praise of the martyrdom of Eleazar (7.16-23) a rhetorical question hints at Eleazar's mastering of the passions and faith in God: 'For what philosopher is there, who lives by the whole rule of philosophy and trusts in God (καὶ πεπιστευκὼς θεῷ)...' In 17.2 it is said of the mother with her sons that she 'broke down the violence of the tyrant, thwarted his wicked devices and demonstrated the nobility of faith (δείξασα τὴν τῆς πίστεως γενναιότητα)'. These passages lead to the conclusion that the πίστις of the martyr is a motif in *4 Maccabees*. The evidence is not very extensive considering the much larger context of *4 Maccabees* in comparison to LXX Dan. 3.39-40 and

1. The three men in the furnace: 13.9-10; 16.3 (only Mishael), 21; cf. 18.12; Isaac: 7.14; cf. 18.11; Isaac and Abraham: 13.12; 16.20; Abraham alone: 14.20; 15.28; cf. 9.21; cf. Daniel in the lions' den: 16.3, 21; cf. 18.13.
2. See for πίστις in relation to Gen. 22 and Dan. 3 above p. 112, 118.

2 Macc. 7.37–8.5. It is nevertheless significant as an exception to the very common terminology of εὐσέβεια etc. which expresses the loyalty of the martyrs to God and his law. The fact that this terminology is present in two of the few passages on the effective meaning of the death of the martyrs (9.24; 17.20-22; cf. also 6.31 in connection with 6.28-29) indicates again that the triad of ἱλαστήριον, αἷμα and πίστις is traditional in a martyrological context, and that therefore πίστις probably refers to the faithfulness of the martyr until death.[1]

4. *Conclusion*

The investigation of possible parallels to the three key words in ἱλαστήριον διὰ πίστεως ἐν τῷ αὐτοῦ αἵματι in Rom. 3.25 results in the conclusion that the traditional background of the formula probably consists of ideas concerning martyrdom. Two of the three writings of the Septuagint in which these ideas are expressed and which were discussed above (2 Macc. 7.37–8.5; *4 Maccabees*) contain the three key words of Rom 3.25 or related terms. LXX Dan. 3.39-40 combines πέποιθα and ἐξιλάσκομαι, but also shares cultic vocabulary with 4 Maccabees. Concerning the setting of the formula we noticed that the passages in Daniel 3 and 2 Maccabees and *4 Macc.* 6.28-29 are situated in an intercessory prayer on behalf of the people, shortly before the death of the martyr. The way in which Paul has assimilated these traditional conceptions must be investigated further. Probably the combination of the effective meaning of Jesus' death and the motif of his faithfulness until death occurs elsewhere in the Pauline corpus (cf. Rom. 5.18-19; Gal. 2.20; 3; faithfulness and vindication in 2 Cor. 4.13-14; Phil. 2.8-9; cf. 1 Tim. 3.16; Rev. 2.10; Heb. 11.33-39 with a reference to a better resurrection in v. 35)[2] and other early Christian writings as well (Heb. 2.17; 12.2; 2 Tim. 2.10-13?). Heb. 2.17 with Jesus as πιστὸς ἀρχιερεύς in combination with the phrase ἱλάσκεσθαι τὰς ἁμαρτίας τοῦ λαοῦ shares also the

1. Against Hay '*Pistis*', who concludes that the most common meaning of πίστις etc. in Judaeo-Hellenistic literature is 'objective basis for faith'. The context must be taken into consideration to establish the meaning. In a martyrological context the meaning 'pledge' or 'evidence' is very improbable.
2. See Longenecker, 'Obedience of Christ'; Hays, *Faith*; Hooker, 'ΠΙΣΤΙΣ'; Davies, *Faith and Obedience*.

conception of the priestly 'office' of the martyr (cf. *4 Macc.* 5.4, 35; 7.11-12 and 17.9, where in contradiction to 2 Macc. 6.18 Eleazar is called a priest). These conclusions confirm that the triad of exceptional quality (that is, faith or faithfulness), effective death, and vindication, which we supposed above, was traditional indeed. The resurrection of the martyrs is a recurrent motif in 2 and *4 Maccabees* and the young men from Daniel 3 were saved before dying.[1] Further research should establish whether Heb. 12.2-4, Rev. 1.5, Ign. *Eph.* 20.1 and maybe other passages can be regarded as formulations of this triad.[2]

Post Scriptum

Since the completion of the manuscript several contributions have been published which are pertinent to the subject. I can only mention very briefly some of these studies here. W. Kraus (*Der Tod Jesu als Heiligtumsweihe. Eine Untersuchung zum Umfeld der Sühnevorstellung in Römer 3, 25-26a* [WMANT, 66; Neukirchen-Vluyn: Neukirchener Verlag, 1991]) considers διὰ [τῆς] πίστεως in Rom. 3.25 as a Pauline addition to the pre-Pauline formula, which should be read against the background of Leviticus 16 and Ezekiel 43. Kraus understands ἱλαστήριον as *Sühneort* and the blood of Jesus as a reference to the dedication of the temple. According to D.A. Campbell (*The Rhetoric of Righteousness in Romans 3.21-26* [JSNTSup, 65; Sheffield: JSOT Press, 1992]) an apologetic and Jewish theology of the Cross is presented in Rom. 3.21-26; διὰ πίστεως refers to the faithfulness of Jesus Christ (cf. also Appendix 3, pp. 219-28: 4 Maccabees should be dated after 135 CE). The last point is also emphasized by I.G. Wallis, *Where Opposites Meet. The Faith of Jesus Christ in Early Christian Traditions* (PhD Dissertation Sheffield, 1991); see on Romans pp. 71-100. See also the well-founded remarks

---

1. In *Mart. Pol.* 14-15 the Prayer of Azariah is alluded to in order to show that Polycarp deserves a postmortem vindication. See J.W. van Henten, 'Zum Einfluss jüdischer Martyrien auf die Literatur des frühen Christentums', in W. Haase and H. Temporini (eds.), *Aufstieg und Niedergang der römischen Welt*, II. 27 (Berlin: de Gruyter, 1993), pp. 719-23.

2. I thank Professor H.J. de Jonge, Professor P.W. van der Horst, Dr G. Mussies and Dr O.J. Schrier for their very helpful comment on the draft of this article and Dr M.C. de Boer for his assistance with the English.

by C. Breytenbach, 'Versöhnung, Stellvertretung und Sühne. Semantische und traditionsgeschichtliche Bemerkungen am Beispiel der paulinischen Briefe', *NTS* 39 (1993), pp. 59-79.

ON HEARING THE GOSPEL BOTH IN THE SILENCE
OF THE TRADITION AND IN ITS ELOQUENCE

J. Louis Martyn

I

In the course of collecting early christological traditions preserved in Galatians, Rien de Jonge has remarked that the extraordinarily volatile letter 'very much presents Paul's own theology, [while containing a surprising number of] references to earlier expressions of the faith shared by Paul and his opponents'.[1] It is a perceptive comment, suggesting that the reader of Galatians must constantly bring three factors into view, recognizing them to be both interrelated and distinct from one another. Paul is a theologian; in his letter to the Galatians his theology is polemically directed against the theology of certain persons who have invaded his Galatian churches; the nature of his polemic is partly determined by the fact that there is a body of early Christian tradition which is highly valued both by himself and by those opponents. The resulting interpretive challenge is intriguing—given the finely nuanced interplay between traditions cited by Paul and polemics crafted by him, certain passages in the letter virtually cry out for a redaction-critical reading.

None of these is more insistent than Paul's initial and famous reference to rectification in Gal. 2.16.[2] It is one of the most tightly

---

1.   M. de Jonge, *Christology in Context: The Earliest Christian Response to Jesus* (Philadelphia: Westminster Press, 1988), p. 39.

2.   There are three rectification passages in Galatians: 2.15-21; 3.6-29; 5.4-5. The bibliography on rectification in Paul's thought is almost endless; the studies on which I have drawn directly are mentioned in the notes. A point of importance is that in this essay *dikaioō* and *diklaiosunē* are usually rendered 'to rectify' and 'rectification', leaving behind the widespread practice of speaking of 'justification' and 'righteousness'. In writing to the Galatians Paul is careful to remove *dikaioō* and *diklaiosunē* from two settings—the courtroom in which there is a legal norm and the religious/

concentrated theological statements in all of Paul's letters. It is also the
earliest of his references to rectification, and thus the text in which we
are privileged to see this crucial element of his theology taking shape.[1]
To these observations one now adds a third: Gal. 2.16 is made to
order for redaction-critical interpretation. In it the apostle says in
effect to his erstwhile opponent Peter—and at a second and immediate
level to the Teachers who have invaded his Galatian churches—'you
and I share a Jewish-Christian tradition about rectification; I am going
to cite this shared tradition, and I am going to draw out the way in
which it speaks to the present situation, precisely in order to insist on
adherence to the truth of the gospel'.[2] Taking for granted some of the
results of detailed exegesis, I can begin with the following somewhat
paraphrastic translation of Gal. 2.15-16:

> You and I, Peter, are by nature Jews, and thus Jewish Christians; we are
> not 'Gentile Sinners'. We have the Law!
> Yet , as Jewish Christians, we ourselves know
> that the human being[3] is not rectified by observance of the Law,
> but rather[4] by the faith of Christ Jesus.

philosophical classroom in which there is a moral norm. Precisely what it is that has
gone wrong, and precisely what is involved in God's making it right are matters that
become clear only in the progression from the first rectification passage to the
second. See the last part of section III below.

1.   That Galatians antedates 1 Corinthians is clear from a comparison of Gal.
2.10 with 1 Cor. 16.1-2; cf. D. Georgi, *Remembering the Poor: The History of
Paul's Collection for Jerusalem* (Nashville: Abingdon Press, 1991).

2.   On the nomenclature 'the Teachers' see J.L. Martyn, 'A Law-Observant
Mission to Gentiles: The Background of Galatians', *SJT* 38 (1985), pp. 307-24. The
persons often referred to as 'the opponents' are Christian Jews with their own mission
to Gentiles, not merely opponents of Paul. Gal. 2.15-21 is the only passage in the letter
in which Paul addresses the Teachers rather than the Galatians. Just as he once spoke
sharply to Peter in the presence of the assembled church of Antioch, so he now
speaks sharply to the Teachers in the assembled presence of each of the Galatian
churches.

3.   The identity of this human being is a matter of great import. In the underlying
Jewish-Christian tradition it is the Israelite. In Paul's interpretation it is the human
being. In neither view, then, is it the Gentile, distinguished from the Jew, *pace*
J. Gager (*The Origins of Anti-Semitism* [Oxford: Oxford University Press, 1985],
p. 233), who follows the suggestions of L. Gaston and M. Barth.

4.   Heikki Räisänen has argued correctly for the adversative force of *ean mē*,
against J.D.G. Dunn's suggestion that it be taken here to mean 'except', see the next
note.

Thus, even we have placed our trust in Christ Jesus,
in order that the source of our rectification
might be the faith of Christ
and not observance of the Law;
for not a single person will be rectified by observance of the Law.

Although Paul does not provide quotation marks, so to speak, his sentence would be ineffective nonsense if he were referring in no way to shared traditions: 'we ourselves know *that...*' One cannot say where the tradition ends and Paul's situational redaction begins; indeed one suspects that the sentence is not the sort that recommends such a literary exercise.[1] Still, the interpreter does well to begin by taking Paul at his word. He is confronting Peter (and the Teachers) with rectification tradition they hold in common, and he is saying that this commonly held tradition speaks sharply to the developments in Antioch (and Galatia) because Peter (and the Teachers) are not being true to it.

II

We have, then, our initial redaction-critical question. Is Paul referring

---

1. In 'The New Perspective on Paul', *BJRL* 65 (1983), pp. 95-122, J.D.G. Dunn, has argued, to be sure, that such a literary division can be made (pp. 111-13). Taking *ean me* in 2.16a to mean 'except', he thinks that that part of the verse is Jewish-Christian tradition: 'one is not rectified by works of the Law except [unless] those works be accompanied by faith in Christ Jesus...' In 2.16b, Dunn continues, Paul 'pushes what began as a [Jewish-Christian] qualification on covenantal nomism into an outright [Pauline] antithesis' (p. 113). It is an interesting suggestion, but one that falters, I think, on three grounds. (a) One can be almost certain that *ean me* is to be taken here with its adversative force, 'but rather' (see H. Räisänen, 'Galatians 2.16 and Paul's Break with Judaism', *NTS* 31 [1985], pp. 543-53). (b) Exploring the huge realm of possibility, one might indeed entertain the thought that on occasion some Jewish Christians told their neighbors they would not be justified by keeping the Law unless they added faith in Christ. In fact, however, Dunn cites no Jewish-Christian tradition to support such a hypothesis, and support from data external to Gal. 2.16 itself is exactly what is needed. (c) Finally, when one looks behind Gal. 2.16 to Jewish–Christian rectification traditions we know Paul to have known, one sees that none of them refers to a circumstance in which rectification does *not* occur (Mt. 5.20 is another matter). See below the discussion of Rom. 3.25; Rom. 4.25; 1 Cor. 6.11, none of which contains a negative. Paul is responsible for all of the negatives in Gal. 2.16 (drawing the third from Ps. 142.2). On the theological implications of Dunn's analysis see J.L. Martyn, 'Events in Galatia', in *Pauline Theology* (ed. J. Bassler; Minneapolis: Fortress Press, 1991), I, pp. 160-79.

to a Jewish-Christian rectification tradition to which we have access,
which we know Paul to have known, and which is sufficiently well-
formed to enable us to compare it with Paul's reading of it? In fact his
own letters present us with several snippets of such tradition, and
three prove to be of considerable importance: Rom. 3.25; 4.25; 1 Cor.
6.11:[1]

> Rom. 3.25 (plus 26a)
> Christ Jesus, whom God put forward as a sacrifice of atonement by his
> blood. He did this to demonstrate the power of his rectitude; in his divine
> forbearance, that is to say, he has forgiven the sins previously
> committed...

> Rom. 4.25
> Jesus our Lord...who was handed over to death for our trespasses and
> was raised for our rectification.

> 1 Cor. 6.11
> And this is what some of you used to be (fornicators, idolaters,
> ...thieves...drunkards ...robbers; v. 9). But you were washed, you were
> sanctified, you were rectified in the name of the Lord Jesus Christ and in
> the Spirit of our God.[2]

---

1.   On pre-Pauline, Christian rectification traditions see P. Stuhlmacher,
Gerechtigkeit Gottes bei Paulus (Göttingen: Vandenhoeck & Ruprecht, 1965),
pp. 185-88; K. Kertelge, *'Rechtfertigung' bei Paulus* (Münster: Aschendorff, 1966),
pp. 45-62; 242-45; several articles in *Rechtfertigung: Festschrift für Ernst
Käsemann* (ed. J. Friedrich *et al.*; Tübingen: Mohr [Paul Siebeck], 1976): F. Hahn,
'Taufe und Rechtfertigung', pp. 95-124 (104-117); D. Lührmann, 'Christologie und
Rechfertigung', pp. 351-63 (359); G. Strecker, 'Befreiung und Rechfertigung',
pp. 479-508 (501-505). See also J. Reumann (with responses by J. Fitzmyer and
J. Quinn), *Righteousness in the New Testament* (Philadelphia: Fortress Press, 1982),
pp. 27-40; U. Schnelle, *Gerechtigkeit und Christusgegenwart* (Göttingen:
Vanderhoeck & Ruprecht, 2nd edn, 1986). Formulae lying outside the letters of Paul
are left aside in the present essay. It is impossible to know the relative ages of the
three formulae cited below; we can say only that they are of Jewish-Christian origin;
the application of the formula in 1 Cor. 6.11 to Gentiles (fornicators, idolaters, etc.) is
a secondary move on Paul's part.
2.   On the texts in Romans see particularly the commentaries of E. Käsemann,
U. Wilckens, P.W. Meyer (*Harper's Bible Commentary* [ed. J.L. Mays; San
Francisco: Harper & Row, 1988], pp. 1130-67); J.D.G. Dunn. N.A. Dahl has
argued that Rom. 3.25; 4.25, along with Rom. 8.32 and Gal. 3.13-14 reflect the use
of Akedah traditions by Jewish Christians ('The Atonement—an Adequate Reward
for the Akedah? [Rom. 8.32]', in *Neotestamentica et Semitica: Studies in Honor of
Matthew Black* [ed. E.E. Ellis and M. Wilcox; Edinburgh: T.& T. Clark, 1969],

While these Jewish-Christian formulae show variations, a picture of considerable coherence does emerge from them.[1]

a. *Rectification is an act of God.* Drawing heavily on traditions in the Old Testament and on strands of Jewish thinking about rectification, the Jewish Christians who worded these formulae speak about an act of God.[2] There are rich traditions, to be sure, having to do with human deeds of rectitude (e.g. Tob. 4.5-6; Wis. 2.12). The makers of these formulae do not draw on those traditions. They speak about God's action (cf. Judg. 5.11; Isa. 46.13).

b. *In that act God sets right things that have gone wrong.* In accordance with the causative force of the *hiphil* of the Hebrew verb *tsadaq* (clearly reflected also in Jewish traditions expressed in Greek) the authors of the Jewish-Christian formulae speak of an action by which God changes the human scene, creating integrity by making right things that have gone wrong.

c. *What has made things wrong is human transgression.* Here we have a point that requires emphasis. The human scene envisaged in these Jewish-Christian formulae is that of the Jewish nation, and in that scene the need of rectification has arisen from the fact that members of God's people have transgressed commandments explicitly issued to them by God, thus proving unfaithful to the covenant.[3] Nothing in any one of the formulae reflects a concern with Gentiles or with a mission to Gentiles (the reference to idolatry etc. in 1 Cor. 6.9 is a frame provided by Paul).[4] If one thinks that the formulae were

pp. 15-29); the hypothesis may have some force in the case of Rom. 8.32, but it is of dubious pertinence to the other passages.

1. Of these formulae the one cited in Rom. 3.25 may be of special importance for the present task. Since a very good case has been made for identifying its *Sitz im Leben* as that of the eucharist, one may take it to be a tradition connecting the celebration of the eucharist with the matter of rectification; and that connection is the formal frame within which Paul confronted Peter in the Antioch church.

2. Did the formula cited by Paul in Rom. 3.25 contain the phrase *dia pisteos* (NRSV 'effective through faith')? If so, then like the rest of the formula it must have referred to God's rectifying act, *his* active faithfulness to the covenant.

3. The covenantal theology of the formula cited in Rom. 3.25 is noted by numerous interpreters; the pathbreaking work is that of A. Pluta, *Gottes Bundestreue: Ein Schlüsselbegriff im Röm 3.25a* (Stuttgart: Katholisches Bibelwerk, 1969); see also E. Käsemann, *Romans* (Grand Rapids: Eerdmans, 1980), p. 100.

4. *Pace* S.K. Williams, *Jesus' Death as Saving Event* (Missoula, MT: Scholars Press, 1975), pp. 26-34 (32 n. 70), who takes 'the sins previously committed'

penned by theologians influenced by apocalyptic thought, then the
dominant pattern is sure to have been what Martin de Boer has correctly identified as forensic apocalyptic.[1] Members of God's covenant
people have sinned, and that is what has caused things to go wrong.

   d. *What makes transgressing members of God's people right is God's
forgiveness.* Given Israel's sins, the need is for divine acquittal, forgiveness, remission of sins and cleansing, so that the covenant can be
unburdened and a new life begun.[2] Rectification is now accomplished,

---

(Rom. 3.25) to be those of Gentiles. A linguistic investigation of the final phrase, *en
te anoche tou theou* (3.26a), could indeed lead one to Jewish texts in which God's
exasperating patience with Gentile sins raises the issue of theodicy (e.g. Isa. 64.10-
12). In general terms, moreover, it is certainly possible that Jewish Christians were
sometimes dismayed—together with their Jewish neighbors —at God's failure to act
immediately against Gentile oppressors. The formula of Rom. 3.25, however, was
very probably at home in the joyful setting of a eucharistic celebration held in a
Jewish-Christian church; and what was being celebrated was God's gracious act in
renewing the covenant with those who were citing and hearing the formula, the
members of that Jewish-Christian church. It was their sins with which God had been
patient until he enacted the rectifying sacrifice in Christ's blood (cf. *anoche* in Rom.
2.4). See Kertelge, *Rechtfertigung*, pp. 59-62. In 'The Atonement'—An Adequate
Reward for the Akedah? (Rom. 8.32)', N.A. Dahl finds in Rom. 3.25 a reference to
Israel's sins (p. 26); he also thinks, however, that Gal. 3.13-14 rests on a Jewish-
Christian formula in which the atoning death of the messiah was seen first to be
effective for Israelites, and secondly to bring about the inclusion of Gentiles in
Abraham's seed, the messiah himself. In the case of Gal. 3.13-14 Dahl's proposed
Jewish-Christian formula includes too many motifs that were almost certainly put
forward by Paul for the Galatian situation, such as the 'curse' link between Deut.
27.26 and Deut. 21.23, the *hina* clauses of Gal. 3.14, and the singular *sperma* of
Gal. 3.16.
   1.   M.C. de Boer, 'Paul and Jewish Apocalyptic Eschatology', in J. Marcus and
M.L. Soards (eds.), *Apocalyptic and the New Testament* (JSNTSup, 24; Sheffield:
JSOT Press, 1989), pp. 169-90.
   2.   This is a juncture at which the thesis of F. Thielman may be taken into
account (*From Plight to Solution* [Leiden: Brill, 1989]), for that thesis may have at
least marginal pertinence to the Jewish-Christian authors of the rectification
formulae. They may have worked to some degree from plight to solution, though
the terms would be far better put by speaking of sin and salvation. In any case,
Thielman's thesis is unconvincing as regards *Paul*. It is a matter in connection with
which one recalls that Karl Barth was an exegete as well as a systematic theologian;
for over a considerable period of time he correctly emphasized that Paul saw Adam
in the light of Christ, sin in the light of grace, and so on. See, for example, *Church
Dogmatics* (Edinburgh: T. & T. Clark, 1957; German, 1942), II, 2: 'it is only by

however, not by a sacrifice executed by a human being (such as the high priest acting on the Day of Atonement), but rather by Christ's death; and that death is understood to have been God's sacrificial act taken at his initiative; it is the deed in which God has forgiven the sins formerly committed in Israel, wiping the slate clean (Rom. 3.25). In this deed of God, guilty members of his people are changed by being the recipients of washing and of sanctification (1 Cor. 6.11; cf. 1QS 3.3-6).[1] This deed is itself, therefore, our rectification (Rom. 4.25).

e. *God's rectification is therefore God's mercy.* This definition is one of the points at which the Jewish-Christian formulae are similar to passages in the Qumran scrolls:[2]

1 Cor. 6.11
(There was guilt as the result of many sins…) but you have been washed, you have been sanctified, you have been rectified in the name of the Lord Jesus Christ…

1QS 11.13-15
He will draw me near by his grace, and by his mercy will he bring my rectification. He will judge me in the rectitude of his truth, and in the greatness of his goodness he will pardon all my sins. Through his rectitude he will cleanse me of the uncleanness of man, and of the sins of the children of men, that I may confess to God his rectitude…

1QH 4.34-37
When I thought of my guilty deeds…I said 'In my sins I am lost…' But then, when I remembered the strength of your hand and the fullness of your mercy, I rose again and stood upright…for you will pardon iniquity and you will purify man of sin through your rectification.[3]

---

grace that the lack of grace can be recognized as such' (p. 92); 'the doctrine of election…defines grace as the starting-point for all reflection and utterance…' (p. 93). In recent decades Barth's point has been emphasized in a certain way by E.P. Sanders, *Paul and Palestinian Judaism* (Philadelphia: Fortress Press, 1977), pp. 442-47.

1. Cf. E.P. Sanders, *Judaism: Practice and Belief* (London: SCM Press, 1992), p. 252; the three verbs in 1 Cor. 6.11 are usually taken to be synonyms, though J. Fitzmyer is dubious (Reumann, *Righteousness*, p. 204).

2. See O. Betz, 'Rechtferigung in Qumran', in *Rechtfertigung*, pp. 17-36; E.P. Sanders, *Paul and Palestinian Judaism*, pp. 305-12. The translations given below are those of G. Vermes, *The Dead Sea Scrolls in English* (New York: Penguin Books, 1968) with minor changes; see also E. Lohse, *Die Texte aus Qumran* (Darmstadt: Wissenschaftliche Buchgesellschaft, 1971).

3. On the understanding of sin in Qumran see J. Becker, *Das Heil Gottes*

1QS 11.12

As for me, if I stumble, the mercies of God shall be my eternal salvation.
If I stagger because of the sin of flesh, my rectification shall be by the
rectitude of God...

The last passage is of particular importance because it places in
parallel God's mercy and God's rectification (in Qumran fundamentally a confident, eschatological hope). The Jewish-Christian formulae
do something similar, equating rectification with God's forgiving
initiative in cleansing one from sins. They thus stand in a long and
impressive line of tradition; God's deed of rectification is God's
merciful forgiveness of transgressions for which atonement has been
made (cf. e.g. *Ps. Sol.* 3.3-12).

   f. *The Law is not mentioned because its continuing validity is taken
for granted; the God who has made things right in Christ is the God
of Israel, the author of the covenantal Law.* The ways in which the
formulae draw on Old Testament traditions, and the fact that they were
made by Christians who were distinctly Jewish tell us that the transgressions referred to were identified as transgressions on the basis of
the Law.[1] Moreover, while it may seem obvious, we must reiterate
that for the Jewish-Christian authors the God who has now enacted his
rectifying forgiveness is the God of Israel, the God of the covenant, the
author of the Law. By enacting his rectifying forgiveness in the death
and resurrection of Christ, God has established his right over his
creation Israel, thus restoring the integrity of the nomistic covenant.

   There is thus no thought that God's rectification removes one from
the realm of God's Law.[2] The three rectification formulae do not

---

(Göttingen: Vandenhoeck & Ruprecht, 1964), pp. 144-48; and the critique in
Sanders, *Paul and Palestinian Judaism*, pp. 272-84.

   1. In 'Not Jewish Christianity and Gentile Christianity but Types of
Jewish/Gentile Christianity' (*CBQ* 45 [1983], pp. 74-79), R.E. Brown had made
some suggestions that are helpful for the identification of churches outside of
Palestine. The church of Jerusalem was, however, another matter; and the same is
true of the churches in Judea that were children of the *euaggelion tēs peritomēs* (Gal.
1.22; 2.7, 9). All were thoroughly Jewish-Christian communities, and the formulae
we are discussing seem clearly to have been authored in them.

   2.   The thought of being removed from the realm of the Law would have
horrified both the Qumran covenantors and the Jewish-Christian authors of the three
rectification formulae. The one whom the Qumran psalmist praises because he will
'pardon iniquity and purify from sin by...[his]...rectification' (1QH 4.37 cited
above) is the one who has engraved his Law on the psalmist's heart (1QH 4.10).

mention the Law either positively or negatively, because taking the Law for granted, they express the *novum*—God's gracious and rectifying forgiveness of sins in Christ.

g. *God has accomplished his rectifying forgiveness in Christ, specifically in Christ's death and resurrection.* Just as in the formulae, silence about the Law shows that the Law's continuance is taken for granted, so that silence also indicates that rectification is not attributed to the Law (a point that will prove crucial to Paul). God has provided his rectifying forgiveness by acting in the atoning blood sacrifice that is Christ's death (Rom. 3.25), or in the event of Christ's resurrection (Rom. 4.25). And that accomplishment of God is made real for those who are being baptized when the name of the Lord Jesus is pronounced over them and the Spirit of Christ descends on them (1 Cor. 6.11). Thus the Jewish Christians responsible for these formulae see an indelible connection—even an identity—between God's deed of

Similarly, for Jewish-Christians the God who has graciously rectified sinners in the sacrificial death of his Son is the one who graciously gave the Law, engraving it forever on the hearts of his people.

It is at this point one may pause in order to ask an important question about the assumption that God's rectification is an act taken by him in the context of the Law. Does this assumption mean that the authors of the Jewish-Christian formulae fail to present God's rectifying deed in Christ as an act of grace? Hardly. Like the Qumran convenantors (and other Jewish sages who deal with the subject of rectification) these Jewish Christians celebrate a new instance of God's grace in the undisturbed context of God's gracious Law. Just as the covenantors could throw themselves on the merciful rectification of God, without dreaming of abandoning God's Law, so the authors of the traditions preserved in 1 Cor. 6.11, Rom. 3.25, and Rom. 4.25, celebrate rectification in Christ without contemplating the possibility that that deed of God might stand in tension with God's giving of the Law, or with their observance of it. Modern Christian interpreters sometimes say of Qumran that strict adherence to the Law spoils the confession of hope solely directed to God's rectification, turning it into something other than true *sola gratia*. But that is a reading forgetful of the fact that Qumran exemplifies the way in which Israel traditionally put together the deepest belief in God's mercy and the strictest observance of God's Law (cf. Sanders, *Paul and Palestinian Judaism*, p. 292). In a word, the covenantors do not move away from the confession of God's gracious rectification to the demand for punctilious observance of the Law, thus allowing the latter to 'spoil' the former. On the contrary, they are representative Jews in holding the two together: observance of the Law and confession of God's mercy. *Mutatis mutandis* the Jewish Christians from whom Paul inherited 1 Cor. 6.11, Rom. 3.25 and Rom. 4.25 did essentially the same.

rectification and God's deed in Christ.[1]

h. In these formulae one finds, then, *God's messianic grace in the context of God's Law*. For that reason the authors of these formulae would have found a polemic against rectification by Law observance entirely beside the point. They were making no such claim. Indeed, the Jewish-Christian tradition about rectification is a stranger to polemics. It seems to have been formulated in Jewish-Christian churches largely free of internal strife.

i. *God's rectifying forgiveness in Christ is confessed without explicit reference to faith*. Just as the formulae make no reference to the Law, so they do not mention faith, either on the part of members of the Jewish-Christian communities or on the part of Jesus Christ.[2] There is, therefore, no hint of a polemical antinomy such as one that would place opposite one another Christ's faithful deed on our behalf and our observance of the Law.

These nine points provide, with a reasonable degree of probability, the major outlines of a Jewish-Christian rectification tradition that antedated both Paul and the Teachers, a tradition that was shared by both of them, a tradition that was indeed revered by both of them. Can we speak with some confidence about the ways in which the Teachers and Paul interpreted this shared tradition?

---

1.   On J.D.G. Dunn's thesis that Jewish-Christian tradition attributed rectification to Law observance *supplemented by* faith in Jesus see p. 131 n. 1.

2.   In n. 2 p. 133 I have already mentioned the question whether the phrase *dia pisteos* (NRSV: 'effective through faith') was included in the pre-Pauline formula of Rom. 3.25. It is an issue much discussed and unlikely ever to be settled to the satisfaction of all interpreters. I am myself inclined to see the phrase as a Pauline insertion, but an impressive argument for including it in the formula can indeed be made on formal grounds (see, e.g., U. Wilckens, *Der Brief an die Römer* [3 vols.; Zürich: Benziger Verlag, 1978–1982], I, p. 190). The weightiest interpretation of the phrase as pre-Pauline is that of A. Pluta (*Gottes Bundestreue*), who takes it as a reference to *God's* covenantal faithfulness. Although not completely convinced by Pluta's argument, U. Wilckens perceptively notes the possibility of a partial parallel in 1 Jn 1.9— 'If we confess our sins, he [God] is faithful (*pistos*) and just *(dikaios)*, and will forgive our sins and cleanse us from all unrighteousness' (*Römer*, I, p. 194). Less weighty is the argument of S.K. Williams (*Jesus' Death as Saving Event*) that the phrase is a pre-Pauline reference to the faith *of Jesus* demonstrated in his death. In short, if *dia pisteos* is to be taken as part of the Jewish-Christian tradition, Pluta's argument stands: that phrase referred, as did the formula as a whole, to God's trustworthy deed in Christ, his rectifying act of faithfulness to his covenantal people. In that tradition it meant neither Jesus' faith nor faith on the part of the human being.

III

A detailed answer to that question would carry us far beyond the limits of a brief essay. Regarding the Teachers' reading of the rectification tradition, I can mention two points:

First, we can be confident that the Teachers find in the tradition what we have seen actually to be there—the affirmation of God's forgiveness of Israel's sins in the sacrificial death of his Messiah. For the Teachers, as for the Jewish-Christian authors of the tradition, Jesus' death is the totally adequate sacrifice made by God himself, the sacrifice in which God accomplished the forgiveness of sins for Israel, the people among whom observance of the Law was and is simply taken for granted.

Second, however, the Teachers hear the Jewish-Christian tradition in a new context in which observance of the Law is not—and cannot be—taken for granted, for they are engaged in a mission to pagan Gentiles. And because they carry out their mission by inviting the Gentiles to enter the people of Israel, they necessarily posit an explicit relation between rectification and observance of the Law. Where the Jewish-Christian tradition affirmed God's deed in Christ for an Israel in which Law-observance was simply taken for granted, the Teachers understand God's deed of forgiveness in Christ to be for Israel, including all Gentiles who transfer from their pagan existence into God's Law-observant people. That rectifying transfer, then, clearly necessitates the Gentiles taking up observance of the Law. Now Paul's interpretation of this Jewish-Christian rectification tradition is more complex;[1] we can consider here a few matters of import.

The Teachers' use of the Jewish-Christian tradition does not cause Paul to give it up. Nor does he provide the slightest hint that he disagrees with this tradition. Precisely the contrary; he calls the Jewish-Christian rectification tradition down on the heads of the Teachers. The way in which he does that proves to be of considerable interest.

As he writes to his Galatian churches, the setting in which Paul hears this Jewish-Christian tradition is both similar to and fundamen-

1. See again the works of Stuhlmacher, Kertelge and others mentioned in n. 1 p. 132.

tally different from the setting in which the Teachers hear it. On the one hand, since both Paul and the Teachers are active in missions to Gentiles, like the Teachers Paul necessarily hears the tradition in that new context.

On the other hand, however, even that context is quite different for Paul. In stark contrast to the Teachers, Paul perceives every day that in his Gentile mission-field God is creating churches—actively making things right, that is, in the whole of the world—apart from observance of the Law. It is easy to see, then, that Paul does not hear a rectification tradition that speaks about the Israelite, the Jew, the transgressor of God's covenantal Law who, because of his transgression, stands in need of forgiveness. As one notes in Gal. 2.16, Paul hears a tradition that speaks to and about *anthropos*, the human being, both Jew and Gentile, without any distinction between the two (cf. Gal. 3.28). And exactly how can he hear the tradition in this way?

He notes in the Jewish-Christian rectification tradition a striking instance of *silence*: the tradition, referring emphatically to God's deed of rectification, does not even mention the Law; specifically, it does not attribute rectification to observance of the Law.[1] In the light of God's work as Paul observes it every day, he sees, then, that the tradition's silence about the Law is no mystery. It is indeed an instance of silence which he hears as though it were a clean clap of divine thunder; for in this silence he senses not only that the tradition itself is speaking generically about the human being; he senses also that it is saying 'the human being is not rectified by observance of the Law...'

The Jewish-Christian tradition is silent with regard to the Law; it is eloquent with regard to Christ; and Paul is as sensitive to the latter as he is to the former. Given the Teachers' work in his Galatian churches, Paul hears the tradition's nomistic silence and its christological eloquence in a new way. He now hears God's voice formulating a new antinomy that links the verb 'to be rectified' both to a negative statement and to a positive one: the human being,

> is not rectified by observance of the Law
> but rather by *pistis Christou Iēsou*.

And to formulate the positive member of this gospel antinomy Paul

---

1. Paul has no objection to the pattern of Law-observance in the Jewish-Christian churches of Judea (Gal. 1.22); for, as the rectification tradition itself shows, these churches do not credit their being set right to their keeping of the Law.

coins an eloquent expression of his own, *pistis Christou.*[1]

Recent decades have seen an extended and vigorous debate as to the force of this expression, some interpreters taking it to mean human faith in Christ (a construction they usually call an objective genitive), some finding a reference to the faith of Christ (usually termed subjective, but best identified, somewhat loosely, as an authorial genitive).[2] In the present essay two points can be mentioned:

First, the Jewish-Christian rectification tradition on which Paul is drawing had affirmed God's rectifying deed by the death (and resurrection) of Christ. If Paul is hearing that tradition anew, without violating it fundamentally, a simple conclusion is to be drawn. When he says that God has made things right by *pistis Christou Iēsou,* he is referring to God's rectifying act in Christ (centrally in his death, which Paul always understands to be part of a holistic event including his resurrection). *Pistis Christou,* in short, arises in Paul's vocabulary as his way of reflecting the tradition's reference to Christ's role in God's deed of rectification.[3]

1. On the exegetical use of the term 'antinomy' see J.L. Martyn, 'Apocalyptic Antinomies in Paul's Letter to the Galatians', *NTS* 31 (1985), pp. 410-24.

2. To trace this debate one will do well to begin with Kertelge, *Rechtfertigung,* pp. 162-219, noting Haussleiter's move from subjective genitive to genitive of authorship. From Kertelge one can then make one's way to the items mentioned in the texts and notes of R.B. Hays, '*Pistis* and Pauline Christology: What is at Stake?' and J.D.G. Dunn, 'Once More *Pistis Christou*', and to those papers themselves, both in the *Seminar Papers* for the SBL meeting of November, 1991. As P.W. Meyer has pointed out in remarks made at that meeting, the objective genitive, strictly defined, demands not only a verbal ruling noun, but also one whose cognate verb is transitive. The verb *pisteuo* is transitive only with the meaning 'to entrust' followed by two accusatives. In the case of *pistis Christou* it may be better, then, to speak of a genitive of authorship or of origin. Everyone would agree that Paul sometimes speaks of our faith; and in Gal. 3.2 and 5 he identifies the generative source of that faith: the proclamation of Christ's death. From those references, then, and also from Gal. 3.22-25, one could draw a conclusion not far from that of J. Haussleiter: 'Christus wirkt den Glauben, indem er sich mitteilt...Und nun bleibt er wirksam hinter dem Glauben stehen, dessen rettende Kraft darin liegt, dass der lebendige Christus wie sein Urheber, so sein Träger ist' (cited from Kertelge, p. 164, n. 18).

3. In theory one could consider the possibility, I suppose, that where the tradition spoke of an act of *God,* making things right in Christ's death, Paul heard a reference to an act of *the human being,* having faith in Christ. I see, however, no exegetical ground firm enough to support this hypothesis, and much to oppose it,

Second, that interpretation is firmly supported by a comparison of Gal. 2.16 with Gal. 2.21. Gal. 2.16 is simply the opening sentence in the first rectification passage in the letter, the final sentence of that passage being 2.21. Both are pithy references to God's deed of making things right, and both are antinomous in form:

2.16	2.21
the human being	
is not rectified by	if rectification were
observance of *the Law*,	through *the Law*,
but rather by	then
pistis Christou Iēsou...	*Christ died* for no purpose at all.

If end corresponds to beginning, then in 2.16, as in 2.21, Paul is referring to an opposition between rectification by Law observance and rectification by the deed of God in Christ. It follows that *pistis Christou* is an expression by which Paul speaks of Christ's atoning faithfulness, as, on the cross, he died faithfully for us while looking faithfully to God. In Paul's own words,

> The Lord Jesus Christ, 'who gave up his very life for our sins', so that he might snatch us out of the grasp of the present evil age, thus acting in accordance with the intention of God our Father (1.4).

The result of this interpretation of *pistis Christou* is crucial to an understanding not only of Galatians, but also of the whole of Paul's theology. God has set things right without laying down a prior condition of any sort. God's rectifying act, that is to say, is no more God's response to human faith in Christ than it is God's response to human observance of the Law. God's rectification is not God's response at all. It is the first move; it is God's initiative, carried out by him in Christ's faithful death.

The antimony of Gal. 2.16, then—*erga nomou* versus *pistis Christou*—is like all of the antinomies of the new creation: it does not set over against one another two human alternatives, to observe the Law or to have faith in Christ. The opposites, as one sees from Gal. 1.1 onwards, are an act of God, Christ's faithful death, and an act of the human being, observance of the Law. The one has the power to rectify, to make things right, the other does not.

pace J.D.G. Dunn and other supporters of the so-called objective genitive. See previous and following notes.

To be sure, as Paul will say in Gal. 3.2, Christ's faithful death for us has the power to elicit faithful trust on our part. Thus in 2.16 itself he speaks in the second instance of our placing our trust in Christ:

Thus even we have placed our trust in Christ Jesus, in order that the source of our rectification might be the faith of Christ and not observance of the Law.

The point is that the Christ in whom we faithfully place our trust is the Christ who has already faithfully died on our behalf (cf. Rom. 5.8) and whose gracefully prevenient death for us is the rectifying event that has elicited our faith.[1]

Finally, there is the matter of defining rectification, of indicating plainly what it is. Here one notes that in composing his first rectification passage, Paul provides his own arresting instance of silence. He uses the verb 'to be rectified' three times in v. 16, a fourth time in v. 17; and, as a fifth reference, he employs the noun 'rectification' in v. 21; yet he speaks in this paragraph only of the means or the source of rectification, giving not a hint as to what rectification itself might be. Why this silence?

It is surely an instance of sophisticated rhetoric; Paul says nothing about the Jewish-Christian definition of rectification as forgiveness, in order in a non-polemical way to clear the deck for a new definition; and that new definition does in fact emerge in the second rectification passage, Gal. 3.6-29 (to which I will add 4.3). One recalls that the Jewish-Christian tradition presents a drama in which there are three actors: sinful human beings, Christ and the God of the covenant who

1.   Paul never remotely suggests that any human act—whether that of observing the Law or that of placing one's trust in Christ—can make things right. In Christ's faithful death God has made things right, and his doing that is what both demonstrates his rectitude and elicits our faithful trust in him. One must thus emphasize—especially in light of the debate mentioned above—that, while Paul attached great significance to our trusting Christ, he did not understand that trust to be an act of which we are the autonomous authors. When we trust God, we signal that we ourselves have been invaded by God's presuppositionless grace, and we confess that the locus of God's invasion is especially our will! Far from presupposing freedom of the will (cf. Hos. 5.4), Paul speaks of the freeing of the will for the glad service of God and neighbor. And that freeing of the will reflects one of Paul's major convictions: our trust in God has been awakened, kindled by God's trustworthy deed in Christ. See H. Schlier, *Der Brief an die Galater* (Göttingen: Vandenhoeck & Ruprecht, 1961), who, in interpreting *akoē pisteōs* in Gal. 3.2, speaks perceptively of '[die] Offenbarung, die den Glauben entzündet' (p. 122).

has accomplished in the blood sacrifice of Christ the true forgiveness of human sins. As we have noted, Paul does not polemicize against that tradition.

In his second rectification passage, however, he does go well beyond it, forming a new definition of rectification, and that new definition involves a dramatic shift. For in Galatians 3 we find a drama in which there are four actors: human beings, Christ, God and anti-God powers:

> The Law that has the power to curse (3.10);
> the Law as it pronounces its curse on the crucified Christ (3.13);
> sin functioning as the prison warden over the whole of creation (3.22);
> the elements of the cosmos that enslave both Jew and Gentile (4.3).[1]

With the appearance of these anti-God powers the landscape is changed quite fundamentally, indicating what has really gone wrong and what is really involved in God's making it right in the whole of the cosmos. In Galatians it is the movement from the first rectification passage to the second that confirms the major thesis of E. Käsemann: for Paul God's rectification in Christ 'is the rightful *power* with which God makes his cause to *triumph* in the world that has fallen away from him...'[2] In a word, the cosmic landscape is now shown to be a battlefield, and the need of human beings proves to be not so much forgiveness of their sins as deliverance from malignant powers that hold them in bondage.

The change to this battlefield is particularly impressive as regards the way in which Paul perceives the relation of Christ's death to the Law. To be sure, continuing Jewish-Christian atonement tradition, Paul still says that Christ died 'for us' (3.13); but now Christ's death is seen to have happened in collision with the Law, and we are not said to need

---

1.   Note that from Gal. 3.10–4.5 Paul uses the expression *hypo tina einai*, 'to be under the power of someone or something', no less than eight times, thus referring seriatim to anti-God powers that enslave all human beings.

2.   E. Käsemann, '"The Righteousness of God" in Paul', *New Testament Questions of Today* (London: SCM Press, 1969), pp. 168-82 (180, emphasis added). The fact that the formulaic *dikaiosunē theou* does not appear in Galatians is thus of no consequence. The view of God's rectification as God's deed of power is present in a multitude of texts, ranging from pre-apocalyptic traditions in ancient Israel to the Dead Sea Scrolls and beyond. Translators are correct, for example, to render *sidqot yahweh* in Judg. 5.11 (the Song of Deborah) 'the triumphs of the Lord' (NRSV); in a word, the institution of the holy war is the deep soil in which cosmological apocalyptic took root in Israel.

forgiveness but rather deliverance from a genuine slavery that involves the Law. In this second rectification passage, the Law proves to be not so much a norm which we have transgressed—although transgressions are involved (3.19)—as a tyrant insofar as it has placed us under the power of its curse. And by his death Christ is not said to have accomplished our forgiveness, but rather our redemption from slavery. With the apocalyptic shift to a scene in which there are real powers arraigned against God, rectification acquires, then, a new synonym, *exagoradzō,* 'to redeem by delivering from slavery' (3.13; 4.5).[1] And, as we have noted, one of the powers from whose tyranny Christ has delivered us is the Law in its role as the pronouncer of a curse on the whole of humanity.

The shifts involved in moving from the first rectification passage to the second provide, then, a major clue to the genesis of Paul's view of rectification; for in 3.6-29 Paul 'circumscribes the forensic apocalyptic eschatology of the...Teachers with a cosmological apocalyptic eschatology of his own'.[2] By his death on the nomistically cursed cross Christ has brought us out of the state of slavery to anti-God powers. Rectification thus remains for Paul God's act in the death of Christ; but now, having taken silent leave of the Jewish-Christian concern with the forgiveness of nomistic transgressions, Paul sees in Christ's death God's liberating invasion of the territory of tyranny.[3]

IV

Paul's use of rectification language has been thought to constitute a doctrine, and about that doctrine numerous interpreters have made

1.   Paul effects the same kind of shift at Gal. 1.4b. Having quoted Jewish-Christian tradition in which Christ is said to have given his life 'for our sins' (1.4a), Paul changes the frame of reference to that of apocalyptic deliverance from the powerful grasp of the present evil age (*exelētai*). While he does not use in this shift the language of rectification, one can say that the theological integrity of the letter warrants one's taking *exaireomai* as yet another Pauline synonym for rectification. And when we are speaking of synonyms, we must at least mention two further ones: for Paul God makes things right by bringing life where there was death (Gal. 3.21; Rom. 4.17) and by creating community where there was division (Gal. 3.28; note *heis*).

2.   M.C. de Boer, 'Paul and Jewish Apocalyptic Eschatology', p. 185.

3.   When Paul takes silent leave of the Jewish-Christian concern with forgiveness, he also leaves behind the role of repentance as a major key to the rectification of what has gone wrong. As Hosea knew, an enslaved people cannot repent (Hos. 5.4).

three claims: (a) it was polemical in its very nature, a *Kampflehre*; (b) it led to wholly unnecessary divisions in the early history of the church; and (c) being itself unnecessary, it proves on inspection to have been marginal to the core of Paul's gospel. Is any light shed on these claims by the redaction-critical reading of Gal. 2.16, and by the comparison with one another of the first two rectification passages in Galatians?

a. The polemical nature of Gal. 2.16 is beyond dispute. When Paul says, 'the human being is not rectified by observance of the Law, but rather by the faith of Christ Jesus, he is clearly involved in a battle marked by considerable *odium theologicum* (Gal. 5.12).

b. It is scarcely surprising, then, that the doctrine of rectification did indeed play a role in early Christian tensions (e.g. Jas 2.18-26). Historians have had some reason for suggesting that those tensions— variously qualified and supplemented—had a hand in the ultimate divorce between the largely Gentile church of the Mediterranean basin and the older, distinctly Jewish churches of Jerusalem, Judea and eventually of Pella and parts of Syria. None of these developments indicates, however, that Paul was himself an enemy of Jewish Christianity. The truth lies with the precise opposite. No one in the early church held more tenaciously to the vision of church unity than did Paul, and no one paid a higher price for that vision. At the famous meeting in Jerusalem, for example, it was Paul who was consumed by the comprehensive vision of God's great work proceeding along two parallel paths between which he envisioned only mutual support and respect. In his early work he was at peace with the Jewish-Christian churches of Judea (Gal. 1.22-24), and to the end of his life he was certain first that the unified church of God was drawn both from Jews and from Gentiles (Rom. 9.24), and secondly that that unity demanded concrete expression in the collection he gathered from his own churches for the church in Jerusalem (the delivery of which led eventually to his death; Rom. 15.25-33).

Given the history of Pauline interpretation, then, one can scarcely overemphasize that the redaction-critical reading of Gal. 2.16 shows Paul formulating a polemic neither against Judaism nor against Jewish Christianity. At the genesis of Paul's doctrine of rectification the apostle understands himself to be in accord with Jewish-Christian rectification tradition, *as* that tradition is newly heard in light of God's gospel-invasion of the whole of the world.

c. Comparing Gal. 2.16-21 with Gal. 3.6-29, and seeing that the two passages present a theological integrity, we have found in the progression from the first to the second an essential clue to the polemical character of Paul's doctrine of rectification. In the first rectification passage Paul emphasizes the antinomy between Christ's faithful death and observance of the Law. In the second passage he then brings that antinomy into the perspective of cosmic apocalyptic in which God can and does carry out his rectification only by acting in Christ against real enemies (3.13; cf. 4.3-5). But that means that Paul's rectification polemic against the Teachers in 2.16 is nothing other than a reflection of God's rectifying polemic against his enemies, among which Paul understandably attends particularly to the curse of the Law. Having earlier said that God does not make things right by means of the Law, Paul now says that God has had to make things right by entering into combat against the Law, in so far as it enacts its curse; and Christ's death on the Law-cursed cross is the point at which God has done that.

It is thus the polemical act of *God* in Christ that causes Paul's doctrine of rectification to be polemical, and that means that one cannot minimize the latter without doing the same to the former. We have no evidence, it is true, that before writing to the Galatians Paul ever spoke directly and explicitly on the subject of rectification. Once his combat with the Teachers in Galatia led him, however, to craft that way of preaching the gospel of God's triumph, he never gave it up.[1]

For while Paul may very well have been a person to whom compromise was foreign territory, his personal idiosyncrasies do not explain his theological tenacity. At root, he was sure that his call to be an apostolic soldier was a reflection of God's being himself *the* soldier, intent on making things right. It is God's declaration of war in Christ against all of the forces enslaving the human race that formed the foundation of Paul's militant doctrine of rectification. In short, God's rectifying declaration of war in Christ is what gave Paul total confidence that in the end Christ will hand over the kingdom to God the Father, after he has destroyed every ruler and every authority and power (1 Cor. 15.24).

---

1. To the instances of *dikaiosunē* and *dikaioō* in 1 and 2 Corinthians one adds some synonyms, such as the expression *katargeō pasan archēn* ...(1 Cor. 15.24).

How Controversial Was Paul's Christology?

James D.G. Dunn

1. *Introduction*

It is Christian belief in Jesus and particularly in the significance of Jesus which most clearly marks out Christianity from all other religions, including its two close relations, Judaism and Islam. Christology, in other words, marks the natural fault line and main breach between Christianity and Judaism in particular. A natural corollary to this indisputable fact is the inference that this must have been true of Christology more or less from the first. Already with the first christological claims, Jew and Christian, including not least Christian Jew, were bound to have been at loggerheads. But is the corollary well founded?

The deduction, that Christian claims for Jesus were a bone of contention from the first, can, of course, find ready support within the New Testament. The Gospel traditions are united in recounting how Jesus was rejected by the Jewish authorities in being handed over to the Romans for execution. And Paul in particular notes how 'Christ crucified' was 'a stumbling block to Jews and folly to Gentiles' (1 Cor. 1.23). Later on he castigates his opponents in Corinth, probably influenced in at least some degree by the Christian Jews of Jerusalem and Palestine, for preaching 'another Jesus' (2 Cor.11.4).[1] And his talk of Christ as having become accursed (by the law) probably echoes some early internal Jewish polemic against the attempts by the earliest Christian Jews to interpret Jesus' death in a positive way (Gal. 3.13).[2] An obvious conclusion to draw from these texts is that

---

1. On Paul's opponents in 2 Corinthians see e.g. V.P. Furnish, *2 Corinthians* (AB,1 32A; Garden City, NY: Doubleday, 1984), pp. 49-54.

2. See e.g. G.J. Brooke, 'The Temple Scroll and the New Testament', in G.J. Brooke (ed.), *Temple Scroll Studies* (JSPSup, 7; Sheffield: JSOT Press 1989),

already by the time of Paul the claims made for Christ by the first generation Christians were highly controversial and made a breach with Judaism unavoidable.

The conclusion is reinforced by those who argue that the distinctive features of Christology were already present in Jesus' own self-understanding or that the most decisive developments in Christology had already taken place within the first generation of Christianity. Influential here has been M. Hengel's claim that 'more happened in this period of less than two decades than in the whole of the next seven centuries, up to the time when the doctrine of the early church was completed'.[1] If that is actually true, notwithstanding the tremendous developments in christological thought from the second century onwards and the tremendous deepening of the breach between Christianity and Judaism which took place during that period, then once again it is hard to see how Paul's Christology in particular could have avoided being highly controversial.

Congruent with Hengel's thesis is the more recent restatement of the older view that the payment of divine honours to and worship of Jesus was an early feature of Christology which must have been sufficient of itself to cause a breach with monotheistic Judaism.[2] Here again the argument is in effect that the decisive make-or-break issues were already being posed during the time of Paul's ministry and writings. Indeed, it can hardly mean other than that Paul himself, the most important and controversial of the early principal figures in Christianity's expansion and self-definition, played an active role in sharpening the issues which focused in Christology. On this reckoning, the split between Christianity and Judaism over Christology was all over bar the shouting by the time Paul disappeared from the scene, with only the 'i's to be dotted and the 't's crossed for the full extent of the divisions to become clear to all.

But again we have to ask, is this an accurate reconstruction of the

pp. 181-99 (181-82), with bibliography in n. 3.

1. M. Hengel, *The Son of God* (London: SCM Press, 1976), p. 2 (italicized in Hengel's text); see e.g. I.H. Marshall, *The Origins of New Testament Christology* (Leicester: Inter-Varsity Press, 1976).

2. See e.g. various contributors to H.H. Rowdon (ed.), *Christ the Lord: Studies in Christology presented to Donald Guthrie* (Leicester: Inter-Varsity Press, 1982); L.W. Hurtado, *One God, One Lord: Early Christian Devotion and Ancient Jewish Monotheism* (Philadelphia: Fortress Press, 1988).

course of events? The impression given in Acts is that while Christian preaching of Jesus and the resurrection caused some embarrassment, it was not a make-or-break issue (cf. e.g. Acts 5.34-39; 23.6-9). The first real make-or-break issue seems to have been what was perceived as the Hellenists' attack on the temple (Acts 6–7). Not unnaturally, it was the more immediate political and economic reality embodied in the temple as well as its power as a religious symbol which proved the more sensitive and explosive issue.[1] Paul himself recalls persecuting the church not out of disdain for the church's Christology, but out of 'zeal' for the law (Gal. 1.13-14; Phil. 3.6). And subsequently in Paul's own mission and writings the crucial issue vis-à-vis the parent faith (Judaism) seems uniformly to have been the law (as in Galatians and Romans, the two Pauline letters in which the tensions between the gospel and traditional Judaism come most clearly to the fore).[2] Nor should we forget the findings of recent research in the Corinthian epistles, to the effect that social issues, as much if not more than doctrinal issues, were at the heart of the problems confronting Paul there.[3]

So the question that arises is to what extent was Christology an issue between Paul and his opponents? Was Paul's Christology quite so controversial as the usual reconstructions of the Pauline controversies argue, and as such texts as those cited above seem to imply? We can only answer this question by looking afresh at the key christological motifs in Paul.

2. *Jesus as Messiah*

So far as the question of this essay is concerned, the most striking feature of Paul's Christology at this point is the degree to which messiah/ Christ has become virtually a proper name for Paul—'Jesus Christ', or 'Christ Jesus', with 'Christ' having a titular significance ('the Christ') only rarely. The bare statistics are almost sufficient to make the point on their own (confining the sample to the undisputed Paulines).

---

1. See further my *The Partings of the Ways between Christianity and Judaism* (London: SCM Press; Philadelphia: Trinity Press International; 1991), chs. 3–4.
2. See my *Partings*, ch. 7.
3. See Furnish, *2 Corinthians*, p. 53.

Christ Jesus/Jesus Christ	68
+ Lord	43
Christ (without article)	112
the Christ	46

That is, of some 269 occurrences of 'Christ', only 46 (17%) speak of 'the Christ'. Moreover, in a high proportion of the 46 instances, the presence of the definite article is dictated by syntactical convention;[1] W. Grundman accepts a titular significance in only seven of these cases (Rom. 9.5; 15.3, 7; 1 Cor. 1.13; 10.4; 11.3; 12.12),[2] and F. Hahn adds a further six (Rom. 9.3; 1 Cor. 10.9; 2 Cor. 11.2; Gal. 5.24; Phil. 1.15, 17).[3] Even if one or two more should be drawn in (Rom. 14.18), the disproportion between Paul's use of 'Christ' with the definite article and without is still striking. Perhaps most striking of all is the fact that the fuller name Jesus Christ/Christ Jesus never has the definite article in Paul; Paul never says 'Jesus, the Christ', or 'the Christ, Jesus'.

The situation is clear: the title ('the Christ') has been elided into a proper name, usually with hardly an echo of the titular significance. That must mean that the claim, or rather the argument that Jesus is the Christ, was no longer an issue for Paul. To call Jesus 'Christ' was not a controversial assertion in the context in which Paul was writing. Had it been so Paul must have argued the point or defended the claim. But nowhere does he do so, or apparently feel the need to do so.

Here is an astonishing fact, but its astonishing character has been dulled for modern students of the New Testament because it has been so familiar for such a long time. We know that the claim of Jesus as messiah was a controversial matter during Jesus' life—at least towards the end, since, evidently it was the political character of the claim which provided the justification for Jesus' execution (Mk 14.61-64; 15.2, 26, 32, pars.).[4] We also know that the claim subsequently became decisive in the final break with the synagogue mirrored in Jn 9.22.[5] But at the time of Paul or in the context of Paul's mission the

1. Cf. BDF, §260(1).
2. *TDNT*, IX, p. 541.
3. *Exegetisches Wörterbuch zum Neuen Testament* (ed. H. Balz and G. Schneider; Stuttgart: Kohlhammer; 1980–83), III, p. 1159.
4. See e.g. A.E. Harvey, *Jesus and the Constraints of History* (London: Gerald Duckworth, 1982), ch. 2; M. de Jonge, *Christology in Context: The Earliest Christian Response to Jesus* (Philadelphia: Westminster Press, 1988), pp. 208-11.
5. On Jn 9.22 see particularly the line of exegesis established by J.L. Martyn,

question of whether Jesus was indeed the Christ seems not to have been an issue.

The same point emerges from a glance at the earlier formulae which Paul cites. In particular, in Rom. 1.3, a passage where Paul seems to be at pains to cite something on which all were agreed as a sign of his 'good faith',[1] Jesus' Davidic pedigree can be simply taken for granted. It was evidently non-controversial across the spectrum of early Christianity, and could thus be used in a formula which united all who believed in Jesus. Subsequent credal formulae were the result of tremendous controversy and political infighting in later centuries. But there is no trace of that here.

What is to be made of this? It can hardly be concluded that Paul was simply operating (in the diaspora) far away from where the controversy actually still raged, or that the controversy would have been so meaningless to Greek-speaking Gentiles that it lost all point in the Gentile mission. For the Jewish and Gentile missions were by no means distinct in the diaspora, as Galatians and Romans again remind us. The issues of Jewish conviction and hope were by no means marginal among the early Gentile-dominated churches, as we shall see in a moment. And in Paul's letters we hear clear echoes of other matters of controversy between Paul and his Palestinian and Jewish interlocutors (principally regarding the law). Nor can it mean that an earlier controversy had already died down, especially if the messianic hope was so central to and significant for Jewish self-understanding.

The more obvious answer is that the identification of Jesus as messiah was not after all so controversial as a point of issue between Christian Jews and their fellow Jews. For one thing, Jewish eschatological hope was not consistently messianic in character as has traditionally been assumed. M. de Jonge has been among those who have reminded us how diverse was Jewish expectation, and indeed how diverse were the hopes for an anointed one or anointed ones.[2] Perhaps we should ask, therefore, whether the messianic status accorded to Jesus was any more controversial than the significance accorded to the Teacher of Righteousness at Qumran or to Phinehas by the Zealots or to bar Kokhba in the second Jewish revolt. Or whether the claim of the first

History and Theology in the Fourth Gospel (Nashville: Abingdon Press, 1979), ch. 2.

　1.　See e.g. my *Romans* (WBC, 38A; Dallas: Word Books, 1988), pp. 5-6.

　2.　M. de Jonge, 'The Earliest Christian use of Christos: Some Suggestions', *NTS* 32 (1986), pp. 321-43 (329-33); also *Christology in Context*, pp. 166-67.

Christians to find Jesus and his fate foreshadowed in the prophets was perceived as a threat to Jewish identity and hope or simply as an invitation to recognize the wealth of meaning in their common scriptures (cf. particularly Acts 17.11). The answer seems to be that it was quite possible to put forward Jesus as candidate for messianic status without thereby undermining Jewish identity and the alternative (whether competing or complementary) expressions of Jewish hope.

This conclusion is probably borne out by other indications. For example, the name by which the new movement was known: within Judaism, as 'the Way' (Acts 9.2; 19.9; 22.4, 22) or 'Nazarenes' (24.5). It was as those who followed a particular pattern of life or teaching, or who followed Jesus the Nazarene, that the first Christian Jews were known among their fellows, not because their claim that this Jesus was messiah made them so distinctive. On the other hand, the title 'Christians' (*Christianoi*) is precisely not a Jewish title, but a Latin formation (*Christiani*), coined no doubt by the Antioch authorities who heard this word as characterizing this new group, without fully understanding its significance—followers of 'Christ', Christ's people, a political rather than a theological designation—like *Herodianoi,* Herodians, those who identified themselves with the cause of Herod.[1]

So too Paul can list 'the Christ' (one of his few titular usages) as the chiefmost of Israel's blessing (Rom. 9.5) without any sense or hint that this was a blessing different in character from the other blessings ('the adoption, the glory and the covenants, the law, the service and the promises'), or that the Christians had somehow stolen the title from Israel.[2] And subsequently he can re-express the Jewish hope in non-messianic terms, indeed in unspecifically Christian terms, as hope for 'the deliverer' to 'come out of Zion' (Rom. 11.26). The fact that the Christians believed that the messiah had already come was of less significance at this point than the common hope for the still future coming of the Messiah.

1.   This point has been made by E.A. Judge in a paper at the New Testament Conference in Sheffield (September, 1991) and to the New Testament Seminar in Durham (December, 1991). He cites the further parallel of the 'Augustiani' who demonstrated on Nero's behalf (Tacitus, *Ann.* 14.15.5).

2.   It is the self-evidently Jewish character of the reference to 'the Christ' here which makes it so hard to believe that Paul or his Roman readers would have taken the following benediction as addressed to anyone other than the one 'God over all' (see further my *Romans*, pp. 528-29).

In short, it would appear that the claim to Jesus' messiahship could be contained within the spectrum of competing claims which were a feature of the closing decades of Second Temple Judaism.

What then about 1 Cor. 1.23—'Christ crucified, a stumbling block to Jews'? To which we might add Rom. 9.32-33—'They [Israel] have stumbled over the stone of stumbling; as it is written, "Behold, I place in Sion a stone of stumbling and a rock of offence..."' Also Gal. 5.11—'the stumbling block of the cross'. Clearly there was something offensive to Jewish sensibilities about the Christian claims regarding Christ. But equally clearly the offence lay more in his death, the manner of it (cf. again Gal. 3.13), than in the attribution to him of the messiah/ Christ title. Or to be more precise, the offence lay not in the fact that messiahship was attributed to someone, but primarily in the fact that it was attributed to one who had been crucified. I must therefore turn to this aspect of Paul's teaching as the second main area of inquiry.

Before I do so, however, I should clarify what the stumbling block consisted of. At first it might seem that it was the very claim made by some of their number which was offensive to the majority of Jews. But when we look at Paul's use of the metaphor elsewhere a rather different picture emerges.

Paul uses the same metaphor in 1 Corinthians 8 and Romans 14 when talking about the problem posed to some Christian Jews by the fact that Christian Gentiles (and other Christian Jews) ate food prohibited to devout Jews by law and tradition (idol meat and 'unclean' food). 'If food is a cause of my brother's stumbling, I will never eat meat, lest I cause my brother to stumble' (1 Cor. 8.13). 'It is right not to eat meat or drink wine or do anything that makes your brother stumble' (Rom. 14.21). What was the stumbling block? As with 1 Cor. 1.23, first impressions might be misleading. At first sight it appears that it was the simple fact that the 'strong' felt free to eat which was so offensive to the 'weak'; the more scrupulous would have been offended simply at the sight of other believers eating what was unacceptable to them. But on closer inspection it becomes clear that the only offence Paul had in mind was when the weak actually ate the idol meat or unclean food in spite of a bad conscience (1 Cor. 8.10; Rom. 14.23). In other words, the stumbling block was not merely the strong sense of disagreement or distaste on the part of the 'weak' for the actions of the 'strong', but the action of actually joining in a practice of which they did not approve.

The parallel can be drawn at once with 1 Cor. 1.23. The offence for most Jews was not simply the message of a crucified Messiah, the fact that some other Jews (and Gentiles) believed and preached that Jesus, crucified and all, was Messiah.[1] It was the prospect of accepting that claim for themselves which was the stumbling block. They stumbled not over the beliefs of others, but at the challenge to share that belief for themselves. If we now link this back into the picture already drawn, it becomes evident that there was a much higher degree of tolerance among most Jews for the messianic claims (at least) of the first Christians. They found the thought of accepting these claims for themselves offensive and stumbled over them. But that did not mean they could not entertain the thought with some equanimity that other Jews held such beliefs. In the sectarian atmosphere of late Second Temple Judaism there must have been some such degree of *de facto* tolerance for the competing claims of the diverse groups among Jews as a whole. Disputes regarding the law and the temple were far more serious. Disagreement regarding the messianic status, or otherwise, of Jesus was evidently not a matter of such central concern.

3. *Jesus' Death as Atonement*

It is generally recognized that the cross stands at the centre of Paul's gospel. We need think only of such passages as 2 Cor. 5.14-21 and Gal. 2.19-3.1, as well as those cited earlier.[2] From this it is easy to deduce, and again particularly from 1 Cor. 1.23 and Gal. 3.13, that it was the proclamation not so much of Jesus as *Messiah*, but of Jesus as Messiah *crucified* which would have been so offensive to Paul's fellow Jews. It would be the significance claimed for Jesus' death, not least as validated by the resurrection, which would have been so controversial among more traditionally minded Jews. But again we must ask whether this conclusion represents a wholly rounded view of Paul's teaching on the subject.

---

1. This is the usual way of taking 1 Cor. 1.23; e.g. G.D. Fee, *1 Corinthians* (NICNT; Grand Rapids: Eerdmans, 1987): 'To the Jew the message of a crucified Messiah was the ultimate scandal' (p. 75).

2. For recent detailed treatments see particularly K. Grayston, *Dying, We Live: A New Inquiry into the Death of Christ in the New Testament* (London: Darton, Longman & Todd, 1990), ch. 2; C.B. Cousar, *A Theology of the Cross: The Death of Jesus in the Pauline Letters* (Minneapolis: Fortress Press, 1990).

The most striking feature here is the degree to which Paul's theology of the death of Christ is contained in pre-Pauline, that is already
traditional formulae. This is clearest of all in the letter in which Paul
works out the theology of his gospel at greatest length—Romans. It is
generally agreed that Rom. 3.21-26 is the theological heart of the
exposition. And it is also widely agreed that the core of that passage is
an earlier formulation reworked by Paul.[1] What is noteworthy, and
too little noticed by commentators, is the brevity of the treatment. It is
an astonishing fact indeed that after two full chapters of carefully
argued indictment, building up to the devastating climax of 3.9-20,
Paul can resolve the dilemma thus posed in the space of a mere six
verses, and by means of citing an established description of Jesus'
death. Evidently the solution he was proposing was so uncontroversial
that there was no need for him to argue it in any detail. Evidently it
was a way of understanding the death of Jesus which was widely
shared among the earliest Christian churches—by Christian Jews as
well.

Some would argue that Paul has subtly shifted the terms of the
formula he uses in Rom. 3.25-26.[2] But any shift could itself hardly
have been controversial, otherwise the point of citing the formula in
the first place (to demonstrate common ground with his readers and
other Christians) would have been self-defeating. And the more
controversial a shift in emphasis, the more Paul would have had to
argue for or to defend it. The most widely agreed shift is the addition
of 'through faith' in v. 25.[3] And Paul does proceed to argue for that
emphasis (3.27–5.1); but that is not properly speaking a christological
issue, more one regarding the relation of faith to the law, as the
elaboration itself makes plain (3.27–4.16).

Moreover, we should note that there are many elements of conscious
controversy in Romans, as Paul's frequent use of the diatribe indicates
(2.1-5, 17-29; 3.27–4.2; 9.19-21; 11.17-24). And the chief interlocu-
tor in most of these cases is one whom Paul characterizes as a typical
'Jew' (2.17), where it is clear that it is not just (or not at all) the
Christian Jew whom Paul has in mind, but his fellow countrymen

1.   See e.g. my *Romans*, pp. 163-64, and those cited there.
2.   So e.g. P. Stuhlmacher, *Der Brief an die Römer* (NTD, 6; Göttingen:
Vandenhoeck & Ruprecht, 1989), pp. 55-56; see others in my *Romans*, p. 175.
3.   See those cited e.g. by B.F. Meyer, 'The pre-Pauline Formula in Rom. 3.25-
26a', *NTS* 29 (1983), pp. 198-208.

generally. Paul was in no doubt that there were features of his gospel which would cause offence among his fellow Jews. What is striking here, however, is that the death of Christ does not feature in any of these diatribes; Paul does not resort to the diatribe when referring to the cross as such. Again the implication is clear. The basic understanding of the death of Christ, as widely agreed among the early Christians generally, including, presumably, those Christian Jews resident in Palestine, was not a matter of particular controversy between Christians and Jews.

Much the same seems to be true of Paul's other main documentation of the controversy between Jew and Christian—Galatians. It opens with what once again appears to be a common formula indicating the significance of Christ's self-sacrifice (Gal. 1.4).[1] And once again we have to deduce that Paul cites the formula in the introduction precisely because it indicated common ground, precisely because it was non-controversial—and this in a letter where, more than any other, Paul was conscious of the tensions between faith in Christ and the tradi-tional Jewish heritage. Controversy there was in plenty, but, as the whole letter shows clearly, the controversy focused entirely on the law. The cross was caught up in that, as Gal. 3.13 indicates. But here too the brevity of the reference indicates that the controversy centred more on the law than on the cross. That Christ hanging on the tree could be called 'accursed' by the law (Deut. 21.23) was actually com-mon ground between Jew and Christian (cf. Acts 5.30; 10.39). The real dispute was whether that fact said anything at all about Gentiles and the law.[2]

The evidence here is remarkably like the evidence considered above in relation to Jesus as Messiah. In both cases there is a taken-for-granted quality in Paul's references. In both cases that could indicate an earlier controversy which had already died down, with results so conclusive that they could be assumed rather than argued for. But given the time scale and continuing points of tension between Jew and Christian throughout that period such a conclusion is hardly justified. The only other obvious conclusion is that the Christian claims were in

1. K. Wengst, *Christologische Formeln und Lieder des Urchristentums* (Gütersloh: Gütersloher Verlagshaus, 1972), pp. 56-57.
2. Gal. 2.21 has to be understood in light of 3.13; see my *Jesus, Paul and the Law: Studies in Mark and Galatians* (London: SPCK; Louisville: Westminster Press, 1990), pp. 230-32, 249, and n. 34.

themselves not, or not yet, a matter of controversy. Even when Christians themselves would see the controversial matters as direct corollaries of their understanding of Jesus' death (Rom. 3.27ff.; Gal. 3.14ff.), the Christology as such was more the calm at the centre of the storm than the centre of the storm itself.

The point at which we might have expected a breach to open up on this front between the first Christians and the rest of Judaism is the attribution to Jesus' death of significance as a sacrifice, particularly if it carried the implication that, in consequence, the temple sacrifices were no longer necessary. This is certainly the conclusion drawn by the writer to the Hebrews, and the polemical character of his exposition is clear (Heb. 8.1–10.18). But in Paul, once again it is significant that his theology of Jesus' death as sacrifice is contained almost wholly in already traditional formulae (Rom. 3.25; 4.25; 8.32; 1 Cor. 15.3; Gal. 1.4; 1 Thess. 5.9-10), or in passing reference (Rom. 8.3; 1 Cor. 5.7), or in allusive references to Christ's 'blood' and to his death 'for sins' or 'for us' (Rom. 5.6-9; 2 Cor. 5.14-15, 21; Gal. 2.20; 3.13).[1] So much so that several have argued that Paul himself did not entertain a theology of Christ's death as sacrifice,[2] or that at least the centre of his own gospel lies more in the concept of reconciliation than in atonement.[3] Neither deduction is justified. What is characteristic and central to someone's theology need not be distinctive; what is fundamental can also be shared, and as shared, little referred to; what is axiomatic is often taken for granted. The more appropriate conclusion is, once again, that Paul did not need to elaborate the point because it was common ground, shared with other Christian Jews, and as thus shared, consequently non-controversial.

It is not to be denied that there is something of a historical problem here, whose solution is far from clear. When was it that early Christian understanding of Jesus' death as a sacrifice became a make-or-break issue within Judaism? It is frequently assumed that it was a

---

1. See further my 'Paul's Understanding of the Death of Jesus as Sacrifice', in *Sacrifice in Redemption: Durham Essays in Theology* (Cambridge: Cambridge University Press, 1991), pp. 35-56.

2. E. Käsemann, *Perspectives on Paul* (London: SCM Press, 1971), pp. 42-45; G. Friedrich, *Die Verkundigung des Todes Jesu im Neuen Testament* (Neukirchen–Vluyn: Neukirchener Verlag, 1982), pp. 47, 66, 70-71, 75, 77.

3. See particularly R.P. Martin, *Reconciliation: A Study in Paul's Theology* (London: Marshall , Morgan & Scott; Atlanta: John Knox, 1981).

factor of significance more or less from the first—even already in Jesus' own teaching. As soon as Jesus' death was seen as a sacrifice for sins, the implication would be widely understood that in consequence there was no need for other sacrifice. Jesus' death made sacrifice and temple of no continuing relevance.[1] This was certainly the case for Hebrews, as already indicated. But was it so from the first among the infant Christian movement in Jerusalem?

A crucial consideration here must be the fact that the earliest Christians stayed on in Jerusalem, and evidently continued to attend the temple at the hour of sacrifice (Acts 3.1). It would no doubt be they who also preserved Jesus' teaching about the conditions for acceptable sacrifice in the temple (Mt. 5.23-24)—presumably because the teaching was of continuing relevance, that is, because they continued to offer sacrifice in the temple. Since Jerusalem was the temple, the holy mount of Zion, it would be primarily for the temple that any Jews would stay in Jerusalem. Or to put the point the other way round, it is certainly hard to envisage a group who were at fundamental odds with the temple and its sacrificial cult staying on in Jerusalem, or a group who made controversial claims regarding the cult, being allowed to stay in Jerusalem as undisturbed as the continuing Christian community evidently were (until the approach or outbreak of the Jewish revolt at least). We know of two groups who did make such controversial claims regarding the temple (the Qumran Essenes, and the Christian Hellenists) and we know how things worked out for them. They either chose to leave Jerusalem and centre their work elsewhere, or they were forced to do so.[2]

It is hard to avoid the conclusion that whatever the first Christians believed and taught about Jesus' death, it was not sufficiently controversial in character for them to feel the need to abandon the temple. And that presumably was the teaching which we find encapsulated in the formulae which Paul echoes on so many occasions. Even in the case of Paul's own potentially more controversial views of Jesus' death, or at least the certainly more controversial corollaries, Paul himself, according to Acts, was able to join in the temple ritual, including the offering of sacrifice towards the end of his career (Acts 21.26). If Acts provides an accurate record of Paul's final days at this

---

1. See particularly the discussion by M. Hengel, *The Atonement: The Origins of the Doctrine in the New Testament* (London: SCM Press, 1981), ch. 2.
2. See further my *Partings*, ch. 4.

point (and why not?—cf. 1 Cor. 9.19-21), that must mean that even Paul himself did not think of his Christology in its implications for the cult as particularly controversial. It is true, still according to Acts, that Paul's tactic or compromise on his last visit to Jerusalem failed (Acts 21.27ff.); but the breaking point had nothing to do with Christology, it was rather, once again, all to do with Paul's known openness to and involvement with Gentiles and consequent breach of the law (Acts 21.28).

So the question still remains: how controversial was Paul's understanding of the death of Jesus in the eyes of his fellow Christian and other Jews?

The position can be better understood when it is realised that the death of a Jew of some public significance on a cross was nothing very unusual in that period,[1] and also that there were other Jewish deaths which were seen as having significance in terms of sacrifice.

In the first case, we may recall, in particular, that in the previous century no less than about 800 Jews were crucified by Alexander Jannaeus in the centre of Jerusalem. What is of especial interest here is that the episode is recalled in the Dead Sea Scrolls, in 1QpNah. i.6-8. The interest focuses in two points. One is that the victims are described as 'those who seek smooth things'—usually taken as a reference to the Pharisees (regarded as opponents by the Qumran writers).[2] The other is that their execution ('hanged alive on the tree') recalls Deut. 21.23, just as is the case with Acts 5.30 and Acts 10.39. It is likely, then, that Deut. 21.23 was used to invoke a curse on various Jews who had been crucified as part of the intra-Jewish polemic between different Jewish factions during this period.[3] And since so many Jews had fallen victim to this barbaric Roman form of execution, it is quite possible that such polemic was regarded as a piece of exaggerated rhetoric and 'mud-slinging' more than a serious point of real critique.[4] The implication would then be as before—that the death

1. Details in M. Hengel, *Crucifixion* (London: SCM Press, 1977), p. 26 n. 17.
2. See e.g. E. Schürer, in G. Vermes and F. Millar (eds.), *The History of the Jewish People in the Age of Jesus Christ* (Edinburgh: T. & T. Clark, 1973), I, p. 224 and n. 22; see also above in n. 2 p. 146.
3. Cf. Hengel, *Crucifixion*, pp. 84-85.
4. This remains true despite Hengel's observation that 'the cross never became the symbol of Jewish suffering; the influence of Deut. 21.23 made this impossible. So a crucified messiah could not be accepted either... the theme of the crucified

of Jesus on the cross allowed a good deal of cheap propaganda by the propagandists among the Jewish factions hostile to the followers of the Nazarene. But otherwise the death of Jesus on a cross would not have been seen as a matter of major substance or in itself an occasion for controversy for the majority of the first Christians' fellow Jews.

If anything, indeed, the death of Jesus at the hand of the Romans gave his death a potential significance in terms of martyr theology. We know that the Maccabean martyrs were a focus of a good deal of reflection in such terms (2 Macc. 7; *4 Macc.* 6–18). Moreover, their deaths could be spoken of in sacrificial terms (cf. particularly 2 Macc. 7.37-38; *4 Macc.* 17.21). This is the theology Paul echoes in Rom. 5.6-8—Christ as the one who gives his life willingly on behalf of others.[1] The language in *4 Macc.* 17.21 is in fact the same as that used in the pre-Pauline formulation in Rom. 3.25 (*hilasterion*),[2] and the language of reconciliation is used in 2 Macc. 7.33 (cf. 8.29) in a way not altogether dissimilar to that in 2 Cor. 5.18-20. Here again, then, the implication must be that to see Jesus' death in sacrificial and martyr terms was not a claim which would necessarily cause much controversy within Second Temple Judaism.

In short, despite its importance for Paul's theology, it would appear that his Christology of the cross was not particularly controversial, either as between Paul and his fellow Jews who believed Jesus to be Messiah, or indeed as between Paul and those more traditional Jews with whom he maintained debate and argument.

---

faithful plays no part in Jewish legends about martyrs' (*Crucifixion*, p. 85). Since so many loyal Jews had been subjected to this cruellest of punishments, including Jews on different sides of the various factional divisions, it would have been impossible for crucifixion to be used as a fully fledged weapon of polemic against a particular individual who had been crucified, without it being turned against the users. The comparative silence in our sources (to which Hengel draws attention) simply reflects these sensitivities.

1.   See my *Romans*, pp. 254-57.

2.   D. Hill, *Greek Words and Hebrew Meanings: Studies in the Semantics of Soteriological Terms* (SNTMS, 5; Cambridge: Cambridge University Press, 1967), pp. 41-48; S.K. Williams, *Jesus' Death as a Saving Event: The Background and Origin of a Concept* (Missoula, MT: Scholars Press, 1975), pp. 76-90.

4. *The Divine Significance of Jesus*

Here controversy seems inevitable. The argument seems to be straightforward. As soon as Jesus was seen as a heavenly figure, that must have begun to put an unbearable strain on infant Christianity's Jewish credentials. And particularly when he was seen as a heavenly figure with divine significance, ranked together with God in Christian piety and devotion; that must have been highly controversial and unacceptable to the fundamental axiom of Jewish monotheism.[1] But was it so? We know that such claims became unacceptable to the Jewish authorities reflected in John's Gospel, making a breach with the synagogue unavoidable: 'This was why the Jews sought all the more to kill him, because he...called God his own Father, making himself equal with God' (Jn 5.18); 'It is not for a good work that we stone you but for blasphemy; because you, being a man, make yourself God' (Jn 10.33). But such texts certainly reflect a later situation than that of Paul.[2] In contrast, what is striking once again is the total absence of any indication that Paul's Christology of exaltation was a sticking point with his Jewish (Christian) opponents. 'Christ crucified' was controversial, as we have seen; but we have no indication that Christ exalted was seen as a problem for Jews as a whole.

I have already dealt with the key evidence elsewhere and can thus prevent this essay becoming too long by summarizing it briefly.[3] The point is simply that the idea of a particular historical individual being exalted to heaven, particularly a hero of the faith, was by no means strange to late Second Temple Judaism. The hope of resurrection was shared with Pharisees (Mk 12.18-20; Acts 23.6), and the suggestion that a particular individual had been raised from the dead could apparently be entertained outside Christian circles (Mk 6.14; Lk. 9.8). Enoch and Elijah were thought to have been translated to heaven (Gen. 5.24; 2 Kgs 2.11), and the righteous expected to be numbered with the sons of God/angels (Wis. 5.5, 15-16). Enoch was also thought to have been transformed by his translation to heaven (*Jub.* 4.22-23; *1 En.* 12–16; *2 En.* 22.8), and Moses to have been made 'equal in glory to the holy ones (angels)' (Sir. 45.2).

---

1. See again those cited above on p. 148 nn. 1-2.
2. This judgment reflects the broad consensus; see e.g. my *Partings*, pp. 220-29.
3. For more detailed treatment see particularly *Partings*, ch. 10.

We cannot even say that the claim that a historic figure was now participating in divine functions would have been regarded as especially controversial and unacceptable in Jewish circles. Enoch and Elijah were both thought to have a part to play in the final judgment (*1 En.* 90.31; *Apoc. Elij.* 24.11-15). In one of the Dead Sea Scrolls Melchizedek seems to have been depicted as the angelic leader of the holy ones who execute judgment on Belial and his host (11QMelch 13-14). And in the *Testament of Abraham* 11 and 13 Adam and Abel are depicted in similarly exalted roles. Nor should we forget that the twelve and the saints generally are also said to have a share in the final judgment according to Mt. 19.28/Lk. 22.30 and 1 Cor. 6.2-3. Or that power to bestow the Holy Spirit was attributed by the Baptist to the Coming One (Mk 1.8 par.) and by Simon Magus to Peter (Acts 8.17-20).

How much more than this was being claimed by hailing Jesus as Lord? The echoes of Joel 2.32 in Rom. 10.13 and of Isa. 45.23 in Phil. 2.10 are undoubtedly of tremendous significance in Christology. But the question still persists. How controversial was the attribution of lordship to the exalted Christ? Paul after all speaks of God as 'the *God* and Father of our *Lord* Jesus Christ (e.g. Rom. 15.6; 2 Cor. 1.3; 11.31): even Jesus as Lord has God as his God. The climax of the celebration of Christ's lordship is 'the glory of God the Father' (Phil. 2.11). And the climax of Jesus' own rule over all things is to be Jesus' own subjection 'to the one who put all things under him, that God may be all in all' (1 Cor. 15.25-28). Evidently there was in all this nothing so threatening to traditional Jewish belief in God, nothing so controversial as to have left any mark of controversy between Paul and his fellow Jews or Christian Jews in particular. The same is true of Paul's characteristic 'in Christ' language.[1] Quite what his fellow Jews made of this incorporative and Adam Christology is far from clear. But they have left no record of any criticism of Paul on the subject.

The Wisdom language used of Jesus, as is generally agreed, in 1 Cor. 8.6 and Col. 1.15-20,[2] leaves the same impression. Whether

1. Cf. M. Casey, *From Jewish Prophet to Gentile God: The Origins and Development of New Testament Christology* (Cambridge: James Clarke; Louisville: Westminster Press, 1991), pp. 129-31.
2. See now J. Habermann, *Präexistenzaussagen im Neuen Testament* (Frankfurt: Peter Lang, 1990), chs. 3 and 5.

Jewish Wisdom writers already conceived of divine Wisdom as a 'hypostasis' or simply as a vigorous personification for divine action, the point remains the same. The use of such language in reference to Jesus does not seem to have crossed a critical boundary in Jewish eyes. The fact that Wisdom had already been identified with the Torah in such circles (Sir. 24.23; Bar. 4.1) is clear enough indication of how relaxed the Jewish Wisdom writers were on the subject. If the identification of a book with divine Wisdom could be taken easily in their stride, would the identification of a man in a similar way be any more puzzling or controversial? Paul himself evidently had no difficulty whatsoever in affirming the one Lordship of Christ in such Wisdom terms in the very same breath as he affirmed the *Shema,* the fundamental Jewish axiom of the oneness of God (1 Cor. 8.6). Once again, where we would expect at least some indication that this Christology was controversial, had that been the case, we find absolutely no hint or suggestion of it. Even to speak of Jesus in the language of pre-existent Wisdom was not particularly controversial in Jewish ears.

What then about the association of Jesus as Lord with the Lord God in greetings and benedictions (as for example in Rom. 1.7 and 1 Thess. 3.11-13)? And what of the devotion and prayer to Jesus?[1] The most relevant point here probably has to be that the devotion to Christ seems to have been contained within the constraints of Jewish monotheism. It consists more of hymns *about* Christ than hymns *to* Christ (especially Phil. 2.6-11 and Col. 1.15-20), more of prayer *through* Christ than prayer *to* Christ (Rom. 1.8; 7.25; 2 Cor. 1.20; Col. 3.17). At the time of Paul, therefore, should we speak, as does Pliny fifty or so years later, of Christians reciting a hymn 'to Christ as to a god' (Pliny, *Ep.* 10.96.7); or is the parallel more that of veneration offered to and through the Virgin and the saints in the still later church? Even after Paul, Judaism could encompass the thought of Enoch or the Messiah as fulfilling the role of the man-like figure in the vision of Daniel 7 (*1 En.* 37–71; *4 Ezra* 13.32),[2] that is, one who takes the throne beside God and who can thus in some degree be associated with God in devotion and in the bestowal of blessing as well as in judgment. Within the 'broad church' of that range of Judaism, how

1. See again particularly Hurtado, *One God, One Lord,* pp. 11-15, 99-114.
2. The tradition that rabbi Akiba thought the second throne of Dan. 7.9 was for (the son of) David is found in *b. Hag.* 14a and *b. Sanh.* 38b.

controversial would have been Paul's attribution of divine agency to the exalted Jesus, how controversial would have been the degree of devotion which he offered? Once again a crucial consideration must be the absence on any protest within the sphere of Paul's mission—no consciousness of Paul's part that he was transgressing some clearly drawn line; no suggestion that other Jews must have found such language and devotion repugnant; in a word, no hint of controversy.

If we were to broaden out the discussion to Paul's interaction with the wider Hellenistic world (rather than just traditional Judaism) the range of discussion would be different, but the outcome would not. Thus, in 1 Corinthians 1–2 the issue is more one of what counts as 'wisdom' than of Christology as such; the earlier attempts to demonstrate a counter Christology maintained by Paul's opponents have not been successful.[1] As for 1 Corinthians 15, there is certainly controversy over the resurrection—that is, the (future) resurrection of believers; whereas the belief that Jesus had already been raised seems to have been common ground (15.5-12). In each case, as in 1 Corinthians 10–11, the Christology could be assumed; it was what the different opinions within Corinth made of these common emphases in Christology which caused the controversy.

In 2 Cor. 11.4 Paul does speak of 'another Jesus' and again there is clear evidence of sharp controversy, as serious as that voiced in Galatians. But in this case the 'other Jesus' seems to be Paul's way of describing what he regards as an exaggerated emphasis on the resurrected and exalted Christ; or to be more precise, the implications of such an emphasis for concepts of apostolic ministry (2 Cor. 10–13). In contrast, it is Paul who calls for the stress to be laid elsewhere—on the cross, on the Christ crucified in weakness; not as a way of defending a distinctively different Christology (as we have already seen, the fact of Christ's death was part of the faith common to all Christians at that time), but as a way of justifying a different model of apostleship, not over Christology as such.[2]

So I could continue. The issue in 1 (and 2) Thessalonians is not

1. So particularly U. Wilckens, *Weisheit und Torheit* (Tübingen: Mohr, 1959).
2. 'It is not even clear that this verse (2 Cor. 11.4) warrants the identification of "Christology" as the basic difference between Paul and his opponents in Corinth... since nowhere else in 2 Corinthians is Christology taken up as a topic in and for itself, not even in 3.7-18, 4.4-6, 9-14, [and] 5.14-19, where the real theme is the nature of Paul's apostolic service' (Furnish, *2 Corinthians*, p. 501).

christological (the belief in the parousia is common ground), but chronological (how soon will it happen). There is no apparent christological issue in Philippians at all. And in Colossians, speculation about the status of Jesus within the heavenly sphere may be implied, but whether we can speak of 'false teachers' and 'opponents' is far from clear.[1]

In general, within the context of hellenistic syncretism it is not apparent that the initial claims made by the first Christians for Christ would have been so controversial. A society which could cater for 'many gods and many lords' (1 Cor. 8.6) would not be particularly put out or non-plussed by the earliest christological affirmations. In fact, it was only towards the end of the first century and the beginning of the second that Christian assertions of the lordship of Christ seem to have become a matter of controversy and persecution. But that was because of the political challenge which these Christian claims were seen to pose. To affirm the lordship of Jesus was now to deny the lordship of Caesar and thus to challenge the empire which Caesar represented. To sing or speak to Jesus 'as to a god' had the unacceptable corollary that the local temples were being deserted and the sacrificial rites neglected, with potential hazard for the civic and political constitution of the communities involved. Prior to that, however, the points of tension were not particularly christological as such, but simply the fact that in the eyes of the Roman intelligentsia Christianity was merely another example of a 'pernicious superstition' imported from the middle east.

5. Conclusions

This essay has been an attempt to bring more clearly into focus the extent to which Christology was at the centre of earliest Christian controversy and dispute with others. Its findings say nothing to disturb the centrality of Christology for Christianity in general or even to question that Christology inevitably was (and is) the cutting edge of Christian theology and its distinctive claims. It simply draws attention to the fact that the fundamental christological claims do not seem initially to have created as much disagreement or to have provoked as

1. See particularly M.D. Hooker, 'Were There False Teachers in Colossae?', in *From Adam to Christ: Essays on Paul* (Cambridge: Cambridge University Press, 1990), pp. 121-36.

much hostility as we would have expected. Nor have I any wish to deny that it was Christology which became the absolutely crucial factor in the final parting of the ways.[1] However, it does seem that initially the foci of controversy seem to have been elsewhere (the temple, the law).

Perhaps is is inevitable that it was the issues which impinged most immediately on daily practice which became the points of tension. In the same way, in the period prior to Jesus' ministry, the various messianic (and non-messianic) expectations of the various strands of Second Temple Judaism seem to have functioned simply as part of the rich tapestry of first century Judaism. In these cases too the disagreements which touched the different groups most directly were those relating to temple, festivals and Torah. Perhaps it is simply a reflection of how human dialogue works, that the course of debate begins with the more immediate points of disagreement and only thereafter presses back behind these more obvious issues into the underlying presuppositions. That was certainly how the christological debates themselves progressed in the subsequent centuries. Be that as it may, it does not appear that the christological claims made by Paul were initially seen as particularly controversial in themselves.

It is a particular pleasure to be part of this homage to Marinus de Jonge. Since we first became acquainted at the SNTS meeting in Aberdeen in 1975 it has been my privilege and pride to call him friend. I offer him this little piece in gratitude and respect for his rich contributions to NT scholarship, not least in the area of Christology, and with all good wishes for many more years of fruitful publication.

---

1. Precisely the contrary — see my *Partings*, chs. 11–12.

Χριστός IN 1 CORINTHIANS 10.4, 9

E. Earle Ellis

The use of Χριστός in 1 Cor. 10.4, 9 raises a number of theological issues, among which are the term's personal or titular connotations and its theological implications for Christ's pre-existence and for his identification with the divine attribute of wisdom. Usually in Paul's writings 'Christ' refers to the person.[1] Even when titular connotations are prominent as in Rom. 9.5, the qualified form, Χριστὸς κατὰ σάρκα, shows that the term carried broader implications. So also in 1 Cor. 10.4, 9 it is not limited in its meaning to the eschatological figure 'from the seed of David' (Rom. 1.3) but refers inclusively to the person of Jesus whether in his eschatological or, possibly, in his pre-existent being. But does not the typological context of 1 Corinthians 10 preclude a reference to a pre-existent person?[2]

1 Cor. 10.1-13 is a midrash on certain Pentateuchal texts that is

---

1. So M. de Jonge, 'The Earliest Christian Use of *Christos*', in *Jewish Eschatology, Early Christian Christology and the Testaments of the Twelve Patriarchs* (Leiden: Brill, 1991), p. 103: 'In [Paul's] argumentation the titular use of Χριστός plays little or no role...' Similarly N.A. Dahl, *Jesus the Christ* (Minneapolis: Fortress Press, 1991), pp. 15-18; M. Hengel, 'Χριστός bei Paulus und in der "vorpaulinischen" Überlieferung', in M.D. Hooker (ed.), *Paul and Paulinism* (Festschrift C.K. Barrett; London: SPCK, 1982), pp. 137-38.

2. As is supposed, for example, by J.D.G. Dunn (*Christology in the Making* [London: SCM Press, 1980], pp. 183-84), who reflects an adoptionist Christology first advanced in the patristic church and argued in this century by the 'history of religions' school. Cf. A. Grillmeier, *Christ in Christian Tradition*, I (Atlanta: John Knox, 1975), pp. 77-78; E. Venables, 'Paul of Samosata' in *A Dictionary of Christian Biography* (ed. W. Smith and H. Wack; 4 vols.; London: J. Murray, 1877–87), I, pp. 253-54; W. Bousset, *Kyrios Christos* (Nashville: Abingdon Press, 1970), pp. 49-54; J.D.G. Dunn, *Unity and Diversity in the New Testament* (London: SCM Press, 1977), pp. 50-54; P.E. Hughes, *The True Image* (Grand Rapids: Eerdmans, 1989), pp. 249-59.

probably preformed[1] and that is here applied to the situation in Paul's church at Corinth. It exhibits the following pattern:

1a	Introductory formula
1b-5	Opening 'texts' = interpretive summary of biblical texts (Exodus 13–17; Num. 14.29)[2]
6-7a	Commentary/application
7b	Supplementary text (Exod. 32.6)
8-13	Commentary/application

An extended application (vv. 14–22, 29-31) concludes (v. 31) with *inter alia* an allusion to 1 Cor. 10.1b-5. The passage explicitly identifies the exodus events of redemption and judgment as 'types (τύποι) for us', as happening 'typically' (τυπικῶς) and 'written for our admonition' (10.6,11). It uses the terms 'technically [as an] "advance presentation" intimating eschatological events'.[3] Does it, however, place Christ only on the eschatological side of this typology? If so, in 1 Cor. 10.9 it should read, 'Neither let us tempt Christ (Χριστόν) as some of them [at the exodus] tempted Yahweh'. But, in fact, the verse reads, 'Neither let us tempt Christ (Χριστόν)[4] as some of them tempted him'. It leaves the term, 'him' unexpressed but clearly implied and thus places Christ both at the exodus and in the (present) eschatological reality at Corinth.

This understanding of 1 Cor. 10.9 illumines the meaning of 10.4bc:

---

1. Cf. E.E. Ellis, 'Traditions in 1 Corinthians', *NTS* 32 (1986), pp. 490-91; W.A. Meeks, ' "And Rose up to Play": Midrash and Paraenesis in 1 Corinthians 10.1-22', *JSNT* 16 (1982), pp. 64-78; J. Habermann, *Präexistenzaussagen im Neuen Testament* (Frankfurt: Peter Lang, 1990), pp. 196-202.

2. The midrash at Gal. 4.21–5.1 has a similar opening 'text' (vv. 21-22). Cf. E.E. Ellis, *The Old Testament in Early Christianity* (Tübingen: Mohr [Paul Siebeck], 1991), pp. 98-99; *idem, Prophecy and Hermeneutic in Early Christianity* (Tübingen: Mohr [Paul Siebeck], 1978 = Grand Rapids: Baker, 1993), p. 156.

3. L. Goppelt, 'τύπος', *TDNT* VIII, pp. 251-52, cf. *idem, Typos: The Typological Interpretation of the Old Testament in the New* (Grand Rapids: Eerdmans, 1982), pp. 218ff.

4. Following E. Nestle and K. Aland (eds.), *Novum Testamentum Graece* (Stuttgart: Deutche Bibelgesellschaft, 26th edn, 1979), p. 456; B.M. Metzger, *A Textual Commentary on the Greek New Testament* (New York: United Bible Societies, 1971), p. 560; L. Zuntz, *The Text of the Epistles* (London: British Academy, 1953), pp. 126-27: 'κύριον then is a (later) "Alexandrian" corruption...' Cf. G.D. Fee, *The First Epistle to the Corinthians* (Grand Rapids: Eerdmans, 1987), p. 457. Otherwise: A. Robertson and A. Plummer, *First Epistle of St Paul to the Corinthians* (ICC; Edinburgh: T. & T. Clark, 1914), pp. 205-206.

'For they were drinking from the spiritual following rock, and the rock was Christ'. Among the later rabbis 'the following rock' became an elaborate legend that may be derived in part from a word-play of the Targum[1] and in part from interpretations of Exodus 15–17 and Numbers 20–21 in later biblical texts.[2] While Paul may have known the Targum, his mention of 'the spiritual following rock' (πνευματικῆς ἀκολουθούσης πέτρας) probably owes more to the biblical inter-pretations, especially to the identification of Yahweh as Israel's redeeming and judging rock in Deuteronomy 32 and in Psalm 78, where the rock is linked to the wilderness experiences (Ps. 78.20, 35).[3]

The term, 'spiritual', strengthens this understanding of 1 Cor. 10.4. Ordinarily in Paul's letters it refers to eschatological realities and particularly to the gifts of the Holy Spirit.[4] In 1 Cor. 10.4 it also points to the activity of the divine Spirit standing behind and effecting the miracle of the water from the rock:

> In 10.4 food and drink are 'spiritual' in the same sense as the 'rock' men-tioned immediately thereafter. In this way the things named are designated as phenomena that point and allude to πνεῦμα. As such they denote the phenomena of miracle, revelation and prophecy that concern an event effected by God.[5]

That is, in agreement with the Old Testament Paul could, by metonymy, have called the miraculous work of God, that is, the rock, by the name of God. Surprisingly, he identifies the rock not with God nor with the Spirit but with Christ.[6] To make clear that he does not

1.   *Targ. Onk.* on Num. 21.16ff. Cf. *T. Suk.* 3. 11ff.; *Sifre* 95 on Num. 11.21; Ps.-Philo, *The Biblical Antiquities* (c. 50–100 CE) 10.7; 11.15. Cf. Ellis, *Prophecy*, pp. 2029-12.

2.   E.g. Pss. 77.20; 78.15ff.; 105.41; Isa. 48.21.

3.   Deut. 32.3-4, 9-18; 1 Cor. 10.13 may allude to Deut. 32.4 LXX; 10.4 to Deut. 32.13; 10.20 cites Deut. 32.17. Cf. 2 Sam. 22.2-3, 47; 23.3; Pss. 18.2; 78.20.

4.   E.g. Rom. 1.11; 15.27; 1 Cor. 14.1; 15.44; Eph. 1.3; Col. 3.16.

5.   H.F. von Soden, 'Sakrament und Ethik bei Paulus', in K.H. Rengstorf (ed.), *Das Paulusbild in der neueren deutschen Forschung* (Darmstadt: Wissenschaftliche Buchgesellschaft, 1969), p. 365. A partial English translation of the article is provided in W.A. Meeks (ed.), *The Writings of St Paul* (New York: Norton, 1972), pp. 257-68. Cf. F. Godet, *Commentary on First Corinthians* (2 vols. in 1; Grand Rapids: Kregel, 1977 [1889]), pp. 484ff.

6.   Elsewhere Paul can also equate the Spirit, in certain respects, with Christ. Cf. 1 Cor. 6.17; 12.4-6; 15.45; Ellis, *Prophecy*, pp. 66-69.

mean the physical rock itself, he uses the qualifier 'spiritual'. As he does in 1 Cor. 10.9, Paul places Christ on both sides of the typology, associating him on the one hand with the eschatological meal of the Lord's Supper (10.16–17) and on the other hand with the miraculous food and drink in the exodus (10.4). In this way he affirms or presupposes the pre-existence of the person of Christ.[1] Does he, in agreement with some contemporary Jewish exposition, also identify the rock (and thus Christ) as the divine wisdom?[2]

The Alexandrian philosopher and exegete, Philo (c. 20 BCE–50 CE), commented on Deut. 8.15-16: 'For the flinty rock is the wisdom of God...from which he gives water to souls that love God... But the primal existence is God and next is the word of God.'[3] Again on Deut. 32.13 he writes: '[Moses] uses the word "rock" to express the solid and indestructible wisdom of God... In another place he uses a synonym for this rock and calls it "manna". Manna is the divine word (λόγον)'.[4] Although Philo works within a different hermeneutic, both he and Paul might still be drawing on common Jewish tradition.[5] If 1 Cor. 10.4 stood alone, it would not in itself establish that Paul here reflects a wisdom Christology. However, other Pauline texts are more explicit. Col. 1.15-20, which is also a preformed tradition,[6] clearly

1. Cf. Habermann , *Präexistenzaussagen*, pp. 212-23 and the literature cited; F. Lang, *Die Briefe an die Korinther* (Göttingen: Vandenhoeck & Ruprecht, 1986), p. 124; C. Wolff, *Der erste Brief des Paulus an die Korinther II* (Berlin: Evangelische Verlags Anstalt, 1982), p. 42. This modifies and goes beyond my previous comment on this verse in E.E. Ellis, *Paul's Use of the Old Testament* (Grand Rapids: Baker, 1991 [1957]), p. 131. In this matter I accept the criticism of Anthony Hanson and would now agree with him that 'the real presence of the pre-existent Jesus', that is of his person, best explains Paul's meaning here. However, *pace* Hanson, I remain convinced that 'typology' provides the frame by which Paul relates the events of the exodus to those of the eschaton. Cf. A.T. Hanson, *Jesus Christ in the Old Testament* (London: SPCK, 1965), pp. 6-7, 17ff., 172-78; *idem*, *Studies in Paul's Technique and Theology* (London: SPCK, 1874), pp. 115-16; Ellis, *Old Testament*, pp. 61ff., 72-73, 105-109, 141-57.
2. So H. Conzelmann, *1 Corinthians* (Philadelphia: Fortress Press, 1975), p. 167; C.K. Barrett, *The First Epistle to the Corinthians* (London: A. & C. Black), pp. 222-23. Otherwise: Fee, *The First Epistle*, pp. 448-49.
3. Philo, *Leg. All.* 2.86.
4. Philo, *Det. Pot. Ins.* 115, 118.
5. So Conzelmann, *I Corinthians*, p. 167.
6. Cf. E.E. Ellis, *The Making of the New Testament Documents,* forthcoming; G.E. Cannon, *The Use of Traditional Materials in Colossians* (Macon, GA: Mercer,

reflects a wisdom Christology that is made explicit in Col. 2.3.[1] More significant is 1 Cor. 8.6.

Despite some shifts in argument and the incorporation of preformed materials,[2] 1 Cor. 8.1-11.1 was very probably composed by Paul as a unified piece.[3] Consequently, 1 Cor. 10.4 may be understood in the light of 1 Cor. 8.6:

> But for us there is one God the Father
> From whom are all things and we for him
> And one Lord Jesus Christ
> Through whom are all things and we through him.

A Stoic ascription to the logos, that is, to the world soul is strikingly similar:

> From you are all things
> In you are all things
> For you are all things.[4]

This philosophical conception was reshaped by pre-Christian Judaism and ascribed to divine wisdom. It is reflected by Philo, who speaks of God 'by (ὑπό) whom' and the word or wisdom 'through (διά) whom' all was created,[5] and by Wis. 9.1, which states that God 'made all things by your word and by your wisdom formed man'. It also appears in 1 Cor. 8.6 where Paul ascribes the Genesis creation to the mediation of Christ.[6] However, the apostle makes a radical change of reference:

1983), pp. 19-37. When Paul uses a non-Pauline tradition, however, he thereby affirms it and makes it his own.

1.   See the discussion and the literature cited in P.T. O'Brien, *Colossians, Philemon* (WBC, 44; Waco, TX: Word Books 1982), pp. 32-42, 95-96.

2.   Ellis, 'Traditions', pp. 491, 494-95 (on 1 Cor. 8.6 and 10.1-13).

3.   So H. Probst, *Paulus und der Brief* (Tübingen: Mohr [Paul Siebeck], 1991), pp. 376-79 (from rhetorical considerations); P.J. Tomson, *Paul and the Jewish Law* (Minneapolis: Fortress Press, 1990), pp. 190-93; H. Merklein, 'Die Einheitlichkeit des ersten Korintherbriefes', *ZNW* 75 (1984), pp. 163-73; Fee, *The First Epistle*, pp. 357-63; Conzelmann, *1 Corinthians*, pp. 137-38. Otherwise: W. Schmithals, *Gnosticism in Corinth* (Nashville: Abingdon Press, 1971), p. 100; J. Weiss, *Der erste Korintherbrief* (Göttingen: Vandenhoeck & Ruprecht, 1970 [1910]), pp. xxxix-xliii. They think that two Pauline letters have been combined in 1 Cor. 8.1–11.1.

4.   Marcus Aurelius (+ AD 180), *Meditations* 4, 23.

5.   Philo, *Cher.* 127; *idem, Det. Pot. Ins.* 54.

6.   Cf. Ellis, 'Traditions', pp. 494-95.

Philo has the Word, Wisdom and variously predicated further powers and beings. Paul on the other hand knows only one central Hypostasis, who combines in himself the traits of Messiah, Wisdom, Word, Spirit and World Soul and also of the κύριος Yahweh and of the Lord and Savior of the mystery-cults, and to whom are subjected all other beings that exist. Only the Spirit works independently alongside Christ, and he is actually the counterpart of Christ.[1]

If a wisdom Christology is present at 1 Cor. 8.6, as is most likely,[2] it may be inferred at 10.4, 9 where Christ is also given a predication and a function that were ascribed in the Old Testament to Yahweh and in pre-Christian Judaism to the divine wisdom. It is in this framework that Paul's argument can be best understood—it was Christ who was both the redeemer and the judge of Israel at the exodus, and he will also perform these functions in the congregation of 'the Israel of God' at Corinth. As in Jude 5, Christ in 1 Corinthians 10 is the manifestation of Yahweh in his roles as redeemer and destroyer (cf. Exod. 12.23; Deut. 32.39; 1 Sam. 2.6; Isa. 45.6-7).

1. H. Windisch, 'Die Weisheit und die paulinische Christologie', in A. Deissman (ed.), *Neutestamentliche Studien* (Festschrift G. Heinrici; Leipzig: Hinrichs, 1914), pp. 220-34, 234.
2. Cf. R.A. Horsley, 'The Background of the Confessional Formula at I Kor. 8, 6', *ZNW* 69 (1978), pp. 130-35.

CHRISTOLOGIES AND ANTHROPOLOGIES OF PAUL, LUKE–ACTS AND MARCION

J. Christiaan Beker

It gives me great pleasure to participate in a Festschrift for Rien de Jonge. I met Rien some twelve years ago at a conference in Louvain. Since that encounter he has become not only a good friend, but also a wise counsellor who has advised me repeatedly in my academic pursuits. And all this happened, notwithstanding the fact that I, as a former student at the University of Utrecht, had been indoctrinated early on to avoid contact with Leiden University, Utrecht's rival!

I intend in this essay to contribute to Rien's interest in Christology by suggesting that the range and depth of one's Christology depends on the depth of one's anthropology.

It is interesting in this respect that two of Paul's most ardent admirers and pupils, Luke and Marcion, undertook to interpret their hero in such radically different ways, and in a period of church history when Paul increasingly had become a suspicious figure who was largely silenced by the emerging early Catholic Church (cf., for instance, the apologists).

1. *The Apostle Paul*

Paul's insight into the human condition has a profundity which has no equal in the New Testament or, for that matter, in the history of Western thought. Indeed, we must not forget that Paul was the originator of this anthropological thought—unlike Augustine and Luther, who each in their own way elaborated Paul's thought, Paul did not stand on the shoulders of Christian predecessors with respect to his anthropology!

To be sure, Paul's anthropology was decisively shaped by the apocalyptic traditions of Judaism. For instance, it has been noticed that his reflections on the salvation-historical place of Israel in God's plan (cf. Romans 9–11) are quite similar to those of the Qumran sectarians with respect to their predestinarian outlook. However, it is especially the apocalyptic concept of the two ages—the antithesis between 'the present evil age' (Gal. 1.4) and the future new age of 'life' and 'the new creation' (Gal. 6.15; 2 Cor. 5.17) which dominates Paul's thought. Indeed, the fabric of Paul's thought is permeated by an apocalyptic substrate. His thinking strains forward to the coming apocalyptic triumph of God when everything in creation that resists God's glory and sovereignty will be overcome, and the whole creation will be at peace in being embraced by the everlasting arms of God.

There can be no doubt that Paul's anthropology is the direct consequence of the apocalyptic texture of his Christology. In other words, Paul interprets the death and resurrection of Christ as an event which not only brings about a collision between the old aeon and the new aeon, but also splits them radically apart. Thus the Christ-event is appropriated in terms of an apocalyptic understanding of reality, that is, in terms of power structures which dominate and determine human life, that is, the powers of sin, death, the law and the flesh. Whatever their specific functions and differentiations may be, the alliance of these powers all have the same outcome—death.

Lest we think that Paul's apocalyptic thinking and his anthropology are the products of a fatalistic determinism, which simply makes people the tragic victims of supernatural powers, over which they have no control and reduces them to puppets and robots in the world, we must be aware that such a Gnostic dualism is far from Paul's mind. Indeed, he was able to discern 'the worm at the core of the apple', as Paul W. Meyer puts it,[1] a discernment which was evoked in him by God's 'revelation of his Son to me' (Gal. 1.16).

Thus, in an important sense, Paul's anthropological thought moves 'from solution to plight' (E.P. Sanders), that is, it moves from the new constitution of Paul's self in the Christ-event to a reconsideration of the old self. This old self, which Paul describes in depth in Romans 7, is portrayed against a cosmic universal background and leads Paul to the conclusion of Rom. 3.9: 'All people are under the power of sin.'

---

1. 'The Worm at the Core of the Apple: Exegetical Reflections on Romans 7', in *The Conversation Continues: Studies in Paul and John in Honour of J. Louis Martyn* (Nashville: Abingdon Press, 1990), p. 62.

In other words, the reason Paul steers midway between a Gnostic, dualistic determinism and a Stoic, rational optimism is due to Paul's understanding of sin's cunning. He constructs, as it were, a narrative of sin's strategy. Rom. 1.18-32, in conjunction with Rom. 7.7-25, shows how sin's strategy aims at deception and illusion. For sin manages to create a deceptive reversal of subject and object, that is, of relations between dominions. We—as subjects—encounter in our human freedom the various objects of our desire which are accompanied by possible transgressions of what is proper and just. However, we imagine that we—the dominating subjects—possess a perpetual freedom to resist or obey the lure of transgressions. Indeed, we imagine ourselves to be the original Adam or Eve in the garden primeval, claiming perpetual innocence in each successive moment of our lives, and pretending continually that we can regain our innocence and freedom over sin after each transgression. And so we usurp in our hubris God's role as Lord of the cosmos.

Sin, then, subtly creates in us the illusion of freedom and autonomy, as if we possess a permanent free choice and a permanent mastery over sin. However, we fail to realize that sin has imperceptibly invaded us and has become the dominating subject which now rules us as its object.

In other words, sin's deceptive itinerary has moved from sin as transgression to sin as power, that is, from sins that can be repaired through repentance, deeds of contrition, or the removal of ignorance to sin as a captivating power. Suddenly, sin has become the agent, which now determines all our choices and actions.

In Paul's language, sin has become a new 'lordship', that is, an apocalyptic power, which rules and overrules us. Indeed, for Paul sin is basically 'the root of all evil'. It manifests itself as the power of idolatry, that is, donating to the finite infinite status (Paul Tillich), or, in Paul's words, exchanging God's glory for transient, finite glory (Rom. 1.25), which carries as its consequence the total disorientation of the human condition. It affects the whole range of our intrapersonal, social and ecological worlds. In the words of L. Binschwanger, my *Eigenwelt, Mitwelt und Umwelt.* Indeed, the idolatrous glorification of the ego's power and 'lordship' causes immense suffering in our world. The 'exchange of the truth of God for a lie' (Rom. 1.25) produces in us the illusion of omnipotence, a 'boasting' which Paul applies especially to the pride of religious persons who, in their possession of the law or of wisdom, elevate themselves in the name of God (Rom. 2.17; 3.27; 4.2; 1 Cor. 1.18–2.16; 3.18-23; 8.1-3).

The only power which is able to break this lordship of sin is God's redemptive act in Christ. Indeed, according to Paul, Christians confess Jesus Christ as 'Lord' because his lordship overpowers the lordship of the idolatrous world, breaks the bondage of the human will and establishes 'the new creation', that is, the body of Christ where people receive a new identity and regain 'in Christ' that status in the world for which God created them. They are now able 'to present their bodies as a living sacrifice, holy and acceptable to God' (Rom. 12.1) so that they can exercise, in Käsemann's phrase, their 'Worship in Everyday Life'.[1]

Thus, Paul was able to sketch the narrative of sin's deceitful itinerary because the Christ-event transformed his life and the life of the created world. His anthropology moves indeed from solution to plight, but unless we recognize the reciprocal relation between solution and plight, we will fail to grasp both the depth of Paul's understanding of the human condition 'under sin' and the radicality of his soteriological Christology. According to Paul, the break between the cosmic ages, which God's action in Christ brings about is so total and so definitive that its discontinuity with the structures of the old age signifies on the anthropological level a similar discontinuity in the human condition before and after Christ.

2. *Luke–Acts and Paul*

A comparison of Paul with his greatest admirers can only be adequate if we keep in mind the various contingent situations that these pupils of Paul had to face.

Luke's portrait of Paul in Acts is heavily influenced by his overall salvation-historical theme, which is unfolded in terms of three interrelated subthemes: (1) the theme of the unity of the church (which includes Luke's anti-heretical stance), (2) the theme of the political legitimacy of the church (Luke's pro-Roman attitude), and (3) the theme of the theological legitimacy of the church (the continuity between the church and Israel). And so Luke portrays Paul

---

1.   The title of the essay found in *New Testament Questions of Today* (Philadelphia: Fortress Press, 1969 [1924]), pp. 188-95.

as the great ecumenical missionary who, in bringing the gospel to Rome, almost single-handedly fulfills God's mandate to bring the gospel 'to the ends of the earth' (1.8). Moreover, Luke's Paul is a loyal Roman citizen who receives constant protection under Roman law and, more importantly, has always been faithful to the best traditions of Judaism because his gospel fulfills what Judaism has been hoping for, that is, the resurrection of the dead.

And finally, Paul's gospel message is in complete harmony with all other apostolic witnesses to Jesus. Indeed, Paul is continuously engaged in safeguarding the continuity of the apostolic tradition by maintaining the original harmonious unity of the apostolic beginnings of the church.

In what manner, then, does Luke portray the human condition, and how does it compare with Paul's own anthropology? J.W. Taeger points out that the concepts 'body' and 'flesh' determine Paul's anthropology: They express the human connectedness with the world and are in no way neutral concepts.[1]

In Luke, to the contrary, the concepts 'heart' and 'soul' are primary and are, like 'body' and 'flesh', basically neutral entities which do not qualify human existence in a negative sense, but only express *its possibilities*.[2] Luke does not parallel Paul with his notion of the human being as alienated from the world and dominated by the powers.[3] And so, Luke advocates a moral understanding of sin: he speaks of *sins*, of specific acts of transgressions and ignorance, which can be corrected by repentance (Lk. 5.32; 15.7), that is, by a change in one's moral life.

Whereas in Paul the being of a person determines his deeds, in Luke the reverse occurs—a person's deeds qualify his being. Luke's fundamental anthropological optimism is well described by Taeger: 'Whereas according to Paul the human being is a *salvandus*, someone who must be redeemed, for Luke the human being is *corrigendus*, someone who can be corrected.'[4]

Luke's Christology conforms to his anthropology in that the proclamation of Jesus Christ effects conversions as basic corrections

---

1. J.W. Taeger, 'Paulus und Lukas über den Menschen', *ZNW* 71 (1990), pp. 96-108. The quotation comes from p. 99.
2. Taeger, 'Paulus und Lukas', p. 99. Emphasis mine.
3. Taeger, 'Paulus und Lukas', p. 101.
4. Taeger, 'Paulus und Lukas', p. 104.

of one's prior ignorance or as developments of one's essential kinship with God (Acts 17.28-30; cf. Acts 14.14-18). And thus, faith is often described as a type of intellectual persuasion and assent (Acts 2.36; 28.23).

Where Paul emphasizes the apocalyptic discontinuity in both his Christology and anthropology, Luke describes the Christ-event as God's means to correct and/or develop what human beings already inherently possess. Therefore, the continuity within Luke's anthropology and soteriological Christology discloses an almost complete absence of Paul's apocalyptic categories.

Indeed, the reciprocal relation of anthropology and Christology is evident in both Paul and Luke. Paul, but not Luke, would have underscored Anselm's dictum: *Nondum considerasti quanti ponderis peccatum est.*

3. *Marcion and Paul*

It is not my intent to explore the whole range of Marcion's thought as, for instance, rendered by Harnack in his magisterial work on Marcion.[1]

John Knox gives a helpful summary of Marcion's general theological position:

1. the creator of the world, although a real God, must be distinguished from the higher God, unknown except as he was revealed in Christ;
2. the creator of the world is a just God, but severe and harsh; the God whom Christ revealed is a Father, a God of love;
3. Judgment is the prerogative of the creator; redemption is the free gift of the God of love;
4. the Jewish Scriptures represent a true revelation of the creator, but they do not speak of or for the God whom alone Christians ought to worship and from whom alone salvation from the present wicked world is to be received;
5. the revelation in Christ was intended not merely to supplement or 'fulfill' Judaism, but entirely to displace it—the one had no connection with the other;

---

1. A. von Harnack, *Maricon: Das Evangelium vom fremden Gott* (TU, 45; Leipzig: Hinrichs, 1924).

6. the Son of the Father did not actually take sinful flesh, but only appeared to do so;
7. there is no resurrection of the flesh; and
8. Paul was the only true apostle to whom Christ committed his gospel—other 'apostles' were false and had misled the church.[1]

Marcion was an extreme Paulinist. He adopted Paul's apocalyptic aeonic theology in emphasizing the total disjunction between the age of the creator God of (inconsistent) justice and the alien God of love, who made himself manifest in Christ and whose sole true apostle was Paul.

Marcion's soteriology so dominated his thought that it not only overshadowed Paul's reflections on sin, but also Paul's cosmology (cf. Marcion's words in Tertullian, *Adv. Marc.* 1.17: 'One work is sufficient for our god; he has delivered man by his supreme and most excellent goodness [*summa et praecipua bonitate sua*; my translation]').

> The freeing of mankind which Marcion ascribed to his higher God implied as its antithesis not the bondage to sin with which the Bible is concerned, but a different bondage—one might say a physical, rather than a spiritual, bondage. Evil for Marcion is not so much moral as physical evil; not sin so much as suffering. Marcion was more concerned over the ugliness and misery of man's environment than the ugly passions of man's heart. Contempt of the flesh is more characteristic of this type of piety rather than a sense of sin as revealed in the Bible—in Psalm 51 or Romans 7, for example.[2]

In other words, Marcion's dualistic separation of soteriology from cosmology meant as well a fundamental separation from Paul's thought. It led him to a docetic Christology. Nevertheless he insisted on the reality of Christ's death, since Jesus conformed to the terms of the creator's law in order to 'purchase' mankind from sin and death, and so Christ becomes the victim of the creator's curse.[3]

Marcion's docetic Christology produced a dualistic anthropology,

---

1.   *Marcion and the New Testament: An Essay in the Early History of the Canon* (Chicago: University of Chicago Press, 1942), p. 7.
2.   E.C. Blackman, *Marcion and his Influence* (London: SPCK, 1948), pp. 105-106.
3.   Cf. R.J. Hoffmann, *Marcion: On the Restitution of Christianity* (Chico, CA: Scholars Press, 1984), p. 179.

because everything which was created by the creator God had no place in the realm of the God of love. Therefore, we must notice that Marcion's extreme asceticism was the result of his Christology. 'The believer must reject everything of this world and its Creator. Marcion's asceticism is the consequence of faith, because it is based on utter contempt for everything in creation.'[1]

4. Conclusion

The analysis of Luke–Acts and Marcion has demonstrated not only the radical difference in the anthropologies of these admirers of Paul, but also the reciprocal relation between their Christologies and anthropologies.

Indeed, the difference in a person's assessment of the human condition determines the difference in that person's Christology.

At this point one may object that a fair evaluation of the difference between Luke–Acts and Marcion requires cognizance of the different contingent situations which these authors faced. Otherwise, we fall victim to an ahistorical and abstract form of investigation.

However, we must be aware that both authors write at approximately the same time (Luke–Acts in the late first or early second century AD; Marcion, c. 140 AD); that both are equally concerned with the transmission of Paul's heritage; and that both address the early Catholic Church, which is in the process of consolidating itself. In other words, both authors face similar contingent circumstances, even when we must acknowledge that this process is more advanced in Marcion's time.

Whereas Luke is attempting to *accommodate* the gospel to the social world of Rome and thus prepares the way for the second century apologists in emphasizing the harmonious unity of the church, its political innocence and its theological legitimacy, Marcion is engaged in *polemics*; he aggressively fights for 'the purity' of the gospel and thus attacks in the name of the only true apostle, Paul, the false transmission of the gospel by the Catholic Church of his time.

This state of affairs prompts an inevitable question—is the coherent core of Paul's gospel simply determined by the contingent situations to which Luke and Marcion respond so differently? And if that is true,

1. E.U. Schüle, 'Der Ursprung des Bösen bei Marcion', *Zeitschrift für Religions und Geistesgeschichte* 16 (1964), p. 26.

then we must conclude that, if social circumstances determine the substance of the gospel, the gospel's coherent core is sacrificed on the altar of what one deems to be relevant to the needs of a particular time and audience.

Indeed, when Luke with his overall eirenic concern harmonizes Paul with the other apostolic witnesses of the church and subjugates him to them, and when Marcion with his polemic program divorces Paul's 'pure' gospel from its salvation-historical moorings in the Hebrew Scriptures, both authors distort the Paul whom they so admire.

More precisely, Luke and Marcion manifest not only a close interrelation, but also a radical collision between their anthropologies and Christologies. Luke casts Paul's anthropology within a framework which celebrates human possibilities, and views the gospel essentially as the correction of these possibilities, whereas Marcion, to the contrary, renders Paul's anthropology within a scenario, which defines human beings simply as strangers to the God of love, and views the gospel as redeeming them from their material plight as victims of the creator God.

In this manner, their mutual differences signify as well a betrayal of Paul's anthropology and Christology. For both Luke and Marcion betray not only Paul's insight into the nature of sin as that bondage which alienates humankind from the worship of God's glory, but also his joyful affirmation that God's intervention in Christ so transforms humankind that it can execute its God-given mission in the world.

THE TWO PAROUSIAS OF CHRIST:
JUSTIN MARTYR AND MATTHEW

Graham N. Stanton

Justin Martyr's *Dialogue with Trypho* provides invaluable insights into the development of early Christian thought and the impact on it of Greek philosophy and rhetoric, the textual traditions of Old Testament writings, and the early reception of New Testament writings. However, there is an even more important reason why the *Dialogue* deserves closer scholarly attention than it has received recently: it is the first surviving Christian writing to tackle fully the issues which separated Christians and Jews in the period after the 'parting of the ways'.

Justin wrote his *Dialogue* some five to ten years before his martyrdom in c. 165 CE. He set his extended discussions with the learned Jew Trypho some twenty years earlier, in the period immediately after the end of the second Jewish Revolt against the Romans. According to Eusebius (*Hist. Eccl.* IV.18.2), who may have gained his information from the missing preface to the *Dialogue*, the discussions took place in Ephesus. This chronological and geographical setting may be a wholly artificial device invoked for literary purposes. The sparse references in the *Dialogue* to Justin's travels and to the geographical location of his discussions with Trypho also fit several other coastal cities in the eastern Mediterranean. On the other hand, however, there is nothing in the extant text (and no other relevant evidence) which rules out the strong probability that part of the *Dialogue* is based on discussions Justin had with a learned Jew in Ephesus shortly after 135 CE. In many passages Trypho is undoubtedly no more than a straw man. He is frequently allowed to ask a question or to raise an objection simply in order to allow Justin to press home his own Christian line of apologetic. But both Justin and his opponent are usually well-informed about contemporary Judaism, and there are good reasons for concluding that the *Dialogue* often records genuine Jewish objections to Christianity.[1]

One of the many interesting christological themes of Justin's *Dialogue* is the extended use of a schema of two parousias, a theme which has not received the attention it deserves.[2] In a large number of passages Justin stresses that Christ's first coming without honour and glory is in sharp contrast to his second coming in glory and upon the clouds.[3] This theme is developed as a Christian response to Trypho's objection that the life of the Christian Messiah did not fulfil scriptural prophecies. This Jewish objection and the Christian response in terms of the 'two-advents' schema appears explicitly for the first time in the *Dialogue*. The two-parousias schema was developed in a number of ways by later Christian writers, often with a similar setting in controversy.[4]

In this article I shall explore this theme within Justin's *Dialogue*, and more briefly his *Apology*. I shall try to show that in spite of the highly stylised way the two-parousias schema is developed in the *Dialogue*, it is used by Justin to counter Jewish insistence that Christian messianic claims do not correspond with the prophecies of Scripture. I shall then suggest, more tentatively, that an early form of this schema is found in Matthew's Gospel where it has been developed for similar reasons.

It is a pleasure to offer this essay to Marinus de Jonge, to whom I owe a great deal. Even if he is not persuaded by the more speculative parts of this article, I am confident that he will approve of my attempt to set New Testament passages in a wider context than is often the case in current scholarship.

---

1. See further G.N. Stanton, 'Aspects of Early Christian–Jewish Polemic and Apologetic', *NTS* 31 (1985), pp. 377-92, which is now included in *A Gospel for a New People: Studies in Matthew* (Edinburgh: T. & T. Clark, 1992), pp. 232-55.

2. On Justin's Christology, see D. C. Trakatellis, *The Pre-Existence of Christ in Justin Martyr: An Exegetical Study with Reference to the Humiliation and Exaltation Christology* (Missoula, MT: Scholars Press, 1976). Trakatellis discusses the 'two parousias' only in passing on pp. 159-60.

3. See *Dialogue* 14.8; 31.1; 32.2; 34.2; 36.1; 40.4; 49.2; 49.7; 52.1; 52.4; 110.2; 120.4; 121.3.

4. See, for example, Tertullian, *Adv. Jud.* 13 and 14; Origen, *Contra Celsum*, I. 56 and II. 29 (discussed below). In Nicholas de Lyra's early fourteenth century treatise *Against the Jews*, the Christian response to the Jewish objection that Dan 7.13 does not apply to Jesus is that there is a second coming. See A.L. Williams, *Adversus Judaeos* (Cambridge: Cambridge University Press, 1935), p. 411.

I

In *Dialogue* 31 Justin asks his Jewish opponent Trypho a rhetorical question: 'If great power accompanies the dispensation (οἰκονομία) brought in by the suffering of Jesus Christ, how great will be that which will be seen in his advent (παρουσία) in glory?' Justin then answers his own question by quoting Dan. 7.9-28.[1]

Trypho accepts Justin's exegesis of Daniel 7, but immediately raises an objection:

> Sir, these and other similar passages of Scripture compel us to await One who is great and glorious, and takes over the everlasting kingdom from the Ancient of days as Son of man. But this your so-called Christ is without honour and glory, so that he has even fallen into the uttermost curse that is in the law of God, for he was crucified (*Dialogue* 32.1).

In other words, Trypho insists that since the life of Jesus does not correspond to scriptural prophecies concerning the coming of the Messiah, Jesus cannot be the promised Messiah.

In reply, Justin refers Trypho to two points he had made earlier—he recalls his earlier use (at 13.4) of Isaiah 53 as scriptural support for the ignominious death suffered by Jesus. He also refers to his earlier exposition (at 14.8) of the two advents of Christ: 'one in which he was pierced by you, and a second when you will recognize him whom you pierced, and all your tribes will lament...'(Zech. 12.10-14).[2]

In *Dialogue* 14.8 Justin had insisted that some passages in the

---

1.   I have used and quoted J.C.T. Otto's edition of the Greek text, *Corpus Apologetarum Christianorum Saeculi Secundi*, I (Jena: Frider Mauke, 1847). With some minor modifications English translations are from A. Lukyn Willams, *Justin Martyr: The Dialogue with Trypho* (London: SPCK, 1930). See in particular, O. Skarsaune, *The Proof from Prophecy: A Study in Justin Martyr's Proof-Text Tradition: Text-Type, Provenance, Theological Profile* (Leiden: Brill, 1987). I have learned a great deal from Skarsaune's fine study. However he does not note the important parallels in Origen's *Contra Celsum* and in Matthew's Gospel which are discussed in this article.

2.   Skarsaune, *The Proof from Prophecy*, p. 78 notes that in references to Zechariah 12.10–12 at *Dialogue* 14.8; 32.2; and 64.7 Justin reads ἐπιγνώσεσθε instead of ἐπιβλέψονται (LXX). He suggests that Justin may have taken the reading from the καιγε recension of the LXX. While this explanation is plausible, it is also possible that Justin has altered the verb deliberately in order to allow for a possible eventual positive response on the part of the Jewish people.

prophets (including Isa. 55.3-13 which he quotes) referred to the first coming of Christ 'without honour and without form and mortal', while others refer to his second coming 'in glory and upon the clouds'[1]: 'your people will see and will recognize him whom they pierced, as Hosea [obviously a mistake for Zechariah], one of the Twelve prophets, and Daniel foretold'.

This exchange between Justin and Trypho in *Dialogue* 31, together with the points made in the related parts of chs. 13 and 14, form the backdrop to a number of passages in later parts of the *Dialogue*. This key passage may be interpreted in two ways: Trypho's comments may reflect a genuine Jewish objection to Christian claims, or Justin may be allowing Trypho to intervene merely so that he can set out one of his major christological themes.

At first sight the latter explanation looks more probable. The numerous two parousias passages in the *Dialogue* are highly stylised. Similar phrases are repeated a number of times. The simple rhetorical strategy of 'negative comparison' is used: the first coming 'without glory', and 'without honour' is contrasted with the second coming 'in glory' and 'as judge'.[2] References to the first coming of Christ usually allude to Isa. 53. 2-3; phrases from Dan. 7.13 -14 or Zech. 12.10-12 (or both, as at *Dialogue* 14.8) are prominent in the references to Christ's second coming.

However, several considerations taken cumulatively suggest that first appearances are deceptive and that the two-parousias schema is Justin's response to known or to perceived Jewish objections. First, in a large number of passages in the *Dialogue* readers are reminded that one of the main issues on which Justin and Trypho are at odds is whether the life of Jesus corresponds to scriptural prophecies

1. In the *Dialogue* 'glory' is regularly associated with references to the coming of the Son of man which are clearly based on Dan 7.13-14. Skarsaune (*The Proof from Prophecy*, p. 286 n. 101) notes that δόξα is not found in any of Justin's OT testimonies concerning the second parousia; since it is found in the *Anabathmoi Iakobou II* source of the Pseudo-Clementines (*Recognitions* I. 49. 2ff. and I. 69. 3-4), the two traditions are related. I do not doubt this. However, attachment of δόξα to references and allusions to Dan 7.13-14 seems to have been a well established convention in both Christian and Jewish exegesis. See Mt. 19.28; 25.31; *I En.* 45.3; 49.2; 55.4; 61.8; 62.5; 69.27, 29; 71 7.

2. Skarsaune, *The Proof from Prophecy*, p. 155 sets out the key phrases in a convenient chart.

concerning the coming of the Messiah (36.1; 39.7; 49.1, 7; 89.1 and 90.1; 110.1-2, for example). The two parousias passages are part of this broader theme which is one of the central issues in the *Dialogue* as a whole.

For my present purposes the 'messianic' passages can be divided into three groups. (a) In two cases Justin and Trypho are able to agree that scriptural prophecies refer to a future coming of the Messiah. As noted above, at 32.1, Trypho accepts Justin's interpretation of Daniel 7 and similar (unnamed) passages; at 39.7 Trypho refers back to this earlier agreement. At 49.2 Justin elicits (and receives) Trypho's agreement that Mal. 4.5 refers to the role of Elijah as the forerunner of the promised Messiah. (b) Trypho (or his teachers) agree implicitly that three further passages refer to the coming Messiah—Zech. 12. 10-12 (*Dialogue* 32.1-2); Gen. 49.8-12 (*Dialogue* 52, 53, and 55.1; 120.4-5) and Micah 4 (*Dialogue* 109, 110.1-2). In each case Justin claims that these passages refer in part to the first coming of Christ, and in part to his future coming. (c) Justin insists on a messianic interpretation of a large number of further passages. In many cases Justin is aware that his Christian interpretation is at odds with Jewish non-messianic interpretation. In *Dialogue* 32–6 and 83, for example, he attempts to refute Jewish claims that Psalms 24, 72 and 110.1-12 refer to Solomon and/or Hezekiah. In none of the passages in this third group is the two parousias schema used.

In all three cases Justin is almost certainly well aware of current Jewish interpretation of the biblical passages he cites. Some caution, however, is necessary since the clearest evidence for Jewish exegesis of the passages in question is often found in targumic or rabbinic traditions which are difficult to date.[1] On the other hand, I do not know of a single case where Justin's own assumptions concerning current Jewish messianic (or non-messianic) interpretation of scriptural passages is demonstrably at odds with the relevant Jewish evidence. In short, there are good grounds for supposing that Justin is

1. For details see Skarsaune, *The Proof from Prophecy*, pp. 260-88 and the revised edition of E. Schürer, 'Messianism', in *The History of the Jewish People in the Age of Jesus Christ* II, (ed. G. Vermes, F. Millar and M. Black, Edinburgh: T. & T. Clark, 1979), §29 pp. 488-549. See also *Judaisms and their Messiahs at the Turn of the Christian Era* (ed. J. Neusner, W.S. Green and E.S. Frerichs; Cambridge: Cambridge University Press, 1987).

using the two-parousias schema with known Christian–Jewish disputes over Scripture in mind.

Secondly, in *I Apol.* 52 Justin uses the two-parousias schema in a quite different way. He argues that since the first coming of Christ which was proclaimed in advance through the prophets has already happened, so 'those things which were similarly prophesied and are yet to happen will certainly take place'. This line of argument is not used in the *Dialogue*, where the strikingly different setting of the two-parousias schema seems to have been elicited by very different circumstances.[1] *I Apol.* 52 shows how Justin might have argued in the *Dialogue* if he had intended solely to give christological instruction.

Thirdly, there is further independent evidence that at the time Justin wrote his *Dialogue* other Jewish objectors were levelling the same charge against Christians, and were receiving a similar response. In the middle of the third century Origen quotes the objection raised by Celsus's Jew (c. 177–180): 'The prophets say that the one who will come will be a great prince, lord of the whole earth and of all nations and armies, but they did not proclaim a pestilent fellow like him (Jesus)' (*Contra Celsum* II, 29) But Origen treats the criticism with disdain by appealing to the 'two-advents' schema he had expounded earlier—there he noted that critics of Christianity who based their case on the interpretation of Scripture 'failed to notice that the prophecies speak of two advents of Christ. In the first he is subject to human passions and deeper humiliation... in the second he is coming in glory and in divinity alone, without any human passions bound up with his divine nature' (*Contra Celsum* I, 56).[2]

In these passages there is no sign of direct dependence on Justin. Even though in his response to Celsus Origen develops one of his own distinctive christological themes, both the Jewish criticism and the

---

1.   Similarly, Skarsaune, *The Proof from Prophecy*, p. 156.

2.   Skarsaune (*The Proof from Prophecy*, pp. 285-86) notes a further important reference to the 'two parousias' in the *Anabathmoi Iakobou II* source of the Pseudo-Clementines: 'He (Moses) therefore intimated that he (Christ) should come, humble indeed in his first coming, but glorious in his second...' (*Recognitions* I, 49). This tradition may well stem from about the same time as Justin's *Dialogue*. Unlike the two parousias schema in the *Dialogue*, however, it is not used explicitly as a Christian response to a Jewish objection.

Christian response are strikingly similar to Trypho's complaint and Justin's reply.[1]

There is, then, a strong cumulative case for concluding that Justin has developed the two-parousias schema as a Christian response to known Jewish objections to Christian messianic claims. While it is probable that in the *Dialogue* Justin has drawn extensively on his own earlier writings or on other sources, the *Dialogue* is the first extant writing in which the two-parousias Christology forms part of Christian–Jewish controversies.[2]

But the roots of such disputes may well be much deeper. Early in the post-Easter period Christians began to claim that their convictions about Jesus were 'in accordance with the Scriptures'. It would not have been difficult for opponents to refute such claims on the basis of Scripture. In particular, in Jewish circles where there were lively expectations concerning the triumphant Davidic Messiah, it would have been natural for opponents to insist that Christian claims concerning the Messiah did not correspond to Scripture.[3] A Christian counter-claim in terms of the 'two advents' of the Messiah, both foretold in Scripture, would have been an obvious response. This line of apologetic may well have been developed long before Justin's day.

---

1. I have quoted H. Chadwick's translation, *Contra Celsum* (Cambridge: Cambridge University Press, 1953), and I have accepted his date for Celsus's lost writing which Origen quotes at length.

2. On the basis of meticulous traditio-historical studies O. Skarsaune has argued that in the *Dialogue* Justin has drawn extensively on two sources: (i) A 'kerygma' source found in many parts of chs. 11–47 and 108–41 which may possibly be related to the Kerygma Petrou, and which contains most of the 'two parousias' passages; (ii) a 'recapitulation' source found in parts of chs. 48–108 (but not 56–60 and 98–106) which may come from Aristo of Pella's lost Controversy of Jason with Papiscus. The presence of 'doublets', especially passages once in a LXX form and once not, and the numerous digressions in the line of argument make it all but certain that Justin has drawn extensively upon earlier sources. However I am not persuaded that one of his two major sources is Aristo's *Controversy*. Origen refers to this writing as a 'little book' (*Contra Celsum* IV, 52), a point overlooked by Skarsaune; on his hypothesis Aristo's *Controversy* was a substantial writing.

3. Luke refers to disputes between Christians and Jews over the interpretation of Scripture, but provides few details: Acts 17.2-3; 18.4; 19.8; 28.23-28.

II

I now want to suggest that an early form of the two-parousias schema is found in Matthew's Gospel as part of the evangelist's response to Jewish criticism of Christian claims. As far as I know, this is a fresh suggestion. Before I set out the evidence which points to Matthew's use of a two-parousias schema, I shall discuss several passages in which Matthew refers to the criticisms of the Jewish religious leaders, in particular the Pharisees, and responds directly or indirectly.

1. At the very end of his Gospel Matthew refers explicitly to the rival explanations of the empty tomb held by Christians and Jews in his own day (28.1-15). The evangelist takes great pains to refute the alternative 'story'. This passage strongly suggests that rival assessments of the significance of Jesus may well be reflected earlier in Matthew's Gospel.

2. Two hostile comments from the opponents of Jesus are of particular interest. They are both found in passages in which Matthew's own redactional hand is evident and are closely related to the double accusation against Jesus which is found in a wide range of early Christian and Jewish writings: Jesus was a magician and a deceiver. The accusation that Jesus was a deceiver was a stock jibe which is found in some Jewish traditions (which are admittedly difficult to date) and in a remarkably wide range of early Christian writings.[1] In many of these writings (most notably Justin *Dialogue* 69, *b.Sanh.* 43a and *b.Sanh.* 107) it is linked with a second critical comment: Jesus was a magician (μάγος).

In Matthew, the opponents of Jesus repeatedly claim that his exorcisms are carried out 'by the prince of demons': 9.34; 10.25; 12.24, 27.[2] In other words, Jesus is a demon-possessed magician or sorcerer. The response is direct and clear: Jesus carries out his exorcisms by the Spirit of God and as a result of the coming of God's kingly rule (12. 28).

Following the burial of Jesus the Pharisees go and ask Pilate to make the tomb secure. They refer to Jesus as 'that deceiver' (ἐκεῖνος

---

1. For details, see G.N. Stanton, 'Aspects of Early Christian–Jewish Polemic and Apologetic', *NTS* 31 (1985), pp. 377-92, which is now included in *A Gospel for a New People*, pp. 232-55.

2. See further Stanton, *A Gospel for a New People*, pp. 171-80.

ὸ πλάνος) and sum up his life as 'deception' (πλάνη, 27.63-64). In this passage the Pharisees, who have hitherto not been mentioned specifically in Matthew's passion narratives, re-emerge as the arch-opponents of Jesus. The evangelist does not take the trouble to respond to this jibe. Presumably he considers that his whole Gospel is sufficient proof of its absurdity.

3. There is a further set of passages in Matthew which are related to disputes with Jewish opponents in the evangelist's day concerning the significance of Jesus. Matthew expands Mark's three references to the title Son of David to nine: 1.1; 9.27; 12.23; 15.22; 20.30, 31 (= Mk 10.47, 48); 21.9, 15; 22.42 (= Mk 12.35) where the title Son of David is implied. Why does Matthew open his Gospel with a reference to Jesus as Son of David and then proceed to add five further references in contexts which are broadly Marcan (9.27; 12.23; 15.22; 21.9, 15)? As several writers have noted, in four of the six redactional passages Matthew connects the Son of David title with the healing ministry of Jesus,[1] but that observation hardly accounts for the evangelist's strong emphasis on this particular christological theme.

Most scholars have overlooked the fact that another motif is equally prominent in the Son of David passages which come from the evangelist's own hand.[2] In four such passages acknowledgment of Jesus as the Son of David by participants in Matthew's story provokes hostility from the Jewish leaders. These four passages come at critical points in the evangelist's presentation of one of his major themes: the conflict between Jesus and the Jewish leaders.[3] This is the very first conflict in

1. So, for example, C. Burger, *Jesus als Davidssohn* (Göttingen: Vandenhoeck & Ruprecht, 1970), pp. 72-106; J.M. Gibbs, 'Purpose and Pattern in Matthew's Use of the Title "Son of God"', *NTS* 10 (1963–64), pp. 446-64; J.D. Kingsbury, 'The Title "Son of David" in Matthew's Gospel', *JBL* 95 (1976), pp. 591-602; D.C. Duling, 'The Therapeutic Son of David: An Element in Matthew's Christological Apologetic', *NTS* 24 (1978), pp. 392-409; U. Luz, 'Eine thetische Skizze der matthäischen Christologie', in C. Breytenbach and H. Paulsen (eds.), *Anfänge der Christologie* (Festschrift F. Hahn; Göttingen: Vandenhoeck & Ruprecht, 1991), pp. 223-26.

2. A notable exception is D. Verseput, 'The Role and Meaning of the "Son of God" Title in Matthew's Gospel', *NTS* 33 (1987), pp. 533-57. Verseput does not discuss the reasons for this link.

3. See J.D. Kingsbury, 'The Developing Conflict between Jesus and the Jewish Leaders in Matthew's Gospel', *CBQ* 49 (1987), pp. 57-73. Kingsbury does not note that confession of Jesus as 'Son of David' provokes hostility from the Jewish leaders.

the Gospel (2.1-6); two passages are found at important turning points in the evangelist's story (9.34; 21.9, 15); the fourth passage (12.23) is an integral part of the important set of claims and counter-claims in ch. 12.

In these four redactional passages acknowledgment of Jesus as Son of David is vigorously opposed by the Jewish religious leaders. Why? And why does the evangelist stress so strongly that Jesus *is* the Son of David? Why does Matthew set out so carefully this fourfold pattern of positive response by some to Jesus' Davidic Messiahship and its rejection by the Jewish leaders?

I suggest that once again we are in contact with claims and counter-claims being made at the time Matthew wrote.[1] The evangelist is well aware that his communities will face fierce opposition to their claims that Jesus was indeed the Davidic Messiah. Matthew insists that this claim is part of the very essence of Christian convictions about the significance of Jesus. But at the same time in several redactional passages he sets out a portrait of the Davidic Messiah which fulfils scriptural prophecies even though it *differs* from many current expectations.[2] The one born 'king of the Jews' is the child Jesus, the Davidic Messiah (2.2-6); in accordance with prophecy Jesus heals every disease and infirmity (8.17); Jesus is the one who is 'meek and lowly in heart' (11.29), the chosen servant of God (12.17-21), 'the humble king' (21.5). All these passages bear the stamp of the evangelist himself. They convey a quite distinctive portrait of Jesus, a portrait elicited, as it were, by objections to Christian claims.[3]

I have set out above three Jewish criticisms which Matthew is anxious to refute: the disciples stole the body of Jesus from the tomb; Jesus was a magician and a deceiver; Jesus was not the Davidic Messiah. I now wish to show that Matthew responds to the latter line of criticism by developing an early form of the two-parousias schema

1.   Several other passages in Matthew may well be a response to hostile allegations: e.g. 1.18-25; 5.17-20.
2.   Jewish messianic expectations were very varied, but there is no doubt that in some circles there were lively hopes for a future triumphant Davidic Messiah. See above, p. 186 n. 1.
3.   See the discussion of these passages by G. Barth in G. Bornkamm, G. Barth and H.J. Held (eds.), *Tradition and Interpretation in Matthew* (London: SCM Press, 1963), pp. 125-31.

which occurs in a more fully developed form in Justin and in Origen.[1] In a series of redactional passages Matthew emphasizes much more strongly than the other evangelists the humility of the earthly life of Jesus the Son of David, the glory of his future coming as Son of Man and judge, and the contrast between the two 'comings'.

The main features of Matthew's distinctive portrait of Jesus as the humble servant of God in his first coming have been sketched above. Matthew's extension of the apocalyptic themes found in his sources is well-known. He repeatedly emphasizes redactionally the future glorious coming of Jesus as Son of Man;[2] he is the only evangelist to use the word παρουσία of the future coming (24.3, 27, 37, 39).

Although Matthew does not refer to the life of Jesus as his παρουσία, he does contrast sharply the humble life of the Davidic Messiah with his future coming in glory in ways which are reminiscent of the later two-parousias schema. The Jesus who must go to Jerusalem and suffer many things (16.21-3) is contrasted much more sharply than in Mark with the Son of Man who will come in the glory of his Father and then reward each person for what he has done (16. 27-8). The 'humble king' who enters Jerusalem (21.5) will come in glory, sit on his throne, and as king he will judge the nations (25.31-46). At the hearing before the Sanhedrin Jesus is asked by the high priest, 'Are you the Christ, the Son of God?' The reply of Jesus is either evasive or hesitant. By adding to Mk 14.62 a strongly adversative πλήν and ἀπ' ἄρτι, Matthew contrasts the present role of Jesus with his future role as Son of Man and judge (27.64).

A further observation lends support to my case. In Matthew's day, as in Justin's, Christians and Jews could agree that certain passages in the prophets referred to the *future* coming of the Messiah, but agreement concerning the 'first coming' was another matter. The burden of proof clearly lay with Christians, for they were making the novel claims. In these circumstances it is no surprise to find that nine out of Matthew's ten distinctive formula quotations claim that the 'first coming', the teaching and the actions of Jesus, is in fulfilment of

---

1. H. Conzelmann (*The Theology of Luke* [London: Faber, 1961], p. 17 n.1) noted that it is quite justifiable to speak of 'two advents' in Luke, even though the actual terminology is not found. However he did not relate this observation to later Christian apologetic.

2. See Stanton, *A Gospel for a New People*, pp. 161-5, 222.

Scripture.[1] And it is no surprise to find that four of the five key passages (all redactional) which set out Matthew's distinctive portrait of Jesus as the humble servant stress that his first coming as the Davidic Messiah did fulfil the prophetic promises of Scripture (2.2-6; 8.17; 12.17-21; 21.5; and, indirectly, 11.29).

We may conclude, then, that in Matthew there is an early form (perhaps the earliest) of the two-parousias schema which was one of the ways Christians countered Jewish claims that the life of Jesus did not correspond to the prophecies concerning the future coming of the Messiah. Matthew's redactional juxtaposition of the present humility of Jesus and his future coming in glory is not related to the incarnational pattern found in other New Testament writings in which the one who was with God humbled himself among men (even to death) and was exalted by God (e.g. Phil 2.6-11; 2 Cor. 8.9). Nor is it related to the pattern of reversal found in Acts: in raising Jesus God reversed the actions of those who put Jesus to death (e.g. Acts 2.23-4; 3.13-15). Matthew simply sets the two contrasting parousias side by side, just as Justin and Origen were to do much later.

The development of the two-parousias schema in the second and third centuries may have been partly influenced by Matthew's Gospel, but there are no signs of direct literary dependence. In Matthew, Justin and Origen, the two-parousias schema is a response to the sharp criticisms of Jewish opponents who insisted that Christian claims about the Davidic Messiahship of Jesus were not in accordance with the prophets.

There is one further observation to be made. Matthew's stark contrast between the humility and meekness of the life of Jesus the Son of David and his glorious future coming as Son of Man and judge reflects (in part) the self-understanding of the communities for which the evangelist wrote his Gospel. Christology and ecclesiology are interrelated.

Matthew's Christian readers are encouraged to live by the conviction that since their Lord who was sent by God (10.40; 21.37) is also the humble servant of God who was confronted at every turn by his opponents, they themselves must reflect that role. Their message and ministry are the same as those of Jesus himself (4.17; 10.7-8). They are 'the little ones' (10.42; 18.6, 10, 14; 25.40), 'the

---

1.   See Stanton, *A Gospel for a New People*, pp. 346-63.

poor in spirit', 'the meek' (5.3, 5), 'the simple unlearned ones' (11.25) who, like Jesus himself, must face fierce opposition (5.10-12; 10.11-42; 23.34), but their cause will be vindicated at the future coming of the Son of Man (25.31-46; and cf. 5.12; 10.41-2), for which they are urged to be ready. They are promised that until that final vindication takes place, the risen and exalted Lord is with them (28.20).

In many ways Matthew's Christology is very different from Justin's. But there are some similarities. Both writers are keenly aware of Jewish objections to Christian claims about Jesus. Their Christology has been shaped (in part) by the experiences and self-understanding of minority communities at odds with their Jewish neighbours.[1]

There is no evidence of a direct link between Matthew's early form of the two-parousias schema, and Justin's richer version. Quite independently, two early Christian writers have developed a similar christological theme as an apologetic response to Jewish polemic. If there is any merit in these suggestions, there is a further corollary. They suggest that students of earliest Christianity may find it advantageous from time to time to work back (with due caution) from the clearer fuller evidence which second-century writers often provide, to New Testament passages which are much less easy to interpret and to place in a specific social setting.[2]

1. Some of the christological themes of the fourth evangelist are related to a similar social setting.

2. After completing the above study I came upon a further, second-century example of the 'two parousias' schema in the Muratorian Canon. In lines 23-26 the four Gospels are all said to declare the two comings of Christ: 'the first despised in lowliness, which has come to pass, the second glorious in kingly power which is yet to come'. However this passage is not related to Jewish criticisms of Christian messianic claims.

THE SON OF MAN IN Q*

Christopher Tuckett

I

The problem of the use of the phrase Son of Man in the Gospels is perhaps one of the most intractable in contemporary Gospel studies and the secondary literature on the subject is enormous. It is however probably fair to say that the prime interest in the topic for many today is at the level of what the term may have meant within the preaching of the historical Jesus.[1] Thus for many, the burning questions are whether Jesus used the term and what he may have meant by it (when probably speaking in Aramaic). In the present context, such problems will be shelved. Rather, I wish to consider the possible meaning of the term in 'Q', that is in the stratum of the tradition which is believed by many to lie behind the Gospels of Matthew and Luke.[2] Further, it is

*   It is both a pleasure and a privilege to offer this article, an earlier version of which was first read as a paper at the British NT conference in Bristol in 1989, to Professor Rien de Jonge in grateful thanks for all the friendship and inspiration he has provided. In accordance with what is becoming standard convention, I give references to passages in Q using the Lukan chapter and verse numbers, though without making any assumptions thereby about whether Matthew or Luke has preserved the Q version more accurately.

1.   For a valuable summary of the problem at this level, see M. de Jonge, *Jesus, The Servant–Messiah* (New Haven: Yale University Press, 1991), pp. 50-54.

2.   This is not the place to defend the existence of a 'Q' source in the Gospels against those who deny it. I have tried to discuss the matter elsewhere, for example in my *The Revival of the Griesbach Hypothesis* (Cambridge: Cambridge University Press, 1983) and in 'The Existence of Q', in a forthcoming collection edited by R.A. Piper. Thus, for present purposes, I shall assume that Matthew–Luke agreements which are not due to common dependence on the Gospel of Mark are to be explained by dependence on some sort of 'Q' source. The nature, and unity, of 'Q' are of course disputed issues. For a survey of the Christology of Q in general, see M. de Jonge, *Christology in Context: The Earliest Christian Response to Jesus*

commonly agreed that the measure of verbal agreement between Matthew and Luke is at times so close as to demand the theory that 'Q' must have been a Greek 'text'.[1] Thus the meaning of Son of Man in any Aramaic form of the tradition will not be considered here.

Q studies have in recent years been notable for the attempt to try to find distinguishing 'theological' characteristics in the Q tradition in the Gospels to see if one can isolate a peculiar 'Q theology' or identify a particular group of Christians (perhaps a 'Q community') responsible for the preservation and handing on of the Q tradition. Within such studies, the problem of the use of Son of Man has been a highly controversial one with a variety of different theories and a mush-rooming secondary literature. The phenomenon of the use of the term Son of Man was in fact the point of access for one of the earliest redaction-critical studies of Q, *viz.* the dissertation of H.E. Tödt.[2] Tödt did not attempt to give a 'redaction'-critical study of Q in the strict sense of 'redaction' (as referring to alterations to an underlying tradition). He took the Q material as an undifferentiated whole and argued that, within Q, the Son of Man sayings occupied an extremely important role. Tödt assumed that, originally, Jesus had spoken of the Son of Man as a figure other than himself who would appear at the endtime to vindicate his cause. On the basis of their Easter experience, the Q Christians became convinced that the Son of Man figure was none other than Jesus himself. Thus the identification of the Son of Man with Jesus was first made by the Q community and a 'Son of Man Christology' (by which Tödt meant primarily an idea of Jesus returning as Son of Man at an eschatological future event) was an extremely important aspect of the ideology of the Q Christians. In Tödt's words, 'Son of Man Christology and Q belong together both in their concepts and in their history of tradition.'[3]

Since Tödt wrote, several developments in Q studies have taken place. Although his work is often regarded as one of the first to apply insights from so-called 'redaction criticism' to the study of Q, Tödt took the Q material as a unity and saw all that material as potentially

(Philadelphia: Westminster Press, 1988), pp. 71-90.

1. See, for example, J.S. Kloppenborg, *The Formation of Q* (Philadelphia: Fortress Press, 1987), pp. 51-64.

2. H.E. Tödt, *The Son of Man in the Synoptic Tradition* (London: SCM Press, 1965).

3. Tödt, *The Son of Man*, p. 269.

contributing to an understanding of the beliefs of the Q Christians. Thus Tödt did not attempt to split the Q material into 'tradition' and 'redaction'. However, more recent studies of Q have shown an ever-increasing tendency to see Q as a much more complex and dynamic entity—hence many today would prefer to regard Q as a stream of the tradition which has its own tradition-history, and would postulate the existence of more than one stratum within Q. At the very least, many would wish to distinguish between a Q-tradition and a Q-redaction; others would go further and argue for three or more stages in the development of Q. Further, within such theories, the problem of the Son of Man sayings has at times played an important role. Thus many have suggested that Son of Man sayings do not characterize Q's redaction but only Q's tradition. Son of Man ideas have therefore been quietly relegated away by some from the forefront of discussions about Q.

Those such as Tödt, and more recently P. Hoffmann, who have not made much of possible distinctions between tradition and redaction within Q, have ascribed great significance to Son of Man for Q's Christology.[1] By contrast, another of the early redaction-critical studies of Q, by D. Lührmann, came to a different conclusion.[2] On the basis of various criteria, Lührmann attempted to identify specific redactional activity and a redactional stratum within Q, whereby earlier traditions were taken up and, in part, modified. Lührmann argued that the identification of the Son of Man as Jesus had already taken place prior to the redactional stratum of Q which was concerned with polemic against 'this generation'. In this polemic, use of Son of Man sayings was only one means amongst several employed by the Q redaction and hence these sayings are not necessarily of great significance in isolating the distinctive features of that redaction.[3]

---

1. See P. Hoffmann, *Studien zur Theologie der Logienquelle* (Münster: Aschendorff, 1972).

2. D. Lührmann, *Die Redaktion der Logienquelle* (Neukirchen–Vluyn: Neukirchener Verlag, 1969), especially pp. 40-41 n. 6.

3. It should however be noted that Lührmann himself did not argue that all the Son of Man sayings were present in Q's tradition: at least one saying (Q 11.30) is regarded by Lührmann as a redactional creation by the Q-redaction: cf. *Redaktion*, pp. 41-42. All Lührmann claimed was that *the identification of the coming Son of Man as Jesus* had already occurred in the pre-Q tradition. Lührmann's own use of the distinction between tradition and redaction is in fact far more flexible: cf. p. 202 nn. 1 and 2 below.

The view that the Son of Man sayings are all pre-redactional within Q has however been argued in great detail in an influential article by H. Schürmann.[1] Schürmann postulates a fairly uniform four-fold development of the tradition whereby individual sayings (stage 1) are interpreted by the addition of further sayings, *Kommentarworte* (stage 2) before being incorporated into slightly larger collections of sayings (stage 3) and then finally into the full speech complexes of Q (stage 4). Schürmann argues in detail that the Son of Man sayings all belong at stage 2—they act as *Kommentarworte* to individual sayings but not as comments to the larger collections of sayings in Q.

The use of the term Son of Man has also played an important role in the writings of H. Koester in relation to the history of the Q tradition.[2] Koester argues that there are many parallels between Q sayings and the *Gospel of Thomas*; however, the *Gospel of Thomas* has no parallel to any of the Q sayings which refer to the apocalyptic expectation of the Son of Man. Hence these eschatological sayings must be secondary accretions to Q. The original form of the tradition had no eschatological Son of Man. Koester also buttresses his argument by referring to Vielhauer's claim that none of the Son of Man sayings is authentic—*all* of them are secondary, post-Easter inventions of the early church.[3] Hence, according to Koester, Q and the *Gospel of Thomas* must both go back to a common, Wisdom-type 'sayings gospel', similar to (if not identical with) the kind of collection which may have been used by the Corinthians whom Paul addresses in 1 Cor.1–4.

More recent studies have tended to be similar to Schürmann's in postulating a multi-stage development in Q, and for some the Son of

---

1. H. Schürmann, 'Beobachtungen zum Menscensohntitel in der Redequelle', in R. Pesch and R. Schnackenburg (eds.) *Jesus und der Menschensohn* (Festschrift A. Vögtle; Freiburg: Herder, 1975), pp. 124-47.

2. See his early article 'One Jesus and Four Primitive Gospels', *HTR* 61 (1968), pp. 203-47, repr. in Koester and J.M. Robinson, *Trajectories through Early Christianity* (Philadelphia: Fortress Press, 1971), pp. 158-204. Most recently, Koester has restated his theories in his *Ancient Christian Gospels* (London: SCM Press, 1990), appealing for support for his general theories to Lührmann and Kloppenborg. See especially, pp. 86ff., 128ff.

3. See P. Vielhauer, 'Gottesreich und Menschensohn in der Verkündigung Jesus', and 'Jesus und der Menschensohn', in *Aufsätze zum Neuen Testament* (Munich: Chr. Kaiser Verlag, 1965), pp. 55-91 and 92-140.

Man sayings play a critical role. A. Polag[1] distinguishes at least three layers in Q with Son of Man sayings playing an important role in the distinction between at least the first two layers—in the earliest tradition (the *Primartradition*), Son of Man means simply 'a certain man' with no other overtones of meaning; later, when traditions were collected together into larger discourses and the sayings were translated into Greek (at the stage of what Polag calls the *Hauptsammlung*), the phrase took on more apocalyptic overtones, though new sayings were not actually created.

Three stages in the development of Q are also postulated by A.D. Jacobson.[2] He argues that a major 'compositional' stage in Q focussed on the theme of rejection using the Deuteronomistic scheme of the violent fate suffered by all the prophets, connected in Q with the motif of Wisdom as the sender-out of the prophets. (This stage in Jacobson's reconstruction is very similar to Lührmann's 'redactional' stage of polemic against 'this generation'.) For Jacobson, this was followed by two further stages, or redactions: an 'enthusiastic' stage stressing the importance of miracles, and a further counter-corrective in the temptation narrative. For Jacobson, however, the Son of Man sayings pre-date the Deuteronomic-Wisdom stage.[3] J.S. Kloppenborg's full-length study of Q also postulates at least three stages in Q's growth.[4] Kloppenborg agrees with Jacobson in indentifying a Deuteronomic-Wisdom stratum; but in his reconstruction, the eschatological Son of Man sayings are often *part of* this stratum which takes up (and modifies) an earlier stage in Q characterized by sapiental sayings directed to the community. Like Jacobson, Kloppenborg also sees the temptation narrative as being added in the final editing stage.

The net effect of the arguments of Lührmann, Schürmann and others has been to shift attention away from Son of Man in studies of Q's Christology. The view that Son of Man belonged only to Q's tradition was said by Neirynck in his survey of recent developments in Q

---

1. A. Polag, *Die Christologie der Logienquelle* (Neukirchen–Vluyn: Neukirchener Verlag, 1977).

2. A.D. Jacobson, *Wisdom Christology in Q* (PhD dissertation, Claremont Graduate School, 1978).

3. See also A.D. Jacobson, 'The Literary Unity of Q', *JBL* 101 (1982), pp. 365-89 (388-89).

4. Kloppenborg, *Formation, passim.*

studies in 1981 to be the 'prevailing view'.[1] The main purpose of this article will be to question how far we should relegate the Son of Man to oblivion in relation to Q's Christology. There are, however, some important preliminary problems to consider first.

II

For example, one must note that the possibility of different strata within Q raises acutely the question of what one is talking about when one refers to 'Q', or speaks for the possible significance of a Son of Man Christology in 'Q'. If, as many argue, Q underwent a series of recensions, Q^1, Q^2, Q^3 etc., then any claim that 'a Son of Man Christology is or is not important for Q' must be clarified: is such a claim being made at the level of Q^1, Q^2 or Q^3? In order to prevent ambiguity, I would suggest that one should reserve the siglum 'Q' for the form of the tradition at or near its 'final' form, that is, the form lying immediately behind the Gospels of Matthew and Luke. Stages in the 'pre-Q' tradition should then be regarded as clearly *pre*-Q, and hence not Q itself.

If that is the case then in at least one of the proposed stratifications of Q considered above, namely that of H. Koester, there is a very close relationship between a Son of Man Christology and 'Q'. For the implication of Koester's theory is that Son of Man *is* thoroughly characteristic of the 'final' stage of the editing of Q. Koester is effectively arguing for a relatively simple two-stage process in the development of Q, with an earlier 'sapiental' layer (with all the parallels in the *Gospel of Thomas*) being overtaken later by an eschatological layer (with the eschatological Son of Man sayings). This is of course quite similar in general terms to Kloppenborg's theory of the development of Q, but quite different from Schürmann's theories about the place of the Son of Man sayings in that development. For the latter, the Son of Man sayings all come in at an early stage in the development. For Koester they are effectively 'redactional' (though he does not use the term);[2] they are dismissed by Koester not because they are unimportant

1. F. Neirynck, 'Recent Developments in the Study of Q', in J. Delobel (ed.), *LOGIA: Les Paroles de Jésus—The Sayings of Jesus* (BETL, 59; Leuven: Leuven University Press, 1982), pp. 29-75 (70).

2. In turn, this makes Koester's views about the Son of Man in 'Q' significantly different from those of Lührmann, despite Koester's own claim (for

for Q, but because Koester himself is as much concerned with the pre-Q tradition as with Q itself.

One must, however, beware of ascribing too much significance to any alleged stratification of Q. If indeed 'Q' is to be regarded as Q in (approximately) its 'final' form, then one must be wary of dismissing all 'pre-Q' elements as having nothing to contribute to 'Q''s theology.[1] At the level of the study of the Gospels themselves, everyone today is aware of the danger of focusing attention exclusively on an evangelist's changes to his tradition in seeking to delineate his overall theology. Such a restriction of attention can lead to a badly distorted result, and hence any analysis of 'redaction' must include an attempt to adopt a more 'literary' approach as well, viewing the evangelist's work as a whole and accepting that a decision to include a tradition, perhaps unaltered, is potentially just as important in assessing the evangelist's theology as any redactional changes made. The same applies to 'Q'. Assigning one part of Q to 'tradition' does not mean that the Q editor(s) did not regard it as significant. The decision to include a tradition must be seen as potentially just as important as a decision to alter a tradition.[2] The latter may be important if it can be shown that the redaction has altered the views of the tradition.[3] However, if there

example in *Ancient Christian Gospels*, p. 135), to be following Lührmann. As we saw above Lührmann tends to play down the importance of the eschatological Son of Man for the Christology of Q's redactional layer.

1.   The relative importance of exclusive attention to the redaction of Q has been debated by Hoffmann and Lührmann: cf. Hoffmann, *Studien*, p. 99, and Lührmann's reply in 'Liebet eure Feinde (Lk 6, 27-36/Mt 5, 39-48)', *ZTK* 69 (1972), pp. 412-38 (423 n. 44), where he tones down his stress on the tradition/redaction distinction. I have tried to discuss the issue of the importance of the stratification of Q further in 'On the Stratification of Q', *Sem* 55 (1991), pp. 213-22.

2.   See also my *Reading the New Testament* (London: SPCK, 1987), pp. 120ff. In relation to Q specifically, see also now Lührmann, 'The Gospel of Mark and the Sayings of Source Q', *JBL* 108 (1989), pp. 51-71, on p. 60, where Lührmann clarifies his methodology considerably in stressing the importance of the whole of Q, and taking Q as a unified 'text', rather than distinguishing too sharply between tradition and redaction. Cf. too the decision of de Jonge (*Christology*, p. 73) to treat Q as undifferentiated whole in seeking to delineate the Christology of Q.

3.   Such a claim becomes particularly difficult to assert when no actual change of wording by the later editor is postulated. This is essentially the view of Polag in relation to the Son of Man sayings (cf. p. 199 n. 1 above), on which see especially the critique of A. Vögtle, 'Bezeugt die Logienquelle die authentische Redeweise Jesu vom "Menschensohn"?' *LOGIA*, pp. 77-99 (82). A methodologically similar

are no such indications then the presence of a traditional element should be allowed to contribute at least something to the views of the person(s) responsible for the final composition. In seeking to identify the views of the final editor, it may be possible at times to isolate redactional additions to earlier traditions, especially if a seam in the tradition is visible. Otherwise one may have to rely on a consideration of the text as a whole, seeing which themes and motifs dominate the whole and trying to identify elements which make a significant contribution to the literary structuring of Q in its present form.

In the next section of this article I consider some of the Son of Man sayings in Q to see if they support a theory that these sayings are less significant for the formation of Q than was claimed by, for example, Tödt.[1] Further, I shall look at a cross-section of *all* the Son of Man sayings and not confine attention only to the so-called 'eschatological' Son of Man sayings. As with the distinction between tradition and redaction in Q, one should perhaps not drive too much of a wedge between the eschatological and non-eschatological sayings. If one is considering the problem of the Son of Man in Q, and if one defines 'Q' as the 'final' stage in any development of the Q tradition, then it is clear that the Son of Man in Q is Jesus and Jesus alone. (Whether this was also the case in the pre-Q tradition is of course debated.) Further, if one may assume that, for Q, the phrase Son of Man meant something and was not a wholly meaningless cipher, then presumably the

proposal is made by Schürmann, 'Beobachtungen', p. 134, in relation to Q 11.30: in the present Q context, Son of Man must refer to the present preaching of the earthly Jesus (cf. the two references to Jonah in 11.30 and 11.32, where it is clear that in the latter Jonah is a preacher of repentance); but in the earlier tradition Son of Man must have been a eschatological judging figure. Hence the Son of Man saying in 11.30 must be earlier than the Q redactional stage which placed 11.30 alongside 11.32. But how can one know what Son of Man 'must have' meant at the earlier stage without any indication of a different wording to that of the present context where, as Schürmann says, Son of Man must refer to Jesus in his present activity? Schürmann's claim of a change in the reference is simply presupposed.

1. My approach is then very close to that of A. Yarbro Collins in her fine article 'Son of Man Sayings in the Sayings Source', in M.P. Horgan and P.J. Kopelski (eds.), *To Touch the Text* (Festschrift J.A. Fitzmyer; New York, 1989), pp. 369-89. (I am also very grateful to Professor Yarbro Collins for making a copy of her article available to me at a time when it was difficult for me to obtain the published version.) Further my results are in many respects very similar to hers, though at times the details of the arguments I offer are slightly different.

fact that some Son of Man sayings, which do not explicitly refer to eschatological activity as such, still refer to Jesus as Son of Man indicates that it is the same figure in mind who will be involved in eschatological activity.[1] Whether this is the only point of the usage of the term Son of Man (so Hoffmann) is quite another matter. But it would be foolish to try to deny that, for Q, the 'earthly Son of Man' is not also the same as the figure described in the eschatological Son of Man sayings—hence the common use of the same phrase to refer to Jesus makes it meaningful to consider the Son of Man sayings together.

III

1. *Q 6.22* (the beatitude pronouncing blessing on those suffering 'for the sake of me/the Son of Man'). It is widely agreed that Luke's 'because of the Son of Man' here is more original than Matthew's 'because of me': Luke does not appear to have a tendency to add references to Son of Man with no basis in his tradition, whereas Matthew does apparently sometimes change a Son of Man reference to a personal pronoun (cf. Mt. 10.32-33/Lk. 12.8-9; Mt. 16.21/Mk 8.31).[2] Hence Q does probably have a reference to Son of Man here.

The beatitude itself is widely regarded as separate in origin from the other three with which it is now joined in Luke/Q, being a secondary expansion of them.[3] However, even within the beatitude itself,

1. Cf. Hoffmann's critique (*Studien*, pp. 143ff.) of Tödt's theories about the significance of the present Son of Man sayings in the tradition.
2. S. Schulz, *Q—Die Spruchquelle der Evangelisten* (Zürich: Theologischer Verlag, 1972), p. 453 n. 377 with further literature; J.S. Kloppenborg, 'Blessing and Marginality: The "Persecution Beatitude" in Q, Thomas and Early Christianity', *FFNT* 2 (1986), pp. 36-56 (41). M.D. Goulder (*Luke—A New Paradigm* [Sheffield: JSOT Press, 1989], p. 353), argues that Luke has changed Matthew 'I' to Son of Man. He appeals to Luke's apparent dislike of ἕνεκεν ἐμοῦ phrases elsewhere in the tradition (cf. Mk 10.30 diff. Lk. 18.29; Mk 13.9 diff. Lk. 21.12), though Goulder admits that Luke does retain the phrase in Lk. 9.24 (= Mk. 8.35). However, the use of Son of Man is unusual for Luke. Goulder claims that this is 'the title Jesus had so far laid claim to (5.24; 6.5)'. But in Luke's story world, 'Son of God' has been far more strongly emphasized via the angelic voice of 1.35, the voice of God himself in 3.21 and in the temptation narrative of 4.1-1. Cf. too Lk. 4.41 (following Mark). A 'Son of God' reference in 6.22 would be easy to envisage as LkR; a Son of Man reference is much harder to see in this way.
3. D.R. Catchpole, 'Jesus and the Community of Israel—The Inaugural

there may be different strata visible. Many have followed O.H. Steck in seeing the final phrase in 6.23c, referring to the violence suffered by the prophets in the past, as a secondary addition to an earlier form of the beatitude.[1] It is somewhat redundant alongside v. 23b which provides a sufficient motive clause for the exhortation to rejoice in v. 23a and for the claim that those being presently persecuted are blessed. In any case these need no supplement with an additional reference to specifically prophetic suffering. There is thus a seam between v. 23b and v. 23c, and the position of 23c at the very end of the beatitude makes it probable that this is a secondary comment appended to an earlier form of the beatitude. The connection of the overall theme of the violence suffered by the prophets is well known and v. 23c is widely accepted as an important facet of the stratum of Q which emphasized this via a Deuteronomic view of history.

What though of the Son of Man reference itself? This does not occur in v. 23c but in v. 22. Schürmann sees no hiatus between vv. 22-23ab and 23c; instead he sees the whole beatitude as a secondary *Kommentarwort* added to the primary tradition of vv. 20-21. Further, since Son of Man does not occur in the rest of the Q complex (that is the section 6.20-23 + 27-35 or even 27-49) it must be part of a pre-formed unit, later adopted without change.[2] Such a theory is not altogether convincing. The lack of any explicit reference to Son of Man later in the sermon is not decisive. If we are right to allow some interplay between the eschatological and non-eschatological Son of Man sayings, then the fact that Jesus is referred to here as Son of Man implies to the reader/listener that he is also the one who will come in

---

Discourse in Q', *BJRL* (1986), pp. 296-316 (299-300) with further literature; also M.E. Boring, 'The Historical-Critical Method's "Criteria of Authenticity": The Beatitudes in Q and Thomas as a Test Case', *Sem* 44 (1988), pp. 9-44 (28ff.).

1. O.H. Steck, *Israel und das gewaltsame Geschick der Propheten* (Neukirchen–Vluyn: Neukirchener Verlag, 1967), pp. 257-60; Schulz, *Q*, p. 456 n. 404; Jacobson, *Wisdom Christology*, pp. 53-54; Kloppenborg, 'Persecution Beatitude', pp. 44-45; M. Sato, *Q und Prophetie* (Tübingen: Mohr, 1988), p. 258.

2. Schürmann, 'Beobachtungen', pp. 130-31. So too Yarbro Collins ('Son of Man Sayings', pp. 376-77) takes the beatitude as a unity. She refers to the motif of the violence suffered by the prophets as part of the argument for seeing the whole beatitude, and hence the Son of Man reference, as important for Q. However, the clear seam visible between v. 23b and v. 23c may mean that one must proceed a little more cautiously.

the future at the final judgment (cf. Q 12.40; 17.23ff.).[1] All four beatitudes are concerned with the promise of the eschatological reversal of fortunes which is promised by Jesus. This in turn correlates closely with the more negative warnings about judgment at the end of the sermon in 6.47-49. Thus the whole sermon may be seen as dominated by a grand *inclusio*, setting the whole under the rubric of eschatological promises and warnings, part of which is for Q related to Jesus' role as the coming Son of Man.[2] In any case Schürmann himself has argued that there is an integral relationship between the wording of the final beatitude in 6.22-23b and the section which probably follows in Q, that is, the section on love-of-enemies.[3] All this

1.   This is not to say necessarily that Q 6.22 should be regarded as an eschatological Son of Man saying *in toto*. Insofar as the traditional three-fold division of Son of Man sayings (into present, suffering and eschatological sayings) is valid, I would argue that 6.22 has primary reference to the present and hence should be taken as a present Son of Man saying. However the saying defies neat categorization. The 'present' of the saying refers to the time of the suffering of the disciples, probably in the post-Easter (but pre-eschatological) situation. Still, the fact that the same phrase in used in all three sets of sayings makes it not unreasonable to assume that, at least for Q which contains both present and future sayings, there is an element of overlap between the sayings. The recent discussion of D.R.A. Hare (*The Son of Man Tradition* [Minneapolis: Fortress Press, 1990]), seems to me to suffer from seeing the issue in too black-and-white terms and not to allow for any interplay between the various interpretative possibilities, or to allow for the possibility that allusions to eschatological activity might be carried by the phrase Son of Man itself in some sayings, at least in the Christian gospel tradition.

2.   I would prefer this more general idea to Catchpole's suggestion of a very specifically *christological inclusio*, whereby the Son of Man reference in 6.22 correlates with the reference to Jesus as Κύριος in 6.46 which is in turn to be related to the references in Q 12.42-46 and 19.11-27 where the κύριος figure of the parables is defined as the Son of Man (cf. Q 12.39-40). There is certainly eschatological warning at the end of the Great Sermon in 6.47-49; but the reference in 6.46 is more plausibly seen to Jesus as the authoritative *present* speaker who demands obedience now. However, the existence of such an *inclusio* may answer the criticism of Hare (*Son of Man*, pp. 219-20), who argues that the eschatological Son of Man cannot have been that important for Q if no such reference appears in the eschatological section of the great programmatic discourse in Q, *viz.* Q 6.46-49. The answer must be that 6.46-49 is not to be seen in isolation within the discourse, but precisely by the literary arrangement of the redactor, is related strongly to the opening beatitudes, *with* the reference to Jesus as Son of Man!

3.   For the verbal and conceptual links here, see his *Das Lukasevangelium* (Freiburg: Herder, 1969), p. 346; see also Lührmann, 'Liebet eure Feinde', pp. 414-15.

suggests that the beatitude as a whole, with the Son of Man reference, plays an important role within the much wider Q context. As such it is hard to see it as simply a traditional vestige with no significance for Q's final composition.

In a recent article devoted to this beatitude, Kloppenborg has argued that the Son of Man clause may also be secondary to the rest.[1] In earlier studies Kloppenborg appeared to argue that only v. 23c was secondary, with the residue as part of his 'sapiental stratum' in Q[2] (though whether it is appropriate to regard the very eschatologically-oriented beatitudes as really 'sapiental' is somewhat doubtful)[3]. In his more recent article, however, Kloppenborg (following Colpe) assigns the Son of Man phrase in v. 22 to a secondary development (though whether this is at the same stage as v. 23c is not clarified); the rest of the beatitude Kloppenborg sees as plausible within the context of the pre-Easter Jesus.[4] Colpe, however, argues that 'because of me' was the earliest form of the tradition, which was then later changed to a 'because of the Son of Man'. But the 'I' form is more naturally explained as MattR and there is no other example of a 'for the sake of the Son of Man' being added to a tradition secondarily. In any case the ἕνεκεν phrase is in some respects essential to the beatitude in order to specify that those addressed are being persecuted and ostracized because of their commitment to Jesus.[5] Thus some equivalent to the ἕνεκεν phrase seems essential to make this clear (unless, of course, it is implied in the second person address: Jesus' disciples, not any who suffer social ostracism, are called blessed). Thus Kloppenborg's suggestion of an original beatitude lacking such a clause seems unconvincing.

Standard critical opinion is that the beatitude is a post-Easter formulation, reflecting the situation of Christians suffering in some way for their faith. However, the beatitude has undergone one gloss in v. 23c and hence must pre-date the gloss itself. Verse 23c is most plausibly to be assigned to a Q-editorial stage in the light of the prominence of the theme of prophetic suffering elsewhere in Q. Hence

1. Kloppenborg, 'Persecution Beatitude'.
2. Cf. Kloppenborg, *Formation*, p. 173; also his 'The Formation of Q and Antique Instructional Genres', *JBL* 105 (1986), pp. 443-62 (452).
3. *Pace* Kloppenborg, *Formation*, pp. 188-89.
4. Kloppenborg, 'Persecution Beatitude', pp. 45-46. Cf. C. Colpe, ὁ υἱὸς τοῦ ἀνθρώπου, *TWNT*, VIII, p. 446 n. 308.
5. See Sato, *Q und Prophetie*, p. 258.

the tradition must have included the Son of Man saying. However, the structural importance which the beatitude now has in the wider Q context shows that the Son of Man is clearly still of central importance at the stage when much larger units in Q were being formed—and that stage cannot be easily distinguished from the stage of the final editing of Q.

2. *Q 9.58* ('Foxes have holes and the birds of the air have nests but the Son of Man has nowhere to lay his head'). Schürmann sees this saying as a *Kommentarwort* prefixed to the double saying in Q 9.59-62.[1] However, it is doubtful whether 9.61-62 belonged to Q at all (and the verses contain a significant number of Lukanisms).[2] Many would agree that 9.59-60, especially v. 60, stem from the earliest stage of the tradition with very strong claims to authenticity.[3] If so, Schürmann may well be right to the extent that 9.57-58 is a secondary comment added to an earlier 9.59-60. However, the present order of the sayings—with vv. 57-58 before vv. 59-60 (an order attested in both Matthew and Luke and hence probably in Q)—suggests that this is not just a case of a *Kommentarwort* interpreting a single saying. Most likely the change in order serves to make the Son of Man saying function as an introduction to the whole mission discourse which follows.[4] The homeless Son of Man with nowhere to lay his head thus functions as the exemplary paradigm for the disciples who are called by Jesus to go out without provisions, dependent on the hospitality of others and open to rejection. The Son of Man saying may well be secondary, at least at the level of its time of entry into the wider context. However, contra Schürmann, this secondary position seems to be of great significance in the structuring of the 'final' form of Q and hence of great importance for Q's composition.

3. *Q 12.8-9 + 12.10* ('Whoever confesses me before men, I/the Son of Man will confess...' + 'whoever speaks a word against the Son of

1. Schürmann, 'Beobachtungen', pp. 132-33.

2. Kloppenborg, *Q Parallels* (Sonoma, CA: Polebridge Press, 1988), p. 64, gives a good summary of the arguments for and against, with references to other literature.

3. See M. Hengel, *The Charismatic Leader and his Followers* (Edinburgh: T. & T. Clark, 1981).

4. J. Wanke, '"Kommentarworte": Äleste Kommentierungen von Herrenworten', *BZ* 24 (1980), pp. 208-33 (216); Sato; *Q und Prophetie*, p. 37; Yarbro Collins, 'Son of Man Sayings', p. 337. It will be seen that I follow Yarbro Collins' analysis closely here.

Man will be forgiven...'). The problems raised by these sayings are legion and they cannot be dealt with in full here. Most agree that Luke's form of 12.8, the Son of Man, is more likely to preserve the Q wording than Matthew's 'I' form;[1] also Luke's order probably best represents the order of the sayings in Q. Many too have argued that 12.4-7 may have constituted a primitive unit (with its own history of development[2]) which has been expanded by the sayings in 12.8-9 at one stage. The well-known aporia between 12.8-9 (where present attitudes to Jesus appear to have decisive, eschatological significance) and 12.10 (where opposition to the Son of Man [who presumably is Jesus] is forgivable)[3] may be explicable (at one level anyway) if 12.10 is a later secondary comment appended to 12.4-9 partly on the basis of a Stichwort connection with 12.8. So far then this would support Schürmann's theory whereby the Son of Man saying in 12.8-9 is a *Kommentarwort*, added secondarily to an earlier tradition but prior to the final editing.

1.   Schulz, *Q*, p. 68 n. 66, and many others. Goulder (*Luke*, p. 530) thinks that Luke changed Matthew's wording under the influence of Mt. 16.27, thereby introducing the Son of Man and the 'angels'. This seems very unlikely. Mt. 16.27 appears to exercise no influence on Luke when Luke deals with Mk 8.38 (the Markan parallels to Mt. 16.27), so it is difficult to envisage why Matthean influence should take place here. Why too should any change of Mt. 10.32 be regarded by Luke as necessary at all? Goulder refers to Son of Man as the more 'numinous' term—but does Luke elsewhere prefer more 'numinous' christological terminology? And does *Luke* regard Son of Man as 'numinous'?
    Another recent attempt to defend the originality of the Matthean wording is that of P. Hoffmann, 'Jesus versus Menschensohn', in L. Oberlinner and P. Fiedler (eds.), *Salz der Erde—Licht der Welt* (Festschrift A. Vögtle; Stuttgart: Katholisches Bibelwerk, 1991), pp. 165-202. Hoffmann argues that Son of Man would have fitted Matthew's purposes well if it were in his source, and that Luke's change can be explained by Luke's adapting the tradition in line with his belief that the Son of Man is constantly ready to be witnessing on behalf of Christians being martyred (cf. Acts 7.58). Hoffmann makes a powerful case. Yet his theory has to assume coincidental, but independent, redaction of the saying by Mark (cf. Mk 8.38) and Luke into a Son of Man form; further, Luke uses the Markan *Son of Man* form of the saying with clear reference to the Parousia in Lk. 9.26, from which it is most natural to assume that Luke interprets Lk. 12.8 in the same way.
2.   Cf. D. Zeller, *Die weisheitliche Mahnsprüche bei den Synoptikern* (Würzburg: Echter Verlag, 1977), pp. 94ff.; R.A. Piper, *Wisdom in the Q-Tradition* (Cambridge: Cambridge University Press, 1989), pp. 52ff.
3.   See Kloppenburg, *Formation*, pp. 211-14 for a clear statement of the problems.

But can one then deny that 12.10 is part of the final compositional
stage in Q? Schürmann denies any connection between v. 10 and
vv. 2-3 which introduce the unit. But it is just as plausible to see v. 10
as connected with vv. 2-3 in order to make the whole unit relate more
specifically to Christian preaching.[1] If (as many assume) the contrast
implied in v. 10 between speaking against the Son of Man and
speaking against the Holy Spirit is a contrast between the pre- and
post-Easter situations of the disciples,[2] then this would correlate well
with the concerns of vv. 2-3 which stress the contrast between the
present (in context, pre-Easter) situation of hiddenness, secrecy,
darkness and whispering, and the future (that is post-Easter) situation
of clear, unambiguous proclamation.[3]

(I find it hard to accept Kloppenborg's claim that vv. 8-9 and v. 10
constitute secondary expansions of a community-directed speech, added
in the same stratum of the tradition and making prophetic threats against
outsiders.[4] Those addressed in v. 9 are not necessarily 'opponents', but
people who are facing the same opposition as the Christian confessors of
v. 8 but who do not have the necessary boldness: the language of
'denying' seems to presuppose a prior commitment on the part of those
addressed.[5] Verse 10 seems to be directed to more active opponents of
the Christian movement. Kloppenborg may be making the 'polemical'
stratum of Q too uniform. The polemic of Q is directed quite as much
against waverers and those who would claim to be disinterested and
neutral as against any active opponents of the Christian cause.)

Many would see 12.10 as exercising some interpretative role on
12.8-9, perhaps qualifying and correcting it to assert that whilst
rejection of the earthly Jesus by Jewish opponents in the past was not
decisive, rejection of the disciples' preaching in the post-Easter situation
is.[6] This would cohere well with other parts of Q which stress the

---

1. See Yarbro Collins, 'Son of Man Sayings', p. 379.
2. So e.g. Tödt, *Son of Man*, p. 119; Schulz, *Q*, p. 248; Hoffmann, *Studien*,
p. 152, and many others.
3. The close connection of v. 10 with vv. 2-3 seems to me to make it more sen-
sible to take the unit in Q as vv. 2-10, rather than try to relate vv. 2-3 to vv. 8-9 as
Piper (*Wisdom*) pp. 58-59, does.
4. *Formation*, pp. 206ff.
5. Cf. H. Schlier 'ἀρνέομαι', *TWNT* I, p. 409: 'Verleugnung kann nur dort
stattfinden, wo vorher Anerkennung und Verpflichtung bestanden hat'.
6. Cf. Hoffmann, *Studien*, p. 152; Schürmann, 'Beobachtungen', p. 137 and
others.

importance of the disciples' preaching: cf. Q 10.16 and indeed the whole of the mission discourse in Q 10.2-12, where the disciples are bidden to continue Jesus' preaching of the imminence of the Kingdom.[1] Given the close correlation between v. 10 and vv. 2-3, there is thus little to stand in the way of the theory that v. 10 has been added in Q at a final stage of the development of the tradition, exercising a significant role in the composition of the wider unit and correlating with other important parts of Q. By contrast 12.8-9 may be present already in the pre-Q tradition though its concerns cohere well with other parts of Q: the implied attack on the neutral, the wavering and the uncommitted can be paralleled from a number of other Q passages, for example, Q 6.46; 11.23; 11.24-26;[2] 13.26; 17.27[3]. Thus Son of Man is part of both the pre-redactional stage (v. 8-9) and the compositional stage (v. 10). And for those who would see the distinction as significant, it is the eschatological Son of Man which is the earlier of the two.

4. *Q 12.40* ('The Son of Man is coming at an hour you do not expect') It is quite likely that the parable of the thief in the night together with its interpretation may be composite. Verse 40 represents an application of the parable which is not entirely apposite and hence may be a secondary addition to the parable.[4] Schürmann argues that the verse functions as a conclusion only to the smaller unit comprising Lk. 12.35-39 which he takes as Q.[5]

The issue of whether Lk. 12.35-38 belonged (perhaps in part) to Q is perhaps not an insignificant issue here. In view of the reminiscences of this parable in Matthew's version of the parable of the thief with the note about the 'watch' in which the thief is coming (Mt. 24.43 cf.

---

1. Indeed one could say that the very existence of Q itself is a witness to the crucial importance for the Q Christians of the continuation of Jesus' preaching in the post-Easter situation by the later disciples.

2. Cf. R. Laufen, *Die Doppelüberlieferungen der Logienquelle und des Markusevangeliums* (Bonn: Peter Hanstein, 1980), pp. 144-47.

3. Cf. D.R. Catchpole, 'The Son of Man's Search for Faith (Luke xviii.8b)', *NovT* 19 (1977), pp. 81-104 (85); and my *Revival*, pp. 169-70. I hope to develop this aspect of the background to the Q material in a forthcoming study of Q.

4. Schürmann, 'Beobachtungen', p. 138; Kloppenborg, *Formation*, pp. 149-50 with further literature. Cf. the discrepancy between the parable, which talks of a theft being prevented by being prepared and watching, and the interpretation, which talks of the coming of the Son of Man whose coming cannot be prevented.

5. Schürmann, 'Beobachtungen', p. 138.

Lk. 12.38) and the note about staying awake (Mt. 24.43 cf. Lk. 12.37), it is indeed quite plausible that Lk. 12.35-38 did (at least in part) belong to Q.[1] On the other hand, part of the argument for such a theory is that the parable coheres so well with other Q material that, at one level, not a great deal is gained for understanding Q by including the parable: it simply confirms the picture already established.

However, the presence of the parable in Q may imply the existence of a rather more extended section of parabolic teaching here in Q on a single subject, and this in turn must imply that the subject is of some importance for the editor responsible for the present form of Q. Schürmann claims that Lk. 12.35-39 + 12.40 was subsequently expanded by the parable in 12.42-46 at a later stage in the development of Q. This is, however, simply asserted by Schürmann and there seems to be little direct evidence. In fact 12.40 coheres extremely closely with 12.42-46 in terms of subject matter—both concern the unexpected return of the Son of Man (12.40)/the master (κύριος) of the story (12.42-46) which will involve potential disaster for those who are unprepared.[2] It seems therefore much more economical to see 12.40 as added at the same time as 12.42-46 and, given the way in which the theme covered here runs through the whole of this substantial section in Q, to assign this to the stage of Q's 'final' composition. The Son of Man saying in 12.40 is thus important for Q's redaction and cannot be dismissed as only of significance at a pre-redactional stage.

5. *Q 17.23-24 + 26-30* (the comparison of the day(s) of the Son of Man with lightning [v. 24] and with the time of Noah and Lot [vv. 26-30]). This section of Q also raises a host of exegetical problems, not all of which can be discussed here. I remain convinced that in vv. 23-24 we do indeed have Q material and that the statement of the false opinions expressed in v. 23 ('Lo here! Lo there!') did form part of Q

1. See my *Revival*, pp. 181-82.

2. This is simply noted as just one possibility by Yarbro Collins ('Son of Man Sayings', p. 381), who would then see this as an 'allegorizing interpretation'. The other possibility she mentions is that the unit appears here via a catchword association (via 'thief') with the preceding saying about treasure in Q 12.33-34. Collins is uneasy about ascribing Lk. 12.35-38 to Q. But if one does take this as Q, then the whole section comprising Lk. 12.35-46 becomes a unit of appreciable length with its own internal coherence and unity of theme, viz. the coming of the master (= Jesus as the Son of Man) in a scene which will involve judgment. With this in mind, Q 12.40 is an integral part of the whole sequence which, by virtue of its size, must have considerable significance for the composition of Q in its present form.

and is not just a Markan vestige in Matthew and Luke.[1] The situation is complicated by the existence of a Markan doublet of the saying though one must beware of confusing the issues of authenticity (in relation to Jesus) and relative priority (within possible strata of Q). In absolute terms it may well be that the appended 'lightning' saying in Q 17.24 is secondary in the sense of being undominical. The false opinions seem to relate to specifically messianic expectations, whereas the lightning saying confronts these expectations with an assertion about the nature of the coming of the Son of Man.[2] Further, there is no indication that the change in reference is a deliberate part of the saying (as if it said 'you are looking for a messianic figure, but the one who will come will be the Son of Man'). Rather, the contrast is between the manner of the coming of what is assumed to be the same figure: the one expected will not come 'here' or 'there' but in an unmistakeable way. Thus it may be that the Q saying in v. 24 is a post-Easter addition to the tradition, presupposing the identification of Jesus as both messiah and Son of Man.[3] However, a post-Easter origin does not determine the place of the saying within the development of Q.

Many have argued that, unlike the situation elsewhere in Q, it is Matthew who may preserve the more original Q order here by placing the 'vultures' saying immediately after the lightning saying: Luke may have objected to the association of the coming of the Son of Man with vultures, and the Lukan introduction to the saying in v. 37 (ποῦ) may be a reflection of the original Q context which concerned the place of the Son of Man's coming.[4] If so it may be that the vulture saying acts as a *Kommentarwort* to the lightning saying preceding it,[5] even if the lightning saying itself may be a Kommentarwort on v. 23.

What then of the relationship between the Son of Man saying in vv. 23-24 and the Son of Man sayings in vv. 26-30?[6] In an earlier study I

---

1. Cf. the doublet in Mt. 24.23, 26. For this as part of Q, cf. Schulz, *Q*, pp. 278-79; Kloppenborg, *Formation*, p. 155; full bibliography in Laufen, *Doppelüber-lieferungen*, p. 361.

2. Kloppenborg, *Formation*, pp.159-60.

3. Cf. Vielhauer, *Aufsätze*, p.75.

4. Kloppenborg, *Formation*, p. 156; D.R. Catchpole, 'The Law and the Prophets in Q', in G.F. Hawsthorne and O. Betz (eds.), *Tradition and Interpretation in the New Testament* (Festschrift E.E. Ellis; Grand Rapids: Eerdmans, 1987), pp. 95-109 (103); Piper, *Wisdom*, p. 139.

5. Yarbro Collins, 'Son of Man Sayings', p. 379.

6. I remain convinced that the Lot saying in vv. 28-30 was part of Q: see my

argued that vv. 23-24 (+ 37) + 26-30 should be seen as an integral
whole, stressing the theme of the suddenness of the coming of the Son
of Man.[1] In particular I argued against the view of Schürmann who
claimed that vv. 26-30 describe the coming of the Son of Man as
judgmental, in contrast to vv. 23-24. I would still wish to argue that
vv. 23-24 + 37 + 26-30 constitute a coherent unity focusing on the
theme of suddenness, but I have been persuaded by the arguments of
Piper and Catchpole that there is a slight shift of emphasis from
vv. 23-24 to vv. 26-30, from geographical to temporal concerns,[2]
from an assertion of universal visibility to one of suddenness.
However, both Catchpole and Piper concede that the lightning saying
and the vulture saying can and do cohere reasonably well into the
wider Q context which is concerned with the sudden unexpected
coming of the Son of Man in judgment. The best explanation of this
small shift of emphasis is that vv. 23-24 comes from an earlier
tradition, and is taken up by a later editor and pressed into service
within a wider composition with a slightly different emphasis.[3]
Further, the concerns of the wider composition cohere very closely
with other parts of Q, notably 12.39-46 (or perhaps Lk. 12.35-38 + Q
12.39-46), which also stress the sudden unexpected nature of the Son
of Man's coming.[4] These thematic links make it hard to deny that it is

Revival, p.169; Catchpole, 'Law and Prophets', p. 102. I find it therefore unnecessary to postulate a post-Q expansion of the Q-tradition in Luke's form of the latter
(cf. Lührmann, *Redaktion*, p. 74; Yarbro Collins, 'Son of Man Sayings', p. 380).

    1. Tuckett, *Revival*, pp. 172-73.
    2. Catchpole, 'Law and Prophets', p. 105; Piper, *Wisdom*, p. 141.
    3. It is just this slight shift of emphasis that perhaps gives greater weight to the
claim that the Noah (and probably Lot) sayings represent a secondary addition within
the growth of Q. Collins ('Son of Man Sayings', p. 380) appears to take the Noah
saying as effectively parallel to the earlier lightning saying, formed by analogy with
it, and hence (apparently) secondary. But the fact that the lightning saying itself may
be secondary (in relation to the question it responds to), and the apparent coherence
(according to Yarbro Collins) between the lightning saying and the Noah saying,
then makes it difficult to distinguish the two in terms of their relatives dates within
the growth of Q. It is precisely the slight unevenness visible between the two sayings
which enables the layers to be detected.
    4. See my *Revival*, p. 182.

this concern which is of primary importance for the Q-editor(s), that is, those responsible for the editing and composition of the final form of Q.

IV

The results emerging from 17.23ff. are typical for the whole of Q. Son of Man sayings appear embedded in Q at all stages of the tradition insofar as these are visible to us. Son of Man *is* a feature of Q's redaction/composition (cf. Q 17.26-30; 11.30;[1] the composition of the Sermon on the Mount; the programmatic use of Q 9.58 in relation to the mission charge). Son of Man is also present in the traditions used by the Q-editor(s) (cf. Q 6.22; 17.23-24). Contra Koester one cannot ascribe all the Son of Man sayings, nor even just the eschatological Son of Man sayings (cf. Q 17.23-24!) to a later strand within Q. Contra Schürmann, one cannot write off Son of Man from the '*Endredaktion*' of Q (unless one can identify such a stage much more precisely and distinguish it more clearly from earlier stages in the composition of Q.)[2] Son of Man *is* important for Q and hence Tödt's claim of long ago about the importance (in general terms) of a Son of Man Christology for Q may still be justified (even if his more precise suggestions about the identification between Jesus and the Son of Man being first made by the Q Christians is more debatable). What this analysis does not do is give any support to the view that any of the non-eschatological Son of Man sayings go back to the earliest forms of the tradition—but that is another story.

1.   Although I have not analysed the saying here, I would agree with Lührmann (cf. p. 197 n. 3 above) and others, that Q 11.30 is a redactional creation by Q to link the tradition about the rejection of the sign with that of the double saying Q 11.31-32 involving (in part) Jonah.

2.   Cf. Neirynck's rhetorical question in relation to Schürmann's theories: 'If these larger complexes [in Q] are all pre-redactional...what is then the *Endredaktion?*' ('Recent Developments', p. 71). The final stage in Q is often thought to include (perhaps only) the addition of the Temptation narrative. I have tried to discuss this issue in 'The Temptation Narrative in Q', in F. van Segbroek *et al.*, (eds.), *The Four Gospels 1992* (Festschrift F. Neirynck; BETL, 100; Leuven: Leuven University Press, 1992), pp. 479-507, arguing that there is no need to see this story as a later addition within Q.

'BEGINNING WITH MOSES AND FROM ALL THE PROPHETS'

Morna D. Hooker

I

In his account of the encounter between the Risen Christ and two
disciples on the Emmaus road, Luke tells us how, 'beginning from
Moses and from all the prophets, [Jesus] explained to them in the
whole of scripture the things concerning himself' (Lk. 24.27). There is
no doubt that Scripture plays a significant role in Luke's understanding
of Jesus, though its importance is not always immediately apparent,
because there are far more scriptural allusions than quotations in his
writings. In this essay I shall confine myself to the Gospel, and
concentrate on those passages which are specifically Lukan.

The first two chapters of Luke's Gospel highlight the problem of
tracing Old Testament influence: the whole section is clearly saturated
in Old Testament ideas and phraseology, yet there is no specific quotation. These two chapters, often referred to as 'the birth narratives',
are perhaps better described as the prologue to the Gospel—like the
equivalent chapters in Matthew and the opening verses of Mark and
John, they provide us with key information as to who Jesus is, information which will enable us, the readers, to comprehend the rest of
the Gospel, but which is hidden from almost all the participants in the
story.[1] Not surprisingly, there is a difference between all these introductory sections and what follows—a difference so marked in the case
of Luke and John that there has been considerable debate as to
whether they are in fact later additions to the story. In all four
Gospels, the truth about Jesus is unfolded in these chapters, and we
learn that he is the Christ, the Son of God. Each of the evangelists

---

1.　See M.D. Hooker, 'The Beginning of the Gospel', in A.J. Malherbe and W.
Meeks (eds.), *The Future of Christology: Essays in Honor of Leander E. Keck*
(Minneapolis: Fortress Press, 1993), pp. 18-28.

emphasizes that the coming of Christ is the fulfilment of past hopes and promises, though each of them does so in a different way: Mark introduces the Gospel with a quotation which he attributes to Isaiah; John opens with a clear allusion to Gen. 1.1, and writes what we may perhaps term a 'midrash' on Gen. 1.1-5 and Exod. 33.12–34.8;[1] Matthew quotes five passages in full, introducing each with a 'fulfilment' formula;[2] and what Matthew does in a somewhat heavy-handed way, Luke does in a much more agile fashion, using Old Testament imagery and vocabulary. Although there is no specific reference to the scriptures in the first two chapters of Luke, there is no mistaking the fact that the language—in particular, the language used by Gabriel and by men and women filled with the Holy Spirit—is reminiscent of that used in the Septuagint. Some of the events echo Old Testament stories (notably, the story of Hannah and Elkanah in 1 Samuel 1–2) or spell out the fulfilment of Old Testament hopes.

In emphasizing the importance of chs. 1–2 for understanding Luke's Gospel, I am clearly disagreeing with Conzelmann, who ignores these two chapters in his interpretation of Luke's theology.[3] But it is precisely because he leaves these two chapters on one side in his analysis that he is led to the conclusion that Luke is making sharp divisions between the three epochs of history—those of Israel, the ministry of Jesus and the church. In fact, Luke seems go out of his way to stress the links between the epochs, first, by emphasizing that the Scriptures were fulfilled in the birth, life, death and resurrection of Jesus, and secondly, by indicating that the mission of the apostles mirrored that of Jesus himself.

These first two chapters fulfil another function, however, for they look forward as well as back. Luke's use of scriptural allusions serves to assure us that what happens in Jesus is the continuation of God's work in the past and the fulfilment of his promises, but these same

1. P. Borgen, 'Observations on the Targumic character of the Prologue of John', *NTS* 16 (1970), pp. 288-95; M.D. Hooker, 'John's Prologue and the Messianic Secret', *NTS* 21 (1974), pp. 40-58.

2. Mt. 1.22-23; 2.5-6,15,17-18, 23. A similar formula is used six times in the rest of the Gospel, at 4.14; 8.17;12.17;13.14, 35; 21.4; 27.9.

3. H. Conzelmann, *The Theology of Saint Luke* (London: Faber, 1960). Contrast P. S. Minear, 'Luke's Use of the Birth Stories' in L.E. Keck and J.L. Martyn (eds.), *Studies in Luke–Acts: Essays Presented in Honor of Paul Schubert* (Nashville: Abingdon Press, 1966; London: SPCK, 1968), pp. 111-30; S. Farris, *The Hymns of Luke's Infancy Narratives* (JSNTSup, 9; Sheffield: JSOT Press, 1985), pp. 151-60.

allusions act as prophecies of what is to come, for the words of
Gabriel and of the men and women who are inspired by the Holy
Spirit describe what the ministry of Jesus will achieve.[1]

Even though the only words in Luke 1–2 italicized in Nestle–Aland's
26th edition of the Greek New Testament as an Old Testament
quotation are those taken from Num. 6.3 and applied to John the
Baptist in 1.15, therefore, these two chapters are of great importance
for understanding Luke's approach to the Old Testament. What we
learn here is that the time of Israel's salvation has arrived; that John
the Baptist will prepare the way of the Lord, as did Elijah of old; that
Jesus will be called the Son of the Most High; that he will inherit the
throne of David, and that his kingdom will have no end; that he is
born through the power of the Holy Spirit; that his coming involves
the putting of things to rights, which will mean the reversal of fortunes for high and low; that through him the promises made to
Abraham will be fulfilled. The focus throughout is on Jesus, and the
echoes of the Old Testament are thus christological.

This brief summary of the themes of Luke 1–2 reminds us of how
very Jewish these chapters are: Jesus is the fulfilment of Jewish hopes.
Moreover, it is only in 2.32, where Simeon speaks of a light which
brings revelation to Gentiles, that we find a hint that the coming of
Jesus will mean their salvation. This Jewishness is something of a
surprise in what is often described as a 'Gentile' Gospel, and may
seem to provide support for those who believe that the introductory
chapters are a later addition. In fact, however, when we examine the
rest of the book carefully, we find that it contains very little about
salvation for the Gentiles. It is true that there are hints of that theme,
but they are only hints, and almost all of them are promises for the
future.[2] It is not until the very end of the Gospel, at 24.47, that the

1. Cf. P. Schubert, 'The Structure and Significance of Luke 24', in
Neutestamentliche Studien für Rudolf Bultmann (BZNW, 21; Berlin: Töpelmann,
1954), pp. 165-86.

2. Exceptions are the stories of the healing of the Roman centurion's servant in
7.1-10, and of the Samaritan leper in 17.11-19; the demoniac in 8.26-39 may also
have been understood to be a Gentile. Other hints are found at 3.6, where 'all flesh'
is to see the salvation of God, in 4.16-30, where Jesus refers to Elijah and Elisha
assisting Gentiles, and in the story Jesus tells in 10.30-37 about a good Samaritan.
Those who flock into the kingdom of God in 13.28-30 could be Gentiles, as could
those who receive a late invitation to the dinner party in 14.15-24 and the 'others' to
whom the vineyard is given in 20.16, though Luke may have understood any of

theme is brought out into the open with the command of the Risen Christ to his disciples to preach to all nations. Significantly, Luke omits the whole of Mark 7, which contains Jesus' teaching about clean and unclean food and the healing of the Syro-Phoenician woman's daughter. It would seem as though Luke has deliberately saved references to Gentiles for his second volume, where their response to the gospel becomes the dominant theme. Because he has two books, he is able to spell out how the gospel was preached to the Jew first, and subsequently to the Gentiles.[1]

In view of this emphasis on the fulfilment of Jewish promises, it is no surprise to find that Jesus is said to have been born in Bethlehem: even though Luke's account of how this came about seems most unlikely, it is clear that all is done in order that Jesus should be a true son of David. Following his circumcision, Jesus is taken to Jerusalem to be presented to the Lord. Describing what took place in the temple, Luke points out no fewer than five times that what was done there was in accordance with the prescriptions of the law.[2] Thus he presents Jesus as a quintessential Jew, born of David's line, in the city of David, and from his birth obedient to the Mosaic law.

It has sometimes been argued that this picture is in conflict with the rest of the Gospel. S.G. Wilson, for example, came to the conclusion that Luke is confused on the issue of the law, and 'presents Jesus as sometimes opposed to and sometimes in league with the law'.[3] It seems to us, however, that Luke himself sees no conflict between Jesus and the law. In 4.1-13 he includes the story of the temptation, in which Jesus rebuts Satan's attack by appealing three times to Deuteronomy. Although in subsequent chapters Jesus (and his disciples) are accused by the Jewish authorities of breaking the law, the real cause of these disputes is the interpretation of the law. Thus in 6.9, and again in 14.3, Jesus poses the question 'Is it lawful to heal on the sabbath?', and

---

these to refer to Jewish outsiders. Although the 'seventy' or 'seventy-two' in 10.1 are often interpreted as missionaries to the Gentiles, Luke appears to have thought of them as having been sent through Jewish territory!

1.   Acts 13.46; cf. Rom.1.16.

2.   The phrase κατὰ τὸν νόμον (or a variant) is used in 2.22, 27 and 39, ἐν (τῷ) νόμῳ Κυρίου in vv. 23 and 24.

3.   S.G. Wilson, *Luke and the Law* (Cambridge: Cambridge University Press, 1983), p. 57.

it is clear that the implied answer is 'yes'.[1] On two occasions, prominent
Jews come to Jesus asking how they might inherit eternal life. On the
first occasion (10.25-28), Jesus throws the question back, asking 'What
is written in the law? How do you understand it?' When his questioner
replies with a summary of the law, to the effect that one must love
God and love one's neighbour as oneself, Jesus gives his approval.
When the question is put a second time (18.18-27), Jesus himself
replies by reciting the last five commandments. Clearly there is no
contradiction between the law and Jesus in either passage. Yet the
teaching of Jesus makes new demands which go beyond those of the
law. In the first story, we find him making the requirements of the
law more stringent in the parable of the Good Samaritan, told in
response to the question 'Who is my neighbour?' (10.29ff.). In the
second, when his questioner claims to have kept the commandments
from his youth, he is told to give all his possessions to the poor and
follow Jesus: if he wishes to enter the kingdom of heaven, obedience
to the law is insufficient.

A very similar picture emerges in Mark, where Jesus is presented as
faithful to the law, but in disagreement with the religious authorities
over its interpretation.[2] In Mark, however, there are two passages
where Jesus apparently challenges the teaching of the law itself. The
first occurs in Mark 7, where Jesus responds to the Pharisees' criticism of his disciples for eating with unwashed hands by accusing his
opponents of concentrating on human traditions and neglecting the
commandments of God; afterwards, when the disciples question Jesus
in private, he spells out the significance of his teaching, and Mark adds
the comment 'By saying this he declared all foods clean' (v.19),
showing that he understood Jesus to be challenging the law itself (not
simply human tradition), by doing away with kosher food.[3] The
second is in Mark 10, where Jesus responds to the Pharisees' question
about divorce by setting the divine command in Gen. 2.24 above the
Mosaic provision in Deut. 24.1; the final saying, in v. 9, prohibits

---

1.   Cf. 13.10-17.
2.   Cf. M.D. Hooker, 'Mark', in D.A. Carson and H.G.M. Williamson (eds.), *It
is Written: Scripture Citing Scripture: Essays in Honour of Barnabas Lindars*
(Cambridge: Cambridge University Press 1988), pp. 220-30.
3.   The fact that the teaching was delivered in private to the disciples suggests
that whatever we may decide about the rest of the passage, the interpretation in
vv. 17-23 belongs to the period of the church.

what Moses allowed. In vv. 11-12, Mark again describes private teaching given to the disciples, in which Jesus declares that a man (or a woman!) who takes advantage of the Mosaic provision that a man may divorce his wife is guilty of adultery if he marries someone else. When we turn back to Luke, however, we find that he has omitted the first of these passages altogether—a surprising omission, if Luke was using Mark as a source, since teaching about clean and unclean clearly backs up the Church's decisions about table-fellowship with Gentiles in Acts. We have noted already, however, that Luke prefers to save this development in understanding for his second volume. The question about divorce and Jesus' response are also missing from Luke; only the saying in Mk 10.11-12 survives, in Lk. 16.18. But the very different context given to it by Luke indicates that he does not regard it as in any sense challenging the law, for it follows immediately after the statement that 'it is easier for heaven and earth to pass away, than for one letter of the law to lose its force'. Since heaven and earth have not passed away, this saying must be understood (*pace* the contortions of various commentators!) as an affirmation that Jesus maintains the authority of the law, in spite of the arrival of the kingdom of God (v.16). In this particular instance, the coming of the kingdom tightens the demands of the law by forbidding remarriage after divorce.

It would seem, then, that Luke's portrayal of Jesus in his Gospel corresponds with his insistence in ch. 2 that everything following his birth was done in accordance with the law.

II

Many of the Old Testament quotations used by Luke are found also in Matthew and Mark: a full investigation would need to consider whether there are significant variations.[1] The two most interesting concern quotations from Isaiah, the first in 3.4-6, where Luke extends the passage from Isaiah 40 cited by Matthew and Mark; the extra lines stress the significance of what is taking place and point forward to the salvation which will be seen by the whole of humanity. The second occurs in Lk. 8.10, where instead of the quotation of Isa. 6.9-10 found in Mk 4.12 we have only an echo of Isaiah: ἵνα βλέποντες μὴ

1. Cf. C.K. Barrett, 'Luke', in *It is Written: Scripture Citing Scripture*, pp. 231-44.

βλέπωσιν καὶ ἀκούοντες μὴ συνιῶσιν. In Matthew, by contrast, where the quotation is attributed to Isaiah, it is considerably extended (13.14-15). But Luke makes use of the full quotation elsewhere, for it occurs at the climax of the story he tells in his second volume—in Acts 28.26-27 it forms Paul's final comment on his own preaching and on the failure of the Jewish people to respond to the gospel. Those who see without perceiving and who hear without comprehending are no longer Jesus' contemporaries, but the Jews of the next generation who reject Paul's message, and that which is hidden from them is now given, not to the disciples, but to the Gentiles (v. 28). As elsewhere, the fact that Luke wrote two volumes appears to have enabled him to avoid using something in the context of the ministry of Jesus which is more appropriate within the life of the early Church.

Two other quotations from Isaiah used in Luke's Gospel do not occur in either Matthew or Mark. The first is found in the story of Jesus' sermon in the synagogue at Nazareth in 4.16-30, where he reads from Isa. 61.1-2, a passage which seems to have been of considerable importance for the early church.[1] It is often pointed out that the reading stops immediately before the reference to God's day of vengeance in Isa. 61.2. The quotation follows the LXX of Isaiah 61, but omits one phrase ('to heal the broken-hearted') and includes another ('to set at liberty those who are oppressed') taken from Isa. 58.6; this minor variation is probably of no great significance. Jesus' exposition of the text consists in the claim that Isaiah's words have been fulfilled today, in the hearing of those in the synagogue. How are we to understand this fulfilment? Jesus has said nothing and done nothing in the synagogue except read the passage—how, then, is Scripture fulfilled? The answer must be that it is fulfilled because Jesus here and now accepts it as the programme for his ministry, identifying his mission with that of the prophetic figure described in Isaiah 61. He is able to accept it because the Spirit of the Lord is indeed on him—something we know, because Luke has continually emphasized it, and backed up his statements with evidence: he has told us of the descent of the Spirit—in bodily form—at Jesus' baptism (3.22); in 4.1 he emphasized that Jesus was full of the Spirit and was led by the Spirit, as a result of which he was able to withstand the temptations of Satan; and in 4.14 he told us that Jesus returned in the

---

1. Cf. Mt.11.5-6= Lk. 7.22, and echoes in Mt. 5.3-4 and Lk. 6.20-21.

power of the Spirit into Galilee, where he taught in their synagogues and everyone sang his praises (vv. 14-15). The Spirit of the Lord is indeed 'on' Jesus;[1] the rest of the quotation tells us what he is anointed to do, by providing a manifesto for Jesus' ministry.

The story has a partial parallel in Mk 6.1-6 and Mt. 13.54-58, but Luke has placed his much fuller version considerably earlier in his narrative, at the very beginning of his account of Jesus' ministry, and we can see why. In the succeeding chapters we find references to exorcisms and healings, together with the cures of a leper, of a paralytic, and of a man with a paralysed hand; we read of Jesus calling Levi to follow him, and then joining a party of 'sinners' in Levi's house; we are given an account of the teaching Jesus addressed to his disciples, who are described as 'poor' and 'hungry'; we hear how he healed a centurion's servant and raised a widow's son to life. By the time John the Baptist sends messengers to him in 7.18ff. asking whether he is the expected one or not, Jesus has preached the good news and set the prisoners of Satan[2] free: he has thus completed the task set out for him in Isa. 61.1-2, except that Luke has not recorded any instances of the one form of healing which is specifically mentioned, which is the restoration of sight to the blind. It can hardly be accidental that when John's disciples pose their question, Luke tells us that Jesus promptly healed many people from their diseases and plagues and evil spirits, and bestowed sight on the blind, so establishing beyond all doubt that he is indeed the one who was to come (7.21).[3] Jesus' next words sum up his activity in language which echoes not only Isa. 29.18-19 and 35.5-6, but 61.1-2 as well. Is this echo of the quotation of Isaiah 61 part of a deliberate *inclusio*? Certainly it seems that the programme spelt out in Luke 4 has been carried out, and that 7.18-23 is intended to underline this fact.

Jesus' exposition of Isaiah 61 in Luke 4 raises various interesting questions. Why, for example, does he quote the wrong proverb? The saying 'physician heal yourself' is surely irrelevant here, for Jesus has no need of healing. The appropriate proverb is found in *Gospel of Thomas* 31: 'No prophet is acceptable in his village; no physician heals those who know him'; this would have led neatly into Jesus' description

1. The Greek ἐπ' echoes the phrase used at the baptism.
2. Cf. 13.16.
3. It is significant that Matthew, whose account is very closely parallel to Luke's at this point, does not include a parallel to vv. 20-21.

of the way in which both Elijah and Elisha ministered to Gentiles rather than to Jews. But here is another puzzle, for though Jesus appeals to the examples of Elijah and Elisha in helping Gentiles, Luke depicts Jesus himself as apparently confining his own ministry to Jews. The references to Elijah and Elisha thus point forward to the mission to the Gentiles which lies beyond Jesus' rejection, death and resurrection,[1] but these latter events are themselves 'foretold' in the saying in v. 24, in the fury of his countrymen and their attempt to lynch him, and in his escape from their hands. This perhaps explains the form of the saying in v. 23, for at the end of the Gospel it will be Jesus himself who needs healing.[2] The story is thus a mini-presentation of the whole Gospel, with one interesting reversal—instead of Jesus' death and resurrection leading to the mission to the Gentiles, it is the promise of salvation for the Gentiles which stirs up his countrymen's hostility, and so leads to their attempt to kill him.

An interesting parallel to this story of biblical interpretation is found in Acts 8, where the Ethiopian eunuch reads from Isa. 53.7-8, and asks Philip to explain to him whom the passage is about. As in Luke 4, the quotation stops abruptly; if in that passage the exclusion of Isaiah's reference to 'the day of God's vengeance' is seen as deliberate, the same logic demands that in Acts 8 the choice of these particular lines of Isaiah 53 and these only must also be understood as deliberate. The passage is used simply as a proof-text about Jesus, not as a key to the meaning of his death: 'and beginning from this passage Philip preached to him the good news of Jesus'.

The second important quotation from Isaiah found in Luke alone[3] among the Gospels occurs in 22.37. In the upper room, Jesus warns his disciples that they can no longer expect to be received and welcomed as messengers of the kingdom; they must equip themselves with swords, because the words of Scripture, 'He was reckoned with the

---

1. B.J. Koet, *Five Studies on Interpretation of Scripture in Luke–Acts* (Leuven: Leuven University Press/Uitgeverij Peeters, 1989), pp. 24-55, denies that the references to Elijah and Elisha are intended as prefigurations of the Gentile mission or of judgment on Israel, and argues that they are intended to encourage Jesus' hearers at Nazareth to respond to his message. But they certainly do not function this way in the Gospel, where indeed they lead Jesus' audience to fury: the passage suggests rather that some Gentiles will respond to the gospel and some Jews reject it, and so exclude themselves from salvation.

2. Cf. the similar jibe in 23.35.

3. We assume that Mk 15.28 is a later addition to the text.

transgressors', must be fulfilled in him. The most obvious meaning of this highly enigmatic passage appears to be that Jesus is saying to his disciples, 'Buy swords, so that I can be arrested in the company of apparent gangsters'.[1] Most commentators shy away from this interpretation, probably because they dislike the highly mechanistic manner of fulfilling Scripture which it apparently attributes to Jesus.[2] They suggest instead that the passage refers to Jesus' crucifixion with two thieves,[3] or that it is a reference to the passion narrative in general.[4] Neither of these solutions offers an explanation of the present context of the words, where they follow Jesus' instruction to his disciples to buy swords.

Whatever explanation we adopt, the interesting factor about this passage is the way in which it is used. We have here the one clear reference to Isaiah 53 in the whole of Luke—indeed, in all four Gospels—and it is used simply as a proof-text. There is no reference to the so-called Servant's vicarious suffering or to any atonement brought about through his death. As with the longer passage quoted in Acts, Luke does not exploit the theological significance of the passage, but simply refers to it being 'fulfilled'.

III

If the beginning of the Gospel is an important clue to Luke's theology, so too is the end; in the resurrection appearances in the final chapter of Luke the fulfilment of Scripture is again an important theme, but now it is linked with a new theme—that of the fulfilment of Jesus' own words. There are three scenes. The first, in vv. 1-12, is set at the empty tomb. A comparison with Matthew and Mark reveals notable differences, one of which is significant for our purposes. Instead of

1. So P.S. Minear, 'A Note on Lk. 22.35-36', *NovT* 7 (1964), pp .128-34.

2. Minear's own suggestion is not that the command is an artificial literary device, but rather that it is intended to disclose the fact that the disciples have disobeyed Jesus' earlier instructions; 'Lk. 22.35-36', pp. 132-33.

3. As in the addition to Mark at 15.28. So J.A. Fitzmyer, *The Gospel According to Luke X-XXIV* (AB, New York: Doubleday, 1985), *in loc.* Cf. M. Rese, *Alttestamentliche Motive in der Christologie des Lukas* (Gütersloh: Gerd Mohn, 1969), pp. 155-58.

4. See I.H. Marshall, *The Gospel of Luke* (NIGTC, Exeter: Paternoster Press, 1978) *in loc.* Cf. D.J. Moo, *The Old Testament in the Gospel Passion Narratives* (Sheffield: Almond Press, 1983), pp. 132-38.

the command to go into Galilee, we have a reminder of what
happened there: 'Remember how he told you, while he was still in
Galilee, that the Son of man must be delivered into the hands of
sinners and be crucified, and rise on the third day'. These words point
us back to the first passion prediction in 9.22 (echoed in v. 44), where
Jesus announced that 'the Son of man must suffer many things and be
put to death...and the third day be raised'.[1] No explanation for the
suffering is offered: it is simply stated that it is necessary, and the
term used, δεῖ, is repeated in 24.7. The same word occurs in 13.33 ('I
must go on my way today and tomorrow and the third day'—that is to
Jerusalem and to death), in the passion prediction in 17.25, and in
22.37, where Jesus says that Isaiah 53 must be fulfilled. This necessity
is clearly based in Scripture, even though there is no clear reference
in any of the passion predictions to any particular passage—but it is
not Scripture alone that has now been fulfilled but the words of Jesus
himself, for it was he who said what would happen and what was
'necessary'. In other words, Jesus is presented as a prophet whose
prophecies have been vindicated—an idea not unfamiliar in Luke,
where Jesus actually refers to himself as a prophet on two occasions,
each time as a prophet who is rejected by his people (4.24, in the passage we have already considered, and 13.33).[2] We have here an idea
similar to one we met in the birth-narratives, where men and women
filled with the Spirit prophesied about the significance of John the
Baptist and Jesus. But now it is Jesus who has prophesied his own
death and resurrection, and his words that have been fulfilled.

The second scene takes place on the road to Emmaus in vv. 13-27.
Jesus upbraids his companions for their slowness to believe all that the
prophets have spoken (v. 25). Was it not necessary, he asks, that the
messiah should suffer all these things and so enter into his glory?
Once again, the necessity is founded in Scripture: 'and beginning from
Moses and from all the prophets, he interpreted to them in all the
Scriptures the things concerning himself'. This time the words of the
Risen Christ link back to the final passion prediction in 18.31ff.,
where Jesus refers to his coming sufferings, not as something which
'must' happen, but as the fulfilment of 'everything which is written of

1. The predictions in 17.25 and 18.31ff. occur on the journey from Galilee to
Jerusalem.
2. The belief that Jesus is a prophet is raised elsewhere in Luke; see 7.16,39;
9.8,19; 24.19.

the Son of man through the prophets'. The interesting feature in 24.27 is that Jesus refers first to Moses; to what passages can this refer? Luke fails to tell us.[1] The reference is vague but inclusive, and becomes more so, as we progress from the prophets in v. 25 via Moses and all the prophets to all the scriptures in v. 27.

In the third scene, in vv. 36-49, the two ideas of Jesus' own prophecies and those of Scripture are drawn together and coalesce. Jesus appears to the eleven in Jerusalem and reminds them of what he has taught them earlier: 'These were my words to you when I was still with you; I told you that everything written about me in the law of Moses and the prophets and the psalms must be fulfilled' (v. 44). The events in Jerusalem have thus fulfilled not simply what was written in all three parts of Scripture, but the words of Jesus himself. Jesus is thus proved to be the prophet like Moses (Deut. 18.21-22). 'Then he explained to them that it is written that the messiah should suffer and rise from the dead on the third day, and that repentance for the forgiveness of sin should be proclaimed in his name to all the Gentiles, beginning from Jerusalem' (v. 47). Once again, Luke fails to tell us where it is written. Nor do the predictions attributed to Jesus to which this passage refers assist us, since the only saying which Luke has quoted in connection with the sufferings of Jesus is the enigmatic quotation of Isa. 53.12 in 22.37. This dearth of explicit quotations is remarkable, since Luke refers to a number of scriptural passages in other connections in the course of his story. It means that in this final chapter, as in chs. 1–2, we have no precise quotation, even though the conviction that everything is happening according to Scripture is clearly underlined in both passages.

Luke uses these conversations with the Risen Christ to draw out the significance of events. In this sense, ch. 24 forms the epilogue to his Gospel, rather as chs. 1–2 form the prologue. One interesting fact is that whereas we are inclined to think that the Scriptures being appealed to must be in the prophets and psalms, we twice find here reference to Moses. Where does Moses fit in?

---

1. This is hardly surprising, since the only passage he has quoted so far is Isa. 53.12 in 22.37, but it corresponds with T. Holtz's contention that Luke did not have direct access to a text of the Pentateuch; see *Untersuchungen über die alttestamentlichen Zitate bei Lukas* (Berlin: Akademie Verlag, 1968), pp. 60-130, 168-69.

IV

That Moses is an important figure for Luke is indicated already by the way in which the evangelist handles the law. Significant, too, is the way in which he treats the transfiguration story in 9.28-36. Only Luke tells us the subject of the conversation between Jesus, Moses and Elijah, namely Jesus' ἔξοδος, which he was to fulfil in Jerusalem—the unusual term establishes a link between the salvation achieved through Moses and the coming death of Jesus. The voice from heaven, identifying Jesus as God's Son, commands the disciples (as in Matthew and Mark) to 'hear him', words which suggest that Jesus is also understood to be the prophet like Moses who is spoken of in Deut. 18.15. Almost immediately following, in 9.51, we are told that the time for Jesus' ἀνάλημψις approached: the term is reminiscent of the assumptions of both Moses and Elijah, and implies that Jesus, also, will be taken up to glory—the glory in which Moses and Elijah appear in 9.31—though in his case by a painful death. But though we are told that the time has approached, and though Jesus is said to have set his face resolutely towards Jerusalem, Luke now begins a long section in which Jesus meanders around Palestine, often heading in the wrong direction. C.F. Evans made the fascinating suggestion that the stories between 10.1 and 18.14 have been carefully chosen and placed in an order which corresponds with the account of Moses leading Israel through the wilderness in Deuteronomy 1-26.[1] Some of his parallels seem far-fetched, and the notion of Luke carefully collating his material with the text of Deuteronomy is too reminiscent of the methods of a modern scholar to be wholly persuasive. There is more evidence to support his less ambitious suggestion that the first two stories in this section both echo stories of Elijah: in the first, we read how, in contrast to Elijah, Jesus refuses to call down fire on those who reject him (cf. 2 Kgs 1.9-12); then (again unlike Elijah) he refuses to allow a would-be disciple to bury his father (cf. 1 Kgs 19.19-21). When we turn to the story of Christ's ascension in Acts 1, we find Luke emphasizing the way in which, after Jesus had promised his

---

1. See 'The Central Section of St. Luke's Gospel', in D.E. Nineham (ed.) *Studies in the Gospels: Essays in memory of R.H. Lightfoot* (Oxford: Basil Blackwell, 1957), pp. 37-53. Evans' suggestion is, of course, incompatible with Holtz's argument that Luke did not have access to a copy of the Pentateuch.

disciples that they would receive the Holy Spirit, they saw him lifted up into heaven (vv. 9-10), an interesting echo of Elijah's insistence that if Elisha were to inherit his spirit in its full power, he must see him depart into heaven (2 Kgs 2.9-15). These echoes confirm the belief that in 9.51 Luke is deliberately linking the assumption of Jesus with that of Elijah.[1]

In view of the hints at 9.31 and 35, we expect the figure of Moses to be of equal significance with that of Elijah, and certainly there are echoes of the Moses tradition in 10.1–18.30. The appointment of the Seventy is reminiscent of Moses' choice of seventy elders (Exod. 24.1; Num. 11.16); the commandments are quoted and endorsed (10.25-8; 18.18-21); the teaching of Moses is invoked (16.29-31); above all, these chapters contain the bulk of Jesus' teaching, which is delivered with great authority. The command to hear Jesus in 9.35 is repeatedly echoed—if men and women hear him, they hear the words of one sent by God (10.16); psalmists and kings longed to hear what the disciples now hear (10.24); in listening to the word of Jesus, Mary chooses the best part (10.39, 42); those who hear and obey God's word are blessed (11.28); Jesus is greater than Solomon, whose wisdom was listened to by the Queen of the South, and greater than Jonah, whose preaching converted the people of Nineveh (11.29-32); those with ears to hear are commanded to hear (14.35); and finally we are told that those who did not hear Moses and the prophets will not repent, even if one should rise from the dead (16.29-31), words whose true significance depends on knowing the end of the story. When we turn to Acts, we find confirmation is found that Luke thought of Jesus as 'the prophet like Moses' in 3.22, where Deut. 18.15-19 is quoted and applied to Jesus. The reminiscences of Moses go beyond echoes of his teaching, however: we have already noted the reference to Jesus' death as an 'exodus' in 9.31, and in 22.19-20, 28-30, in the context of the last supper, we find Jesus linking his death with a covenant; this theme, associating Jesus' death with the covenant on Sinai, appears first in the disputed words over the second cup, but it is used again in the saying about the kingdom which God has covenanted to him, and which he now covenants to his disciples, appointing them as judges who will sit

---

1.   There are, of course, other hints in Luke that he sees Jesus as the new Elijah, e.g. 7.11-17. Cf. P. Dabeck, 'Siehe, es erschienen Moses und Elias' (Mt. 17.3)', *Bib* 23 (1942), pp. 175-89; J. Drury, *Tradition and Design in Luke's Gospel* (London: Darton, Longman & Todd, 1976), pp.147-48.

on thrones judging the twelve tribes of Israel.[1]

Whether or not we accept the suggestion that the travel narrative is meant to parallel the journey of Moses from Horeb to the promised land, therefore, it would seem that Luke intends to present Jesus as both the prophet like Moses and as the returning Elijah.[2] In doing so, he demonstrates another way in which 'Moses and all the prophets' are fulfilled in Jesus. Just as he spells out in 4.16-7.23 his conviction that the passage from the prophets which Jesus read in Nazareth was fulfilled in his actions, so he indicates in 9.51-62 that Jesus is a new Elijah, and spells out in 9.51-18.30 his belief that he is also the prophet like Moses and that the law of Moses is 'completed' in him. This typology perhaps appears to us to be subtle, but it is no more subtle than the use of septuagintal phraseology in chs. 1-2: Luke's manner of handling the Scriptures and seeing their fulfilment in Jesus is not quite what we, from our twentieth-century perspective, expect. But if the relevance of Moses and the prophets is not immediately obvious, that is hardly surprising, for only in ch. 24 does the Risen Christ open the eyes of the disciples 'to understand the Scriptures'. It may be that modern scholars need similar illumination if they are to understand the subtleties of Luke's manner of expressing his conviction that 'the whole of Scripture' referred to Jesus.

---

1. Cf. Deut.16.18.
2. Mal. 4.4-5 links the figure of Moses and Elijah. It is possible that Luke saw significance in the fact that the end of the travel narrative brings Jesus and his disciples to Jericho (18.35) since Jericho features in both the story of the death of Moses, Deut. 32.49, 34.1,3, and the account of Elijah's assumption, 2 Kgs 2.4.

THE ANOINTED ONE IN NAZARETH

David R. Catchpole

I

In an extended series of contributions to the study of Jesus and his world Marinus de Jonge has laid stress on the recovery of a sense of continuity between Jesus and early Christianity. In his 1985 Presidential Address to the Studiorum Novi Testamenti Societas he urged that the term χριστός, employed very shortly after Jesus' death and resurrection with a full understanding of its inherent connotations in the formula 'Christ died for us', must already have been important during Jesus' lifetime.[1] More recently, in his 1989 Shaffer Lectures at Yale Divinity School, he pressed the point that Jesus' prophetic presentation and inauguration of God's kingdom, his exorcistic powers, his sense of a special relationship with God, could all encourage and coexist with the conviction that he was the Lord's Son of David 'not only in the future, but already during his prophetic work in Galilee'. On this showing, 'it is probable that he regarded himself as the Messiah and Son of David inspired and empowered by the Spirit'.[2] This theme of continuity, which by no means excludes early Christian creativity, provokes further reflection upon a classic Lucan text, in which the theme of the Lord's anointed is presented with impressive literary artistry, namely the episode in Nazareth (Lk. 4.16-30). In connection with this tradition one's mind goes back to the true judgment of George Bernard Shaw, a judgment admittedly based on not entirely true premises and developed in not entirely true directions, that 'it is Luke's Jesus who has won our hearts'.[3] After an encounter with a

---

1.   'The Earliest Christian Use of *Christos*', *NTS* 32 (1986), pp. 321-43 (336).

2.   *Jesus, The Servant-Messiah* (New Haven: Yale University Press, 1991), pp. 67-72, 75.

3.   *Androcles and the Lion* (Harmondsworth: Penguin Books, 1949), p. 41.

recent survey of scholarly discussion of Lk. 4.16-30, running to no
fewer than 318 published studies,[1] it may border on temerity to
attempt anything further. Yet there is a specific question which is
worth addressing: if, as will be argued, Luke is exercising creative
versatility, how far does he still remain connected by a thread of continuity to the mission of Jesus of Nazareth? Is his theological attachment to the ἀρχή inclusive or exclusive of genuine historical
reminiscence?

II

The much-debated relationship or non-relationship between Lk. 4.16-
30 and Mk 6.1-6a should be clarified by a recognition that Marcan
creativity is probably responsible for more or less the whole of that
version of the episode in Nazareth.[2] Although the proverb, 'A prophet
is not without honour, except in his own country', is doubtless able to
circulate independently and to survive, the same can hardly be said for
the tradition as a whole.[3] To put the matter form-critically, what

---

1. C.J. Schreck, 'The Nazareth Pericope: Lk. 4.16-30 in Recent Study', in *The
Gospel of Luke* (ed. F. Neirynck; BETL, 32; Leuven: Leuven University Press, 2nd
edn, 1989), pp. 399-471.
2. This was the main thrust of the work of E. Grässer, 'Jesus in Nazareth
(Mk 6.1-6a): Notes on the Redaction and Theology of St Mark', *NTS* 16 (1969),
pp. 1-23, although at a few points he restricted the extent of Marcan creativity.
3. The supposed uneasiness of the relationship between Mk 6.4 and its context
should not be overplayed. Three tensions are detected by E. Grässer, 'Nazareth',
p. 6: (1) Jesus did not come to Nazareth as a prophet but as a famous teacher and
wonder worker. (2) The redactor's association of the family with those who reject
Jesus is out of line with the initial comment's having come from the other people of
Nazareth. (3) If the people behave in v. 5 in line with the maxim in v. 4, then Jesus'
amazement in v. 6a is out of place. In response: (1) Wisdom and miracles belong to
the prophetic pattern, and are not separate from it. (2) The phrase 'out of line' is not
out of order, but there is a certain tension within Mark's own thought here. The
words καὶ ἐν τοῖς συγγενεῦσιν αὐτοῦ καὶ ἐν τῇ οἰκίᾳ αὐτοῦ extend somewhat
the essential aphorism and pick up the theme of Mk 3.20-21, 31-35. The function of
the question referring objectively to the family is to set up an antithesis between
human thinking and the ultimate truth— also a theme of Mark, cf. Mk 8.33. Since
the critical astonishment of Nazareth residents does not exclude a similar distancing
of Jesus' family from him, the tension in Mark's thought is not acute. (3) The astonishment of Jesus at miracle-inhibiting ἀπιστία matches the Marcan presentation in

purpose would Mk 6.1-6a serve? Its serviceability within any early Christian community is not at all evident. On the other hand, its serviceability within the Marcan scheme, and its use of characteristically Marcan devices and ideas, is more than a little obvious.

1. The synagogue teaching, and the astonishment it provokes (6.2a), recall the MarkR section 1.21-22.[1]
2. The use of a question (6.2b), which remains unanswered precisely because it cannot be answered within the available human framework, recalls that favourite Marcan tactic deployed in 4.41; 8.4, 27.
3. The coupling of the teaching, expressed in σοφία, and the δυνάμεις (6.2b) conforms to Mark's overall interest in such a pairing and indeed his view of the acts of power as expressions of authority—again 1.21-22, 27-28.
4. The instinctive recourse to the matter of origin (6.2bα) as the key to authority fits the thrust of Mk 11.27-33, another

9.14-29, in which Jesus confronts unbelief with an exclamation of rebuke and frustration.

1. A possible clash between ἐξεπλήσσοντο (v. 2a) and ἐσκανδαλίζοντο (v. 3) has sometimes suggested the presence of underlying source material here, maybe even a pre-Marcan tradition of a successful appearance of Jesus in Nazareth, cf. R. Bultmann, *The History of the Synoptic Tradition* (Oxford: Basil Blackwell, 1963), p. 31. Grässer ('Nazareth', p. 5), while not taking up the source idea, insists that ἐκπλήσσειν always represents 'a fact of being overcome, of an ecstasy, of numbness caused by shock', which is different from taking offence. However, the usage of ἐκπλήσσειν elsewhere suggests a range of meaning, and therefore that the one could easily lead into the other. Thus, in Mk 7.37; 11.18 the sense is positive and approving, but in 1.22 it is more equivocal— Jesus' teaching creates an impression of newness over against scribal teaching, specifically within the Pharisaic stronghold of the synagogue, and it is the ensuing miracle which brings about the final favourable response in Mk 1.27. Similarly, in Mk 10.26 ἐκπλήσσειν introduces an objecting question. The capacity of ἐκπλήσσειν to convey a positive appreciation which can then turn sour is well established by Wis. 13.4 (where being impressed by the created order may lead to genuine monotheism but does not prevent idolatry), and three martyrological texts, 2 Macc. 7.12; *4 Macc.* 8.4; 17.16 (where the tyrant's astonished appreciation of the conduct of the loyalists does not prevent his hounding them to death). See also the Aquila versions of Gen. 27.33 (the agonized and horrified question of Isaac); 1 Kgdms 4.13 (Eli's fearful apprehension concerning the ark of God); 13.7; 16.4; 21.1; 28.5.

pericope which has no obvious role and therefore no secure existence as an independent unit.

5. The achievement of acts of power 'through his hands' (6.2bβ) has already emerged as a Marcan commonplace (1.31, 41; 5.23, 41).

6. The raising of a question about Jesus' own identity (6.3) is exactly what Mark does whenever he can, by means either implicit or explicit, for this is the key issue which he takes care to answer in advance for the benefit of the reader (1.1) and then sets about interpreting in what follows—the residents in Nazareth are therefore 'Marcan puppets' in asking a question which presumes that Jesus belongs to a transhuman order of existence. In their bewilderment and resort to earthly realities (6.3), which can only lead to misunderstanding, they join the Marcan queue of *incognoscenti*.

7. The inability of even his relatives to understand Jesus recalls the reflective complex, compositionally constructed as a 'sandwich structure' by the evangelist in 3.20-35.

8. The generalized statement about the acts of power which were, or were not, performed (6.5) is entirely in line with Marcan generalizations in 1.32-34; 3.10; 6.53-56.

9. The amazement of Jesus himself (6.6a), starkly contrasted as it is with the more conventional amazement evoked by Jesus, attracts attention. But this could, given Marcan use of Q 7.1-10, 18-35; 9.57-10.16,[1] be read with the greatest of ease as an echo of themes and terms employed by Q. The case does not rest on the last point, since Marcan responsibility for all but 6.6a must entail responsibility for 6.6a as well.

The conclusion that the evangelist is responsible for virtually all of Mk 6.1-6a has a powerful bearing on the source criticism of Lk. 4.16-30. Lucan dependence on MarkR implies that no alternative non-Marcan source can be envisaged for the overlapping parts of the tradition, namely vv. 16, 22b, 24. Only in two respects is this conclusion threatened.

---

1. W. Schenk, 'Der Einfluss der Logienquelle auf das Markusevangelium', *ZNW* 70 (1979), pp. 141-65.

The first is the famous Matthew/Luke agreement in Ναζαρά (Mt. 4.13/Lk. 4.16). The arguments against the presence here of non-Marcan source material, as proposed by H. Schürmann[1] and in a modified form by C.M. Tuckett,[2] have been put with great vigour by J. Delobel.[3] While the arguments against the presence of source material here are in general very compelling, it must be admitted that they are at their most fragile in respect of the 'special problem'[4] of Ναζαρά: (i) the reading Ναζαρά in Mt. 4.13 is textually uncertain, and might possibly be the result of secondary assimilation to Luke's text; (ii) this 'minor agreement' occurs in the setting of many major disagreements attributable to MattR or LukeR and is not strong enough to support unaided the hypothesis of another source; and (iii) 'la coincidence peut être accidentelle ou due à un copiste'. For the alternative position, it can be argued (i) that the predominance of the alternative versions Ναζαρέτ/Ναζαρέθ in the text of Gospels and Acts would tend to favour the originality of the rarer reading Ναζαρά in Mt. 4.13; (ii) that Mk 1.9 Ναζαρέτ and Mt. 2.23 Ναζαρέτ ought to combine to produce Ναζαρέτ in Mt. 4.13, or at the very least Ναζαρεθ, but they do not; and (iii) that Lucan references to Nazareth are invariably in the Ναζαρέθ/Ναζαρέτ form, cf. Lk. 1.26; 2.4, 39, 51; Acts 10.38, the last instance being particularly significant for our purpose in view of the heavy influence of Lk. 4.16-30 upon Acts 10.34-43 as a whole. So Ναζαρά in Mt. 4.13 looks original and non-MattR, and Ναζαρά in Lk. 4.16 looks non-LukeR. Unless one is going to travel along the otherwise uninviting route towards Lucan use of Matthew,[5] the obvious explanation of ἦλθεν εἰς Ναζαρά is in terms of Q (cf. ἦλθεν εἰς Καφαναούμ, Q 7.1). This will incidentally have the virtue

1. 'Der "Bericht von Anfang": Ein Rekonstruktionsversuch auf Grund von Lk. 4, 14-16', repr. in *Traditionsgeschichtliche Untersuchungen zu den synoptischen Evangelien* (Düsseldorf: Patmos, 1968), pp. 69-80.

2. 'Lk. 4.16-30, Isaiah and Q', in *Logia* (ed. J. Delobel; BETL, 59; Leuven: Leuven University Press, 1982), pp. 343-54; 'On the Relationship between Matthew and Luke', *NTS* 30 (1984), pp. 130-42 (131).

3. 'La rédaction de Lc. IV. 14-16a et le "Bericht vom Anfang"', in *L'Evangile de Luc* (ed. F. Neirynck; BETL, 32; Leuven: Leuven University Press, 2nd edn, 1989), pp. 113-33 (127-28); additional note, pp. 306-12 (310).

4. Schreck, 'Nazareth Pericope', p. 417.

5. M.D. Goulder, *Luke: A New Paradigm* (Sheffield: JSOT Press, 1989), pp. 306-307.

of responding to the need for a transition in Q from the temptation tradition (Q 4.1-13) to the inaugural discourse (Q 6.20-49), matching the transition from the discourse to the centurion tradition which follows. But, and this is what is of immediate importance, it will by no means introduce Q to the body of Lk. 4.16-30.

The second is οὐχὶ υἱός ἐστιν Ἰωσὴφ οὗτος; which matches the reference to ὁ τοῦ τέκτονος υἱός (Mt. 13.55). In spite of recurrent claims to the contrary the MattR change is well grounded in concern to eliminate a possible hint of illegitimacy,[1] and the LukeR change is a consistent following through of the recent and equally LukeR addition of ὡς ἐνομίζετο to the genealogy (Lk. 3.23: νομίζειν also at Lk. 2.44 and seven times in Acts).

Attacks on the exclusively Marcan derivation of Lk. 4.16, 22b, 24 having thus been repulsed, the logic of the rest of the story can now be examined with a view to further decision about Lucan sources and, above all, Lucan theology.

III

The composite quotation from Scripture is all-controlling. All the signs are that this extremely carefully constructed quotation is a literary product and intended to be complete in itself.[2] In effect, there is no encouragement or space for the theory that the unfolding sequence of events is provoked by what is not said about 'the day of vengeance of our God'.[3] What is not said is not significant, and what is said is not provocative. The omission of ἰάσασθαι τοὺς συντετριμμένους τὴν καρδίαν is only partial, for the proverb of Lk. 4.23 characterizes Jesus as ἰατρός, and the verb συντρίβειν is replaced by a genuine synonym θραύειν.[4] But in its place, or rather, *not quite* in its place

1. H.K. McArthur, 'Son of Mary', *NovT* 15 (1973), pp. 81-113.
2. Rightly, U. Busse, *Das Nazareth-Manifest Jesu* (SBS, 91; Stuttgart: Katholisches Bibelwerk, 1977), p. 33.
3. B. Violet, 'Zum rechten Verständnis der Nazarethperikope', *ZNW* 37 (1938), pp. 251-71; J. Jeremias, *Jesus' Promise to the Nations* (SBT, 24; London: SCM Press, 1958), p. 45. Equally, there is no reason to follow A. Strobel (*Kerygma und Apokalyptik* [Göttingen: Vandenhoeck & Ruprecht, 1967], p. 111) in his historicizing guess that the day of vengeance was mentioned and gave rise to the later hostile reaction.
4. The two verbs are indistinguishable in sense, share two possible Hebrew

comes ἀποστεῖλαι τεθραυσμένους ἐν ἀφέσει from Isa. 58.6. The slightly different positioning of this clause, together with the substitution of κηρῦξαι for καλέσαι, serves to produce a clear structure. That is, a major declaration πνεῦμα κυρίου ἐπ' ἐμέ, οὗ ἕνεκεν ἔχρισέν με is immediately amplified by a quartet of statements of purpose using alternately the verbs ἀποστέλλειν and κηρύσσειν—thus:

a εὐαγγελίσασθαι πτωχοῖς ἀπέσταλκέν με
b κηρῦξαι αἰχμαλώτοις ἄφεσιν καὶ τυφλοῖς ἀνάβλεψιν
a′ ἀποστεῖλαι τεθραυσμένους ἐν ἀφέσει
b′ κηρῦξαι ἐνιαυτὸν κυρίου δεκτόν.

Within this major declaration the central and now repeated ἄφεσις (b, a′)[1] achieves a dominant position, while the absence of the one element of the Isa. 58.6 text which has no counterpart in Isa. 61.1, that is, τὴν καρδίαν, and the collocation of αἰχμαλώτοις ἄφεσις and τυφλοῖς ἀνάβλεψις, serves to highlight the achievement of *physical* healing within the programme. That physical healing must, in the light of the suitability of the verb θραύειν to describe physical illness and subjection to an oppressive power,[2] be understood as the scourge of the devil, from which Jesus is set to exercise a ministry of deliverance.[3] So ἄφεσις here is, quite unsurprisingly, it must be said, exactly what Luke indicates in his commentary on Lk. 4.18-19 in Acts 10.38b: 'he went about doing good and healing all that were oppressed by the devil'.[4] No room is left here for a Satan-free mission, nor indeed for an endowment with the Spirit which is not directly and integrally con-

bases, namely קלה and רצץ, the latter being the word which underlies Isa. 58.6 LXX.

1. Compare the bringing together, by means of this shared word, of Lev. 25.13, the jubilee year text, and Deut. 15.2, the sabbath year text, in 11QMelch 2-3.

2. Physical sickness: Wis. 18.20; Josephus, *War* 6.76; *Ant.* 8.390. Oppression by an alien power: Exod. 15.6; Num. 24.17; *3 Macc.* 6.5.

3. Similarly, U. Busse, *Die Wunder des Propheten Jesus* (FzB, 24; Stuttgart: Katholisches Bibelwerk, 2nd edn, 1979), p. 62.

4. Cf. P. Achtemeier, 'The Lucan Perspective on the Miracles of Jesus: A Preliminary Sketch', *JBL* 94 (1975), pp. 547-62: 'There can be no question that Luke does understand Jesus' ministry as a successful battle against Satan', The comment by M. de Jonge and A.S. van der Woude on 11QMelch, a text similarly conditioned by Isa. 61.1-2, could equally be attached to Lk. 4.18-19: 'The destruction of the powers of evil inaugurates the time of salvation'. '11QMelchizedek and the New Testament', *NTS* 12 (1966), pp. 301-26 (305).

nected with miracle performance.[1] Quite the contrary! The mission is
about liberation; at the heart of the mission stands miracle (in this
sense, b/a' has a/b' surrounding it as an *inclusio*), and liberation is
what happens in miracle;[2] talk of 'sending' must not be indulged without taking account of miracle (a, a'), and neither must talk of
'preaching' (b, b'); *all* of this is a drawing out of the implications of
the anointing. Once again, it is exactly what Luke indicates in Acts
10.38a, by pairing the Holy Spirit with power, and by prefacing the

---

1.　Busse, *Wunder*, pp. 59-60. Against C.M. Tuckett, 'Lk. 4.16-30', pp. 347-50,
as earlier E. Schweizer, 'πνεῦμα', *TDNT*, VI (1968), p. 407, and M. Rese,
Alttestamentliche Motive in der Christologie des Lukas (Gütersloh: Gerd Mohn,
1969), p. 145: 'Durch die Streichung will Lk anzeigen, da der Geist des Herrn
prophetischer Geist und nicht wundermachende Macht ist'. Had Luke wanted to
signal a metaphorical meaning, τὴν καρδίαν would have helped, not hindered. Luke
uses καρδία to describe the seat of memory (1.66; 2.19, 51), the place of internal
dialogue (2.35; 3.15; 5.22; 9.47; 12.45; 24.38), the basic disposition (1.17, 51; 6.45;
8.15; 12.34; 16.15; 21.14, 34; 24.25, 32), the person viewed as the recipient of the
word (8.12). The omission of τὴν καρδίαν therefore signals disinterest in
psychological problems: rightly, Busse, *Wunder*, p. 60. It is true that a transferred
sense for τυφλοῖς ἀνάβλεψις is possible, cf. Isa. 42.7, 18, but it is excluded here by
Lk. 7.21-22, a formulation heavily indebted to LukeR. Equally relevant in this
connection is the heavily loaded term χάρις. Not for nothing does Luke explain
Stephen's impressive miracle working activity by his being full of χάρις καὶ
δυνάμις (Acts 6.8), and define the 'witness to ὁ λόγος τῆς χάριτος' preached by
Paul and Barnabas as the granting of signs and wonders. And when he redacts Mk
3.10-11, in Lk. 7.21 he adds in τυφλοῖς πολλοῖς ἐχαρίσατο βλέπειν, a statement
which recalls how λόγοι τῆς χάριτος (4.22) describe the announcement of τυφλοῖς
ἀνάβλεψις (4.18). Finally, readers of the Gospel would shortly become familiar
with the logically related bracketing together by the evangelist (14.13, 21) of 'the
poor', who dominate 4.18, and the physically disabled in the persons of 'the
maimed, the lame and the blind'.

2.　Against the suggestion that Luke, though not his putative source, understands
ἄφεσις more narrowly as forgiveness (thus, C.M. Tuckett, 'Lk. 4.16-30', p. 349),
there is the evidence of the story used shortly afterwards in Lk. 4.38-39/Mk 1.29-31.
By means of the redactional phrase ἐπετίμησεν τῷ πυρετῷ (cf. 4.35, 41) Luke
makes it one of a trio of exorcisms and is quite content to adopt the Marcan
statement καὶ ἀφῆκεν αὐτήν to describe the cure. By means of the *inclusio* formed
by εὐαγγελίσασθαι...ἀπέσταλκεν/ἀποστεῖλαι (v. 18) and εὐαγγελίσασθαι
...ἀπεστάλην (v. 43) Luke ensures that the trio of exorcisms forms a commentary
on the programmatic announcement. Thus for Luke Jesus is the agent of ἄφεσις in
the widest sense of that term.

ministry of deliverance from the devil, in 'God anointed Jesus of Nazareth with the Holy Spirit and with power'.

We may scarcely doubt that a text so deeply impregnated with the thought of Luke is indeed the creation of Luke. While it may be admitted that the interpenetration of OT texts,[1] such as we discover in Lk. 4.18-19, is not exactly typical of the writer of the Gospel[2] (though, one might add, less untypical of the writer of Acts), nevertheless every writer must be allowed the freedom to do something once and only once, and in this case the Lucan imprint is really rather overwhelming. On this foundation we can build with the further reflection that the evangelist wants to underline with all possible firmness the positive reaction which is forthcoming from the audience in Nazareth. As already observed, nothing has been said to provoke any other kind of reaction. In similar vein, the witnessing (ἐμαρτύρουν αὐτῷ) is positive—just as positive as the witnessing to the word of grace in Acts 14.3 (cf. also Acts 15.8; 22.5). And the astonishment (ἐθαύμαζον ἐπί) is positive—more positive than it is in the ambivalent Lk. 11.14 or the critical Lk. 11.38, and just as positive as it is in the LukeR 8.25 (diff. Mk 4.41) where it is paired with a question about the status of Jesus, or in the LukeR 9.43 where it encapsulates in a single word the acclaiming reaction of those who were 'astonished at the majesty of God' exhibited in the miracle of Jesus, or in Acts 4.13 where it is coupled with perplexity about the apparently defective credentials of the ἀγράμματοι καὶ ἰδιῶται. And even the question (οὐχὶ υἱός ἐστιν Ἰωσὴφ οὗτος) is positive, for all that it has an ingredient of bewilderment and bafflement—just as positive as the questions which erupt in Lk. 4.36; 8.25. Given the palpable dependence of the question in 4.22b upon the report of receptivity in 4.22a (ἐμαρτύρουν...καὶ ἐθαύμαζον...καὶ ἔλεγον), and given the eminent reasonableness of the request, 'physician, heal yourself', which Jesus, as it were, puts into the mouths of his audience, there is every reason to keep the implication of the

---

1. Compare the combinations of Isa. 29.18-19; 35.5-6; 61.1 in Q 7.22 and of Exod. 23.20 and Mal. 3.1 in Q 7.27.

2. This point is stressed by a number of writers, including M. Dömer, *Das Heil Gottes* (BBB, 51; Bonn: Peter Hanstein, 1978), pp. 55-56; B.D. Chilton, *God in Strength: Jesus' Announcement of the Kingdom* (SNTU, 1; Freistadt: Plöchl, 1979), p. 147; Tuckett, 'Luke 4.16-30', p. 347.

comparable Marcan question firmly and far removed from the process
of interpreting the Lucan question.[1]

IV

This brings us neatly and naturally to Lk. 4.23 with its double crux,
the function of the proverb, 'Physician, heal yourself', and the
apparently misplaced Capernaum reference by someone who has not
yet visited that town. For all that the double crux makes for difficulty,
it is limpidly clear that v. 23, with the sayings attached to it, has just
as critical a role to play in defining the manner of the mission as
vv. 18-19 has in defining its matter.

The similarity of Luke's ἰατρέ, θεράπευσον σεαυτόν and
Plutarch's use of Euripides' slogan ἄλλων ἰατρός, αὐτὸς ἕλκεσιν
βρύων led John Nolland[2] to see the one as the closest parallel for the
other, and then to insist on the importance for Lk. 4.23 of the context
in which Plutarch used the proverb. The problem with this view is not
the transformation of the Euripidean slogan into the Lucan imperative
form, but the dissonance of the contexts. For the texts in Plutarch[3]
have invariably a moralizing tone, an insistence that irreproachable
moral probity is the *sine qua non* for teaching. The text in Luke, on
the other hand, has no concern whatever with Jesus' personal moral
character and every concern with the location of his work. On this
score the proposal of S.J. Noorda[4] is distinctly preferable. This sets
Lk. 4.23 alongside Dio Chrysostom, *Discourse XLIX*. For Dio, the
role of the philosopher in the political sphere is the concern—to hold

1.   J. Nolland, 'Impressed Unbelievers as Witnesses to Christ (Luke 4.22a)',
JBL 98 (1979), pp. 219-29, has convincingly drawn attention to the typical Lucan
interest in positive testimony to Jesus from those who stand somewhat apart from
his mission.
2.   'Classical and Rabbinic Parallels to "Physician, Heal Yourself" (Lk. 4.23)',
NovT 21 (1979), pp. 193-209.
3.   'How to Tell a Flatterer' 71F, *Moralia I* (trans. F.C. Babbitt; LCL London:
Heinemann, 1927), p. 380; 'How to Profit from One's Enemies' 88D, *Moralia II*
(trans. F.C. Babbitt; LCL; London: Heinemann, 1928), p. 16; 'On Brotherly Love'
480F-481A, *Moralia VI* (trans. W. Helmbold; LCL; London: Heinemann, 1939),
p. 262.
4.   '"Cure Yourself, Doctor!" (Lk 4.23): Classical Parallels to an Alleged
Saying of Jesus', in *Logia* (ed. J. Delobel; BETL, 59; Leuven: Leuven University
Press, 1982), pp. 459-67.

office is an obligation and an opportunity, and for the philosopher an activation of his supreme concern; historically, rulers have often recognized the supreme role of the philosopher by appointing many such as counsellors who, in effect, rule them; by exercising 'the most difficult office of all', namely control over the self, the philosopher is the person who expects to rule. Consequently, 'the function of the real philosopher is nothing else than to rule over human beings'. Dio then envisages a situation in which a philosopher is asked to administer his own city and excuses himself by claiming not to be competent. The inadmissibility of such a position is demonstrated by three parallels. The first is a doctor, claiming to be in general a physician, and then treating others but not himself—he cannot convincingly claim incompetence, and he therefore gives the impression of being unduly interested in the fees and favours which come from patients other than himself. The second is a teacher, claiming indeed to be an able instructor, but teaching other people's sons rather than his own, even though they may benefit less from going to someone less effective than their father. The third is a son, who quite indefensibly neglects his own parents, and gives preference to the parents of others because they are wealthier or more distinguished. From all of this Dio draws the conclusion that the philosopher should accept office, though he mounts a defensive justification of his not having made himself available, on the grounds that he has been quite unavoidably too busy and will in addition soon be leaving the town.

This trio of arguments exhibits an integrated wholeness. The first and the second deal with claims which are not put into effect except outside one's own immediate sphere; no claim can be involved in the third because of the nature of the relationship in question, that between son and parent. The third and the first deal with situations offering the possibility of personal advantage, whether in money or in prestige; this cannot apply to the second, since no alternative commitment is involved. The second and the third deal with family relationships, which the first cannot do because it is alone the self which is in mind. This carefully structured complementariness and wholeness suggests that Nolland is incorrect to say that the passage would have been more effective for the omission of the comments about alternative recompenses. The point is that the claim not to be competent is (i) at variance with the person's overall stance of 'professing to be a physician', and therefore (ii) a smokescreen for some quite different

motive. And the overall purpose of the trio is to show that *the basic
definition* of a person's existence and function, which is expressed in
an explicit claim, must be brought to effect *generally*, and therefore
without excluding those who are *directly related*. In particular, the
refusal of *a call from one's own community* cannot be justified in
terms of acceptable motives. When Lk. 4.23a is tested for conformity
to this pattern of thought it works splendidly. First, the same medical
illustration is used. Secondly, the same application to one's πατρίς is
attached by means of v. 23b. Thirdly, there is an invitation by those
who would benefit. Fourthly, there is presupposed a well-known and
definitive claim about the key person's role, which brings vv. 18-19
into play. Fifthly, the necessity of providing some very good
overriding reason for a refusal is understood, which brings either or
both of v. 24 and vv. 25-27 into play.

With Noorda's proposal concerning the Luke/Dio parallelism as
basis, therefore, the implications for the relationship between v. 23a
and the adjacent material can be drawn out. First, the variety of ways
in which the idea of the doctor's healing himself is used (Plutarch in
one way, Dio in another) shows that v. 23a needs the clarification
provided by v. 23b. Indeed, each needs the other within a complementary whole, since v. 23a makes plain that healings are involved
whereas v. 23b refers only vaguely to ὅσα...γενόμενα, and v. 23a
leaves without explanation the enigmatic word σεαυτόν. Source-
critical separation of strata is therefore not in order, nor any diminution of the logical compactness of v. 23ab. Secondly, the heavy
emphasis on healings within vv. 18-19 has already been noted, and
makes the address ἰατρέ appropriate and the omission of the healing
clause from Isaiah 61 a mark of sophistication rather than a cause of
surprise.[1] Thirdly, as already suggested, the tone of the hypothetical
request in v. 23 must be adjudged entirely positive. The request neither presupposes a rejecting attitude, nor does it implicitly contain a
charge that Jesus has not been doing in Nazareth what he has done in
Capernaum, nor does it presuppose that the request will be rejected,
nor does it register scepticism about the initial claim.

Before moving, as has now become imperative, to the relationship
between v. 23 and vv. 24, 25-27, a word must be said about the so-

---

1. Against Chilton, *God in Strength*, p. 144; Tuckett, 'Lk. 4.16-30', pp. 347-46:
'There is no good reason why Luke should omit the healing clause from Isaiah 61'.

called 'Capernaum crux'. It is hard to suppress a sense that much too much has been made of this. In consequence, an exotic variety of hypotheses has seen the light of day— that v. 23, within the putative source to which it belonged, has been moved from a different pre-Lucan position;[1] or that Luke constructed 4.14-44 as an homogeneous unit so that on the level of Luke's thinking v. 23 presupposes vv. 31-44, rather than vice versa;[2] or that Luke, at work redactionally here, is simply presupposing what took place in the Marcan sequence in advance of Mk 6.1-6a;[3] or that ἐρεῖτε is a strictly temporal future which points forward to Lk. 8.19-21 and the visit of the relatives, whose wish to see Jesus is a wish to see him perform miracles (cf. 9.9; 23.8), and who 'want to take him to Nazareth in order that he may work miracles in what they consider the proper place'[4]—in spite of the attempted assassination in Lk. 4.28-30! Much the most probable solution to the problem involves taking ἐρεῖτε in a rhetorical sense, permitting what might be said to be part of the immediate conversation, as has been accepted by a number of writers,[5] and as is supported by several other Lucan texts in which a response to something previously said or done is envisaged.[6] And, most importantly, all that is needed to give backing and wholly adequate preparation for v. 23b is to be found in Lk. 4.14: 'And Jesus returned in the power of the Spirit into Galilee, and a report concerning him went out through all the surrounding country'. Concerning this narrative statement, (i) 'the power of the Spirit' must, as already argued, be interpreted in terms of the close association in Luke's mind between power, the Spirit and miracle; (ii) while the reference in v. 14a is extremely general, a particular central point of reference is envisaged by v. 14b;[7] (iii) the similar statement in

---

1. Schürmann, 'Nazareth-Perikope', p. 197.
2. Busse, *Wunder*, p. 62.
3. Delobel, 'Rédaction', p. 123.
4. H. Conzelmann, *The Theology of Saint Luke* (London: Faber, 1961), p. 34.
5. H. Schürmann, *Das Lukasevangelium* (HTKNT 3/1; Freiburg: Herder, 1969), p. 237; Busse, *Wunder*, p. 62; D. Hill, 'The Rejection of Jesus at Nazareth, Lk. 4.16-30', *NovT* 13 (1971), pp. 161-80 (171).
6. See Lk. 13.25, 27; 17.7, 8; 19.31; 20.5/Mk 11.31.
7. Cf. Mk 1.28; Lk. 7.17. This observation was made by Schürmann in his 'Bericht vom Anfang' article, and is valid whatever one's view of his overall hypothesis.

Mt. 9.26 serves not only to confirm a central point of reference but also the naturalness of miracle as the event which gives rise to the circulating report; (iv) Capernaum in Mk 1.21 is explicitly defined by redaction in Lk. 4.31 as πόλις τῆς Γαλιλαίας. Doubtless the activity detailed in vv. 31-44 will serve further to confirm the painful and controversial preference for Capernaum which is defended in vv. 24, 25-27, but it is not the frame of reference for v. 23. The latter is entirely provided by v. 14, and thus the 'Capernaum crux' crumbles.

V

From here, then, we can move to vv. 24, 25-27. But this move requires considerable care, given the rather tense relationship between the two OT allusions and the preceding saying which might have been expected formally to function as some kind of a heading. While the figure of the prophet and his treatment ἐν τῇ πατρίδι αὐτοῦ correspond to Elijah and Elisha and their impact ἐν τῷ Ἰσραήλ, the correspondence is not without serious tension—substantially, acceptability (δεκτός) is hardly the issue in the Elijah/Elisha situations, and formally the overlap between ἀμὴν λέγω ὑμῖν and ἐπ' ἀληθείας δὲ λέγω ὑμῖν serves less to associate than to separate and to establish the independence of vv. 25-27 from v. 24. From v. 23 we know what is needed, namely a refutation of the 'if Capernaum, then also Nazareth' request by means of an 'although Capernaum, not Nazareth' answer, but v. 24 does not quite work that way. From this situation of tension we have to move forward with great sensitivity in connecting the Capernaum/Nazareth antithesis to the outside/inside Israel antithesis. What we can say for sure on this is that Luke does not want the Capernaum community to be symbolic of the Gentile world, and therefore he does not want Nazareth to be symbolic of the community of Israel. This is quite evident in that (i) his Jesus proceeds immediately to minister in Capernaum (4.31-44), manifestly as part of a ministry in Israel rather than as a symbol of a ministry in the Gentile world; (ii) his Jesus, like Elisha, cleanses a leper, but unlike Elisha, *within* the community of Israel (cf. his offering sacrifice, Lk. 5.12-16/Mk 1.40-45); (iii) his Jesus, replicating the action of Elijah, is doubly hailed as a great prophet active 'among us' and the means whereby 'God has visited his people' (Lk. 7.11-17); (iv) his Jesus is confirmed as ὁ ἐρχόμενος, the one whom the Baptist had announced in the course of his mission to Israel (Lk. 7.18-23, cf. 3.7-9); (v) his scheme, so vividly illustrated in much quoted passages such as Acts 13.46-47; 18.6-7; 19.9 and 28.28, is one in which the gospel is taken to the Gentiles after having been presented to the Jews and after having been rejected by them, whereas the scheme in Lk. 4.14-15, 16-30 is one in which Jesus works in Capernaum before approaching Nazareth, and turns away from Nazareth before that community rejects him. When these considerations are brought together they seem to suggest that the function of vv. 25-27 is more limited than some commentators suppose. It is not the great climax of the story, so that the Capernaum/Nazareth antithesis is just the springboard for the great leap forward to the climactic theme of the advance to the Gentiles.[1] It is simply and solely, and nothing more than, the double plank supporting the Capernaum/Nazareth antithesis, which is really about something else. What that 'something else' is will need to be defined, but before that happens the detail of the Elijah/Elisha allusions itself needs to be exposed.

Of the two biblical allusions the first, the more extended and dominant, clearly contains the major thrust. Traditional biblical language is to be found in ἐγένετο λιμὸς μέγας[2] and its amplification ἐπὶ τὴν γῆν,[3] to which πᾶς is elsewhere attached.[4] The fact that this language is so traditional does not help the suggestion that Luke intends to foreshadow Acts 11.28 and to show in both contexts how a

---

1. Against J.A. Fitzmyer, *The Gospel according to Luke 1–9* (AB, 28; New York: Doubleday, 1983), p. 537: 'vv. 25-27 provide a justification from the OT for the Christian mission to the Gentiles.' Sensitivity to this matter is well illustrated by the comments of H. Schürmann, *Lukasevangelium*, I, p. 238. A confident observation about 'der Übergang der Heilspredigt von den ablehnenden Juden zu den Heiden' is preceded by the following remark: 'Vielmehr wird mit diesen beiden Beispielen *nur in lockerer Weise* (my italics) der (prophetische) Hinweis angefügt, dass auch Jesus Sendung über Nazareth und Israel hinaus an die Heiden ergehen wird'. Similarly, S.G. Wilson, *The Gentiles and the Gentile Mission in Luke–Acts* (SNTSMS, 23; Cambridge: Cambridge University Press, 1973), pp. 40-41, takes the theme of Jewish rejection and Gentile inclusion to be implicit 'but not made explicit'. Clearly difficulties are being experienced.

2. 4 Kgdms 6.25; 1 Macc. 9.24.

3. Cf. Gen. 12.10; 26.1; 41.30; 42.5; 43.1; 45.6; 47.4; Ruth 1.1; 2 Kgdms 24.13; 4 Kgdms 4.38; 8.1; 2 Chron. 6.26; Ps. 104.16; Amos 8.11; Jer. 14.15.

4. Gen. 41.54, 56, 57; 47.13.

famine serves 'to bring disparate people together',[1] an idea which can only be extracted from Lk. 4.25-27 with the utmost difficulty. The more natural frame of reference for what is said here is that of a people under judgment, as emerges from two very important data. First, the three and a half years of famine is strikingly different from the seven years[2] or three years[3] which figure elsewhere, the latter most notably in the description of the famine in Ahab's reign (1 Kgs 18.2). It is surely right when commentators refer to 'der Zeitraum des Unheils'[4] and 'die apokalyptische Unglückszeit',[5] but more questionable whether 'this apocalyptic detail is meaningless in the Lucan account; the evangelist has simply inherited it'.[6] Secondly, it is a perceptive summing up of a multitude of Old Testament texts which brings Ezekiel to include famine among 'the four sore acts of judgment' (14.21), or Titus in theologizing vein to ask, 'Faction, famine ...what can these things mean but that God is wroth with them and extending his aid to us?'[7] Against this background it can scarcely be doubted that the fact of judgment is the concern of Lk. 4.25, and therefore that the threat of judgment is the primary and overpowering concern to which the attention of the residents of Nazareth is being distracted. That being so, we can go on to discuss the rest of 4.25-26. for which there is, formally at least, the counterpart in 4.27. The full significance of 4.25a, 26 only emerges when the following points are noticed.

First, the experience of the widow in 1 Kgs 17 to which allusion is being made is not this time the raising of her son (1 Kgs 17.17-24), as it is in Sir. 48.5 or Lk. 7.11-17, but the provision of food when she was on the point of death. The reasons for this are (i) that the reference to famine defines the situation; (ii) that the problem of the dying son is unique to the one widow, whereas the shortage of food is common to many, cf. πολλαὶ χῆραι, and the argument requires a shared problem to be in view; (iii) that the experience is linked with Elijah's

---

1. Thus, L.C. Crockett, 'Lk. 4.25-27 and Jewish–Gentile Relations in Luke–Acts', *JBL* 88 (1969), pp. 177-83 (178-79).
2. Gen. 41.27; 2 Kgs 8.1.
3. 2 Sam. 21.1/1 Chron. 21.12.
4. Strobel, *Kerygma*, p. 111.
5. Schürmann, *Lukasevangelium*, I, p. 238; cf. Dömer, *Heil*, pp. 51-52.
6. Fitzmyer, *Luke 1–9*, p. 538.
7. Ezek. 14.21; Josephus, *War* 6.40.

being sent, cf. ἐπέμφθη, and therefore belongs to the start of their contact; (iv) that the widow is often in the OT a type of the person who needs food.[1]

Secondly, the situation of the typical widow[2] is one of intense vulnerability, of 'loneliness and many sorrows' (*4 Macc.* 16.10). At risk, both judicially and materially, and readily associated with the orphan and the resident alien, she becomes identified with the poor. As such she is the subject of repeated divine demands for justice, for God watches over her with special vigilance and maintains her cause. It is therefore almost, but not quite, unthinkable and a mark of the most fearful judgment that widows should be caught up in divinely initiated adversity. But it can indeed happen that 'the Lord does not rejoice over their young men, and has no compassion on their fatherless and widows' (Isa. 9.17).

Thirdly, famine texts in the Old Testament affirm the norm that even during such straitened times those who fear the Lord can count on supplies from God (Pss. 33.18-19; 37.18-19); indeed, as *Ps. Sol.* 15.8 puts it, it is a sign of God on the righteous with a view to their salvation, that famine as well as sword and death are kept far from them.

We have therefore in Lk. 4.25-26 a very pointed and disturbing analysis of a situation in which not a single one of those persons in Israel who might especially count on divine support in times of adversity does in fact receive it. The supply of food to widows is a concern of God, the conviction that in times of famine exceptions may be made is a firm element in faith, and the expectation of such compassionate exemption by God follows from the terms of the covenant, and yet it did not happen. For such an interpretation of the events in 1 Kgs 17 there is no explicit parallel except in Isa. 9.17. The intensity of the judgment here described could scarcely be exceeded.

On this basis we can now press even further with the process of drawing out the implications of Lk. 4.25-27, bearing in mind all the time the need to check whether there is or is not a correspondence with the Acts missionary pattern involving outreach to the Gentiles.

Elijah and Elisha were throughout their careers prophets of Israel (cf. 1 Kgs 18.17; 2 Kgs 5.8). They would serve ill as examples of

1. Deut. 10.18; 24.19-21; 26.12-13; Job 22.9; 31.16-17.
2. G. Stahlin, 'χήρα', *TDNT*, IX (1974), pp. 449-65.

those who became prophets of the nations. Moreover, the actions recalled in these texts scarcely fit a situation of mission. Elijah is involved in 1 Kgs 17.8-16 as a refugee, and engages in no public activity whatever before his return to Israel in 1 Kgs 18.1. Elisha, for his part, makes no move at all to contact Gentiles in general or Naaman in particular— the initiative comes exclusively from the side of Naaman himself (2 Kgs 5.4). Furthermore, significant features of 1 Kgs 17.8-16 and 2 Kgs 5.1-14 alert us to the fact that while miracle is involved in each case, the prophet himself is not presented as a miracle worker. It is, strictly speaking, an 'act of God' or a 'sign from heaven' in each case. God acts, and the prophet merely utters the word (see especially 1 Kgs 17.14 and 2 Kgs 5.7, 10). This strong concentration on God is sensitively registered in Lk. 4.25-26, 27 by means of the two 'divine passives' ἐπέμφθη and ἐκαθαρίσθη,[1] together with the fact that in v. 27 Elisha himself is almost incidental. By ensuring that attention is shifted from the prophet to God, the ground is prepared for an insistence on God's freedom to choose who shall benefit from the exertion of miraculous power.

This divine freedom of choice has been highlighted by a number of writers. For example, C.M. Tuckett declared, 'The point of vv. 25-27 may originally have nothing to do with a Jew-Gentile distinction: rather these verses simply illustrate God's absolute freedom and his refusal to be dictated to or tied down'.[2] It would perhaps be better to say that the Jew-Gentile distinction is important and is introduced precisely in order to remind and challenge a self-consciously Jewish audience, but the main point must be right. Of course, this does not mean that Israel's election as such is rejected. Instead, very specific and limited, but nevertheless heavily loaded, precedents are being adduced to establish a grand principle, which in turn can be given very direct and *ad hominem* application. The principle is not that of 'Gentiles as well as Jews', which is the missionary programme of Acts, but 'Gentiles instead of Jews' in a very limited and well defined context. The application, as far as Nazareth is concerned, is that God is free. He will not be hemmed in by any general scheme, however theologically lofty. He *can* work elsewhere, that is, outside the presumed natural or

1. J. Jeremias, ''Ηλ(ε)ίας', *TDNT*, II (1964), pp. 928-41 (935); Busse, *Wunder*, p. 64.
2. Tuckett, 'Lk. 4.16-30', p. 352.

even necessary setting, as the Old Testament precedents demonstrate. He *will* work elsewhere if overriding concerns, which he freely decides, require. And since it *is* a matter of divine decision, the legitimacy of the prophetic agent or his claim is in no way undermined.

The *Sitz im Leben* of Lk. 4.25-27 is quite unmistakably mission in Israel. Not even a sidelong glance is cast at any mission among Gentiles, and therefore, one has to say, neither the establishing of Jew/Gentile table-fellowship in the setting of Christian mission nor the inclusion of God-fearers are in view when the function of the Elijah/Elisha texts is discerned.[1] The line of thought is a warning, a salutary warning to Jews that their position is not so special that they cannot be bypassed by God. And that line of thought is, in scheme and in substance, notably close to that of some Q traditions— those which set out a pair of matching arguments in support of a basic thesis, sometimes combining male and female cases (Q 12.22-31; 13.18-21), or those which use Gentile personnel to the disadvantage of a Jewish audience (Q 10.13-15; 11.31-32), or those which answer an audience's longing for a sign by issuing a severe warning that their concerns should be focused on the judgment which may blow their lives apart (Q 11.29-30; 17.22-30), or those which take their cue from the Baptist's chiding of those whose comfortable complacency is connected to the covenantal privileges, and whose immediate and overriding need is to come to terms with the far from comfortable prospect of judgment (3.7-9). Nearness to Q should almost certainly not be taken to mean derivation from Q. Rather, the extent to which this pair of Old Testament-based arguments reflects the concerns of the Lucan gospel and connects up with LukeR activity in 4.23, suggests that the evangelist is responsible for an imitation of the approach of Q—an acute, sophisticated and sensitive imitation, but still an imitation.

What, then, of the statement which appears to function as some kind of heading for the Elijah/Elisha arguments: 'And he said, "Truly, I say to you, no prophet is acceptable in his own πατρίς"'? Within this generalizing proverbial statement the word πατρίς cannot stand for any community other than the home town— if it stands for home

---

1. Against P.F. Esler, *Community and Gospel in Luke–Acts* (SNTSMS, 57; Cambridge: Cambridge University Press, 1987), p. 35.

country the proverb effectively ceases to be true.[1] That being so, v. 24 relates logically and easily to v. 23. But, as already observed, v. 23 points up the need for a refutation of the 'if Capernaum, then also Nazareth' request by means of an 'although Capernaum, not Nazareth' answer. The argument in vv. 25-27 works well to that end, but v. 24 does not. Elijah and Elisha were emphatically not cases of prophetic unacceptability (cf. ἐκτός, LukeR in v. 24). That means that v. 24 states a principle explicitly which is different from that which the following arguments demand implicitly. This suggests that v. 24 should after all not be regarded as any kind of heading for the following arguments, but rather a comment explaining what happens when the prophet works within the parameters of the divine design, and particularly when he says the things which Jesus *and Jesus alone* says in vv. 25-27. Thus it functions as a prospective comment on the consequences for him of refusing a sign and warning of judgment. It alerts the reader to what will happen after vv. 25-27 have been uttered. It is a preparation for the grisly outcome which materializes in vv. 28-30. And that is the outcome for Jesus *and Jesus alone*.

On this basis, the theological concern of the story emerges triumphantly over the slight literary disorder. Jesus as the prophetic agent of liberation, liberation effected through the gospel and in the healings and by the Spirit, is the great overarching concern. Luke cannot impress this on his readers too strongly. But there is another, a complementary theme. The word judgment is never uttered and yet it never ceases to be heard. And Jesus is the prophetic preacher of the divine word in Israel, implicitly warning of judgment, implicitly calling for repentance, proving unacceptable, having his word rejected, nearly falling victim to an assassination attempt. Nearly, but not quite and not yet! For even here the divine design dictates that he cannot die prematurely, although he must die eventually. What is all this but a deuteronomic interpretation of the work of the ultimate prophet of liberation?

---

1. *Pace* Dörner, *Heil*, p. 60. This is not to deny that the term as such can stand for home country, which it manifestly can (Jer. 22.10; Ezek. 23.15; 2 Macc. 4.1; *4 Macc.* 1.11, *et al.*), just as it frequently stands for home town (Lev. 25.10; 2 Macc. 8.33; Mk 6.1; Josephus, *Ant.* 5.229, 232, 270, 317, 346). It is merely to affirm that the former sense does not, and the latter sense does, work in this particular setting.

VI

And where does this leave us in respect of the continuity or otherwise between Luke and Jesus? Surely we can drop without hesitation the 'or otherwise'! Luke has with immense skill and artistry painted a picture of someone who, as countless readers would attest, 'has won our hearts', and he is extremely heavily involved in that presentational process. But while the words are the words of Luke, the voice is surely the voice of Jesus. Was he not in profile a prophet? Was he not committed to Israel? Was he not a charismatic endowed with the Spirit? Was he not concerned for the poor as the top priority dictated by Israel's traditions and present traumas? Was he not resistant to demands for signs? Was he not engaged in a ministry of liberation by word and deed? Was he not unswerving in the announcement of judgment and insistent on the demand for repentance? Was he not the first to reflect, as it were, deuteronomically upon his own calling and destiny?

HISTORICAL ISSUES AND THE PROBLEM OF JOHN AND THE SYNOPTICS

D. Moody Smith

I

Marinus de Jonge has repeatedly addressed himself to questions of the history and interpretation of the Johannine literature and has quite recently published an important contribution to Jesus research.[1] Although in the latter volume he does not deal with the Gospel of John, but focuses mainly on Mark and Q, he nevertheless writes that not only material distinctive of Matthew and Luke, but 'even individual pieces of tradition recorded only in the Fourth Gospel, may also go back to an earlier date'.[2] In a much earlier essay, however, de Jonge had dealt sensitively with the important question 'Who are "we"?', taking his direction from the 'we have seen his glory' of Jn 1.14.[3] De Jonge observes that here as elsewhere in the Fourth Gospel and 1 John the apostolic eyewitness is in view, although John's use of the first person plural cannot be limited to that original group.

In paying tribute to our colleague we should not appear to invoke his words to validate our own opinions, but it does seem worthwhile to point out that my interests find a resonance in his work. In this essay it is my intention to set the question of historicity in John over against the problem of John and the Synoptic Gospels, not so much with a

1. See, for example, the collection of his Johannine essays in *Jesus: Stranger from Heaven and Son of God, Jesus Christ and the Christians in the Johannine Perspective* (SBLSBS, 11; Missoula, MT: Scholars Press, 1977); on Jesus himself, *Jesus, The Servant-Messiah* (New Haven: Yale University Press, 1991).

2. De Jonge, *Jesus, The Servant-Messiah*, p. 2.

3. The essay, entitled 'Who Are "We"?' is found in de Jonge's *Jesus: Inspiring and Disturbing Presence* (trans. J. E. Steely; Nashville: Abingdon Press, 1974), pp. 148-66. The earlier part of the essay, which concerns us here, was written in 1968 as a public lecture and published in Dutch that same year.

view to proving John historical, as to suggest that in a number of cases in which John differs from the other Gospels there is not convincing reason for preferring them for historical purposes or on historical grounds. Insofar as John's differences do not seem to be variants from the Synoptics made for theological reasons, they speak on the side of the independence of the Gospel of John, whether or not the evangelist knew, or knew about, the other Gospels.

Over a half-century ago, Percival Gardner-Smith wrote that critics are not likely 'to accept the Johannine account as historical in the narrower sense of the term; the influence of interpretation is too obvious for that; but where the Fourth Gospel differs from the Synoptics it may henceforth be wise to treat its testimony with rather more respect than it has lately received, and perhaps in not a few cases it may prove to be right'.[1] Gardner-Smith's 'henceforth' modestly alluded to his own arguments for the independence of the Fourth Gospel of the Synoptics, which heralded a major change in scholarly opinion. With the publication of C.H. Dodd's *Historical Tradition in the Fourth Gospel*, the view that John wrote independently of the other Gospels, basing his narrative on a separate, if related, tradition, seemed well on the way to becoming canonical.[2] The significance of John's independence of the Synoptics for the historical question was, however, variously expressed, as the differences between Dodd and Rudolf

---

1.   *Saint John and the Synoptic Gospels* (Cambridge: Cambridge University Press, 1938), p. 97.

2.   C.H. Dodd, *Historical Tradition in the Fourth Gospel* (Cambridge: Cambridge University Press, 1963), p. 8 n. 2, refers to Gardner-Smith's work as 'a book which crystallized the doubts of many [regarding John's dependence on the Synoptics], and he exerted an influence out of proportion to its size'. One may cite, in America, R.E. Brown's important commentary as typical of this newly emerging position: *The Gospel according to John* (AB, 29A; Garden City, NY: Doubleday, 1966, 1970); note especially vol. I, pp. xliv-xlvii: 'To summarize, then, in most of the material narrated in both John and the Synoptics, we believe that the evidence does not favor Johannine dependence on the Synoptics or their sources' (p. xlvii.) But already in 1941 R. Bultmann had completed his *Das Evangelium des Johannes* (Göttingen: Vandenhoeck & Ruprecht) for the Kritsch-exegetischer Kommentar series, which thirty years later was to be translated by G.R. Beasley-Murray and others as *The Gospel of John: A Commentary* (Oxford: Basil Blackwell, 1971); in this critically important commentary he finds John's use of the Synoptics an unnecessary hypothesis and at best a late, redactional phenomenon, peripheral rather than central to John's composition.

Bultmann show. For Dodd the possible historical value of the Fourth Gospel was an important implication of its independence with distinct theological overtones, but for Bultmann, the historicity of the Fourth Gospel was, apart from its bare fact claim, negligible and of little theological import. In any event, John's independence could be taken for granted as a beginning point for discussion, and in his efforts to renew the defence of the historicity of the Fourth Gospel, John A.T. Robinson did just that.[1]

For those who follow Johannine scholarship, however, it is scarcely fresh news that John's independence of the Synoptics is no longer taken for granted. Indeed, the latest wave of investigation moves in the opposite direction.[2] In light of this recent movement, I want to examine some of the historical aspects or implications of the problem of their relationship. Obviously, if the Gospel of John was wholly dependent upon the Synoptics for its portrayal of Jesus and his ministry, any deviation from them would imply a diminution of its historical accuracy. Accordingly, the Gospel would be deemed of no value as an independent source. If, on the other hand, John was independent of the Synoptics, the question of its historical value would be worth pursuing. In the latter case, of course, nothing would be necessarily implied about its historical truth, for an independent gospel could be historically valueless or specious. But if, or insofar as, the distinctly Johannine materials present or reflect data or situations that are plausibly or arguably historical, they bespeak the

1. See most recently, and finally, the late Bishop Robinson's *The Priority of John* (ed. J.F. Coakley; London: SCM Press, 1985), where Robinson more or less begins from the premise of John's independence (cf. pp. 10-23). Robinson's 'The New Look on the Fourth Gospel', in his *Twelve New Testament Studies* (SBT, 34; London: SCM Press, 1962), pp. 94-106, was first given as a paper at the Oxford conference on 'The Four Gospels' in 1957. It expresses the same point of view more tentatively. At about the same time, A.J.B. Higgins was writing his brief book, *The Historicity of the Fourth Gospel* (London: Lutterworth, 1960), in which John's independence is presumed.

2. It is represented most impressively by the work of Professor F. Neirynck and his colleagues at the Catholic University of Louvain. On this most recent turn in the discussion of the problem, see my *John among the Gospels: The Relationship in Twentieth-Century Research* (Minneapolis: Fortress Press, 1992). The trend is well represented in the papers presented to the Louvain Biblical Collegium 1990 on John and the Synoptics. See A. Denaux (ed.), *John and the Synoptics* (BETL, 101; Leuven: Leuven University Press, 1992).

independence of John from the Synoptics. While independence does not imply historical value, the attribution of historical plausibility to the distinctive Johannine material does imply independence, although it, of course, does not prove it.

II

In all probability, at least two characteristics of the Gospel of John have led historians of Christian origins to regard it as a document of only secondary historical worth—behind the Synoptic Gospels—if it has any such value at all. In the first place, several of the signs of the Fourth Gospel surpass in their sheer miraculousness the mighty works narrated in the Synoptics. They are more spectacular or incredible. The man at the pool of Bethzatha has been ill for thirty-eight years; the blind man in ch. 9 has been blind from birth; the dead Lazarus has been in the tomb all of four days. Such astounding aspects of Johannine stories seem to be exaggerations based upon the already amazing deeds of Jesus narrated in the Synoptics. If in the Synoptics Jesus supplies ample food for the five thousand from a few loaves and fish (as he does also in John) the fourth evangelist portrays Jesus changing water into wine. But, secondly, even more distinctive than the Johannine Jesus' deeds are his words. In the Synoptics, especially in Mark, Jesus can scarcely be coaxed into talking about himself, whereas in the Fourth Gospel he proclaims his messianic status and argues with opponents about his dignity and role. The familiar 'I am' words of Jesus are altogether typical, and distinctive, of the Gospel of John.

Both these characteristics of the Fourth Gospel are understandably, and rightly, regarded as historically suspect, while at the same time they cast doubt upon the historicity of the Johannine portrayal of Jesus and his ministry generally.[1] While the unhistorical nature of such aspects of the Gospel of John has been granted by most critical scholarship in the course of this century, a similar negative historical evaluation has gradually characterized Synoptic exegesis also. Some Johannine exegetes have sought to turn the situation in Synoptic studies to the advantage of the Fourth Gospel, and its historical worth, by pointing out that John's theological character scarcely differentiates it from the other canonical

---

1. J. Ashton, *Understanding the Fourth Gospel* (Oxford: Clarendon Press, 1991), pp. 36-38, cites Strauss and Baur in documenting the demise of the Fourth Gospel as a historical source in the eyes of nineteenth-century critics.

gospels.[1] This is certainly true, but from the standpoint of one who values historical trustworthiness it may be small consolation!

Obviously, it does not enhance the historical value of John just to devalue the other three. Yet there are a number of points at which it may be argued that John represents, or reflects more accurately, the historical situation or events of Jesus' ministry, even if his purpose is not to narrate something we call 'history' or 'biography'. If one seeks criteria to identify such points, or justify their consideration as historical, three simple ones may be suggested. Elements or items deserve consideration as possibly historical that (1) without reproducing the Synoptics accord with the portrayal of Jesus found in them, (2) do not advance the distinctively Johannine Christology, and (3) are historically plausible in the time, place, and setting of Jesus' ministry. I want to point to such elements or items with brief justification, by way of inventory, without drawing any firm conclusions. For our purposes it is neither necessary nor appropriate to presuppose John's independence in the sense of his ignorance or deliberate ignoring of the Synoptics. It is obvious enough that the evangelist goes his own way. I intend simply to point to certain data and leave the conclusions up to the reader. Nothing of what I say will be entirely new. Gathering and quickly surveying the data in view of the question of John's relation to the Synoptics may, however, be worthwhile.

1.   Already R.E. Brown effectively made this point in one of his early articles, 'The Problem of Historicity in John', *CBQ* 24 (1962), pp. 1-14 (3). His purpose was broader than ours, namely, to show that John's Gospel should be considered representative of a Palestinian, eyewitness historical tradition in some ways as valuable as the Synoptic. (Although his article appeared the year after Dodd's book, it was obviously written before Dodd was published.) Our purpose is simply to argue that at a number of points where John differs from the Synoptics his account is at least as likely—sometimes more likely—to be historically valid. Perhaps closer to our purpose is Brown's 'Incidents that are Units in the Synoptic Gospels but Dispersed in John', *CBQ* 23 (1961), pp. 143-60. Brown's interest in maintaining an important element of historicity at the level of Jesus himself is strongly evident in the first volume of his Anchor Commentary especially, and I think he has never abandoned it, despite the fact that he has later shown greater interest in *The Community of the Beloved Disciple* (New York: Paulist Press, 1979). Likewise, his longtime Union Seminary colleague J.L. Martyn, who in *History and Theology in the Fourth Gospel* (Nashville: Abingdon Press, rev. edn, 1979), portrays the Gospel as a narrative on two levels, the *einmalig* (putatively Jesus') and that of the primitive Johannine church, nevertheless focuses his attention on the latter level.

First, there is the *chronology* of Jesus' ministry. The traditional three-year ministry is, of course, an inference from the Fourth Gospel, for the Synoptics seem to presuppose a ministry of one Passover and of a year or less. John, on the other hand, speaks of three distinct Passovers (2.13; 6.4; 11.55).We commonly say that the three-year scheme of the Fourth Gospel accommodates the evangelist's interest in Jesus' replacement of Jewish festivals.[1] This may be the case, but that fact alone would not necessarily mean that there is not something historically correct about John's time-frame. Moreover, the Synoptic (Markan) framework is generally acknowledged to be literary and theological rather than historical. Did Jesus gather disciples, teach, gain fame as a miracle-worker, and arouse opposition that led to his death in less than a year? Possibly, but the traditional, longer (Johannine) time-frame makes considerable sense, particularly if we take into account a period in which Jesus worked under the influence of John the Baptist, as the Fourth Gospel may imply. The ancient and traditional way of harmonizing the Gospel accounts by accommodating the other three to the Fourth Gospel was an obvious and practical apologetic procedure, but not for that reason necessarily wrong.

Another chronological consideration is, of course, the matter of when, according to the Jewish calendar, Jesus celebrated the Last Supper with his disciples and when he was put to death. As is known, according to the Synoptics the Last Supper was a Passover meal, and Jesus was tried and put to death during the feast. According to John, on the other hand, Jesus' last meal was at most a proleptic Passover feast, for it occurred the evening before Nisan 15. He was then tried and crucified before the Feast (Cf. Mk 14.2), so that the Jewish authorities wanted his body taken down quickly (Jn 19.31). In favor of the Synoptic chronology it is argued that John makes an alteration to have Jesus die while the Passover lambs are slain. Odd that he should make this juxtaposition and not mention it or otherwise indicate why he has done so. Moreover, one would then expect Jesus' expiatory, salvific death to play a larger role, as it does in Paul and even 1 John. Of course, there have been elaborate efforts to explain John's deviation from the Synoptics by recourse to theories about John's midrashic character or diverging Jewish calendars. But is not the

---

1. Cf. already E. Hoskyns, *The Fourth Gospel*, pp. 63-64, cited by Bultmann, *The Gospel of John*, p. 122 n. 3. This is, of course, a recurring theme with many variations in the exegesis of the Fourth Gospel.

simplest explanation that the Synoptics succumb to an understandable pressure to make of the Last Supper a Passover meal, while John represents a more primitive phase in which that had not yet occurred?[1]

Closely related to the three-year Johannine chronology or itinerary of Jesus' ministry is the *geographical locale*, in which Jesus appears frequently and for long periods of time in Judea and Jerusalem. Again, Johannine theological interests are apparently at work. Jerusalem is the headquarters of 'the Jews'. Yet if, in fact, Jesus' ministry went on for two or three years, is it not intrinsically probable that he made more than the one Passover pilgrimage to Jerusalem that the Synoptics report? The three Passover visits reported by John become a probability, even though they advance Johannine Christology. One might also note that Mark (14.49) has Jesus say to the arresting party that he was daily (*kath'hēmeran*) in the temple teaching, a statement that fits the Johannine chronology and setting better than the Markan, where Jesus could have only been there a few days. Jesus' seeming familiarity with persons or places in Jerusalem, reflected precisely in the Markan account of the preparation for this Triumphal Entry (11.3) or the Last Supper (14.13-17), bespeaks a longer acquaintance with the capital city than Mark's narrative seems to allow.

The whole question of *Jesus' relationship to the Baptist* (always called simply 'John') is handled more elaborately in the Fourth Gospel than

1. I here follow Dodd (*Historical Tradition in the Fourth Gospel*, pp. 109-11), who assembles the evidence in favor of John's dating. C.K. Barrett, *The Gospel according to John: An Introduction with Commentary and Notes on the Greek Text* (Philadelphia: Westminster Press 1978), pp. 48-51, makes the case for the historicity of the synoptic dating, following Jeremias and taking issue with Bernard (ICC), who had favored the Johannine. Bultmann's indifference to the historical question is typical: 'Nor is the historical question, which of the two datings is correct (perhaps the Johannine), of any importance for the interpretation of John' (*Gospel of John*, p. 465 n. 1).

There is another significant Johannine variant, in that Jesus is said to be crucified at, or after, the sixth hour (19.14), whereas in Mark he is crucified at the third hour (15.25). Assuming the Jewish reckoning of time in both cases, John would put the crucifixion at noon, when the Passover lambs were slain, arguably a theologically motivated timing, which, however, seems more likely to lie in John's tradition than in the evangelist's redaction. On the other hand, twelve noon would seem a more plausible time for the crucifixion to begin than nine in the morning, particularly since in Mark the trial before Pilate immediately preceded. (This gets us into questions of how early in the morning a Roman prefect would have gone to work and whether that is irrelevant because of the unusual circumstances, etc. These questions cannot be adjudicated here.)

in the Synoptics. For example, in the Fourth Gospel the Baptist goes out of his way to make sure that his own temporal priority to Jesus is not misconstrued (1.15, 30). The one who comes after—Jesus—was before, in the sense of prior to, or greater than. Bultmann, following Matthew Black, suggests the possibility the 'coming after' (*erchesthai opisō*) means following in the sense of discipleship.[1] Thus Jesus would at one time have been a disciple of John, and this was then all the more reason for the evangelist to make their actual, theological relationship clear.[2] If, indeed, Jesus himself baptized, as John more than once states (3.22, 26; 4.1), he clearly identified himself with the movement of which the Baptist was the head. The statement that only Jesus' disciples, not Jesus himself, baptized (4.2) seems a lame afterthought and correction. Moreover, this entire scene (3.22–4.3) portrays Jesus and the Baptist as working, if not side-by-side, at the very same time.[3]

Thus it became necessary to note, probably in light of the contradiction with the Synoptics, that John had not yet been cast into prison (3.24)—again a sort of afterthought.[4] In the Synoptics, of course, John is already out of the way, in prison, before Jesus begins his ministry (Mk 1.14). Here there is a rather strange agreement between John and Luke only, for while Luke notes that Herod imprisoned John (Lk. 3.19-20), he does not make the sharp dichotomy between John's ministry and Jesus', which we might have expected of him (that is, he omits Mk 1.14). One suspects that John (with Luke) knows something, namely, that John the Baptist's ministry did not end before Jesus' began, that they were for a while contemporaries, and that John would have appeared the originator and leader of a movement Jesus joined. Thus the Fourth Evangelist needs to set matters straight theologically because he knows the somewhat embarrassing history! Certainly John's historical assumptions about the relation of Jesus and John do

1. Bultmann, *The Gospel of John*, p. 75 n. 4.
2. Bultmann, *The Gospel of John*, p. 108.
3. Dodd (*Historical Tradition in the Fourth Gospel*, pp. 285-86), takes the representation of Jesus as baptizing to derive from old tradition, if it is not historical. Bultmann (*The Gospel of John*, p. 168) conjures with the possibility that 3.22 is derived from old tradition, but nevertheless views the entire section 3.22-26 as a literary composition of the evangelist designed to show Jesus' superiority over the Baptist.
4. Bultmann (*The Gospel of John*, p. 171) proposes that 3.24 is the insertion of the ecclesiastical redactor, for the evangelist shows no interest in harmonizing his account with the Synoptics. Dodd (*Historical Tradition in the Fourth Gospel*, pp. 279-80) also takes 3.24 to be 'an editorial note' but from the evangelist.

not serve his Christology nearly so well as the Markan premise of the clean sequence of Jesus and John, with no overlap, would have. Yet given the conditions of first-century Palestinian Judaism, the more complex relationship predicated by the Fourth Evangelist seems entirely reasonable. What is missing from John's Gospel, of course, is the apocalyptic character of John's preaching, as well as that of Jesus, which we know so well from the Synoptics. But this is exactly what we would expect in John. Furthermore, just that apocalyptic outlook would explain the close relationship of John and Jesus, which the Fourth Gospel describes more fully than do the others. John strongly implies that Jesus was a baptist, and I am inclined to agree!

Moreover, it is arguable that John the Baptist's statement, 'I did not know him' (1.33), reflects the historical fact that John had not known Jesus prior to this encounter. In Matthew (3.14), however, it is clearly presumed that John had prior knowledge of Jesus and of who he was. Although Mark does not state that John had such prior knowledge, Matthew may have inferred it from Mk 1.7-8. While Luke does not go beyond Mark in this narrative, he had earlier described Mary as a relative of John's mother Elizabeth (1.36), leaving the reader to presume John's knowledge of Jesus, to whom he would have been related. In the Fourth Gospel John comes to know who Jesus is, but only by virtue of the descent of the Spirit (1.33-4).

The portrayal of Jesus' relationship to John the Baptist raises the question of Jesus' own disciples, inasmuch as the Fourth Evangelist has two of them sent to Jesus by John the Baptist. That this happened in the way, and with the words of introduction (1.29, 36), John reports is unlikely. Yet that some of Jesus' disciples had been attracted to, or were followers of, the Baptist is altogether probable, given the similarities between them. Moreover, the Johannine account is, as interpreters have noted for centuries, better motivated. In Mark (followed by Matthew) Jesus calls disciples who apparently have never before seen him, and they follow. Traditional harmonization has explained this implausible sequence by proposing that Mark's (and Matthew's) narrative assumes John's. As unlikely as this may be, it is a way of taking account of the problem and acknowledging that John supplies an answer to an important question that Mark leaves unanswered—and unasked.

Moreover, while assuming the existence of the twelve, John clearly acknowledges that Jesus had other disciples, indeed, some who deserted him (6.66). Is it likely that John would have fabricated such a scene had he not known it, or at least the fact of their desertion, as a given.[1] Of course, we now tend to look first at John's own situation to explain and identify such deserters, but if the evangelist had such contemporaries in mind, he could easily have had Jesus predict them in the farewell discourses rather than insert them into his Galilean ministry.

John not only knows there were disciples who deserted Jesus. He also knows that the loyal disciples did not understand Jesus during his earthly ministry, but only after his crucifixion and resurrection.[2] Mark, of course, knows this as well. But John differs from Mark in his presentation of this state of affairs. In Mark, Jesus clearly predicts his coming death (and resurrection) and seemingly holds the disciples accountable for their failure to understand. John, however, regards the disciples as unable to understand, because the crucial events have, after all, not occurred, and the Holy Spirit or Paraclete has not yet come. Although John's presentation of Jesus is in some ways highly anachronistic—and much more so than the Synoptics—John does not have Jesus predict his own death so openly; rather he alludes to it more obliquely (3.14-15; 12.32), and the disciples are not clearly and culpably obtuse for not understanding. In this respect John seems closer to what must have been the actual situation of Jesus' disciples during his ministry. They did not understand because as yet they could not. Incidentally, in this connection Peter's confession in John does not betray that disciple's failure to understand and his culpability as it does in Mark, and John otherwise shows no particular desire to elevate or exonerate Peter. (Ch. 21 might be regarded as an exception, but even there Peter is subordinated to the beloved disciple, who as one who all along does understand in that sense at least represents the postresurrection church.)

Perhaps less important than Jesus' relationship to his disciples, but nevertheless interesting, is his relationship to his family—mother, brothers and father. Suffice it to say that, as in the Synoptics

1.   Dodd (*Historical Tradition in the Fourth Gospel*, pp. 220-21) thinks that 6.66 has some traditional and historical basis, thanking W.L. Knox for the original suggestion.

2.   On the disciples' inability to understand earlier, see F.F. Segovia, '"Peace I Leave with You; My Peace I Give to You": Discipleship in the Fourth Gospel', in F.F. Segovia (ed.), *Discipleship in the New Testament* (Philadelphia: Fortress Press, 1985), pp. 76-102 (92-94); also M. de Jonge, *Jesus: Stranger from Heaven and Son of God*, pp. 7-9.

(Mk 3.21, 31-35) Jesus puts distance between himself and his mother and brothers in incidents that are, however, distinctive of the Fourth Gospel (2.1-11; 7.1-10).

Another of Jesus' relationships that stands out as significant involves *the women who appear in the Fourth Gospel*.[1] Jesus' mother (never called 'Mary' in the Fourth Gospel) plays a larger and more positive role in the Johannine narrative than in the Synoptic, but one that is not contradictory to the Synoptic accounts. Jesus' encounter and conversation with the Samaritan woman at Jacob's Well (ch. 4) is, of course, unique to the Fourth Gospel. (Luke shares an interest in Samaria, as well as Jesus' female followers, with the Fourth Gospel, but without their sharing the same narratives.) But here the Johannine Jesus manifests typically human characteristics. He is tired from the journey in the heat of the day, as well as thirsty, and strikes up a conversation with the approaching woman, asking her for a drink. That Jesus should initiate a conversation with a woman, much less a Samaritan, is out of keeping with Jewish custom, as the story eventually indicates (4.9, 27), but this state of affairs does not necessarily speak against the historicity of the incident. Indeed, Jesus' approach to the Samaritan woman, his apparent openness to her, is congruent with and complements the Synoptic, especially the Lukan, picture of Jesus. *That* Jesus might have behaved in this way. The reader may be pleasantly surprised, but he is not confused. The conversation that develops is, of course, replete with Johannine theological themes and reflects the style and vocabulary of the Fourth Evangelist. One would be hard pressed to argue that John presents an account of an actual conversation between Jesus and this woman.

The sisters of Lazarus, Mary and Martha of Bethany, appear only in John and Luke (10.38-42). But only in John are they said to be sisters of Lazarus and to reside in Bethany. In John as in Luke they play host to Jesus and thus appear as his friends. In fact, Jesus is said to love them, even as he loves Lazarus (Jn 11.5). In John only, of course, this Mary anoints the feet of Jesus and wipes them with her hair (12.1-8; cf. Lk. 7.36-50, where the woman is not named). In John the apparent personal relationship between Jesus and this family in Bethany is the

1. See the remarkable essay by R.E. Brown, 'Roles of Women in the Fourth Gospel', in *The Community of the Beloved Disciple*, pp. 183-98. Brown underscores the evidence that women are fully, and perhaps uniquely, recognized as disciples of Jesus in the Gospel of John.

basis of a theologically important narrative: Jesus raises the brother Lazarus from the dead. But whatever one makes of this episode, it scarcely calls into question the verisimilitude of the relationship. Obviously, verisimilitude is not the same as historical factuality, but it is its *sine qua non*. That Mary and Martha appear also in Luke, in a somewhat different narrative, enhances the credibility of the Johannine notices. It is, of course, possible that John has here taken up the sisters from Luke, made the Lazarus of the Lukan parable (16.19-31) their brother, and constructed the narratives we now read in his Gospel. (But such a proposal involves us in the larger question of the relationship of Luke to John, which presents difficulties for it, that is, the distinctively Lukan material or L, is scarcely paralleled in John.)

Then there is Mary Magdalene, who in John, as in the other Gospels, appears at the cross and at the empty tomb. (In Luke she is not yet named at the cross, but only Luke indicates that she had an earlier relationship with Jesus; cf. Lk. 8.2.) In John she becomes the first witness of an appearance of the risen Christ (20.11-18). This is also the case in Mt. 28.9-10, although there her role is not stressed. Again, it is possible that John has taken a small item from Matthew and enlarged it greatly, but again we encounter the problem of explaining John's larger relationship—or lack of it—to the other Gospel.[1] Certainly John has ascribed a larger role to Mary Magdalene. She now stands out along with the mother of Jesus, the Samaritan woman, and the sisters Mary and Martha as one of the prominent people of the Gospel story. Is it more reasonable to believe that John in his social and theological setting enhanced their roles because of his nascent feminist interests or that he reflects here, albeit in ways different from the Synoptics, Jesus' actual relationships with women who followed him?

The *Johannine passion narrative* contains a number of interesting divergences from the Synoptics. We have already noticed the flagrant difference in the dating of the Last Supper and Jesus' crucifixion. The other most striking Johannine departure is the omission of any trial before the Sanhedrin following Jesus' arrest. Ironically, John's dating of the arrest before the feast lightens one of the major objections to the historicity of such a trial. Obviously, there is also an element of

1. Brown (*The Gospel according to John*, pp. 1002-3), regards Mt. 28.9-10 as a later insertion into the Matthean narrative, among other reasons, because v. 8 leads so nicely into v. 11 if it is omitted. Thus Jn 20.14-18 would be an independent version of the same tradition and not a Johannine development of a Matthean episode.

confusion in John, for Jesus is sent to Annas the father-in-law of the high priest Caiaphas (18.12-13), but subsequently in the same episode Annas is referred to as high priest. At the end Jesus is sent off bound by Annas to Caiaphas the high priest, but nothing is said about what happened there. Is the Markan (and Matthean) account of the trial to be assumed in reading John? Apparently Luke did not assume it; at least he moves the whole Sanhedrin scene to the morning after and at the same time removes its juridicial elements (22.66-71). How is John's omission to be explained? On the one hand, we are told that the Jewish trial scene is superfluous in John, because all along Jesus has been on trial before the Jews.[1] Moreover, a Jewish verdict against Jesus seems to be presumed in the trial before Pilate (18.30-31), but whether it is based on the verdict of a missing trial scene or the conclusion of the case against Jesus made throughout the Gospel is hard to say. On the other hand, John's omission of the trial is a problem for the exegete because its inclusion would seemingly have fulfilled his purpose and design so well. Jesus is condemned because he finally claims to be the Messiah, the claim that has got him in trouble with the authorities since the beginning of his ministry in the Fourth Gospel. Of course, the Markan episode presents severe historical problems as to its time, execution and verdict—much more so than the Johannine. Whether John knew Mark or not, his version is to be preferred on historical grounds.[2]

Other distinctive elements of John's account are historically plausible. A (Roman) cohort is involved in Jesus' arrest (18.3). Overkill perhaps, but Roman involvement, especially at Passover, might be expected. After his condemnation, Jesus leaves for the place of execution, bearing his own cross (19.17), the usual procedure in a crucifixion. Of course, in the Synoptics (Mk 15.21 par.) Simon of Cyrene is impressed to carry Jesus' cross. Traditional exegesis has long combined the two; Jesus starts out as in John, but subsequently

1. Cf. Barrett, *The Gospel according to St John*, pp. 523-24. Moreover, according to Barrett (p. 524), 'there is little in his story that cannot be explained as a Johannine modification of a narrative not unlike Mark's'. On the Gospel of John as a juridical proceeding, see A.E. Harvey, *Jesus on Trial: A Study in the Fourth Gospel* (London: SPCK, 1976). In a paper read before the 1990 Louvain Colloquium on John and the Synoptics, A. Dauer argued that John 10 presupposes, or is based upon, a narrative of the Jewish trial similar to, but not identical with, Mark's. See his 'Spuren der (synoptischen) Synedriumsverhandlung im 4. Evangelium. Das Verhältnis zu den Synoptikeen', in *John and the Synoptics*, pp. 307-39
2. As Dodd contends, *Historical Tradition in the Fourth Gospel*, pp. 88-96, 120.

needs help, as Mark describes.[1] This is, in fact, quite possible, although we can scarcely get beyond conjecture in the matter. Only John tells of the intention to break the legs of the three crucified men in order to speed their death, again a common practice. The soldiers in the detail dispatched to do this found Jesus already dead, and this finding agrees with what we read in Mark, namely, that Pilate was surprised to learn that Jesus had already died (Mk 15.44). Again, we have to be content with the observation that John's report of the crucifragium could be historically true. That it was invented to provide fulfillment of Scripture (Ps. 34.21; cf. Exod. 12.46 and Num. 9.12; Zech. 12.10) is possible, but I think less likely than that those passages were used to interpret an historical event, or at least one conveyed as such by tradition. (Such Old Testament testimonia in the Fourth Gospel seem to be traditional rather than the composition of the evangelist, because they frequently have Synoptic or other New Testament parallels.)

Missing from the broader Johannine passion is, of course, the cleansing of the temple, which had already taken place on Jesus' first Passover pilgrimage to Jerusalem. Traditional Christian exegesis has resolved the seeming contradiction between John and the Synoptics by having Jesus cleanse the temple twice—an unlikely solution. John A.T. Robinson's proposal that the Fourth Gospel is correct on this point and the Synoptics wrong has found few takers because of Robinson's other views, but it is by no means outlandish.[2] Most of us have preferred to think that Jesus' action in the temple led directly to his arrest and execution at the same Passover. But it remains possible that Jesus' action at an earlier Passover caught the attention of the temple authorities and caused them to lie in wait for him on his return. (Such a scenario is all the more credible on E.P. Sanders' view that the displacement of the old temple with a new one was a central item of Jesus' eschatological agenda.[3]) However that may be, it remains arguable and perhaps even likely, that John's departures from the Synoptics in the passion narrative reflect a more accurate view of what actually took place.

1. Brown (*The Gospel according to John*, p. 899) observes that 'serious scholars of the caliber of Dodd and Taylor judge...[this] solution a perfectly reasonable interpretation of the evidence'.

2. Robinson, *The Priority of John*, pp. 127-31, 185-86.

3. E.P. Sanders, *Jesus and Judaism* (Philadelphia: Fortress Press, 1985), pp. 61-76.

Turning briefly to the *resurrection narratives*, we find a new and different situation, for here as nowhere else in the Gospel all John's episodes have Synoptic parallels, whether close or more remote. The arrival of the beloved disciple and Peter at the empty tomb, probably a Johannine composition, seems to be the outstanding exception, but even that is already suggested by Luke (24.12, 24). At this point in the narrative, if anywhere, John's account appears to be clearly secondary to the Synoptics. I have already observed that in the Fourth Gospel Jesus' initial resurrection appearance is to Mary Magdalene, but even here John's dramatic account can be viewed as a development of Matthew's rather brief and colorless notice of Jesus' appearance to Mary Magdalene and the other Mary at the tomb.

The most striking and original Johannine resurrection account is, however, in the appendix (21.1-14). This story, paralleled only in the call narrative of Lk. 5.1-11, is presented as the third resurrection appearance of Jesus (21.14), although it is actually the fourth counting the one to Mary Magdalene. In part because of the Lukan parallel, it has been understood by some exegetes, pre-eminently Robert Fortna, as a sign story that has been transferred to the resurrection period.[1] But the Gospel of Mark and the Gospel of Peter anticipate a Galilean resurrection appearance of Jesus. Indeed, Peter's account seems to anticipate just such a scene by the sea as we find in the Fourth Gospel. John's narrative is on the face of it more likely to be a traditional resurrection narrative than the rather obviously Matthean composition that concludes the First Gospel. In fact, this appearance narrative is exactly the one that Mark's Gospel leads us to expect, even to the extent that Peter plays a leading role. (The women are told in Mk 16.7 to tell Jesus' disciples and Peter.) One might facetiously suggest that the lost ending of Mark's Gospel somehow became the appendix to John's! I am not going to suggest that, but more, soberly, that the narrative of Jn 21.1-14 may well be the earliest account of Jesus' appearance to his disciples that we possess.[2]

---

1. R.T. Fortna, *The Gospel of Signs: A Reconstruction of the Narrative Source Underlying the Fourth Gospel* (SNTSMS, 11; Cambridge: Cambridge University Press, 1970), pp. 87-88. In his more recent *The Fourth Gospel and its Predecessor: From Narrative Source to Present Gospel* (Philadelphia: Fortress Press, 1988), pp. 65-79, Fortna maintains his position, but acknowledges its more hypothetical character in relation to his other proposals (p. 66).

2. Bultmann, *The Gospel of John*, p. 705: 'The early Easter story, related in

III

If this rather brief survey of the Gospel of John seems to confirm the impression of John's independence with which I started, that should come as no surprise. I have, in effect, been spelling out the basis for that impression. In conclusion, I return to the question of John and the Synoptics, which has hovered in the background all along. What conclusion may be drawn by way of summary? Simply, that where John possesses, reflects or advances data or a point of view different from, or at odds with, the Synoptic Gospels or tradition, its statements or narratives deserve serious consideration as quite possibly historically superior to the Synoptics. The distinctive Johannine Christology, on the other hand, is usually found in the discourses and dialogues of Jesus, which on other grounds seem to be compositions of the evangelist. They scarcely represent the utterances of the historical Jesus.

Are we then to infer that John is independent of the Synoptics? Not necessarily, particularly if independence means ignorance. But if independence means not being determined or even overly influenced by the Synoptics, John certainly seems to live up to that standard, especially in his use of an array of historical data concerning which there is little reason to prefer the Synoptics. Indeed, as we have seen there is often good reason to prefer John.[1]

---

vv. 1-14, manifestly originally told of the first (and only?) appearance of the risen Jesus to the disciples'. Moreover, 'that this story, or a variant of it, formed the original conclusion of Mark (and of the Gospel of Peter) has a certain probability' (p. 705 n. 5). Bultmann is not being facetious.

1. That the Johannine account of Jesus' words and works is a theologically freighted narrative is clear enough, and no longer needs any defense. Yet this fact does not determine, or should not determine, its value as a historical source on specific points. In this regard the statement of R. Pesch, 'The Gospel in Jerusalem: Mk 14.12-26 as the Oldest Tradition of the Early Church', in P. Stuhlmacher (ed.), *The Gospel and the Gospels* (Grand Rapids: Eerdmans, 1991), p. 116, is very much to the point:

> The linkage of theology to history—in subordination to the biblical witness of the canon—is the linkage to the faith-interpreted history of God with his people... The stubbornly factual character of that history and of the concrete speech of the word of God resists the arbitrariness of our willful arrangements—even in the language of legend, which by no means lacks a relationship to history simply because it is not interested in the historical accuracy of the course of events portrayed in the world of the narrative but is very interested in the meaning of the history as faith understands.

JOHN 6:
TRADITION, INTERPRETATION AND COMPOSITION

Peder Borgen

In 1975 I had the privilege of reading a paper at the twenty-sixth Biblical Conference at Louvain, Belgium, under the chairmanship of Professor M. de Jonge to whom this volume is dedicated. Ten years later I served as the local host of the 40th General Meeting of *Studiorum Novi Testamenti Societas* at the University of Trondheim, Norway, and the President in charge was Professor de Jonge. On many other occasions I have had the privilege of learning greatly from his scholarship and of being enriched by his friendship. It is therefore with pleasure and gratitude I make a contribution to his Festschrift. In the essay I shall add some insights on a question which has engaged me for many years, the intriguing ch. 6 in the Gospel of John.

There are many puzzling problems in this chapter. First, the collective designations of people vary. In 6.1-40 one reads about the disciples (vv. 1-21), the crowd, ὁ ὄχλος, the men, οἱ ἄνθρωποι, and then, in 6.41-58 the term 'the Jews', οἱ Ἰουδαῖοι, is used. Finally, when the general reaction to Jesus' discourse is told in 6.60-71, only the reaction by many among the disciples, οἱ μαθηταί, etc. are mentioned. Secondly, the term 'sign', σημεῖον (σημεῖα), seems to have different meanings in vv. 2 and 14, and in v. 26, and v. 30. Although the crowd, according to v. 14 has seen a sign, they still ask for a sign in v. 30, and Jesus says in v. 26 that the crowd does not seek him because they saw a sign, although according to vv. 14-15 they saw the sign and therefore thought he was a prophet and wanted to make him king. Thirdly, there is the long-debated question of relating the eucharistic formulations in vv. 51ff. to the preceding section of Jesus' discourse.[1]

---

1. See commentaries and the survey given by L. Schenke, 'Die literarische Vorgeschichte von Joh 6.26-58', *BZ* 29 (1985), pp. 68-75.

In *Bread from Heaven*[1] I concentrated on the analysis of Jn 6.31-58, understood as an exposition of the scriptural quotation in v. 31b, 'bread from heaven he gave them to eat'. There is a need for looking more closely at ch. 6 as a whole and its thematic ties at the end of ch. 5, however. More recent scholarly analysis both by others and myself should also be brought into the investigation.

Jesus is not just the Prophet-like-Moses, Jn 6. 1-21

The persons mentioned in this section are: Jesus, the disciples (with name specifications in vv. 5-8), a lad (v. 9), a large crowd (vv. 2 and 5: ὁ ὄχλος πολύς) and the people (vv. 10 and 14 οἱ ἄνθρωποι, numbering 5000, v. 10). In v. 4 there is a reference to 'the Jews'. The two stories narrate actions and reactions among Jesus, the disciples and the crowd. Oral dialogue takes place between Jesus and Philip/Andreas in vv. 5-10a, and words said by Jesus as a greeting to the disciples are recorded in v. 20. There is no dialogue between Jesus and the large crowd/the people, but a report on what the people said (among themselves) is given in v.14: 'they said, "This is indeed the prophet who is to come into the world"'.

This section begins with a general statement about 'the signs which Jesus did on those who were diseased' (v. 2) and then one particular sign follows, the feeding of the 5000 (vv. 3-13). In vv. 14-21 effects of the event are described—on the one hand the effect on the people and subsequently on Jesus (vv. 14-15), and on the other hand on the disciples and Jesus (vv. 16-21).

The story of the feeding of the 5000 in Jn 6.1-13 renders one version of a tradition which is narrated in all the four gospels, Mt. 14.13-21; Mk 6.32-44, and Lk. 9.10-17. The brief subsequent section, Jn 6.14-15, has no parallel in the Synoptic Gospels. These verses show the effect which the event had on the crowd, and how Jesus reacted to the crowd's understanding and action. The crowd understood the feeding miracle to have a meaning beyond itself. They thought the event bore witness to Jesus being prophet and king (like Moses[2]), 'When the people saw the sign which he had done, they said, "This is indeed the prophet who is to come into the world!"' (v. 14); 'Perceiving then that they

1.   P. Borgen, *Bread from Heaven* (NovTSup, 10; Leiden: Brill, 1981 [1965]).
2.   See especially W.A. Meeks, *The Prophet-King* (NovTSup, 14; Leiden: Brill, 1967).

were about to come and take him by force to make him king, Jesus withdrew again to the hills by himself"' (v. 15).

In Jn 6.16-21 the crowd is not in the picture, but 'his disciples' who are seen as a distinct group. They got into a boat and crossed the sea. While a strong wind was blowing and the sea was becoming rough, Jesus came to them 'walking on the sea and drawing near to the boat' (v. 19).

The two stories primarily tell how Jesus acted in feeding the crowd and how they reacted—they wanted to make him a king. This led to a responding action on Jesus' part—he withdrew to the hills. The reaction of the disciples was also in the form of an action—they went away across the sea.

While maintaining that the evangelist interpreted the feeding miracle meaningfully, J. Painter thinks that the same evangelist reported the story of the sea-crossing because it was already attached to the feeding story in the received tradition. But, according to Painter, the evangelist used the story to good effect as it dramatically separates Jesus from the crowd which had followed him into the desert.[1]

When Painter interprets the sea-crossing (6.16-21) as an extension of the story of the miraculous feeding (6.1-15), he does not take seriously the fact that the disciples and Jesus are the persons mentioned in the sea-crossing, and not the crowd. The story of the crossing of the sea, therefore, has quite a central function. It makes clear that although Jesus withdrew from the crowd, the opposite happened to the disciples: he acted by miraculously coming to them.[2] Here, as elsewhere, John has made the traditional story express an idea which was central to him. The crowd misjudged the meaning of the feeding miracle, while the disciples had an authentic and epiphanic encounter with Jesus.

The works done by Jesus are called signs. What is the definition of the term 'sign', σημεῖον, in this context? John describes the miracles of Jesus both by the term 'works', ἔργα, as in 5.36, and by the term

1. J. Painter, *The Quest for the Messiah* (Edinburgh: T. & T. Clark, 1991), pp. 226-27. The same view was already expressed in Painter's article, 'Tradition and Interpretation in John 6', *NTS* 35 (1989), pp. 430-31.
2. See Borgen, *Bread from Heaven*, p. 180, n. 1: 'According to v. 15, the feeding miracle brought the people to the non-spiritual and external wish to make Jesus king. For the disciples, on the other hand, it resulted in a theophanic encounter with the Son of God, vv. 16-21'. C.K. Barrett (*St John* [London: SPCK, 2nd edn, 1978], pp. 279-80) finds this interpretation to be plausible.

'signs', σημεῖα, as in 6.2. The term 'sign' suggests that the miracle has a function beyond itself in the form of carrying a certain meaning or creating a certain effect. The meanings or effects may vary somewhat, and the precise and detailed description of the term must therefore be made within the context in which it is used. In 6.14-15 the designation 'sign' indicates that the feeding miracle was understood to have a function beyond itself and to activate the people's expectations of a coming prophet/king. By withdrawing from the people at that point Jesus made it clear that they had misunderstood the significance of his actions.

The Son of Man—the Father's Accredited Envoy, Jn 6.22-27

Verses 6.22-24 seem at first to be very confused, and the apparent obscurity has caused several variant readings to appear in the manuscripts.[1] The structure of the verses takes on meaning, however, when one realizes that John here repeats phrases from and makes references to the preceding stories and adds interpreting words.[2] In this way it is seen that in v. 22 he refers to the story of the crossing of the sea by the disciples (vv. 16-21). In vv. 23-24a he refers to the story about the feeding, while in v. 24b-25a the crowd is brought to the destination of the disciples' crossing, Capernaum. Some of the repeated words are common to both stories, of course. In the following the words from the two stories are in bold type.

From the crossing of the sea:

v. 22   **ὁ ὄχλος** ὁ ἑστηκὼς **πέραν τῆς θαλάσσης** εἶδον
ὅτι **πλοιάριον** ἄλλο οὐκ ἦν ἐκεῖ εἰ μὴ ἕν, καὶ
ὅτι οὐ συνεισῆλθεν **τοῖς μαθηταῖς αὐτοῦ ὁ Ιησοῦς εἰς τὸ**
πλοῖον
ἀλλὰ μόνοι οἱ **μαθηταὶ αὐτοῦ** ἀπῆλθον

From the feeding of the 5000

v. 23   ἄλλα ἦλθεν **πλοιάρια** ἐκ Τιβεριάδος ἐγγὺς τοῦ τόπου
ὅπου ἔφαγον ἄρτον [εὐχαριστήσαντος τοῦ
κυρίου].[3]

---

1. See Barrett, *St John*, p. 285.
2. Cf. R. Schnackenburg, *Das Johannesevangelium* (Frieburg: Herder, 1971), II, pp. 44-47. Schnackenburg attempts to reconstruct a picture of the details in the movements of the crowd(s) as to timing and geography. His analysis demonstrates, however, that the text as it stands is not consistent.
3. See R. Schnackenburg, *Johannesevangelium*, about the words in brackets

v. 24   ὅτε οὖν εἶδεν ὁ **ὄχλος** ὅτι **Ἰησοῦς** οὐκ ἔστιν ἐκεῖ
         οὐδὲ οἱ μαθηταὶ αὐτοῦ

To Capernaum
         ἐνέβησαν αὐτοὶ **εἰς τὰ πλοιάρια** καὶ **ἦλθον εἰς**
         Καφαρναοὺμ ζητοῦντες Ἰησοῦν.
v. 25   καὶ εὑρόντες αὐτὸν **πέραν τῆς θαλάσσης** εἶπον αὐτῷ

The elaborations emphasize that Jesus was not found with his disciples when they crossed the sea. Neither was he present at the place where the feeding miracle took place. After searching in vain in these two places, the crowd looked for Jesus in Capernaum where they found him. Then they asked where he had been:

> (v. 25) 'And having found him...they said to him,
> "Rabbi, when did you come here?"
> (v. 26) Jesus answered them,
> "Truly, truly, I say to you,
> You seek (ητεῖτε) me, not because you saw signs, but because
> you ate your fill from the loaves.
> (v. 27) Do not labour for the food which perishes,
> but for the food which endures to eternal life,
> which the Son of Man will give to you;
> for this is the one whom God the Father has sealed"'.

Jesus criticizes the crowd for having searched for him for the wrong reason (v. 26) and then he challenges them not to labour for perishable food, but for food which endures to eternal life, which the Son of Man will give, for on him God the Father set his seal.

It is important to notice that the main point in v. 27 is not the search by the crowd nor the choice with which Jesus confronts them but the seal which God the Father set on the Son of Man. In order to understand this saying the term σφραγίω, 'to seal', must be examined. The use of the word here is debated by the exegetes.[1] B.F. Westcott has suggested that the sealing refers to Jesus' consecration unto death by the Father.[2] A similar argument is entertained by J. Marsh, who sees the aorist as a 'prophetic perfect', which refers to the future glory

---

which are lacking in some mss and may be an added gloss.

1.   For the following, see F.J. Moloney, *The Johannine Son of Man* (Biblioteca di Scienze Religiose,14; Rome: LAS, 2nd edn, 1978), pp. 113-14.

2.   B.F. Westcott, *The Gospel according to John* (London: Murray, 1908), p. 100.

of the cross and resurrection.[1] For B. Lindars the sealing tells that
Jesus is chosen or marked out.[2] M.-J. Lagrange and G.H.C. Macgregor
think that it is the authority of Jesus' miracle-working power that is
referred to, including the miracle of the incarnation itself.[3]
R.E. Brown emphasizes the idea that God sets his seal on the Son, not
so much by way of approval, but more by way of consecration.[4]
C.K. Barrett understands 'the sealing' to mean that it is 'God the
Father who attests the authority and truth of Jesus'.[5]

Molony follows Barrett and defines the meaning in this way: 'What
is being said here is: "You must work for the bread which endures for
eternity; that bread will be given to you in the revelation of the Son of
Man. It is to the Son of Man, and to him alone, that God has given
such authority; what he reveals is the authentic revelation of God"'.[6]
This understanding by Barrett and Moloney is appropriate to the use
of the term σφραγίω here. An even more precise meaning can be
given, however. In Liddell and Scott's Greek-English Lexicon the
meaning of the word in Jn 6.27 and 2 Cor. 1.22 is defined as 'accredit
as an envoy'.[7] This interpretation is confirmed by the equivalent
Hebrew and Aramaic word חתם, to seal, which, as seen from
M. Jastrow's Dictionary, is the technical term for sealing and signing
as a witness.[8] An understanding along this line has been suggested by
R. Schnackenburg: 'Just as the One Sent by God (3.34) brings the
testimony about the Father (cf. 3.35) from the heavenly world, so also
the Father gives testimony about the Son (5.32, 37; 8.18)'.[9]

The verb in Jn 6.27 has aorist form and refers to the sealing as a
past event. This event is probably the commissioning of the Son of

1.   J. Marsh, *Saint John* (Harmondsworth: Penguin Books 1968), p. 295.
2.   B. Lindars, *The Gospel of John* (London: Oliphants, 1972), p. 255.
3.   M.-J. Lagrange, *Evangile selon saint Jean* (Paris: Gabalda, 1964), p. 173;
G.H.C. Macgregor, *The Gospel of John* (London: Hodder & Stoughton, 1928),
pp. 138-39.
4.   R.E. Brown, *The Gospel according to John, I–XII* (AB 29; Garden City,
NY: Doubleday, 1966), p. 261.
5.   Barrett, *St John*, p. 287.
6.   Moloney, *The Johannine Son of Man*, p. 114.
7.   H.G. Liddell and R. Scott, *A Greek-English Lexicon* (Oxford: Clarendon
Press, 1985 [1940]), p. 1742.
8.   M. Jastrow, *A Dictionary of the Targumim, the Talmud Babli and
Yerushalmi, and the Midrashic Literature* (repr. in Israel, no date), pp. 513-14.
9.   Schnackenburg, *Johannesevangelium*, p. 50.

Man as the Father's emissary, as the Son of Man who descended from
heaven (Jn 3.13).[1] This commissioning is indicated several places in
John, as in Jn. 12.49: 'For I have not spoken of myself, but the Father
who sent me, has himself given me commandment what to say and what
to speak'.[2]

The Manna-bread from Heaven—the Sign of the Son of Man,
Jn 6.28-59

This section, Jn 6.28-59, consists of a dialogue between 'they', that is,
the crowd (vv. 28, 30, 34) and Jesus (vv. 29, 32, 35) which results in
reactions and objections among the Jews (vv. 41, 52) with answers
given by Jesus (vv. 43, 53).

In Jn 6.59 it is reported that Jesus said this in the synagogue, as he
taught at Capernaum. C.K. Barrett comments: 'At v. 24 we learned
that the scene was Capernaum, but the discourse with its interruptions
suggests a less formal occasion than a synagogue sermon'.[3] Against
Barrett, it must be said that questions and answers, direct exegesis and
problem-solving exegesis were part of the discourses in the synagogue.
All these elements are found in rabbinic midrashim, as for example in
Mekilta on Exodus, as well as in Philo's commentaries. A glimpse into

1.	See Borgen, 'The Son of Man Saying in John 3.13-14', in *idem, Logos Was
the True Light and Other Essays on the Gospel of John* (Trondheim: Tapir, 1983),
pp. 138-42, also printed in Borgen, *Philo, John and Paul* (Atlanta, CA: Scholars
Press, 1987), pp. 107-10. As for the concept of agency in John, see Borgen, 'God's
Agent in the Fourth Gospel', in J. Neusner (ed.), *Religions in Antiquity* (Leiden:
Brill, 1968), pp. 136-48, reprinted in *idem, Logos Was the True Light*, pp. 121-32; in
idem, Philo, John and Paul, pp. 171-84; and in J. Ashton (ed.), *The Interpretation of
John* (London: SPCK, 1986), pp. 67-68; J.-A. Bühner, *Der Gesandte und sein Weg
im 4. Evangelium* (Tübingen: Mohr [Paul Siebeck], 1977).
	As Jewish background for the idea of God's, the Father's, sealing of the Son of
Man, one might refer to the figures of Logos, Metatron and Yahoel, upon whom the
name of God was, as understood from exegesis of Exod 23.20: 'for My name is on
him'; Philo, *Migr.Abr.* 173-75; *b.Sanh.* 38b; 3 *En.* 12.5; *Apoc.Abr.* 10. See Borgen,
'Heavenly Ascent in Philo: An Examination of Selected passages', in J. Charlesworth
and C. Evans (eds.), *Biblical Interpretation and the Pseudepigrapha* (JSPSup;
Sheffield: JSOT Press, forthcoming).
2.	See Borgen, 'The Use of Tradition in 12.44-50', *NTS* 26 (1979), pp. 18-35;
repr. in *idem, Logos Was the True Light*, pp. 49-66, and in *idem, Philo, John and
Paul*, pp. 185-204.
3.	Barrett, *St John*, p. 300.

such practice is given by Philo in his description of the Therapeutai. When they assemble, the leader 'examines (ητεῖ) some points in the sacred writings, or also solves (ἐπιλύεται) that which is propounded by another' (*Cont.* 75). The term ητέω and the composite verb ἐπιητέω are used elsewhere in Philo's writings when an exegetical question is asked, such as in *Op. Mund.* 77, 'One might examine (ἐπιητήσειε) the reason because of which...', cf. *Spec. Leg.* 1.214; *Leg. All.* 1.33, 1.48; 1.91; 2.103, and *Quaest. in Gen.* 1.62 (Greek fragment). Answers and solutions are given, and in *Leg. All.* 3.60 the verb λύω is used, corresponding to the use of the composite verb ἐπιλύω used in *Cont.* 75. In *Cont.* 79 the leader is said to have discoursed, διαλέγομαι, and since questions and answers were part of the discourse, the verb means 'discuss'. In Philo's commentary *Questions and Answers on Genesis and Exodus*, a question or a specific view is introduced by simple formulae, for example by phrases such as 'some say' (*Quaes. in Gen.* 1.8; 2.64, and 3.13, cf. *Op. Mund.* 77); or just 'why' (*Quaest. in Gen.* 1.1; 2.13, 64, etc.) or 'what' (*Quaest. in Gen.* 2.15, 59).

Thus in Philo's expositions, such as those seen in the *Allegorical Commentary* and elsewhere, direct exposition of a scriptural quotation often is interrupted by a question or an objection, and in *Quaest. in Gen.* a question is raised at the very outset, and direct exegesis and objections may then be given, as for example in *Quaest. in Gen.* 2.28.

> The question:
> 'What is the meaning of the words
> "He brought the spirit over the earth and the water ceased"?'
> Interpretation:
> 'Some would say that by "spirit" is meant the wind through which the flood ceased.'
> Objection and alternative interpretation:
> 'But I myself do not know of water being diminished by wind...
> Accordingly, (Scripture) now seems to speak of the spirit of the Deity...'

Against this background the following conclusion can be drawn: in Jn 6.30ff. John draws from the gospel tradition the claims that Jesus was asked to give a sign and that he gave his answer.[1] When John elaborates upon this tradition in 6.30-58, he develops the exegesis of an Old Testament quotation into learned midrashic expositions. Thus, the reference to a synagogue as the setting (Jn 6.59) is appropriate.

---

1. See Jn 2.18; Mt. 16.11ff./Mk 8.11ff.; cf. Mt. 21.23ff./Mk 11.27ff./ Lk. 20.1ff.

The analysis of Jn 6.28 should be continued against the background of these observations. Jn 6.28 is a further discussion of the word ἐργάζεσθε in v. 27. The crowd asks Jesus: 'What must we do, then, to "work" the works of God (ἐργαζώμεθα τὰ ἔργα τοῦ θεοῦ)?' Although the term in v. 28 means 'perform a work', and not as in v. 27 'to work for food', it has vv. 22-27 as background—the crowd acted wrongly and misunderstood the multiplication of the loaves to mean that the eschatological manna miracle was of earthly nature. Jesus corrects them and tells them to work for the food which endures to eternal life. In vv. 28ff., the crowd then logically asks what they shall do to receive the proper food.

In Jn 6.28 the crowd asks Jesus to define his understanding of the notion 'the works of God', that is, the works willed by God. In v. 29 Jesus defines the term, but in the singular, 'this is the work (τὸ ἔργον) of God, that you believe in him whom he sent'. On this basis they ask Jesus to provide the legitimation so as to demonstrate that he is to be identified as 'him whom he [God] sent'.[1] The question about the works/work which the crowd was to perform, has in this way been related to what Jesus could do to demonstrate his own identity as the Father's commissioned envoy (v. 30). 'So they said to him, "then what sign do you do (ποιεῖς) that we may see and believe you? What work do you perform (ἐργάζῃ)?"' The dialogue form is appropriate to such a change of meaning given to ἐργάζομαι and ἔργα/ἔργουν in v. 28ff.

In v. 31 they refer to the manna miracle: 'Our fathers ate the manna in the wilderness; as it is written, "He gave them bread from heaven to eat"'. This reference is strange, since according to vv. 14-15, as a reaction to the multiplication of the loaves, they understood Jesus to be a prophet, that is a prophet like Moses (Deut. 18.15, 18). If so, they already had regarded the feeding miracle to be an eschatological event corresponding to the manna miracle in the desert (Exodus 16). Against this background the repeated reference to the manna miracle in Jn 6.30-31 is puzzling, since they seemingly once more ask for the same sign as they already had experienced.

Exegetes have suggested various solutions to this problem. R.E. Brown states that it is difficult to reconcile the request for bread (vv. 30-31) with the indication that this is the same crowd that saw the multiplication of the loaves the day before. In his comments on

---

1. On agency in John, see references on p. 274 n. 1.

v. 14 he writes: 'Most likely this is a reference to the expectation of the prophet-like-Moses...for in v. 31 these people draw a connection between the food supplied by Jesus and the manna given by Moses.'[1] As a response to Brown's interpretation, one must say that in v. 14 the crowd already seems to have understood the feeding miracle as an event corresponding to the manna miracle, since they thought that Jesus was the prophet-like-Moses. If so, Brown does not explain why the crowd in vv. 30ff. again asks Jesus to perform the manna miracle as a sign.

R. Schnackenburg thinks that vv. 2 (signs=healing miracles) and 15 (they wanted to make him king) express the misunderstanding of the signs by the crowd, while v. 14 formulates the understanding as intended by the Evangelist—Jesus was to be confessed as the prophet-like-Moses who actually exceeded Moses. When, according to v. 31, the crowd asks for a sign similar to the manna given in the desert, it is to be seen as a literary device made by the Evangelist.[2] M.J.J. Menken rightly objects to Schnackenburg's interpretation that it is the same crowd who pronounces both the confession of 6.14 and the question of 6.30-31, and John does not indicate in his text a shift from one level of meaning to another.[3]

According to Haenchen the contradiction between the request for a sign in Jn 6.30-31 and the sign mentioned in v. 14 should not be taken seriously.[4]

The contradiction disappears, however, if one understands vv. 30-31

1. Brown, *John I–XII*, p. 234.
2. R. Schnackenburg, *Johannesevangelium*, p. 53: 'Wenn man diese Überleitung als literarisches Vorgehen des Evangelisten betrachtet, fällt die mehrfach erwähnte Schwierigkeit weg (oder wird begreiflich), dass die Teilnehmer an der Speisung ein Verlangen äussern, da sie nach dem von Jesus gewirkten Zeichen und ihrem eigenen Bekenntnis (v. 14) als erfüllt anschen sollten'. See also pp. 31-32. J. Painter, *The Quest*, pp. 230-31 seems mainly to see Jn 6.31 as a verse which introduces the theme of manna as a crucial issue in the subsequent conflict with the Jews, 6.49-58.
3. M.J.J. Menken, 'Some Remarks on the Course of the Dialogue: John 6.25-34', *Tijdschrift voor filosofie en theologie* 48 (1987), p. 141.
4. E. Haenchen, *Das Johannesevangelium: ein Kommentar* (Tübingen: Mohr [Paul Siebeck], 1980), p. 321: 'der Evangelist will hier keine psychologisch durchsichtige Darstellung der Reaktionen bei den Hörern bringen. Die Zeichenforderung der Juden zeigt freilig einmal, wie unfähig die Menschen sind, die erlebten Zeichen als solche zu erfassen. Zum andern schafft der Evangelist sich damit den Übergang zum eigentlichen Thema, dem er zustrebt: das Himmelbrot'.

along the lines suggested by Menken.[1] Then these verses are to be seen precisely as a restatement of the crowd's view that the feeding miracle corresponded to the manna miracle and thus legitimated Jesus as a prophet-like-Moses (vv. 14-15). In their view, since Jesus had already legitimated himself as a prophet by the feeding miracle, they now needed another sign which would demonstrate that he was the one sent by the Father, that is, the Son of Man who was sealed by the Father, God (vv. 27-29). The correct meaning of vv. 14-15 and vv. 30-31 is then: since the feeding miracle was the eschatological manna miracle, Jesus had legitimated himself as the prophet-like-Moses. Now in vv. 27-29 he seemed to imply that he was the Son of Man, the Father's (heavenly) commissioned envoy. Therefore there was the need for (another) sign which would demonstrate that this was the case.[2]

John 6.30ff. can be paraphrased in this way: The crowd said, 'What sign do you do so that we may see, and believe that you are God's heavenly-sent envoy, the Son of Man who is sealed by the Father? The manna sign which we experienced in the feeding miracle was a sign which, in our mind, showed that you were the prophet-like-Moses, but did not legitimate you as God's heavenly-sent envoy, the Son of Man.' You have misunderstood the manna miracle. It was not given by Moses, nor now by the prophet-like-Moses, but it was the gift from heaven, given by the Father, and I am (myself) the manna/bread.'

Thus in vv. 32ff. Jesus, by means of his different exegesis of v. 31b, 'bread from heaven he gave them to eat', demonstrated that the Scriptures bore witness to him (5.39) and that Moses wrote about him (5.46). The giving of the manna, rightly understood, was a sign about Jesus (not just as a prophet-king, but) as the one who came down from heaven.

From 6.30-40 there is an exegetical dialogue between Jesus and 'they',

1. Menken, 'Some Remarks', pp. 145-46.
2. This distinction between two levels of Christology is formulated by M. de Jonge, *Jesus: Stranger from Heaven and Son of God* (Missoula, MA: Scholars Press, 1977): 'it is evident that this identification of Jesus with the Mosaic Prophet, though perhaps pointing in the right direction, does not really explain the secret of Jesus' coming. Jesus' reaction towards the ideas of the crowd in the following discourse is entirely negative. In that chapter not the similarities but the dissimilarities receive all emphasis... it is clear, however, that the unique relationship between Jesus and God is underlined by means of the expression "my Father" (vv. 32, 37, 40, 44 and especially v. 46) and the notion of "descent from heaven" (vv. 33, 41, 42, 50, 51)'.

that is, the crowd, and from vv. 40-58 there are exegetical objections voiced among the Jews, followed by statements given by Jesus.

Jn 6.31-58 has many midrashic features. As shown in my book *Bread from Heaven* there are such features in vv. 32-33. Jesus develops philogical exegesis and states in v. 32 that his Father and not Moses is the subject of the verb 'to give' (ἔδωκεν, Hebrew נתן) in the Old Testament text. Moreover, the verb is not to be read as past tense, δέδωκεν (ἔδωκεν), but in the present tense, δίδωσιν. By means of midrashic exegesis, Jesus corrects the crowd when they refer to the manna/bread from heaven (v. 31) as a sign of the prophet-like-Moses.

Jesus' understanding of the Old Testament quotation follows in v. 33, introduced by γάρ:[1] 'For *the bread* of God is that which (or he who) comes down *from heaven*, and gives life to the world'. (The words from the Old Testament quotation are italicized.) According to Jewish traditions the Torah, given at Sinai, gave life to Israel or the world (*Tanḥ. Shem.* 25; *Mek. Exod.* 15.26; *Exod. R.* 29.9). Thus, 'the bread of God' in Jn 6.33 has the role of the Torah. This understanding presupposes the identification of the manna/bread from heaven with the Torah, as exemplified in Philo, *Mut. Nom.* 253-63 and *Mek. Exod.* 13.17. Moreover, in the expository application in Jn 6.32 the third person plural pronoun 'them' (αὐτοῖς) has been interpreted as 'you' (ὑμῖν).

In Jn 6.34 'they' (the crowd) ask for this Torah-bread from Jesus: 'Lord, give us this bread always'.[2] The exposition in vv. 32-33 made clear that God the Father gives the bread, but does not make explicit what kind of bread it is. The formulations seem to indicate that the bread means the wisdom of life-giving Torah, and the crowd asks Jesus to give them this bread always, presumably as a teacher who gives the people the wisdom of the God-given Torah. Thus they had

1. Cf. Philo, *Det.Pot.Ins.* 47-48, with exegesis of Gen. 4.8: 'it must be read in this way: "Cain rose up and slew himself", not someone else. For (γάρ)...'
2. Painter, *The Quest*, p. 233, asks why according to Jn 6.34 the crowd should think of Jesus as the giver if he has said that it is his Father who gives this bread? Painter's answer is that the crowd, provisionally at least, has accepted Jesus as the emissary of God (6.29), that is the Son of Man. It is not necessary to go quite as far as Painter does, however. Against the background of 6.31-33 the crowd might understand Jesus to be a teacher who through his teaching brings the Torah-manna which gives life. They would then understand Jesus to be a teacher who follows the principle formulated in 5.39: 'You search the Scriptures, because you think that in them you have eternal life'.

not recognized Jesus' identity, that he himself was the one who came down from heaven.[1] Then Jesus makes explicit his exegetical application of the Old Testament quotation (v. 31b) on himself in v. 35: 'I am *the bread* of life; he who comes to me shall not hunger and he who believes in me shall never thirst.'

J. Painter regards Jn 6.35 as the pronouncement to which the dialogues of 6.25-36 lead. According to him, this verse is the text upon which the discourse as a whole is based. Thus the Old Testament quotation in 6.31b does not serve as the text, but v. 31 as a whole is used leading up to the pronouncement of 6.35.[2] It must be said that Painter does not define the relationship between vv. 31 and 35 in an adequate way. The Old Testament quotation in v. 31b and the pronouncement in v. 35a are tied together in the way formulated in 5.39: 'it is they [the Scriptures] that bear witness to me'. Thus, on the basis of this hermeneutical key the pronouncement in Jn 6.35a, 'I am *the bread* of life', renders the precise meaning of the central term in the Old Testament quotation in v. 31b '*bread* from heaven he gave them to eat'. The scriptural text in v. 31b bears witness to Jesus.

Moreover, although v. 35 gives the precise meaning of the Old Testament quotation, it does not function as the text since it does not form the basis for a subsequent expository structure. The Old Testament quotation in v. 31b serves as such a text, however. In a systematic way the words from the Old Testament quotation are repeated and paraphrased. Only words from the first part of the quotation, 'he gave them bread from heaven', are repeated and paraphrased and discussed in vv. 32-48. The last word, 'to eat' is then added, so that the whole quotation is interpreted in vv. 49-58. Moreover, themes from the Old Testament quotation are developed in a systematic way.

1.   *vv. 32-49.* In vv. 32-34 it is made clear that it is the Father who 'gives the bread'. Then in vv. 35-49 the theme is Jesus as the 'bread'.

2.   *vv. 49-58.* In vv. 49-51a the focus is on the effect of the 'eating of the bread'—it gives eternal life. This theme is continued in vv. 51b-58, but here with the emphasis on the idea that the bread is the flesh of Jesus as the 'Son of Man'

---

1.   Against Painter, *The Quest*, p. 233, who thinks that 'the crowd, provisionally at least, has accepted Jesus as the emissary of God (6.29)'.

2.   Painter, *The Quest*, pp. 229, 232.

(referring back to the Son of Man in v. 27) which he 'shall give for the life of the world'.

The conclusion is that the Old Testament quotation in v. 31b serves as a text, while Jesus' word in v. 35 gives the precise expository meaning of the word 'bread' in the quotation.

Painter's hypothesis of a distinction between quest stories as John's first edition and rejection stories as his second edition breaks down in 6.36-40. According to him the quest is made by the crowd, and the 'Jews' (vv. 41 and 52) are the ones who reject. Verse 36 reports that the crowd rejected, however: 'they do not believe'. To Painter this causes embarrassment: 'surprisingly, in the end we are told that the crowd's quest ended in failure, 6.36. But 6.36-40 is made up of a collection of isolated sayings forming a transition to the rejection story of 6.41ff.'[1] According to Painter, 'the Jews' are the group associated with rejection. He does not give a plausible reason why John, who, according to Painter, is himself responsible for both editions, here pointedly states that 'they', that is, *the crowd* (cf. v. 24) rejected Jesus. Painter indicates that the crowd's unbelief in v. 36 shows that the quest story ended in failure. If so, there is no real distinction between the quest story and the rejection story.

In Jn 6.35b-40 the identification of the manna/bread with Jesus (v. 35a) is related to the main point in the dialogue of vv. 29-30, believing in him whom the Father, God, has sent. Verse 35b refers to 'coming' and 'believing'. In v. 36 Jesus accuses the crowd that they 'do not believe'. Then vv. 37-40 combine the idea of 'coming' and 'believing' with the idea of Jesus as 'the one sent by the Father'. The section is an elaboration of the words 'from heaven' in the Old Testament quotation in v. 31b, a phrase which is repeated in v. 38, and is an integral part of the dialogue about the 'Son of Man' and 'the one whom God sent'.

In the study 'God's Agent in the Fourth Gospel',[2] I have shown that in vv. 38-40 halakhic principles of a commissioned envoy are applied to Jesus, the one whom the Father sent. One such principle was that it was a legal presumption that an agent; that is, one who is sent, would carry out his mission in obedience to his sender. In accordance with this principle, Jesus was an obedient agent who did as the Father had

---

1. Painter, *The Quest*, p. 229. See also pp. 236-37.
2. See reference on p. 273 n. 1.

commanded. He said, 'I have 'come down *from heaven* [see v. 31b
'from heaven'] not to do my own will, but the will of him who sent
me'. The will of the sender is then defined in vv. 39-40.

Another halakhic principle of agency is also used, that in the context
of a lawsuit the sender transferred his own rights and the property
concerned to the agent. The will of the sender, the Father, in Jn. 6.39
is based on this transfer: 'This is the will of him who sent me, that all
he has given me...' The transfer is even more pointedly stated in
Jn 17.6: 'thine they were, and thou gavest them to me...' The same
idea is also formulated in 6.37: 'All that the Father gives me...'

The Jews' objection to Jesus' exegesis in 6.41-42 is formulated with
a term from the story about the manna (Exod. 16.2, 7, 8): they
'murmured' (ἐγόγγυζον) (Jn 6.41, cf. v. 43). The objection has the
form of an exegetical problem formulation followed by a solution,
parallels to which are found in the midrashim and in Philo. The
exposition consists of the following points:

1.   The Old Testament quotation: Jn 6.31, 'Bread from heaven
     he gave them to eat'.
2.   The interpretation of the quotation: 6.41, 'he [Jesus] said, "I
     am the bread which came down from heaven"' (words taken
     from vv.35 and 38).
3.   The basis for the questioning of Jesus' exegesis: 6.42, 'They
     said, "Is not this Jesus, the son of Joseph, whose father and
     mother we know?"'
4.   The questioning of the interpretation: 6.42, 'how does he
     now say "I have come down from heaven?"'
5.   The answer to the objection and the solution to the problem:
     6.43ff., 'Jesus answered and said to them, "Do not 'murmur'
     among yourselves..."'
     In Jesus' answer the word 'he who believes in...' in v. 47
     refers back to vv. 35 and 29-30, and the words, 'I am the
     bread of life' in v. 48 repeats v. 35a, which in turn is the
     interpretation of the word 'bread' in the scriptural quotation
     in v. 31b.

In *Bread from Heaven*, I have shown that the corresponding points of
exegetical exchange are found in *Mek. Exod.* 12.1 and 12.2 and in
Philo, *Mut. Nom.* 141a.142b-144.[1]

1.   Borgen, *Bread from Heaven*, pp. 80-83.

It is noticable that the objection in Jn 6.41ff. is not raised by the crowd, but by 'the Jews', οἱ Ἰουδαῖοι. Painter draws extensive conclusions from this introduction of the term 'the Jews' in Jn 6.41: 'It is argued here that the change of terminology from the crowd to the Jews indicates a change of audience and a change of time, and that the note concerning the synagogue in 6.59 indicates a change of location. Jn 6.41-59 reflects the struggle between the Johannine Christians and the synagogue. For this text 'the Jews' is the appropriate term of reference. They do not represent the Galilean crowd which had followed and subsequently come seeking Jesus'.[1] Against Painter it must be said that the reason for this change of terminology cannot be that 'the Jews' rejected Jesus, while the crowd did not. On the basis of the text, it might even be said that 'the Jews' who 'murmured' expressed scepticism about Jesus' exegesis,[2] while 'they', that is, the crowd, rejected Jesus outright as stated in v. 37,[3] and nothing in v. 41 indicates a different time and location from the setting of the preceding verses.

Several scholars think that 'the Jews' in Jn 6.41 refers to 'the crowd' (6.22, 24) and thus does not carry the usual meaning of the Jewish authorities.[4] There is one observation which indicates that the term 'Jews' also here refers to the Jewish authorities, but in the role of midrash scholars. In John 6 the 'crowd' wants to make Jesus a king, they seek him and address him as rabbi, and make requests to him. They do not perform scholarly midrashic exegesis, however, as rabbi Jesus and 'the Jews' do. Thus 'the Jews' in Jn 6.41 and 52 are the midrashic experts, as distinct from the common people, 'the crowd'. As Jesus and 'the Jews' in Jn 5.10-18 had a halakhic and midrashic

1.　Painter, *The Quest*, p. 237.

2.　J. Ashton, *Understanding the Fourth Gospel* (Oxford: Clarendon Press, 1991), p. 200: '...called οἱ Ἰουδαῖοι (6.4, 41, 52), but their 'murmuring' (γογγυσμός, v. 41) is prompted more by bewilderment than by real antagonism'.

3.　Painter, *The Quest*, p. 238, ignores Jesus' word to the crowd that they do not believe (v. 36), and writes: 'The crowd, though it has misunderstood Jesus, requests that Jesus should always give them the bread of which he has been speaking, 6.34. On the other hand the Jews do nothing but raise *objections* to what Jesus has said. They represent a hardening attitude of the synagogue...' Against Painter it must be said that objections do not represent a hardening attitude when compared with the attitude of unbelief of the crowd.

4.　See the survey in U.C. von Wahlde, 'The Johannine "Jews": A Critical Survey', *NTS* 28 (1982), pp. 33-60.

exchange on the commandments about the sabbath in the Law of Moses, so rabbi Jesus and 'the Jews' in 6.41ff. and 51ff. had a scholarly midrashic exchange. The difference is that the Jewish authorities in 5.10-18 persecuted Jesus and sought to kill him, while the Jewish scholars in 6.41 and 52 expressed objection to Jesus' application to himself of the scriptural quotation about the bread from heaven (v. 31b). Thus the attitude of 'the Jews' in Jn 6.41 and 52 are similar to the attitude associated with term in 1.19; 2.18, 22, where the designation expresses scepticism and unbelief, but not hostility. In 6.41, 52 'the Jews' represent those who, as stated in 5.39, execute (professional) midrashic exegesis of the Scriptures, but refuse to accept that the Scriptures bear witness to Jesus.

Jesus' answer leads in 6.49ff. into further elaboration of the application to himself of the scripture quotation in v. 31b. Now the word 'to eat' (φαγεῖν) from v. 31 is introduced and is placed in the center of the exposition to the end, v. 58.[1] As Jesus did in v. 32, he also here criticizes the misunderstanding expressed by the crowd in vv. 14-15, 26 and 31.

In Jn 6.51b the 'bread' of the scripture quotation in v. 31b is interpreted as Jesus' 'flesh'. This application of the scriptures to Jesus is again met with exegetical objection in dispute among 'the Jews' (v. 52). Also the objection here has the form of an exegetical problem formulation followed by a solution, parallels to which are found in the midrash and in Philo. The same five points as found in vv. 41-48 are also found here, except point 3, which in an explicit way had stated the basis for the questioning of Jesus' exegesis in vv. 41-48.

1. The Old Testament quotation: Jn. 6.31, 'Bread from heaven he gave (ἔδωκεν) them to eat (φαγεῖν)'.

2. The interpretation of the quotation: 6.51, 'the *bread* (ὁ ἄρτος) which I *shall give* (δώσω) for the life of the world is my 'flesh' (ἡ σάρξ)'.

3. The basis for the questioning of Jesus' exegesis (the basis is implied in point 4).

1.　Concerning the use of τρωγεῖν in vv. 54-58, see Borgen, *Bread from Heaven*, pp. 92-93.

4. The questioning of the interpretation: 6.52, 'The Jews then disputed among themselves, saying, 'How can this man *give* (δοῦναι) us his 'flesh' (τὴν σάρκα) *to eat* (φαγεῖν)?'

5. The answer to the objection and the solution of the problem: 6.53ff., 'So Jesus said to them, "Truly, truly I say to you..."'.

In 6.53-58 there is an expository elaboration on the theme of eating, introduced in v. 31, tied together with the theme of the Son of Man in vv. 53 and 27, and the theme of the one whom the Father sent in vv. 57 and 29. It should be added that the formula used when raising the question in Jn 6.52, πῶς δύναται, corresponds to the technical midrashic term כיצד.[1]

Although the exposition in Jn 6.31-58 consists of dialogue and scholarly exchanges, there are several unifying threads which demonstrate that the passage is composed as a whole—throughout the words 'Bread from heaven he gave them' (v. 31b) are built into the formulations, and from 6.49 and onwards the word 'to eat' from v. 31 is added. Moreover, the statement 'our fathers ate manna in the wilderness' (v. 31) is repeated with some changes in v. 49 and in v.58. These threads which run through 6.31-58 demonstrate that the passage as a whole is composed to serve as a scriptural debate in response to the question raised in v. 30: 'Then what sign do you do, that we may see, and believe you? What work do you perform?'

The Reaction among the Disciples, Jn 6.60-71

It is surprising that the subsequent section of Jn 6.60-71 reports the reaction among the disciples. They have not been mentioned in 6.25-59, although their presence must then be presupposed. The section refers at several points back to the earlier parts of the chapter. The disciples are mentioned several times in 6.3-21 and also in 6.22-24. The disciples 'murmured' (γογγύζουσιν), 6.61, just as 'the Jews' did (6.41). This 'murmur' has its background in Exod. 16.2 and shows that the scriptural story about the manna still serves as the frame of reference. The words in 6.62 ('If then you see the Son of Man ascending to where

---

1. Borgen, *Bread from Heaven*, pp. 89-90; W. Bacher, *Die exegetische Terminologie der jüdischen Traditionsliteratur* (repr. Darmstadt, 1965; Leipzig, 1899), p. 77.

he was before?') presuppose the words about the Son of Man in 6.27, 53 and the words about (his) descent from heaven (6.38, 41, 51).[1] The term 'flesh' occurs in 6.63 and back in 6.51-56.[2] Some of the disciples 'do not believe' (6.64), just as the crowd (6.36). Jn 6.65 cites a previous saying of Jesus, actually a composite of words from 6.37 and 6.44. In contrast to the unbelief of the crowd (6.36), and of some of the disciples (6.64), Peter, representing 'the twelve', says that they have believed (6.69). Thus Peter gives a positive response to Jesus' words in 6.29: 'This is the work of God, that you believe in him whom he has sent'.

These observations demonstrate that the section 6.60-71 is an integral part of the chapter. How is this function to be defined in a more precise way? At the outset it is to be noticed that the subsequent result of the feeding miracle for the disciples is the walking on the sea in 6.16-21—Jesus miraculously came to the disciples (6.16-21) after he had withdrawn from the crowd who had mistakenly wanted to make him king (6.14-15). The works of Jesus, that is, the healing miracles, the feeding miracle and the walking on the sea, bore witness to him and the disciples experienced an epiphanic encounter with him.

Jesus' words about perishable and life-giving food and about the Father bearing witness about the Son of Man were addressed to the crowd (6.27). His words about believing in him whom God sent, and his application to himself of the scriptural word about the manna-bread from heaven, resulted in unbelief by the crowd and in exegetical objections stated by the Jewish scholars (6.28-58). Thus it remains to learn how the disciples reacted to the witness to the Son of Man given by the Father, who sealed and sent him (6.27-28), and by the Scriptures (6.31-58).

Then from 6.60-71 we learn that the reaction among the disciples was divided—many said that Jesus' discourse was a hard saying, and they subsequently left him. Peter, representing the Twelve, accepted Jesus' words. Thus they accepted that God bore witness about him and

---

1.   It is difficult to define the exact meaning of Jn 6.62 because it has the protasis, but lacks the apodosis. See commentaries and Borgen, *Bread from Heaven*, p. 187; Moloney, *The Johannine Son of Man*, pp. 120-23; and L. Schenke, 'Das Johanneische Schisma und die "Zwolf" (Johannes 6.60-71)', *NTS* 38 (1992), pp. 113ff.

2.   Concerning the meaning of Jn 6.62-63 in relation to 6.51-56, see commentaries, and Borgen, *Bread from Heaven*, pp. 181-83; Schenke, 'Schisma', pp. 109, 114-11.

so also did the Scriptures: 'You have the words of eternal life; and we have believed, and have come to know, that you are the Holy One of God' (6.68-69). As for Jesus' 'words (ῥήματα) of eternal life' it is to be noticed that according to 5.47 the writings of Moses and the words of Jesus coincide: 'but if you do not believe his [Moses'] writings, how shall you believe my words (ῥήματα)?' Moreover, Jn 10.36 makes evident that 'the Holy One of God' means consecrated by God and sent by Him into the world: 'him, whom the Father consecrated (made holy) and sent into the world.'[1] Thus, the christological designation used by Peter has the same meaning as that expressed by the designations used in 6.27, 'on him the Father has set his seal', and in 6.29, 'him whom he has sent'.[2]

The Transition from John 5 to John 6

The transition from John 5 to John 6 represents one of the most striking aporias of the Fourth Gospel. In ch. 5 Jesus was in Jerusalem, and in ch. 6 he is in Galilee and goes to the other side of the Sea of Galilee (6.1ff.). Then he comes to Capernaum (6.24, 59). Moreover, there is in Jn 7.23 a reference back to the healing story in 5.1-18, and both 5.16-18 and 7.1ff. report that 'the Jews' persecuted Jesus and wished to kill him. Scholars such as Bultmann and Schackenburg thus reverse the order of chs. 5 and 6, and Lindars and Ashton regard ch. 6 as an addition made by the evangelist himself.[3]

The present study is an analysis of ch. 6. Thus it would go beyond the limits of this paper to deal with its relationship to ch. 5, especially since such an undertaking would necessitate a thorough examination of this latter chapter. Some observations might be listed, however, as a point of departure for further research on the subject.

It might prove fruitful to investigate whether points in Jn 5.31-47,

1. Cf. Brown, *John I–XII*, p. 298; Schnackenburg, *Johannesevangelium*, II, pp. 110-11; Barrett, *St John*, p. 307.

2. There is no need in this essay to discuss whether John 6 implies an antidocetic polemic. See the commentaries, and Borgen, *Bread from Heaven*, pp. 183-92; Schenke, 'Schisma', pp. 105-21.

3. R. Bultmann, *Das Evangelium des Johannes* (Göttingen, 18th edn, 1964 [1941]), pp. 154-77; Schnackenburg, *Johannesevangelium*, II, pp. 6-114; B. Lindars, *The Gospel of John*, pp. 50, 206-209 and 234; Ashton, *Understanding the Fourth Gospel*, pp. 200-201.

the final part of the discourse of Jesus in 5.19-47, serve as the thematic background of ch. 6. If so, such a thematic connection would indicate that ch. 6 is in its right and original place in the Gospel. These points from ch. 5 may also give an important insight into the composition of ch. 6.

Such an approach was indicated in embryonic form in my book *Bread from Heaven*. I suggested that Jn 6.31-58 might be an elaboration upon and an illustration of points discussed in 5.37-47. The conclusion was: 'The close connection between Jn 5.37-47 and 6.31-58 speaks against any rearrangement of the sequence of chs. 5 and 6 in spite of the obvious geographical discrepancies (ch. 5 in Jerusalem; ch. 6 at the Sea of Galilee, etc).[1]

The most obvious point deals with the interpretation of Scriptures (5.39-40) for which 6.31-58 is an illustration. References back to 5.39 have already been made in the present study. The connection is then as follows: in Jn 5.39-40 a hermeneutical principle is formulated—(v. 39) 'You search the Scriptures, because you think that in them you have eternal life; and it is they that bear witness to me (v. 40); yet you refuse to come to me that you may have life.' The same principle is also found in 5.46-47: 'If you believed Moses, you would believe me , for he wrote of me. But if you do not believe his writings, how will you believe my words?' Then in ch. 6 a quotation from the Scriptures is given in v. 31, 'as it is written, "He gave them bread from heaven to eat",' and midrashic interpretations and diverse responses are seen in vv. 32-59, and various attitudes are also pictured in vv. 60-71. Thus Jn 6.31-58 serves as an illustration of the searching of the Scriptures mentioned in Jn 5.39-40. The phrase ἐρευνᾶτε (τὰς γραφάς) in Jn 5.39 is even a Greek equivalent for the technical term for performing midrashic exegesis.

This link between chs. 5 and 6 provides a basis for investigating whether other connections might be found. Jn. 5.36 might give us a lead. According to this verse Jesus' works bear witness to him: 'the works which the Father has granted me to accomplish, these very works which I am doing, bear me witness that the Father has sent me'. The line here may be drawn to 6.1-13. If so, light might be thrown on the puzzling verse 6.2—why should the evangelist here report that the crowd followed Jesus because they saw the signs which he performed

---

1. Borgen, *Bread from Heaven*, p. 152, with the quotation taken from n. 2.

on those who were diseased? Actually only one healing is reported by him to have taken place in Galilee (4.46-54). Seemingly, E. Haenchen is right when he states that the context does not explain why it is said that a large crowd followed Jesus. The verb ἠκολούθει even has the imperfect form to show that the crowd's following of Jesus was a lasting phenomenon![1] The preceding context, that is Jn 5.36, may provide a clue. This verse says that Jesus' works, τὰ ἔργα, bear witness to him, and 6.1-13 may be meant to illustrate this witnessing function of the works, first by giving a summary statement about Jesus' healing activity in v. 2[2] and then reporting in vv. 3ff. more specifically on how Jesus' feeding miracle bore witness to him.

Also Jn 5.37, 'and the Father who sent me has himself borne witness to me,' might prove to be of interest. Does the evangelist here think of a particular occasion or a particular kind of witness? Scholars have made several different suggestions. It has been mentioned above that Schnackenburg has joined the idea about the testimony of the Father, in Jn 5.37 with Jn 6.27b where it is said that it is the Father, God, who sealed the Son of Man and bore witness to him as his envoy.[3]

If further analysis offers support for these suggestions, then there are three witnesses. First, Jesus' works (v. 36), secondly, the Father who sent him (v. 37), and thirdly, the Scriptures (v. 39-40 and 46-47). It is interesting to note that three corresponding sections seem to be found in ch. 6 since the main focus in vv. 1-21 is on Jesus' works as signs,[4] in vv. 22-27 on the Father and in vv. 28-71 on the Scriptures.

Summary

Jesus is not just the Prophet-like-Moses, Jn 6.1-21

The two traditional stories about the feeding of the multitude and the crossing of the sea in Jn 6.1-21 primarily report how Jesus acted in

---

1. Haenchen, *Das Johannesevangelium*, p. 300: 'Das eine grosse Menge Jesus folgt (Imperfekt der Dauer!), wird hier aus dem Kontekst freilich nicht verständlich'. Cf. Schnackenburg, *Johannesevangelium*, II, p. 17: 'Woher die grosse Volksmenge stammt, die hier unvermittelt auftaucht, wird nicht gesagt. Von einem "Nachfolgen" so vieler Menschen ist sonst nirgends im Joh-Ev die Rede...'
2. Summarizing statements about Jesus' healing activity are found in Mt. 4.23-25; 9.35; Acts 2.22; 10.38. See also Jn 20.30.
3. Schnackenburg, *Johannesevangelium*, II, p. 50.
4. See Borgen, *Bread from Heaven*, p. 180: 'the feeding miracle offers an example of the works mentioned in 5.36'.

feeding the crowd and how they reacted: they thought the feeding was a new manna miracle and that Jesus was the prophet-like-Moses, and they wanted to make him king. This reaction, in turn, led to a further action on Jesus' part—he withdrew to the hills. The reaction of the disciples as a distinct group was also in the form of an action—they went away across the sea and Jesus miraculously came to them.

The Son of Man: The Father's Accredited Envoy, Jn 6.22-27

In 6.22-24 John repeats phrases from and makes references to the preceding stories and inserts additional interpretation. In this way it is seen that in v. 22 he refers to the story of the crossing of the sea by the disciples (vv. 16-21). In vv. 23-24a the story about the feeding is referred to, while in vv. 24b-25a he brings the crowd to the destination of the disciples' crossing, Capernaum. In this way it is shown that the crowd was searching for Jesus.

The concluding point in v. 27 is not the search of the crowd nor the choice as such with which they are confronted by Jesus, but the seal which God the Father put on the Son of Man. The word σφραγίζω and its Hebrew and Aramaic equivalents, are technical terms for sealing and signing as a witness. Thus, the Son of Man (and not the prophet-like-Moses) gives the bread which endures for eternal life.

The Manna-bread from Heaven—the Sign of the Son of Man, Jn 6.28-59

The structure of Jn 6.28-59 is as follows: Against the background of the general statements about 'the Son of Man' and 'the one who is sent' by God (6.27, 29) the question is raised whether Jesus is 'the Son of Man' and 'the one who is sent' by God (6.30). Exchanges on the scriptural story about the giving of the manna follow in 6.31-58, with particular focus on the interpretation of the quotation 'bread from heaven he gave them to eat' (6.31b). In this way it is made clear that Jesus himself is the manna miracle, as the bread/the Son of Man who came down from heaven (6.31-58).

The common people, 'the crowd' addresses Jesus as 'rabbi' (6.25) and asks questions (6.25, 28, 30, 34), while Jesus and 'the Jews' practise scholarly midrashic exegesis. Jesus accuses 'the crowd' of unbelief (6.36), and he criticizes 'the Jews' because they object to his application of the scriptural quotation to himself (6.43ff. and 54ff.).

The Reaction among the Disciples, Jn 6.60-71

From 6.60-71 we learn that the reaction among the disciples was also divided—many disciples left him. Peter, representing the Twelve, accepted Jesus' words. Thus they acknowledged that both God and the Scriptures bore witness about him, 'You have the words of eternal life; and we have believed, and have come to know, that you are the Holy One of God' (6.68-69). Jn 10.36 makes evident that 'the Holy One of God' means consecrated by God and sent by him into the world. Thus, the christological designation used by Peter has the same meaning as that expressed by the designations used in 6.27 and in 6.29.

THE CHRISTOLOGY OF THE FOURTH GOSPEL:
A SURVEY OF RECENT RESEARCH*

Maarten J.J. Menken

Much was and is being published on the Gospel of John.[1] Such a large
number of books and articles is due to two things. First there is the
fascinating character of this writing—whether it attracts or repels—in
which Jesus' person, reduced to its essential traits, is central. Second,
there is the series of problems with which this Gospel confronts the
scholar, such as its literary unity, the sources and traditions that have
been used, its relation with the Synoptic Gospels, its structure and its
background.

Because the person of Jesus is central in John, the theology (in the
literal sense of 'speaking about God') of this Gospel is in fact
Christology—only Jesus, as the one who came from God and who is
now with God, reveals God (see Jn 1.18; 6.46). At the end of the
Gospel, its author reports that he wrote down the signs of Jesus narrated in his book, 'that you may believe that Jesus is the Christ, the
Son of God, and that by believing you may have life in his name'
(20.30-31). Christology, in the sense of speaking of Jesus'
significance, is the heart of the fourth evangelist's message. However,
there is substantial disagreement in recent research when it comes to
determining the exact content of this Christology.

At the two extremes of the range of viewpoints are the opinions of

---

* An earlier, Dutch version of this article, in which the 1990 literature on the
Christology of John was not reviewed, was published under the title 'De christologie
van het vierde evangelie: Een overzicht van resultaten van recent onderzoek',
Nederlands Theologisch Tijdschrift 45 (1991), pp. 16-33.
1. G. Van Belle (*Johannine Bibliography 1966–1985: A Cumulative
Bibliography on the Fourth Gospel* [BETL, 82; Leuven: Leuven University
Press/Peeters, 1988]) lists 6300 publications for the period of 20 years covered in his
bibliography.

R. Bultmann, and of E. Käsemann. The easiest way to characterize their views is by means of Jn 1.14, a verse that is often considered to be the climax of the Prologue: 'And the Word became flesh and dwelt among us, and we have beheld his glory...' Bultmann emphasizes the first part of the verse, the incarnation of the Word.[1] The fundamental paradox, the essential offence of the Fourth Gospel, is that 'in Jesus, God himself is encountered, and that precisely in Jesus as a human being, in whom nothing extraordinary is perceptible, except his bold statement that God is encountered in him'.[2] For Käsemann, the emphasis falls on the second part of the verse, on the divine glory of Jesus.[3] In his view, the humanity of Jesus is hardly important in John; Jesus is here presented as God. The Fourth Gospel is 'naively docetic'. The present discussion on John's Christology is largely determined by these two antipodes, and for a large part the debate consists of attempts to break through the dilemma of opting for one point of view and rejecting the other on the basis of an awareness that both authors touch upon an important aspect of John's Gospel, but at the same time leave out of account equally important aspects.

In this survey the serious, scholarly monographs on the Christology of the entire Fourth Gospel that have been published in the period 1985–1990 will be presented and briefly commented upon.[4] The two Dutch books I shall start with are strictly speaking outside the scope I have outlined, but they are nevertheless important for the investigation of Johannine Christology, because they raise for discussion the hermeneutic point of view from which the evangelist looks at Jesus' person. Then some studies will follow in which a synthesis of Johannine Christology is offered, and an investigation into the christocentric

1.　See R. Bultmann, *Das Evangelium des Johannes* (MeyerK; Göttingen: Vandenhoeck & Ruprecht, 1941), pp. 38-43 and *Theologie des Neuen Testaments* (Tübingen: Mohr, 1958, 3rd edn), pp. 354-445.

2.　Bultmann, *Theologie*, p. 403.

3.　See E. Käsemann, *Jesu letzter Wille nach Johannes 17* (Tübingen: Mohr, 1971, 3rd edn [1966]).

4.　Consequently, monographs on the Christology of separate parts of John, or in which the Christology of the Fourth Gospel is compared with other Christologies, clearly popularizing and manifestly unscholarly monographs, unpublished theses and collections of articles are left out of consideration. In what follows, the adjective 'Johannine' usually means 'of the fourth evangelist'; in the cases in which the term has a broader sense, this will become clear from the context. Page numbers in the text always refer to the pages of the book under discussion.

literary structure of the Gospel. Next, I will review some publications
in which the alternative of a divine or a human Jesus is under
discussion. I shall conclude the presentation with a few studies
concerning special christological issues (Jesus' signs and works, and
the conceptions of Jesus as the prophet and as the Son of Man in
John), and I shall finally try to draw a conclusion. I consider it an
honour and a pleasure to dedicate this survey to Rien de Jonge, who
made such a substantial contribution to our knowledge of the
Christology of early Christianity in general, and that of the Fourth
Gospel in particular.[1]

1. *The Hermeneutics of the Fourth Evangelist*

In his dissertation,[2] L.T. Witkamp asks 'what qualitative meaning the
tradition concerning Jesus had for John and his community, and how
the awareness of tradition is related to their own experiences' (pp. 27-
28). This question has literary, theological and historical aspects.

On the literary level, Witkamp searches for the way in which
traditions about Jesus function in John. He selects a limited number of
passages (1.19-34; 2.13-22; 5.1-18; 9; 10.22-39; 12.20-36 and 13.21-
30), and for each of these passages, he tries to determine what
traditional materials have been incorporated in it. He does so
cautiously—he does not try to reconstruct a *Grundschrift* or a *Semeia-
Quelle*, but he just tries to determine the traditional fragments,
particularly by means of comparison with the Synoptic Gospels (he
does not consider John to be directly dependent on the Synoptics).[3]
Next, he investigates how the traditional materials have been
incorporated into the Gospel, and he concludes that the evangelist
selects, transposes, transforms and interprets his traditions. The

---

1. See M. de Jonge, *Jesus: Stranger from Heaven and Son of God: Jesus
Christ and the Christians in Johannine Perspective* (SBLSBS, 11; Missoula, MT:
Scholars Press, 1977); *Christology in Context: The Earliest Christian Response to
Jesus* (Philadelphia: Westminster Press, 1988); cf. further H.J. de Jonge, 'A
Bibliography of the Writings of Marinus de Jonge 1953–1990', in M. de Jonge,
*Jewish Eschatology, Early Christian Christology and the Testaments of the Twelve
Patriarchs* (NovTSup, 63; Leiden: Brill, 1991), pp. 314-29.

2. L.T. Witkamp, *Jezus van Nazareth in de gemeente van Johannes: Over de
interaktie van traditie en ervaring* (Kampen: Van den Berg, 1986).

3. Here Witkamp closely concurs with B. Lindars; see Lindars' *The Gospel of
John* (NCB; London: Oliphants, 1972).

interpretation is not an addition to the tradition, but an unfolding of its richness in the light of the Johannine community's own experiences.

On the theological level, Witkamp looks for the hermeneutical theory which legitimates this way of dealing with the tradition. On the one hand, John considers the self-revelation of the earthly Jesus to be a unique historical event, as he shows especially in the Prologue (1.1-18). On the other hand, this event is unfolded and deepened after Jesus' death and resurrection by the work of the Spirit. Exegesis of the sayings on the Paraclete (14.16-17, 26; 15.26; 16.8-15) shows that he is the one who after Jesus' death discloses the meaning of the ministry of Jesus to the disciples, and, by means of their testimony, continues the work of Jesus within the community and before the world. 'The Spirit is necessary to disclose the tradition and to make it speak in the community's own time' (p. 326); this also means that the evangelist considered his own Gospel—in which precisely this happens—to be a product of the activity of the Spirit. The figure of the 'beloved disciple' (13.21-30; 19.26-27, 35; 20.2-10; 21) connects the period of Jesus and the period of the Spirit with each other. Already in the time before Easter, this disciple is the true post-Easter believer. 'Within his community, he was recognized as someone who acquired the deepest knowledge of Jesus, that is, pre-eminently experienced his love. It was characteristically his role to be both the bearer of the tradition and its interpreter, with the emphasis on the latter' (p. 359). As the bearer of the tradition and its interpreter, he is the charismatic authority behind the Gospel of John, though not in the literary sense its author.

Finally, Witkamp raises the question of the history of the Johannine community (or communities). Its situation is marked by the conflict with Pharisaic Judaism, which after the catastrophe of 70 made itself into true Judaism and tried to excommunicate other movements within Judaism. The expulsion of the Johannine Christians from the synagogue, which is referred to in 9.22; 12.42 and 16.2, was one of the measures taken by the Pharisaic Jews to secure their own identity. The main cause of the expulsion was the incompatibility of the 'high' Christology of John, in which Jesus as the Son is one with the Father, with the confession of the one God.

In his thesis Witkamp tries to discuss many things, perhaps too many. In my opinion, the main merit of the book is that the author shows how the use of the traditional materials in the Gospel agrees

quite well with the hermeneutical theory which the evangelist
advances, in particular in the sayings on the Paraclete. Consequently,
John is able to give the earthly Jesus the marks of the Christ who is
present in the community, and to retrace the experiences of his community in the history of Jesus.[1] In the discussion between Bultmann
and Käsemann, Witkamp cautiously adopts a middle course: the
believer, in whom the Spirit is working, can find the glorified Christ
in the words and deeds of the earthly Jesus.

The problem raised by Witkamp is also present in the first part of
the commentary on John by H.N. Ridderbos,[2] although here a completely different answer is given. Ridderbos explicitly wants to practise *theological* exegesis, which implies that he is concerned about 'the
tenor of the preaching of the gospel, which the evangelist must have
had in mind when he wrote his Gospel the way he did' (p. 9).
Ridderbos presupposes, mostly because of 1.14, that the evangelist was
an eyewitness of that which he reports. How eyewitness reports are
related to the use of traditions in John's Gospel (a use Ridderbos
acknowledges), is not made clear. What does become clear, is that this
presupposition leads to a highly historicizing exegesis. According to
Ridderbos, the evangelist focusses everything 'on the *person and
identity* of Jesus as the Christ, the Son of God, and on the faith in *his*
name' (p. 17). He explains this 'christological concentration' as the
result of the confrontation between the Johannine community and its
Jewish environment and of the development of the preaching of the
gospel itself. However, he does not accept that John's interpretation of
the history of Jesus refers to both the ministry of the earthly Jesus and
events in the Johannine community.[3] Aside from our defective historical knowledge of this community, the main problem of this view for
Ridderbos is that it does not take sufficiently serious notice of the
incarnation of the Word as a unique event. So he even tries to situate a
detail such as the expulsion from the synagogue in 9.22 within the
scope of Jesus' earthly ministry (pp. 395-98).

---

1.   Witkamp, *Jezus van Nazareth*, pp. 20-22, rightly points in this context to the
influential study of J.L. Martyn, *History and Theology in the Fourth Gospel*
(Nashville: Abingdon Press, 2nd edn, 1979).

2.   H.N. Ridderbos, *Het evangelie naar Johannes: Proeve van een theologische
exegese. Deel 1 (hoofdstuk 1-10)* (Kampen: Kok, 1987).

3.   It is not surprising that in Ridderbos's commentary the 'two-level-theory' of
Martyn (see n. 1 above) is frequently mentioned and rejected.

Ridderbos rightly emphasizes that for the fourth evangelist too the earthly ministry of Jesus is a unique, past event. The fact that John has presented his message in the form of a Gospel narrative makes this obvious; he does not permit the glorified Christ to absorb the earthly Jesus. However, that does not alter the fact that there are elements in his story about Jesus which in their present shape cannot be situated within the actual, historical ministry of Jesus, such as the expulsion from the synagogue just mentioned. The heated debates between Jesus and 'the Jews', in which the question whether Jesus comes from God or not is continuously under discussion, particularly do not fit in with the historical ministry of Jesus, as far as we can reconstruct it, and neither does John's usual negative portrayal of 'the Jews'. No doubt John puts into Jesus' mouth words about himself that exceed by far what the 'historical Jesus' ever said—although for the evangelist they are no more than an unfolding of what was already implicitly present in the words of the 'historical Jesus'. Finally it seems to me that Ridderbos has too little place for the Spirit, about whom Jesus says to his disciples that 'he will teach you all things, and bring to your remembrance all that I have said to you' (14.26; cf. 16.13-15), as the hermeneutical force behind the Gospel of John. For that reason, Ridderbos fails to notice how John makes the story about Jesus into a present reality for his community *without* neglecting the fact that the ministry of Jesus is a unique event.

The critical remarks above do not alter the fact that on various points Ridderbos's commentary contains an interesting exegesis of the Gospel of John. I would especially draw attention to his continual focus on John's picture of the Christ-event as the goal of the history of salvation, and to his non-sacramental interpretation of 6.51c-58 (pp. 274-84).

2. Syntheses of Johannine Christology

In continuity with the review of Ridderbos's commentary, I mention a recent study by L. Morris on the theology of John.[1] Morris describes from a highly historicizing point of view, just like Ridderbos's, what he sees as the theology of the fourth evangelist. Because of the character of John's Gospel, Morris's book is mainly about Johannine

1.   L. Morris, *Jesus Is the Christ: Studies in the Theology of John* (Grand Rapids: Eerdmans; Leicester: IVP, 1989).

Christology. In fact, the author almost limits himself to an indication and a brief discussion of the passages from the Gospel which bear upon the themes considered by him. The book can be a useful introduction for anyone who shares the author's theological way of thinking. However, as a synthesis of Johannine theology, it is too superficial and pays too little attention to the coherence of this theology.

W. Grundmann[1] concentrates his discussion of Johannine Christology around four main points: the Logos, the incorporation of the christological tradition, the 'I am'-sayings and 'the witness of truth'. He regards the Fourth Gospel, at least so far as its broad theological outlines are concerned, as a coherent whole. He considers it as a product of the same *Johanneskreis* from which the Book of Revelation originated earlier. From a traditio-historical point of view, he finds in Revelation the point of departure for the 'I am'-sayings and for the terminology of 'witnessing' of the Gospel of John (pp. 59, 70; cf. e.g. Rev. 1.17-18 and 1.2, 5).

For Grundmann, Jewish Wisdom literature is the most important factor that influenced the Christology of the Fourth Gospel (pp. 17-29). Its impact is visible not only in the Prologue (1.1-18), in which the Logos, just like Wisdom, is presented as the pre-existent mediator of creation and as giver of life and light (esp. Prov. 8.22-36; Sir. 24.1-22), but also in the rest of the Gospel, for example in the incomprehensibility of the heavenly things (3.12-13; cf. Wis. 9.13-17) and in the offer of food and drink (6.35; cf. Sir. 24.19-21). Grundmann regards the parallelism between the relation of the Father and the Son and the relation of the Son and 'his own' as a central element of Johannine Christology: just as the Father and the Son love each other, so the Son and 'his own' love each other (see esp. 10.14-15). Thereby they are accepted into the love of the Father (14.21, 23). According to Grundmann, this idea is already to be found in Wisdom literature: God loves Wisdom, and Wisdom loves those who love her (Wis. 8.3; Prov. 8.17). By their companionship with Wisdom, they acquire God's friendship (Wis. 7.14, 28).

In a clear and balanced way Grundmann presents the main thoughts and motives of John's Christology, such as his view of Jesus as the Son,

---

1. W. Grundmann, *Der Zeuge der Wahrheit: Grundzüge der Christologie des Johannesevangeliums* (ed. W. Wiefel; Berlin: Evangelische Verlagsanstalt, 1985). The manuscript dates from before 1976, the year in which Grundmann died.

MENKEN *The Christology of the Fourth Gospel* 299

sent by the Father to reveal him and to offer life in that revelation, a mission which culminates in Jesus' death on the cross. He shows clearly both how the evangelist is committed to tradition, and uses it in his own, creative fashion. Grundmann's study is somewhat one-sided in so far as he presents sapiential thinking too exclusively as the background of John. Johannine research of the last century has shown very clearly that the question of the religious background of the Fourth Gospel cannot be solved by one single, simple answer. The evangelist has been influenced in various ways and it is his independent, creative incorporation of those influences into a new synthesis, which makes it so difficult to determine them exactly.

Recently, W. Loader[1] has ventured to trace the Christology of the Fourth Gospel in its central structure and in the elaboration of this structure. R. Bultmann[2] found the central structure of the Christology of John in the pattern of the 'redeemer-revealer', sent by God, and in the demythologization of this pattern by the evangelist. If Bultmann's hypothesis of demythologization is not accepted, the question of the unity of the various elements of the Christology of John arises once again. Loader asks that question at the level of the evangelist's redaction. Investigation of a few salient passages (3.31-36; 12.44-50; 17) and a rereading of the entire Gospel lead to the following definition of the central structure of Johannine Christology:

> The Father sends and authorises the Son, who knows the Father, comes from the Father, makes the Father known, brings life and light and truth, completes his Father's work, returns to the Father, exalted, glorified, ascended, sends the disciples and sends the Spirit to enable greater understanding, to equip for mission, and to build up the community of faith (p. 76).

Next, Loader considers some questions which are raised by the central structure. The first one concerns Jesus' death in John: does it mean anything more than Jesus' return to the Father? The theologoumenon 'atonement' appears to be only indirectly important for John. Of more weight is the notion that by dying Jesus accomplishes the work of revelation with which he was charged (4.34; 19.30), and sets an example for the believer (15.18-16.4). The evangelist views Jesus'

---

1. W. Loader, *The Christology of the Fourth Gospel: Structure and Issues* (Beiträge zur biblischen Exegese und Theologie, 23; Frankfurt/ M: Lang, 1989).
2. See n. 1 p. 293.

death mainly as the glorification and exaltation of the Son of Man (13.31-32; 12.32-34): the cross is the way by which he returns to his glory. The traditional 'resurrection on the third day' also belongs to that way (see 20.17), and the gift of the Spirit is linked to it (16.7-11). In his narrative, the evangelist points forward a few times to the complex of glorification and gift of the Spirit as something which exceeds Jesus' preceding ministry (e.g. 7.37-39). According to Loader, this 'exceeding' does not mean that only after his death Jesus gives eternal life to the believers, but it means that his death and resurrection, together with the gift of the Spirit, constitute a 'revelation about revelation' (p. 107): 'The Spirit will bring greater understanding, bring forth the fruit of mission and mediate the presence of the Son and the Father to the believer in the community of faith and sacrament' (pp. 132-33).

The second question concerns the nature of the salvation event in John. In this Gospel, revelation is not a communication of knowledge, but the self-revelation of a person: 'The gift of salvation in John is primarily a person and a relationship with a person, the Son, and through the Son, a relationship with the Father' (p. 145). By means of ideas such as Jesus' pre-existence, his divinity (1.18; 20.28), his unity with and dependence on the Father (5.17-30; 10.22-39), the evangelist emphasizes that God is actually met in the Son. For John, this does not reduce Jesus' real humanity; he takes Jesus' humanity for granted, still without seeing the problems that could arise from the superhuman traits in his picture of Jesus.

The third problem Loader discusses is the character of the Fourth Gospel in the light of its Christology. The evangelist appears to be aware that after, and in the light of, Jesus' return to the Father, and inspired by the Spirit, he is elucidating with his writing the essence of Jesus' ministry for his community: 'the coming of the Son and so the coming of life through faith in him' (p. 201). Finally, Loader very briefly traces how the Johannine Christology arose from a variety of elements, and how this genesis is related to the history of the Johannine community. He also gives a few pointers, worthy of consideration, on how in our days the Fourth Gospel should be treated.

To my mind, Loader's synthetic description of the Christology of the Gospel of John at the level of the redaction of the evangelist can broadly speaking be considered as successful. As Loader himself remarks in his preface, his synchronic description still has to be completed with a traditio-historical approach. Nevertheless, the (almost) exclusively synchronic description as offered by Loader, involves the risk that the structure of the whole will dominate too much the individuality of certain parts. I think Loader did not completely escape that danger. In his description of Johannine Christology, the emphasis is on the 'vertical' aspects, which are no doubt dominant in the gospel: Jesus has been sent as the Son by God, the Father, and he reveals him. In addition to this, however, John's Christology also has 'horizontal' aspects: Jesus is part of a history of salvation; he is the one to whom Moses and the prophets have testified, the Messiah, the king of Israel (1.35-51). Even if it is true 'that Jesus' messiahship is consistently expounded in terms of his being the Son sent from the Father and come to make him known' (p. 79), the fact still remains that John apparently attaches value to presenting Jesus occasionally as the Messiah and not as the Son. Loader does not do enough justice to the line of the history of salvation, and I suppose that this is due to his (almost) exclusively synchronic approach. So this approach should be completed with a diachronic one; then it should be possible to integrate in a more refined description of Johannine Christology those elements which are less dominant but nevertheless clearly present.

Loader rightly asks the question of the position of Jesus' death in John. The problem is that in John both the incarnation and the complex of cross and resurrection are salvation events, and therefore the question arises how the two are related. Loader's answer, rendered above, certainly has its value, but I wonder whether he does not leave some aspects underexposed. For John, Jesus' death is actually the 'end point' of the incarnation (3.16; 6.51). Besides, a (believing) reader of or listener to the Gospel of John is not an eyewitness of Jesus' ministry, but he looks back after the event on the whole of Jesus' work, from the incarnation up to and including his cross and resurrection. He only knows the earthly Jesus as the one who has also been crucified. From that perspective, it perhaps does not make too much difference whether Jesus' gift of life is bound to his incarnation (6.51ab) or to his death (6.51c).

3. *Literary Structure and Christology in John*

In his dissertation, G. Mlakuzhyil[1] has tried to connect the formal literary structure of John's Gospel with its christological content. After having argued that John 1–20 constitutes a literary unit (with John 21 as an appendix), and after having discussed a series of extant proposals for the structure of the Gospel, Mlakuzhyil gives criteria for the structure of the Fourth Gospel. These are successively literary criteria (conclusions, introductions, for example), dramatic techniques (change of scene, of *dramatis personae*, for example) and structural patterns (parallelism, chiasm, concentric and spiral structure). The author rightly holds that a sound analysis of the structure of a literary work must be based on a multitude of criteria and not on just one or a few. Nevertheless, his list is incomplete, as he himself admits (pp. 87 n. 1, 135),[2] and he does not ask himself sufficiently under which conditions his criteria should be applied, and in what order of precedence they should be used.

On the basis of his application of the criteria, Mlakuzhyil arrives at the following division of John. The introduction 1.1–2.11 is followed by 'the Book of Jesus' Signs', consisting of three sections: 2.1–4.54; 5.1–10.42 and 11.1–12.50. The second main part is 'the Book of Jesus' Hour', consisting of the sections 11.1–12.50; 13.1–17.26 and 18.1–20.29. Except for 11.1–12.50 that consists of two parallel subsections, the sections display a 'chiastic' pattern; in all instances, six subsections are arranged according to a pattern A-B-C-C'-B'-A'. The whole is concluded by 20.30-31, and followed by an appendix 21.1-25. A few elements (2.1-11 and 11.1–12.50) obviously have a bridging function, and belong to two parts. To reckon with such a bridging function of parts of the text, is quite compatible with ancient theory on the writing of history,[3] and seems to me an advantage of

1. G. Mlakuzhyil, *The Christocentric Literary Structure of the Fourth Gospel* (AnBib, 117; Rome: Pontificio Instituto Biblico, 1987).

2. Mlakuzhyil pays hardly any attention to, for example, the *size* of parts of the text; on that issue, see my *Numerical Literary Techniques in John: The Fourth Evangelist's Use of Numbers of Words and Syllables* (NovTSup, 55; Leiden: Brill, 1985), and C.J. Labuschagne, 'De numerieke structuuranalyse van de bijbelse geschriften', *Nederlands Theologisch Tijdschrift* 41 (1987), pp. 1-16.

3. Mlakuzhyil (*Structure*, p. 104 n. 38) quotes in this context—just as many others do—Lucianus, *Quomodo historia conscribenda sit*, 55.

Mlakuzhyil's analysis of structure. It enables him to solve problems such as the fact that Jesus' 'hour' appears to have come in both 12.23 and 13.1. For the rest, it must be said that his subsections are very different in size, character and composition, and that sometimes the correspondences between them are minimal (for example, 6.1-71 should correspond to 10.1-21). One wonders how completely and sophisticatedly Mlakuzhyil has applied his own criteria, and whether the Gospel of John actually does have, or should have, such a perfect structure.

The author finally examines the relation between the structure and the Christology of the Gospel. He does so by investigating the development of some important themes (derived from 20.30-31) in relation to the literary structure and by outlining the unfolding of John's christocentric theology throughout the structural development of the Gospel. In fact, this amounts to a brief description of the theology of John and to a brief commentary on John. To me it is not clear what new insight the analysis of the literary structure adds here. I surmise Mlakuzhyil would have done better to relate the structure and the content of the Gospel at an earlier stage. Then his structure could have been tested to a greater extent by the contents of the Gospel, and perhaps his results would have been different.

4. A Divine or a Human Jesus in John?

The question of the structure of John's Gospel is also raised by B. Hinrichs,[1] but in a completely different way. He looks for the structuring principle of the Gospel, for what makes it a consistent whole. If the Gospel of John is well-composed, then the structuring principle should correspond to what is structured, that is, to the theology of the evangelist. Apparently, this evangelist is not concerned about a 'realistic narration'; in that case he would have organized his itinerary in a better way. John concentrates his theology, according to Hinrichs, in Jesus' self-revelation, which occurs in his saying 'I am'. This is sometimes used absolutely (6.20), sometimes with a predicate

1. B. Hinrichs, *'Ich bin': Die Konsistenz des Johannes–Evangeliums in der Konzentration auf das Wort Jesu* (SBS, 133; Stuttgart: KBW, 1988). The author owes much to the commentary on John by his teacher J. Becker, *Das Evangelium nach Johannes* (OTKNT, 4; Gütersloh: Gerd Mohn; Würzburg, Echter Verlag, 1979–1981).

(6.35). Jesus speaks here about his divine being, not subject to the boundaries of space and time that belong to this kosmos. Whoever believes in Jesus, will participate in this being, which is 'eternal life' (6.35; 8.12).

No one will deny that the 'I am'-sayings of Jesus are of great importance in the Fourth Gospel. But whether the interpretation given to them by Hinrichs leads to a better understanding of John seems highly dubious to me, for two reasons:

1. Hinrichs's opinion on the tenor of the 'I am'-sayings forces him to consider all 'I am'-sayings that are not compatible with his view, together with their contexts, as redactional additions. This includes 10.7, 9, 11, 14; 15.1, 5 and even 9.9, because according to him only the Johannine Jesus can say 'I am' (pp. 18-22, 66-82). We may presume that Hinrichs straitjackets these Johannine texts, and that he insufficiently takes into account the possibility that the Johannine 'I am' may have more than just one function. Here, he also pays the price for not taking notice of the tradition history of the formula.

2. Hardly any room is left for a possible significance of Jesus' humanity and of his death on the cross—and that appears to me to be incompatible with the text of the Gospel itself (1.14; 3.14-15, for example). Hinrichs's interpretation of John is very close to a modern version of docetism. According to Hinrichs, Jesus' fleshly appearance constitutes only one dimension of his being. The decisive dimension is actually the one that simply 'is', independent of his coming into earthly existence (p. 38, cf. p. 56).

John's 'high Christology' has also been studied by J.H. Neyrey.[1] In the first part of his book he offers an analysis, along the lines of the usual historical-critical method, of chs. 5, 8, 10 and 11 of John. In each of these chapters, the most recent literary layer contains according to Neyrey a high Christology: Jesus is equal to God; he shares in God's creative power and in his eschatological power. This power consists in raising the dead and judging, and in the possession of eternal and imperishable life, so that Jesus is entitled to divine

1. J.H. Neyrey, *An Ideology of Revolt: John's Christology in Social-Science Perspective* (Philadelphia: Fortress Press, 1988).

honour (5.17-29; 8.21-59; 10.17-18, 28-38; 11.4, 25a). It is true that in older literary layers Jesus is depicted as the one sent by God, but there he is anyhow still considered as a human being. The high Christology implies that Jesus is not of this world, but belongs in heaven, with God (6.63; 8.23).

In the second part of his book, Neyrey wants to gain insight via the Christology into the social setting of the Johannine community. In other words, the confession of Jesus implies an ideology, 'a system of cognitive and moral maps of the universe', with of course 'a social behavior in keeping with this world view' (p. 5). To trace this system and behaviour, Neyrey uses the 'group/grid model', introduced by the anthropologist M. Douglas. '*Group* refers to the degree of societal pressure at work in a given social unit to conform to the society's definitions, classifications and evaluations... *Grid* refers to the degree of socially constrained adherence normally given by members of a society to the prevailing symbol system, its classifications, patterns of perception and evaluations' (p. 119). On the basis of these two variables, it is possible to situate the Johannine community in the different stages of its development. The stages of missionary propaganda, that is, of the formation of a party inside Judaism ('strong group/low grid'), and of Jesus as the replacement of Judaism, that is, of an attempt to reform Judaism ('strong group/rising grid'), are followed by the stage of the high Christology: the community dissociates itself radically from the synagogue and from pseudo-Christians in their own midst, and orients itself on the heavenly Jesus, who is not of this world ('weak group/low grid'). To this stage belongs a world-view in which all value is concentrated in heaven and not on earth, in the spirit and not in the flesh, above and not below (see 6.62-63; 8.23-24). This actually means that Jesus' death on the cross, the tradition, the sacraments and the structure of the church lose their significance. In this stage, the Spirit is valued in an extremely positive way: he leads to the future and to new revelation.

Neyrey's project of locating John's Christology in a social context is in itself very interesting and necessary.[1] Every text has a social context; the better we know the latter, the more we understand the

---

1. This 'sociological exegesis' has already been current for some time, mainly in the USA; for John, see especially the pioneering article (often quoted by Neyrey) of W.A. Meeks, 'The Man from Heaven in Johannine Sectarianism', *JBL* 91 (1972), pp. 44-72.

former. Of course, the question then arises which social science model
is best suited to the task of determing from a text its social context.
Douglas' model is only one out of many possibilities. I do not consider
myself competent to pass judgment on this model; I just notice that
Neyrey accepts it as right with little comment. But apart from the
question of the value of the social science theory used by him, his
views on John raise several objections:

1. The passages that are crucial to Neyrey's view on John, Jn
    6.62-63 and 8.23-24, are nowhere subjected to a thorough
    exegetical analysis. Neyrey's hypothesis that these passages
    show that Jesus is considered as equal to God, as not of this
    world, should be tested.

2. Neyrey practises literary criticism in a thoughtless and con-
    sequently arbitrary way. The supposed distinction of three
    literary layers, to which three stages in the history of the
    Johannine community should correspond, is nowhere
    demonstrated—no literary arguments are given. The argu-
    ments for the distinction, in John 5, 8, 10 and 11, between
    the layer of the high Christology and the previous layers are
    not strong. Neyrey states, for example, that the accusations
    against Jesus in 5.16 and 18 are completely different: viola-
    tion of the sabbath is quite distinct from the claim to be equal
    to God (p. 16). However, he overlooks the fact that v. 18 is,
    via v. 17, a logical continuation of v. 16: Jesus is accused of
    violating the sabbath; he replies by saying that he works on
    the sabbath, just as his Father does; then 'the Jews' try to kill
    him because he violates the sabbath with an appeal to God as
    his Father, which means that he makes himself equal to God.

3. Neyrey supposes that in the stage of the high Christology all
    sorts of ideas from the previous stages are radically rejected.
    If that is true, why then does the evangelist simply leave the
    results of the first two stages in his text? If he exclusively
    considers Jesus as equal to God, why then does he also still
    consider Jesus as Israel's Messiah (1.41, 49)? Neyrey thinks
    that the various stages of development of John's Christology
    do not square with each other, but actually, witness the text
    of the Gospel, at a later stage the results of previous stages
    remain valid.

The studies of Hinrichs and Neyrey lead us to the question of the nature of Johannine Christology: is it docetic or not? U. Schnelle has gone into this problem in his *Habilitationsschrift*.[1] Following P. Weigandt,[2] Schnelle calls a Christology docetic, 'in which the saviour is exclusively of a divine nature, and consequently, not he himself, but his δόκησις appears on earth' (p. 77). He investigates a number of passages from John by means of redaction criticism: the miracle stories and other texts on Jesus' signs, the parts in which—in Schnelle's view—the sacraments are under discussion (3.1-4.1; 6.30-58; 19.34-35), and the Prologue. It appears that the evangelist understands Jesus' miracles as revelation of Jesus' glory *in* our material world; this revelation brings about faith. John connects the sacraments of baptism and eucharist with Jesus himself; they have soteriological meaning. According to 1.14, the climax of the Prologue, the divine Word really became flesh, and in that flesh his glory can be seen.

Schnelle concludes that the Fourth Gospel must be considered as 'in essential parts...a reaction to a docetic Christology', as 'a thoroughgoing theological destruction of docetism' (p. 249). In his view, this means that the *Sitz im Leben* of John's Gospel is a discussion within the church, and not—as often presumed—a conflict between Christians and Jews; for the evangelist, the latter conflict already belonged to the past. Because the question of docetism is under discussion in 1 John as an acute problem (see 1 Jn 2.22; 4.2, 3, 15; 5.1, 5, 6), Schnelle is of the opinion that inside the 'Johannine school' 1 John was written earlier than the Gospel of John.[3]

No doubt Schnelle has thrown light on an important aspect of Johannine Christology. He also has the merit of casting justified doubt on a number of positions which are considered as almost self-evident by many German-speaking New Testament exegetes, such as John's use of a *Semeia-Quelle*, and the attribution of 6.51c-58 to an ecclesiastical redactor. Apart from several disputable details, I think that his book leaves something to be desired on two major points:

1.   U. Schnelle, *Antidoketische Christologie im Johannesevangelium: Eine Untersuchung zur Stellung des vierten Evangeliums in der johanneischen Schule* (FRLANT, 144; Göttingen: Vandenhoeck & Ruprecht, 1987).

2.   P. Weigandt, 'Der Doketismus im Urchristentum und in der theologischen Entwicklung des zweiten Jahrhunderts' (dissertation Heidelberg 1961), pp. 16, 18.

3.   This opinion has also been defended by Schnelle's teacher G. Strecker: 'Die Anfänge der johanneischen Schule', *NTS* 32 (1986), pp. 31-47.

1. In view of the important position of the conflict between
    Jesus and 'the Jews' in John, one can scarcely maintain that
    for the evangelist this conflict belongs to the past. Schnelle is
    being inconsistent. He thinks he can deduce from the text of
    the Gospel both the existence of a 'Johannine school' and of
    anti-docetic polemic at the time of the evangelist, but he
    refuses to deduce a conflict between Jews and Christians as an
    issue contemporary with John (pp. 37-48, 53-59, 249-58). By
    which criteria can one decide whether one problem is acute
    for the evangelist, and the other is not?
2. The portrait of Jesus which John draws in his Gospel, has—as
    Schnelle himself admits (pp. 182-85, 257)—alongside human
    traits a heavy emphasis on his superhuman, divine traits,
    while 1 John contains anti-docetic polemic. The question of
    the sequence in which the two writings were written is then
    probably best answered in this way: some people in the
    Johannine community drew docetic conclusions from the
    Gospel, and 1 John reacts with an explicitly anti-docetic point
    of view.[1] If one supposes, with Schnelle, the reverse order,
    those traits of the portrait of Jesus in the Gospel of John
    which are easily interpreted in a docetic way remain unex-
    plained. Moreover, the anti-docetic elements in John which
    Schnelle indicates, are hardly *explicitly* anti-docetic; it rather
    appears that Jesus' humanity has not yet constituted a prob-
    lem in the Gospel. At most a text such as 19.34-35, which is
    difficult to interpret, might have an anti-docetic point.

In the published version of her dissertation,[2] M.M. Thompson
moves in roughly the same field as Schnelle. She wants to challenge
Käsemann's opinion that John is guilty of a naive docetism, by finding
out, on the basis of the entire Fourth Gospel, how the evangelist views
Jesus' humanity.

For that purpose she examines four themes in John: Jesus' earthly
origin, the incarnation (1.14), Jesus' signs and his death. Jesus' origin

1. So, for example, R.E. Brown, *The Epistles of John* (AB, 30; Garden City,
NY: Doubleday, 1982), pp. 35, 69-115; see also M. de Jonge, *Jesus*, pp. 200-10. An
important question is of course also to what extent exactly terms such as 'docetic'
and 'anti-docetic' can be applied to the Fourth Gospel.
2. M.M. Thompson, *The Humanity of Jesus in the Fourth Gospel*
(Philadelphia: Fortress Press, 1988).

as the son of Joseph from Nazareth in Galilee (1.45 for example) appears to be presupposed in John; for the believer this origin is not incompatible with his heavenly origin, but for the unbeliever it is. At Jn 1.14, Thompson searches for the meaning of σάρζ; from an exegesis of all passages in John in which this word is used, she concludes that it 'refers to the human realm in contrast to the divine and natural existence in contrast to the life given by the spirit' (p. 49), and 'it also connotes what is material or bodily' (p. 50). So the statement: 'the Word became flesh', means that in and through Jesus' human bodily existence, revelation of God took place (cf. 1.18). In John, Jesus' signs are material manifestations of God's glory in Jesus, which should evoke faith (2.11; 11.4, 40); nowhere in John are the signs devalued. Jesus' death is in John the climax of his mission; in it, Jesus is glorified (17.1-5); through it, the world receives life (6.51). In the man (19.5) who really dies on the cross (19.34-35), the believer sees 'the king of the Jews' (19.14).

Thompson concludes: 'None of the passages examined in this study necessarily demands an interpretation which impugns the true humanity of Jesus' (p. 117). After Easter, when the Spirit is working in the community, John looks back on Jesus' life; he sees God's glory in it and he defends this belief against a Jewish environment which refuses to see in Jesus more than a human being.

It seems to me that the importance of Thompson's study consists in her convincing demonstration that Jesus' humanity is *presupposed* from the beginning to the end of John's Gospel. It is not something that needs to be established. What has to be established in the conflict with the synagogue, is that Jesus is more than just a human being: he is the Christ, the Son of God. So, the Fourth Gospel is neither docetic nor anti-docetic. Jesus' humanity is neither called into question in the Gospel of John, nor is it defended, whereas it is defended in 1 John. Although Thompson leaves aside the question of the relation between John's Gospel and the Johannine Epistles, she proves in fact that the discussion on Jesus' humanity arose in the Johannine community only after, and probably as a result of, the Gospel.

The subject of H. Kohler's dissertation[1] is essentially the same as that of the books of Schnelle and Thompson, but this time it is treated from

---

1. H. Kohler, *Kreuz und Menschwerdung im Johannesevangelium: Ein exegetisch-hermeneutischer Versuch zur johanneischen Kreuzestheologie* (ATANT, 72; Zürich: Theologischer Verlag Zürich, 1987).

the perspective of John's view on Jesus' death on the cross: 'On the basis of John's theological treatment of Jesus' death on the cross, it has to be shown how concretely and visibly the Christ is understood in the Fourth Gospel. In that connection, the question of the Johannine theology of the cross is how far the risen one is and remains the crucified one—and not only as the common question how humanly Jesus is depicted' (p. 1).

Kohler starts with an extensive review of recent (German language) research into the Gospel of John, to trace the hermeneutics that are implicitly present in it. A major result is the formulation of the substantial points of difference between the Johannine and the gnostic *Daseinsverständnis* (pp. 137-39). In a second part, Kohler discusses four passages from John that are essential to his theme, namely 20.19-29; 13.1-17; 12.27-36 and 3.14-21. Here, he tries to integrate historical and theological exegesis: 'One should rather, through the historical description, penetrate to the *experimental basis* of the texts, in order to take out, if only approximately, the value of reality they have' (pp. 13-14). In practice, this kind of exegesis often appears to amount to little more than a paraphrasing explanation in inflated theological language; it is not very easy to verify how this language is related to the language of the Gospel. Moreover, Kohler makes the evangelist into someone who practises a kind of Christology without a context: he does not consider that John's message was intended for specific people in a specific situation.[1] Of course, Kohler is right both when he states that the Gospel cannot be reduced to the situation in which it originated, and that the evangelist also writes his story just because of his belief in Jesus (pp. 148-50). However, this does not alter the fact that knowledge of the situation in which the story arose certainly contributes to our understanding of the story in its actual, historically conditioned form.

In addition to these critical notes, it should be said that many elements of Kohler's exegesis are worthy of consideration. At 20.24-29, he calls attention to the fact that, for John, Jesus even as the risen one remains the crucified one, and that Thomas' faith is not considered as imperfect; the beatitude 'Blessed are those who have not seen and have come to believe' (20.29c), is intended for later generations, who believe on the basis of the testimony of the eyewitnesses (pp. 173-97).[2] Kohler gives an exegesis of Jn 13.1-17 in which the intrinsic relation

1. Contrast de Jonge, *Christology in Context.*
2. So also Schnelle, *Antidoketische Christologie,* pp. 156-61, and Thompson, *Humanity,* pp. 75-76.

between the soteriological and the paraenetical interpretation of the footwashing (13.6-10, 12-17) becomes clear (pp. 199-229). Especially on 3.16, he shows how much the incarnation is oriented towards the death on the cross in John (pp. 255-60).

5. *Some Christological Themes*

F. Grob[1] raises the matter of the significance of Jesus' 'work' in the Fourth Gospel, a significance which has often been underestimated in his view. First he wants to prove, on the basis of Jn 3.1-21 and 9.1-41, that there is in John a movement from the less important notion 'sign' to the more important notion 'work'; the latter notion is characteristic of John. He holds that 3.21 has to be interpreted christologically: the one who 'does the truth' is Jesus; his works are 'performed in God'. In 9.1-41, Jesus' works appear to be more than just messianic signs: they are acts of God, a new creation.

Next, Grob discusses the Johannine passages on Jesus' signs. The concept 'sign', as an indication of the acts with which Jesus legitimates himself as the prophet, as the Messiah, is at home in Jewish expectation of the future. It may have been taken over by John from a source, or otherwise from the language of Jewish Christians. In the Gospel, it is mainly put in the mouth of Jews (see e.g. 11.47), or the evangelist uses it in relation to Jewish expectation of the future (see e.g. 6.2, 14). Jesus' signs are mainly significant for the Jewish crowd, and do not appear to convince them (see esp. 12.37). In 4.48 and 6.26, Jesus speaks negatively about signs;[2] in 2.11 and 4.54, the evangelist uses the word in a neutral sense. Signs do indeed evoke faith, according to 2.11 and 20.31, but they only do so with people who already believe.

After this 'humiliation' of Jesus' signs, Grob has cleared the way for the 'exaltation' of Jesus' work. In that framework he discusses 4.1-42 and especially 4.34. God has sent Jesus as his authorized agent to accomplish God's work, the giving of life. Grob extensively

---

1.   F. Grob, *Faire l'œuvre de Dieu: Christologie et éthique dans l'Evangile de Jean* (EHPR, 68; Paris: Presses Universitaires de France, 1986).

2.   Jn 4.48 is often interpreted in that way. According to Grob (pp. 65-74), Jesus' words in 6.26 should mean: 'You think you are looking for me because you have seen signs, but actually you are looking for me because you have eaten and been satisfied', that is, they have noticed that Jesus gives them the eschatological bread and that he is greater than Moses. To me it seems that this explanation is hardly compatible with the context of the verse.

comments on the passage 5.19-30. Verses 19-20 are a parable about a
father teaching his son a craft.[1] This parable is subsequently
interpreted in theological terms; in vv. 21-25 concerning the work of
giving life, in vv. 26-30 concerning the work of judging. Finally,
5.31-47 and 13.1-20 are discussed. The witnesses in favour of Jesus,
who are adduced in the former passage, do not have a juridical
function, but they must make his mission credible. Jesus' works, that
bear witness to him (5.36), are to be understood to mean his whole
ministry, including his death and resurrection. The ethics, mentioned
in the subtitle of Grob's book, are discussed in his exegesis of 13.1-20:
the disciples have to continue Jesus' work in their mutual love.

In my opinion, Grob's study hardly contributes to a better understanding of John's Christology. A lack of logical structure in the book, a
language which may be evocative but in general is not very precise, and
the circumstance that a number of important Johannine passages on
Jesus' 'work' or 'works' are not discussed (especially 10.22-39), are just
some of the factors which give rise to this negative evaluation. Grob's
interpretation of various passages raises doubts (for example, see above
on 3.21 and 6.26). With great ease, Grob mixes up the Jewish expectations of the prophet and that of the Messiah, which should in fact be
distinguished from each other (pp. 49-56). It is quite possible that a
parable is at the basis of Jn 5.19-20, but because of its thorough integra-
tion in the final redaction of the evangelist, the language of the parable
has become theological language. So, one cannot suggest with Grob
(pp. 147-49) that Jesus' pre-existence is not under discussion here.

One of the most problematical aspects of Grob's study is the way he
plays off Jesus' signs against his work(s). It is inconceivable that an
evangelist, who summarizes his narrative as a series of signs that have
been written down in order that the reader or listener might believe
that Jesus is the Christ, the Son of God (20.30-31), would have been
little interested in signs. It is true that in John Jesus himself speaks
about his acts as 'work(s)', and that this concept is a comprehensive
description of his entire ministry (17.4); there can be no doubt, however, that his signs also belong to his works (see 9.16 beside 9.3-4).
They are meant to evoke belief in him as the Christ, the Son of God
(2.11; 20.31), just as his works should evoke belief in him as the one
in whom the Father is, and who is in the Father (10.38; 14.11). Of

1. Grob derived this theory from C.H. Dodd, 'Une parabole cachée dans le
Quatrième Evangile', *RHPR* 42 (1962), pp. 107-15.

both Jesus' signs and his works, it can be said that they make his mission credible. It is impossible, however, to play off, with Grob, the function of Jesus' works to make his mission credible against their juridical function. In the 'lawsuit' between the Johannine Jesus and 'the Jews', Jesus' works, among which his signs, are unmistakably part of the evidence which is favourable to Jesus and incriminates 'the Jews' (see 5.36; 10.25; 15.24).

Jesus' signs in the Gospel of John are the subject of the dissertation of W.J. Bittner.[1] His study bears a resemblance to the works of Schnelle and Kohler. Bittner also emphasizes strongly that according to John faith in Jesus is linked to the sensory perception of Jesus' signs. He interprets 4.48 ('Unless you see signs and wonders, you will not believe') not as a criticism of a faith which is based on miracles, but as a general rule: the way to faith goes via the perception of signs (pp. 122-34). Like Schnelle, Bittner is critical of the hypothesis of John's use of a miracle source.

Bittner starts with an examination of the use of the term σημεῖον outside John. The term appears to indicate something which is perceived and which has an informative content within a specific context. In the Old Testament and in Judaism, the announcement of a sign which then happens in conformity with the announcement belongs especially to the mission of a prophet, in particular of Moses and of 'the prophet like Moses' of Deut. 18.15, 18.

Next, Bittner concentrates on the Fourth Gospel. According to 20.30-31, Jesus' signs, strictly limited by Bittner to his miracles, have a prominent place in it—they lend credibility to the confession that Jesus is the Christ, which means for John that he is the Son of God. The context within which Jesus' signs receive an informative content, which in Bittner's view is unambiguous, is the Old Testament. Jesus' signs can be recognized as the mighty acts of the Davidic Messiah, such as he is described in Isaiah 11 (and in related passages such as Isaiah 42, 49 and 61).[2] The structure of announcement and event,

---

1. W.J. Bittner, *Jesu Zeichen im Johannesevangelium: Die Messias-Erkenntnis im Johannesevangelium vor ihrem jüdischen Hintergrund* (WUNT, 2/26; Tübingen: Mohr, 1987).

2. Bittner (*Jesu Zeichen*, pp. 136-50, 245-58) puts forward some suggestions, which are worthy of consideration, concerning Isaiah 11 (and related passages) as a background to Jesus' miracles, his 'hour', his 'exaltation', and his gathering of the dispersed in John.

From Jesus to John

which is characteristic of a sign, is present here—God announces in the Old Testament these acts of the Messiah, and Jesus accomplishes them. The circumstance that not everyone understands Jesus' acts in this way is, according to Bittner, not a consequence of their ambiguity, but the result of the obduracy of the people, brought about by God according to Jn 12.37-43.

The only sign of Jesus in John that might be interpreted as a sign of the eschatological prophet like Moses and consequently as a political action,[1] is the multiplication of the loaves (6.1-15), but such an interpretation of this sign is explicitly rejected (6.14-15, 22-59). The strange fact then occurs that John names Jesus' miracles with a term ('signs') which was traditionally linked with the eschatological prophet, a qualification which he precisely rejects for Jesus. Bittner explains this as follows: John opposes the belief that Jesus is the eschatological 'prophet like Moses', a belief which was found in his environment and which had political overtones, but he adopts from it the term σημεῖον to indicate Jesus' acts.

No doubt Bittner's study is an important contribution to a better understanding of what John aims at by indicating Jesus' miracles as 'signs', especially because of his attention to the Old Testament and Jewish background. He clearly shows that in John, Jesus' performance of miracles is not a concession to human weakness, but an essential condition for faith. It appears to me, however, that his argument deserves criticism on at least three major points:

1. That the evangelist in 20.30-31 summarizes his whole Gospel under the term 'signs', strongly suggests that he considers at least the immediately preceding stories about the appearances of the risen Jesus as a 'sign' too, and that he does not limit the term strictly to Jesus' miracles.
2. Bittner's idea that signs are unambiguous is problematical. Even when the miraculous character of the act itself is evident (which is not always the case; see Jn 2.9-10), it still remains true that the Old Testament as the context of the sign

1. An obvious parallel is to be found in the announcements of signs by the 'signs-prophets' described by Josephus, *Ant.* 18.85-87; 20.97-99, 167-72, 188; *War* 2.258-63, 433-34; 7.437-41; they appeared in the time before, during and shortly after the Jewish War, and their acts were clearly inspired by the stories of the Exodus. See Bittner, *Jesu Zeichen*, pp. 57-74.

is not univocal. Besides, we are dealing here with the Old Testament as interpreted in Judaism around the beginning of our era, and divergent interpretations were current there. One need only consider Jn 9.16-17: one and the same act of Jesus can be assessed as a violation of the commandment to keep the sabbath, as a miracle that cannot have been done by a sinner, and as the act of a (or the) prophet. Jesus' signs do point in a certain direction, but they do not constitute compelling evidence for his mission. It is not without reason that John ultimately reduces belief and unbelief not to a matter of intelligence, but to the result of God's action (for example, 6.44; 12.39-40).

3. It is not correct that John rejects the qualification of Jesus as the eschatological 'prophet like Moses'. Except in 6.15 where Jesus withdraws from a crowd who interpret the title 'the prophet' as 'king', nowhere in John is the title of prophet rejected for Jesus (see 1.21, 25; 7.40, and maybe also 4.19; 7.52; 9.17)—although it is true that the qualification of Jesus as 'the prophet' is never the final word about him. The use of σημεῖον as an indication of Jesus' miracles might then be positively related to Jesus' prophetic traits—although it remains curious that in John the signs function to legitimate Jesus as the messiah, the Son of God (see 7.31; 20.30-31).

Quite differently from Bittner, M.-E. Boismard[1] wants to show how Jesus is portrayed in the Gospel of John as the one who realizes God's promise of a 'prophet like Moses' (Deut. 18.18-19). Not only is Jesus called 'the prophet' a few times (see above), but also several 'implicit quotations' are to be found from Old Testament words of Moses or stories about him (cf. 12.48-50 with Deut. 18.18-19, for example). Philip's words to Nathanael: 'Of whom Moses in the Law wrote...' (1.45), are also connected with Deut. 18.18. In the writing which is at the basis of John's Gospel, the three miracle stories which are situated in Galilee (2.1-11; 4.46-54; 21.1-14) would have formed the beginning of the description of Jesus' ministry, as a counterpart of the three miracles at the beginning of Moses' ministry in Exod. 4.1-9. Because the expectation of 'the prophet like Moses' has a central place

---

1. M.-E. Boismard, *Moïse ou Jésus: Essai de christologie johannique* (BETL, 84; Leuven: Leuven University Press/Peeters, 1988).

in the theology of the Samaritans, the Johannine interest in Jesus as 'the prophet like Moses' must be somehow related, according to Boismard, to Samaritan influence.

However, the fourth evangelist does not stop short at this Christology of the prophet. Jesus is not only, as the prophet, the one who communicates God's Word or his Wisdom (identified with the Law; see, for example, Sir. 24.23), but he also *is* himself God's Wisdom (see, for example, 6.35 compared with Sir. 24.19-21), the incarnate Word of God, and as such greater than Moses (see 1.14, 17). As the Word of God he is God's only-begotten Son (1.14, 18), and he can even be called 'God' (1.1; 20.28) and pronounce the divine 'I am' (8.24, 28, 58; 13.19, cf. Isa. 43.10).

Boismard does not pretend to offer a complete description of John's Christology; he limits himself to the Christology of the prophet and to what is, in his opinion, a further development of it. He describes it mainly from a synchronic point of view, by considering the Gospel in its final redaction and not in the various stages of its development. Only in the final chapter does he connect his complex theory on the genesis of the Gospel of John, a theory which has met much criticism,[1] with the Christology of the prophet and its further developments.

Boismard shows how John's Christology basically consists of diverse views of Jesus. As was said above, a certain order of precedence can be found in that range of views, and the various conceptions are often connected with each other. Even in the final redaction of the evangelist, a 'primitive' Christology—Jesus as 'the prophet like Moses'—retains certain rights. I doubt, however, whether exactly this type of Christology is present in John to the great degree suggested by Boismard. When he considers the three signs, performed by Jesus in Galilee, as parallel to the three signs of Moses from Exodus 4, he not only moves at the highly hypothetical level of his supposed source, but he is also hardly able—as he himself admits (p. 59)—to point out any similarities of content; the parallelism is limited to the fact that in both cases there are three signs. However, it should be possible to verify a parallel literarily, and it should concern specific similarities of both texts.

1.   See M.-E. Boismard and A. Lamouille, with the collaboration of G. Rochais, *L'Evangile de Jean* (Synopse des quatre évangiles en français, III; Paris: Cerf, 1977); for a thorough criticism, see F. Neirynck, *Jean et les synoptiques: Examen critique de l'exégèse de M.-E. Boismard* (BETL, 49; Leuven: Leuven University Press/Peeters, 1979).

Finally, it must be said that the reader of Boismard's book has to digest implausible theories on a number of details. So Nathanael's confession of Jesus as 'the king of Israel' (1.49) should refer to Jesus as 'son of Joseph', that is, of the patriarch Joseph, who was considered king among the Samaritans (pp. 33-41). The Samaritan testimonies concerning the kingship of Joseph date however from after the time John was written, and they do not speak of a 'son of Joseph' as eschatological saviour. To my mind, it is obvious that 'the king of Israel' here refers to the Davidic Messiah.

R. Rhea[1] concentrates upon another christological title which is used in John: the Son of Man. The format of his study is more that of a pamphlet than of a book: it has only 79 pages, and does not deal with all the passages from John's Gospel in which the Son of Man occurs (he discusses only 5.27; 6.53, 62; 9.35).[2] According to Rhea, the Johannine Son of Man sayings are based on authentic sayings of Jesus. In his view, there is no evidence that the title 'Son of Man' functions in John—or, for that matter, in the authentic synoptic Son of Man sayings—as an apocalyptic title: 'Not only is there a marked absence of apocalyptic imagery in the Gospel, the Evangelist's use of the title betrays a definite theological purpose which is determined by the unique revelatory status of Jesus' (p. 69). The title, which is indeed used in a messianic sense in the Johannine Son of Man sayings, derives from a prophetic background (cf. the use of 'Son of Man' in Ezekiel and in some psalms): 'It is...highly probable that the term Son of Man was a somewhat obscure yet significant phrase which provided a means of referring to prophetic office. It served to indicate the divine presence which had made itself manifest to the human prophet' (p. 70).

Rhea is no doubt right when he emphasizes the revelatory function of the Son of Man in John, at least as long as the concept of revelation includes giving life and judging. It is clear that John integrates the title

1. R. Rhea, *The Johannine Son of Man* (ATANT, 76; Zürich: Theologischer Verlag Zürich, 1990).
2. It is somewhat surprising to see that Rhea frequently refers to secondary literature by means of other, more recent secondary literature, and more than once his portrayal of others' viewpoints is inaccurate. So Rhea supposes R. Bultmann to be of the opinion, 'that the scandal in v. 61 [=6.61] is related to the whole of the preceeding [*sic*] Bread of Life Discourse and its emphasis on the Eucharist' (p. 40). In fact, in Bultmann's reconstruction of the original order of the Fourth Gospel, the pericope 6.60-71 is the closing passage of the complex 10.40-12.33; 8.30-40; 6.60-71; see his *Evangelium des Johannes*, pp. 298-346.

'Son of Man' in the framework of Jesus' descent from and ascent to heaven, on account of which he is able to reveal the Father, which means that he gives life and judges (see, for example, 3.13-18, with the shift from 'the Son of Man' to 'the Son').

This does not mean, however, that John's Son of Man concept is not apocalyptic. It is true that John—with some notable exceptions (1.51; 5.28-29)—avoids typically apocalyptic imagery, but this is, I think, mainly a consequence of his heavy emphasis on realized eschatology. The literary and conceptual similarities between Jn 5.22, 27 and Dan. 7.13-14, 22 show that John here takes up apocalyptic language, to reinterpret it, of course, within the framework of his own character-istic Christology. There are also definite points of contact between John's Son of Man concept and the Son of Man in the synoptic tradi-tion—the Son of Man who is exalted and glorified on the cross (Jn 3.14; 8.28; 12.23, 34 [cf. 32]; 13.31) and ascends into heaven (Jn 3.13; 6.62), may be regarded as a Johannine reinterpretation of the synoptic Son of Man who has to suffer (Mk 8.31) and will come in glory (Mk 8.38).[1] From a too cursory view of John's Son of Man sayings in their present context and function, without taking into account the history of their tradition, Rhea arrives at unjustified conclusions concerning the Johannine Son of Man. The prophetic background, which Rhea supposes and which he fills in in a peculiar way (see the quotation from his p. 70 above), cannot constitute a more or less adequate explanation for John's use of the term 'Son of Man'. Besides, it blurs the clear order of precedence of christological views which John handles and which is especially evident in the series of titles in 1.19-51 and ch. 9; in both passages, 'prophet' (1.21, 25; 9.17) is superseded by Jesus revealing himself as 'Son of Man' (1.51; 9.35). A problem which of course arises from what precedes, but which Rhea does not touch upon, is the relation in John between the concepts of Jesus as 'the Son' and as 'the Son of Man'.

6. *Conclusion*

When we try to survey the fifteen studies presented above, there seem to be several points of agreement. However, it is mostly just a minor

1. See the excursus 'Der Menschensohn im Johannes–Evangelium' in R. Schnackenburg, *Das Johannesevangelium* I (HTKNT 4/1; Freiburg: Herder, 3rd edn 1972), pp. 411-23.

consensus, because on almost all points to be mentioned, there are dissidents among the authors who deal with the theme in question. I nevertheless mention the following points of—modest—agreement:

1. Criticism of a too far-reaching literary-critical division of the Gospel of John into different literary 'layers' gains support. Awareness is increasing of the highly hypothetical character of such an enterprise. It is evident that the fourth evangelist made use of various traditional materials, but it is impossible to determine them exactly. The text of the Gospel as it lies before us, as the product of the final redactor, the evangelist, deserves our primary attention.

2. Scholars try to avoid the dilemma between the positions of Bultmann and Käsemann, mentioned at the beginning of this article, by pointing out that the fourth evangelist perceives God's effective glory *in* the ministry of the man Jesus. John is not describing the paradox of a revealer who does not distinguish himself in any way from other people; the Johannine Jesus does distinguish himself from them, not least by his signs. Neither does John speak of a God who, disguised as a human being, walks on this earth; at least, John never eliminates the continuous offence taken by Jesus' opponents in this Gospel, at the claims of a man who makes himself equal to God (cf. 5.18; 10.33). The evangelist speaks of a human being in whom God can be met, or better, in whom God gives himself to be met.

3. Scholars arrive at this view among other reasons because they recognize the perspective from which the evangelist is writing—after, and in the light of, Easter, as one who knows that he is inspired by the Spirit. Because of this viewpoint, John can give the traits of the glorified Christ to the earthly Jesus without merging them; he can draw his own distinctive portrait of Jesus with a remarkable freedom, a portrait which reacts freely to the tradition, yet is firmly linked to it.

4. It appears that John considers Jesus' signs in a positive way: they constitute a material revelation of his glory (2.11) and they demonstrate, to the one who is prepared to accept it, that Jesus is the Christ, the Son of God (20.31). The signs are not a concession to human weakness, neither do they lead to an

imperfect faith only, but for John they are indispensable in
order to come to true faith.

5. The development of the Johannine Christology is closely
   connected with the development of the Johannine community.
   Social science theories may contribute insight into this
   relationship.

6. Given the fact that Jesus' humanity is taken for granted in the
   Gospel of John, and has become a problem in 1 John, the
   obvious supposition is that the Gospel was written before the
   first letter.

Finally, the survey shows that at least two problems concerning the
Christology of the Fourth Gospel need further clarification:

1. It seems that in the development of Johannine Christology
   elements from former stages (for example, Jesus as prophet,
   Jesus as Messiah) remain valid in later stages. The question is
   then to what extent they have retained any independent
   significance in the final synthesis of the Gospel. A comparable question can be asked concerning the christological
   titles 'the Son' and 'the Son of Man', which seem to be, in the
   evangelist's redaction, of more or less equal value: what is, at
   the redactional level, the individual value and colour of these
   titles?

2. What exactly is the importance of Jesus' death and resurrection
   in the Christology of John, and how are the complex of death
   and resurrection on the one hand and the incarnation on the
   other related to each other?

In order to answer these questions, it is essential that we combine the
study of Johannine Christology at the final, redactional level with
investigation into the tradition history of those elements from which
Johannine Christology has been constructed and into the historical
development of Johannine Christology—so far as this tradition history
and this development can be reconstructed in a reliable way. We may
expect that a combination of a synchronic and a diachronic approach
will really advance research into the Christology of John.[1]

---

1.   I thank Mrs K.M. Court for her correction of the English of this article.

TOWARD THE RENEWAL OF
NEW TESTAMENT CHRISTOLOGY

Leander E. Keck

The study of New Testament Christology will be renewed if it recovers its proper subject matter—Christology—and its proper scope, the New Testament.

The scholarly literature shows that what is called New Testament Christology is, by and large, really the history of christological materials and motifs in early Christianity and their ancestry. This massive preoccupation with history has, to be sure, produced impressive results. In fact, today it is difficult to imagine a study of New Testament Christology which is not influenced by this historical analysis of early Christians' conceptions of Christ and their antecedents. Nevertheless, the time is at hand to take up again what was set aside—an explicitly theological approach to New Testament Christology, one which will be informed by the history of ideas but which will deliberately pursue Christology as a theological discipline. It is doubtful whether the study of New Testament Christology can be renewed in any other way. This essay intends to illumine and substantiate this claim by considering briefly the nature of Christology, then by reviewing the turn to history and its consequences for the study of New Testament Christology, and finally by sketching elements of an alternative.

On the Nature of Christology

Because this essay discusses the renewal of a discipline by recovering its true subject matter, what will be said here about the nature of Christology should be more a reminder than something wholly new. What might be new is that it is being said in just this way, and that it is being applied to the study of Christology in the New Testament.[1]

---

1. The fact that 'New Testament Christology' is used here in the sense of

From Jesus to John

'Christology' is a comprehensive term for the statement of the identity and significance of Jesus. Although the vast preponderance of such statements occur in Christian contexts, this phenomenological definition recognizes that christological statements are implied also whenever Jesus' identity and significance are expressed, be it 'religious genius' or avatar.[1] It is, however, with Christian discourse that this essay is concerned. Among Christians, the scope of Christology has, from the start, been wider than 'the man Jesus' because neither his identity nor his significance could be stated by speaking of him alone, as an isolate. 'Jesus' is really an abbreviation for the person who is the centre of an event whose boundaries are not self-evident (see below)— unless one is prepared to deny that to a person belongs one's appropriation of a heritage on the one hand and one's relationships on the other. What needs clarification, in this context, is the rationale of christological statements about this event, the 'rules of the game'. In view here is the formal structure of Christology, its 'grammar' or perhaps better, the syntax of the signification of Jesus for Christian theology.

'Significance' is intelligible only in relation to something or someone.

'Christology in the New Testament' is a matter of style and nuance; it refers to Christology as the subject matter of a particular body of material. In no way does this usage imply that there is a single Christology in the New Testament.

1.   The identity and significance of Jesus can, of course, be expressed in non-christological ways, as in an attempt to identify and assess his impact on western culture, and through it on the modern world. That would be an historical judgment, comparable to judgments about Moses or Mohammed. A statement of Jesus' identity and significance becomes christological when that significance explicates his religious meaning. Whoever affirms the religious significance of Jesus—a first order statement—implies a christological statement (a second order statement). Schillebeeckx introduces the distinction between first and second order statements in order to account for the inevitability of Christology. On this basis, 'living contact' with Jesus 'was experienced as God-given salvation', which in turn produced reflection on the experience, which yielded 'the creedal affirmation: God himself...has acted decisively in Jesus' (a first order statement); this produces a second order statement designed to explicate the first by focusing on his identity. This whole discussion, however, occurs in a context in which Schillebeeckx wants to explain the movement from a '*theology* of Jesus of Nazareth' to Christology. By the former he means 'reflection upon what Jesus himself had to say'. However, these are two quite different moves, because reflection on Jesus' message is not the same as reflection on a first-order statement grounded in the experience of salvation (E. Schillebeeckx, *Jesus* [New York: Seabury, 1979], pp. 545-50).

Accordingly, the subject matter of Christology is really the syntax of relationships or correlations. In developed Christology this structure of signification is expressed in relation to God (the theological correlation proper), the created order (the cosmological correlation) and humanity (the anthropological correlation);[1] each of these impinges on the others whether or not this impingement is made explicit. Consequently, from statements about God or world or humanity one can infer the appropriate christological correlates, and vice versa.

Of these correlations, two have not received adequate attention—the cosmological and the theological. Nils A. Dahl has rightly observed that the understanding of God has been the neglected factor in the study of New Testament theology as a whole.[2] This is particularly true of the study of New Testament Christology, even though every statement about Christ implicates God, beginning with the designation of Jesus as the anointed. This neglect of the theological correlate has constricted Christology and skewed Christianity as a whole, for it is not enough to say with Melanchthon that 'to know Christ is to know his benefits'.[3] The neglect of the cosmological correlate is even more striking, despite the current interest in the use of wisdom traditions and themes in the New Testament—an interest which thus far has generally remained on the historical plane.

The correlation which receives most attention concerns anthropology—the human condition and the salvific alternative brought (or brought about) by (or through) Jesus. In this connection three observations are called for.

(a) There would be no Christology if there were no soteriology because it is what Christians claim about Jesus as the bringer or effecter of salvation that generates the question of his identity. To oversimplify: soteriology makes Christology necessary; Christology

1. Current sensibility having outlawed the use of 'man' in English theological discourse, 'humanity' must serve as a surrogate, despite its intrinsic inability to function as a real equivalent.

2. N.A. Dahl, 'The Neglected Factor in New Testament Theology', *Reflection* 73, 1 (Yale Divinity School, Nov. 1975), pp. 5-8.

3. In this connection, one should ponder Jean Milet's *God or Christ? The Excesses of Christocentricity* (New York: Crossroad, 1981). He contends that although Christianity is constitutively bi-polar (God *and* Christ), the modern difficulty of thinking cogently about God has produced such a one-sided preoccupation with Christ that virtually one religion has been substituted for another—a religion with a one-sided emphasis on redemption.

makes soteriology possible. To paraphrase: Jesus' significance must be
grounded adequately in his identity. At the same time, Christology is
not reducible to soteriology because, at least in the classical Christian
tradition, Christ is always more than saviour.[1] Even the Gospel
according to John, in which the work of Christ is to manifest his
identity, knows this, for its Christ is the incarnate logos 'through
whom all things were made'.

(b) Just as a grammar allows all sorts of things to be thought, said
or written, so the grammar of Christology permits a variety of things
to be expressed concerning Jesus' identity and significance. The formal
structure is constant,[2] but the material content can vary. Further, each
of these material contents has its own integrity within its linguistic
field. Thus, if the human condition is viewed as bondage, Christ is the
liberator and soteriology will be expressed in the idiom of liberation.
Christology will then show what there is about Christ that makes it
possible for liberation to occur through him. Or, if Christ is hailed as
the great teacher, the human condition will be construed as ignorance
or illusion, so that salvation will be a matter of learning the truth.
Moreover, one of the ways that Christology develops nuance and sub-
tlety is by asserting new mutations of categories. Thus one can speak
of ignorance as bondage, and so construe Christ as the liberator from
unknowing. What must not be overlooked is this—because
Christology and anthropology are always correlates, one cannot agree
with Herbert Braun's claim that anthropology is the constant but
Christology is the variable.[3] A changed Christology entails a changed
anthropology as well.

Being aware of the correlational aspect of Christology allows one to
see the high degree of theological sophistication of many New

1.   It should not be overlooked that the formula, 'Creator, Redeemer and
Sustainer', which is now being substituted, in some Anglo-Saxon quarters, for
'Father, Son and Holy Spirit' not only replaces a trinity of persons with a triadic
functionalism but also constricts the role of the second person to redemption—a
move which lacks clear warrant in the New Testament.

2.   To speak of the constancy of grammar vis-à-vis variable formulations is not
yet to imply that grammar is static; to the contrary, that grammars have histories also
suggests that the 'grammar' of christological discourse too undergoes change (not
the same as the history of Christology, the history of formulations). The matter
deserves exploration, which cannot be undertaken here, however.

3.   H. Braun, 'The Meaning of New Testament Christology', *JTC* 5 (1968),
pp. 89-127.

Testament passages, as in Paul's 'If anyone is in Christ one is a new creation'. Understanding this christologically entails delineating the anthropology-soteriology of 'new creation' (including what is implied about 'old creation') as well as that of being 'in Christ' (including being 'outside Christ'); then one can analyze the effect of juxtaposing these two expressions. Naturally, one cannot recover the steps in Paul's reasoning by which he produced this remarkable statement. That would be only of historical or psychological interest anyway. What one can do is to expose the logic, the grammar, of what his text says, and thereby make its tacit meaning explicit.

(c) Christological correlations tend to obey the law of parsimony. That is, generally speaking, Christology and soteriology-anthropology are not wasted on each other, because the understanding of Jesus' identity and significance should not exceed what is required to resolve the human dilemma. A superficial view of sin requires only a superficial view of salvation, just as a superficial view of Jesus cannot deal with a profound view of sin. This implies, further, that unless a tragic view of sin is correlated with a radical view of salvation grounded in a strong Christology, the human dilemma will be too deep to be dealt with decisively by Christ.

This principle can be applied fruitfully to three quite different Christologies in the New Testament. Over against the fear of the Colossian Christians that the *stoicheia* must be placated even by Christians, the author of the Epistle to the Colossians insists that there is no dimension of the human condition which has not already been dealt with decisively in the event of Christ. Consequently, he explicates a christological hymn in such a way as to show that believers do not live in a world whose hostility outruns Christ's capacity to deliver them. When, however, one reads Matthew in light of this principle, a basic question emerges—is Matthew an exception to the rule, or does it actually lack an integrated Christology, since its view of the human dilemma does not really require all the Christology which the text contains? The virgin birth, for instance, really adds nothing to the identity and significance of Jesus which is required if the human dilemma is centred on the need to acquire the rectitude necessary to enter the kingdom. Again, important light is cast on the vexing problem of Paul's apparent non-use of Jesus' teachings—except in paraenesis—or of his deeds. Given Paul's view of the human predicament as bondage to powers like sin and death, what could be gained by quoting Jesus or by appealing to his precedent, even if thematically appropriate logia and stories had come to the apostle's attention? Where the human condition is bondage, there one needs emancipation, not a teacher or a theologian to explain it or the example of a free man (especially one whose deeds of freedom were followed by his execution!). Furthermore, one may also ask whether the Matthean construal of Jesus would be able to deal salvifically with the Pauline construal of the human condition—especially if the Matthean Jesus is the bringer but not the effecter of salvation. In short, had the syntax of Christology been kept in mind, New Testament study would have been spared a great deal of misplaced worry about Paul's disinterest in Jesus' words and deeds—which is not at all to be confused with an alleged disinterest in Jesus.[1]

Having reminded ourselves, in a rather terse and formal way, of the nature of Christology, of its syntax, the significance of turning away from Christology to history can come into view more perceptively.

From New Testament Christology to the History of Christology in Early Christianity

If the study of New Testament Christology is to become explicitly christological, it must come to terms with a legacy which, apart from the Bultmannian tradition, has been dominated by historical questions. Then it can be free to find its own way. To understand this preoccupation with history, no one is more useful than William Wrede, who insisted that the study of New Testament theology (and hence of Christology as well) must become a purely descriptive, historical enterprise, 'totally indifferent to all dogmatic and systematic theology'.[2]

Wrede called for a turn away from presenting New Testament theology as a compendium of doctrines. The real subject matter was to be '*what was believed, thought, taught, hoped, required and striven*

---

1. These terse, and perhaps cryptic, formulations beg for elaboration and substantiation, which cannot be provided here. That will be provided by my forthcoming book, *Jesus in New Testament Christology*.

2. W. Wrede's essay, published in 1897, has become available in English only recently in *The Nature of New Testament Theology* (trans. and ed. R. Morgan; Naperville, IL: Allenson; London: SCM Press, 1973), p. 69. Morgan's own extensive introduction, which also deals with Schlatter's essay on the same theme, merits careful reading.

for in the earliest period of Christianity, not what certain writings say about faith, doctrine, hope, etc'.[1] The texts were not to be analyzed theologically but used as sources of information in order to describe major types of piety. These, in turn, were to be seen in organic relation to their antecedents in antiquity, on the one hand, and to their subsequent developments in Christianity on the other. 'How the systematic theologian gets on with the results—that is his own affair'.[2] What Wrede called for at the end of the nineteenth century did, to a remarkable degree, come about in the twentieth.

Wrede saw that for the task of reconstructing early Christian religion the New Testament alone was inadequate; all early Christian literature must be consulted. Moreover, the New Testament had to be disassembled so that their component parts or sources, such as Q, also could be assigned their proper place into a sequence that was historical. Subsequently, certain texts themselves were disassembled so that their component parts or sources, such as Q, also could be assigned their proper place in a comprehensive, chronologically ordered history of early Christian sources. Only then could the history of early Christianity, including its theology, be written properly. Non-Christian materials were used intensively not only to illumine the context of early Christianity (and its Christology), but to explain it. With regard to Christology, Wrede's programme was carried out by Bousset's magisterial *Kyrios Christos*,[3] whose sub-title shows the relation to Wrede's programme: 'A History of the Belief in Christ from the Beginning of Christianity to Irenaeus'. Neither the legitimacy nor the importance of this enterprise is in question here, whatever one must say about Bousset's conclusions. It is as valid, and as important, to reconstruct the history of early Christian Christology as it is to reconstruct the history of early Christianity or the social structure of early Christian communities.[4] The point, rather, is that the history of early Christian

1. Wrede, *Nature of New Testament Theology*, pp. 84-85 (his italics).

2. Wrede, *Nature of New Testament Theology*, p. 69.

3. W. Bousset, *Kyrios Christos* (Nashville: Abingdon Press, 1970; orig. German, 1913).

4. This essay's contention that the study of New Testament Christology should become avowedly theological in no way entails a repudiation of historical reconstruction or of sociological reconstruction and analysis, which I have defended elsewhere. To the contrary, my 'On the Ethos of the Early Christians', *JAAR* 42 (1974), pp. 435-52 (= 'Das Ethos der frühen Christen', in W.A. Meeks, (ed.), *Zur Soziologie des Urchristentums* [Munich: Chr. Kaiser Verlag, 1979, pp. 13-36) is a

Christology should not be called New Testament Christology because (a) in such a move the New Testament has in fact disappeared into early Christian literature, (b) the problem for Christology created by the pursuit of the historical task cannot be solved by continued historical inquiry, (c) Christology has been abandoned for something else—the history of titles. Each of these results merits further comment.

a. Replacing the New Testament with 'early Christian literature' has consequences—precisely for historiography—which are as serious as they are subtle. No one will deny that all texts must be treated alike, that there is no privileged status for canonical texts, when one is looking for information, or 'facts', about the past; nor will anyone argue that non-canonical texts are of inferior value for historical inquiry because they are not part of scripture. However, problems arise when this stance becomes more than a procedural principle for carrying out a particular task. Not only is the category 'early Christian literature' an anachronism which has become historically significant only recently and only in the scholarly guild, but relying on it alone obscures precisely the phenomenon being studied, namely, that some of this literature was regularly and increasingly shaping early Christianity, and its Christology, by being used repeatedly as scripture on the way to becoming canon. In fact, were it not for this emerging canon and the results of its complex interaction with the developing church, the rest of the literary products of early Christianity would be of but marginal interest and of even less significance as footnotes to the religious history of antiquity.[1]

Moreover, to excavate the Christology of Q or of the Johannine signs source is surely historically valid and useful, but to treat these as if they were more than momentary efforts which were absorbed into texts which *did* have a future is to skew historical understanding at the

programmatic call for New Testament scholarship to attend to the social realities which shaped early Christianity and which were affected by it. Likewise, over against a tendency on the part of some literary criticism to be a-historical if not plainly anti-historical, I defended the necessity of historical work in 'Will the Historical-Critical Method Survive? Some Observations', in R.A. Spencer (ed.), *Orientation by Disorientation* (Festschrift W.A. Beardslee; Pittsburgh: Pickwick Press, 1980), pp. 115-27. In *The Bible in the Pulpit* (Nashville: Abingdon Press, 1978), I sought to show how the historical-critical method can become fruitful for preaching.

1. For a more extended discussion of this point, see my 'Is the New Testament a Field of Study? or, from Outler to Overbeck and Back', *The Second Century* 1 (1981), pp. 19-35.

outset. Wrede himself insisted that the historian must distinguish what was influential from what was of but passing importance. In other words, sound historiography itself requires that due attention be given to the Christology of texts which were on the way toward becoming canonical. Otherwise, what will be reconstructed is not the history of Christology that was but something else—the history that might have been.

b. The turn to history has, unexpectedly for the most part, called into question the legitimacy of Christology itself because the key historical question became ever more difficult to answer historically, namely, why did these christological materials come to be used of Jesus, a Jesus who was reconstructed historically by separating him from just this early Christology? When Boers reviewed the English translation of Bousset, he formulated the issue so well that he deserves to be quoted fully:

> The fundamental problem of a christology of the New Testament as posed by *Kyrios Christos*...was that the view of Jesus found in the New Testament was not historically true of Jesus himself. This undercuts the basic assumption on which the christology of the New Testament depends, namely, that it is an expression of the truth about the historical Jesus. Thus New Testament christology is confronted by an irresolvable dilemma: to recognize that christology is a composite product of the early Christian communities and not the truth about the historical Jesus is the dissolution of christology itself, but to justify a christology by attempting to confirm that its claims about Jesus are somehow valid is possible only at the expense of not recognizing the early communities as their true authors. New Testament christology since *Kyrios Christos* has been a constant struggle with, and clarification of, this dilemma, whether in conscious recognition of Bousset or not.[1]

C.F.D. Moule, however, takes note of Boers and argues exactly the opposite, contending that 'Jesus was, from the beginning, such a one as appropriately to be described in the ways in which, sooner or later, he did come to be described in the New Testament period'.[2] For Moule, the later Christologies represent 'various stages in the development of perception, not the accretion of 'any alien factors that were not there from the beginning'. Such an accretion would have been an evolution

1. H. Boers, 'Jesus and the Christian Faith: New Testament Christology since Bousset's *Kyrios Christos*', *JBL* 89 (1970), p. 452.

2. C.F.D. Moule, *The Origin of Christology* (Cambridge: Cambridge University Press, 1977), pp. 2-3 (his italics).

of Christology; development, on the other hand, is an organic unfolding, like the transition from bud to flower. The statement of Christology, therefore, did not take the church farther from the fact of Jesus but into it more deeply. Just as Boers' historically couched contention requires critical assessment from the standpoint of Christology, so Moule's theological assertion requires historical confirmation. Neither can be undertaken in this context, however.

It suffices to point out that the unwanted outcome of concentrating on origins is that the historical link between Jesus and Christology has grown weaker rather than stronger. The clearer this result became, or threatened to become, the more vigorously the historical question was pursued, either by attempting to show that Jesus did use certain christological titles of himself, or that what they express agrees with his Christology which was implicit in his sense of identity and authority expressed in his use of 'abba' and 'amen' respectively. The more relentlessly such efforts were pursued, the more difficult it actually became to show that Jesus had used *any* title for himself, or why the early church acknowledged his sense of authority by developing precisely these Christologies. Indeed, the one title with which Jesus might have been comfortable—'prophet'—had no future except in certain strands of Jewish Christianity—but they are not represented in the New Testament.[1] In a word, if the legitimacy of Christology depends on establishing historically the continuity between the historically reconstructed Jesus and the Christology of the church, then the turn to history alone has not only made suspect all Christology which goes beyond that which was in the mind of Jesus but continued historical work is unable to resolve the dilemma.

(c) The consequences of turning to history are most evident in the preoccupation with christological titles. Indeed, it is often assumed that New Testament Christology is a matter of history of titles. Probably no other factor has contributed more to the current aridity of the discipline than this fascination with the palaeontology of christological titles. To reconstruct the history of titles as if this were the study of Christology

1.   According to John Knox, early Christian non-use of 'prophet' for Jesus reflects the fact that this title had been appropriated by the disciples of John the Baptist. ' "The Prophet" in the New Testament Christology', in R.A. Norris (ed.), *Lux in Lumine* (Festschrift N. Pittenger; New York: Seabury, 1966), pp. 22-24. It is more likely, however, that the major strands of early Christianity found 'prophet' incapable of embracing the soteriological correlates which they wanted to express.

is like trying to understand the windows of Chartres cathedral by studying the history of coloured glass. In fact, concentration on titles finally makes the Christologies of the New Testament unintelligible as Christologies, and insignificant theologically. Renewing the discipline of New Testament Christology requires, therefore, liberating it from the tyranny of titles—though obviously they cannot be ignored. Three considerations, at least, warrant this claim.

To begin with, title-dominated study of New Testament Christology reflects an inadequate view of language, because it assumes that meaning resides in words like 'Lord'. Just as this assumption misled Vincent Taylor when he wrote that 'the question, who Jesus is, is approached best by considering how men named Him, for it is by His names that He is revealed and known',[1] so an alternative pointed James Barr in the right direction when he declared that 'it is in sentences that real theological thinking is done'.[2] Furthermore, where titles dominate the scene, the difference between a word and a concept is blurred. A word is identical with a concept only if it is a technical term which has no synonyms. Barr is essentially correct, as Friedrich more or less concedes,[3] when he complains that because Kittel's Dictionary has not thought out this difference, its writers sometimes talk about concepts when they should be discussing words.[4] This confusion can be found also in Hahn's influential monograph,[5] which gave a new legitimacy to this approach, despite the searching criticism pressed by Vielhauer.[6]

Next, concentrating on titles actually hampers the effort to

---

1. V. Taylor, *The Names of Jesus* (London: Macmillan, 1953), p. 1.

2. J. Barr, *The Semantics of Biblical Language* (Oxford: Oxford University Press, 1961), p. 234.

3. G. Friedrich, ' "Begriffsgeschichtliche" Untersuchungen im Theologisches Wörterbuch zum Neuen Testament', *Archiv für Begriffsgeschichte* 20 (1976), pp. 151-77. Friedrich, under whose leadership Kittel's project was completed, also defends the dictionary against Barr's criticism by noting that Kittel followed L. Weisgerber (1927) who contended that word and concept are interrelated. Friedrich's views on the need for a New Testament concept-lexicon are found in 'Das bisher noch fehlende Begriffslexikon zum Neuen Testament', *NTS* 19 (1972/73), pp. 127-52.

4. Barr, *Semantics*, p. 209.

5. F. Hahn, *The Titles of Jesus in Christology* (Cleveland: World Publishing, 1969), especially the chapter on 'Christ'.

6. P. Vielhauer, 'Ein Weg zur neutestamentliche Christologie?' *EvT* 25 (1965), pp. 24-72; 'Zur Frage der christologischen Hoheitstitel', *TLZ* 90 (1965), pp. 569-88.

understand Christology in the New Testament texts. This can be seen in the following five considerations. (1) Concentration on titles cannot deal adequately with christologically important passages in which no title appears, whether they be narratives or sayings in the Gospels or discursive arguments in the Epistles. The Gospels often refer simply to 'Jesus' just as the Epistles use 'Christ' as a proper name; in Matthew the Jesus-Moses theme never gets expressed in a title. So strong has been the influence of titles, however, that frequently scholars have supplied them as if the creators of the text had forgotten to include them. For instance, the concluding scene in Matthew, highly important for the Christology of this book, does not mention any title but is content to mention only 'Jesus'; yet some scholars have provided the 'missing' title in order to read the story in terms of the Danielic 'Son of Man',[1] others in terms of 'Son of God'.[2] In the case of the miracle stories, a 'title' has been introduced which never appears in the New Testament at all—*theios anēr*.[3]

(2) The title-dominated approach does not, and perhaps cannot, deal adequately with the plurality of titles in a given text. Just as the Christology of no major New Testament book coincides with a single title, so it is not the aggregate of titles either. Moreover, the texts show neither embarrassment over the many titles,[4] nor concern to do what their modern interpreters find necessary—instruct the reader about the relation of one title to another.[5]

(3) More important, concentrating on titles can lead one to miss the Christology which is in the text. For example, because Paul uses

1. See, e.g., J.P. Meier, 'Salvation History in Matthew: In Search of a Starting Point', *CBQ* 37 (1975), pp. 210-12.

2. So J.D. Kingsbury, 'The Composition and Christology of Mt. 28.16-20', *JBL* 93 (1974), pp. 573-84.

3. Although the phrase *theios anēr* is absent from the New Testament, its use in recent scholarship is unclear; sometimes it is used virtually as a title, at other times as a category (like 'hero'), a motif, an image or a concept. For an assessment of its role, see J.D. Kingsbury, 'The "Divine Man" as the Key to Mark's Christology: The End of an Era?', *Int* 35 (1981), pp. 243-57. Kingsbury calls it a concept.

4. M. Hengel observed, 'The multiplicity of christological titles does not mean a multiplicity of exclusive 'christologies' but an accumulative glorification of Jesus'. 'Christology and New Testament Chronology', in *Between Jesus and Paul* (London: SCM Press; Philadelphia: Fortress Press, 1983), p. 41.

5. See, e.g., J.D. Kingsbury, *Matthew: Structure, Christology, Kingdom* (Philadelphia: Fortress Press, 1975), ch. 2.

'Christ' virtually as a proper name (except for Rom. 9.4), neither the etymology of *Christos* nor the history of pre-Christian messianic hopes and messianic claimants is relevant for his construal of Jesus. Nothing the Apostle says about the identity and significance of Jesus for the revelation of God's righteousness depends on a christological title. In fact, concentrating on titles does not lead one into Paul's Christology but right past it.

(4) Titular Christology tends to see but half of the christological hermeneutic—that half in which titles are supposed to do the interpreting, namely, of the person and event called 'Jesus'. This is rather odd, since the pre-Christian history of the titles shows that none of them (except 'prophet') really fit Jesus. It is not surprising that scholarship has been unable to show that he applied them to himself. Consequently, the other half of the christological hermeneutic needs to be brought into view—that the Jesus-event interprets the titles. This is obvious in John (e.g. 7.40-43), but it is no less true elsewhere as well (e.g. Mk 9.30-32), but the customary focus on titles will not disclose it. Interestingly enough, the point of this paragraph is tacitly acknowledged by all those treatments of the material which contend that Jesus, in applying titles to himself, simultaneously reinterpreted, 'spiritualized' or transformed them.

(5) In title-dominated study of New Testament Christology, the identity and significance of Jesus in relation to the Old Testament is objectified and concentrated in a way that short-changes the truly significant christological issues. Title-dominated Christology has nothing to contribute, for example, to understanding Paul's dictum that 'Christ is the *telos* of the law' (Rom. 10.4), however *telos* be understood. The author of Hebrews understands this point intuitively, for he not only allows the Jesus-event to reinterpret the title 'priest', but his understanding of why the earthly cultus is now obsolete does not turn on the titles used (Heb. 10.1-10). In fact, it is hard to see what the title approach to New Testament Christology can contribute to the clarification of the complex and important, though widely neglected, issues epitomized by the rubric, 'Christ and the Old Testament'.

The third reason why the study of New Testament Christology must be liberated from the tyranny of titles should now be clear: it bypasses Christology itself, because it does not respect either its formal grammar or its material contents (the correlations). Instead, it deals with matters pertaining to Christology in a piecemeal way. In light of the nature of

Christology, as outlined above, concentrating on titles tells us little that we need to know in order to understand the Christologies in the New Testament, and helps us even less to think christologically. An alternative is needed, and to that I now turn.

The Way Ahead

First of all, a more adequate approach will concentrate on its proper subject matter by respecting the grammar of christological discourse. To do so is not to introduce the old loci system because what will be sought is not a set of doctrines but a systemic grasp of the way the correlates of Christ and God, world, and the human condition are expressed or implied. Nor does an explicitly christological approach require that historical and philogical questions be abandoned; what is required is that Christology is not confused with historical reconstruction of the history of ideas but is free to be what it claims to be— Christology. Otherwise the study of New Testament Christology will continue under the illusion that the history of ideas pertaining to Christology *is* Christology.[1] Attending to the correlates of Christology is, moreover, particularly appropriate to the New Testament because this literature consistently expresses the identity and significance of Jesus in relation to something else—doxology, paraenesis, cult narrative, etc. There are no sections of the New Testament devoted to Christology as a discrete topic in its own right. Attending to the syntax of the signification of Jesus is therefore not an attempt to impose an alien structure on the texts but a way of ordering the relational character of Christology as it appears in the New Testament.

In the second place, the study of Christology in the New Testament should be just that—Christology as it appears, or is implied, in the New Testament. It is the Christology of this particular corpus of texts that must remain central. This deliberate concentration on these texts has a number of consequences, three of which deserve to be noted here.

First, a focus on texts, or in the case of Paul (and to some extent of John as well) a corpus of texts, keeps in view the fragmentary character of Christology in the New Testament.[2] Because the Christology of

---

1. See also E. Güttgemanns, *Der leidende Apostel und sein Herr* (FRLANT, 90; Göttingen: Vandenhoeck & Ruprecht, 1966), pp. 46, 196 for similar observations.
2. E. Käsemann called attention to the fragmentariness of the material in 'The Problem of a New Testament Theology', *NTS* 19 (1973), pp. 241-43.

a text, or corpus of texts, cannot be equated with the Christology of the writer, one should speak of the Christology of persons only in carefully circumscribed contexts. Given the occasional character of the New Testament texts, as well as their several genres and functions, a text's Christology is but a partial expression of what the writer thought about Jesus' identity and significance. Just as there is no reason to think that any Evangelist wrote into his Gospel everything he knew about Jesus, so there is no reason to think that he expressed completely his construal of Jesus' identity and significance in the particular narrative that now bears his name. So too, there is no adequate reason to equate the Christology of a text or of its sources with the Christology of a particular group. To assume that the Christology of Q or John or the Pastoral Epistles is a profile of the Christology of distinct communities, and then to assume that each community had but this one Christology so that one can use discrete Christologies to reconstruct diverse groups is surely an unwarranted procedure. What is characteristic of communities is their capacity to affirm multiple and diverse Christologies simultaneously. It is more likely that various Christian communities had different configurations of Christologies. In any case, the point is that the Christology of individual authors and of communities is largely hidden because what we have is but a set of fragments which cannot be assumed to be representative cross-sections of how the identity and significance of Jesus were construed. Concentrating on the Christology of New Testament texts is an essential way of remembering how much is unknown and remains unknowable.

Secondly, a focus on texts will deal with the text or corpus of texts as they actually exist and, so far as possible, with what they were designed to do. Historical questions customarily treated in introductions, including those of genre, are indeed important because the form and function for which the text was created affected what the writer emphasized and neglected. The current use of literary, discourse and rhetorical analyses accords with this insistence that what must remain in focus is the thought-structure and argument of the text as we have it. Respect for genre entails exploring, for instance, the ways in which narrative creates both possibilities and constraints which are different from argumentative discourses or the vision reports of apocalypses.[1] For example, the fact that in John the

---

1. For a thought-provoking exploration of narrative Christology, see M. Eugene Boring, 'The Christology of Mark: Hermeneutical Issues for Systematic Theology',

protagonist of the story articulates in the first person singular elements of the author's Christology (the 'I am...' form) which a discourse would express in the third person singular ('he is...') poses an interesting question for Johannine Christology: what is the significance of the fact that the disciples do not confess that Jesus is the light, the door, etc. but that instead Jesus proclaims himself in these terms? That is, what is the difference for Christology between Christian predication and Christ's own self-proclamation? That is probably a more fruitful question for understanding John's Christology than asking where the *Ego-eimi* sayings come from. In a word, the central questions to be pursued and answered are: what is the overall construal of Jesus' identity and significance in the text? What is the structure of this Christology and to what extent are the logical correlates expressed? What degree of coherence and completeness does this Christology have? It is the structure and dynamic of a given Christology that should become clear. What is in view here comports with E.P. Sanders' call for a systemic grasp of Paul's theology.[1] A systemic approach will make it clear that a text's Christology is not simply the sum of its parts but a construal of Jesus which must be seen as a whole.

Thirdly, concentrating on the Christology of existing texts in a systemic way makes it manifest that the decisive questions are not the origin of Christology or of particular Christologies. Concretely, it keeps in focus the true subject matter—the construal of Jesus' identity and significance—precisely because inquiry is not deflected into the historical question of whether Jesus' self-interpretation is its origin. Jesus' own construal of his identity and significance is indeed a valid historical question in its own right. Christology, however, brings to expression the Christian construal of Jesus as the focal point of a network of theological correlations. Because the religious and theological significance of Jesus emerges only when one reflects on this event in relation to God, the world and the human condition and its resolution, it is of but secondary importance whether this understanding was derived from Jesus himself (derivation must not be confused with consonance). Neither the effort to understand a Christology, nor to discern its

Sem 30 (1984), pp. 125-53 (136-45).
1. See E.P. Sanders, 'Patterns of Religion in Paul and Rabbinic Judaism: A Holistic Method of Comparison', *HTR* 66 (1973), pp. 445-78; *Paul and Palestinian Judaism* (Philadelphia: Fortress Press; London: SCM Press, 1977), pp. 12-18.

capacity, nor to assess its validity depends on a historian's success in tracing it to the mind of Jesus. Nor, conversely, may a Christology be disallowed because it did not occur to Jesus to avow it. In other words, the Christology of the critically reconstructed historical Jesus is not part of the Christology of the New Testament.[1] The historical relation between Jesus' self-interpretation and the early Christian interpretations of Jesus is another matter.

The New Testament texts have their own ways of making the Jesus-event central to their Christologies, and studying these texts should identify and illumine those ways. Here too, one must guard against introducing modern categories which obscure one's vision and skew the agenda. In this regard, the term 'earthly Jesus' is almost as alien to the texts as 'historical Jesus'. Paul has been falsely accused of having no interest in Jesus, allegedly being preoccupied with the exalted Christ, because his modern interpreters assumed that they already knew what an interest in Jesus would, and should, look like, and so they did not ask sufficiently how Paul himself viewed the matter. What a text includes in the word 'Jesus' (or in the phrase 'Jesus Christ') is exactly what the study of the New Testament Christology should reveal, just as it should clarify why the text does not draw our kind of line between an 'earthly Jesus' and some other. (To insist on this is not to imply that the texts made no distinctions within the 'Jesus event' at all; Rom. 1.3-4 is but one way in which distinctions were made.) Even the current emphasis on the identity of the earthly Jesus and the exalted Christ is not really appropriate for texts which never separated them to begin with. In other words, the subject matter of New Testament Christology can be said to have two poles; the one is 'Jesus', and the other concerns how the various correlations between Jesus and God, the world and the human condition affect the content of this 'Jesus'. The study of New Testament Christology should expose why this polarity exists and how it works itself out in the texts.

Renewing the study of New Testament Christology entails not only

---

1.   A clear instance of a well-known work based on exactly the opposite point of view is Joachim Jeremias, *New Testament Theology* (New York: Charles Scribner's Sons, 1971); volume 1 of this unfinished work bears the title 'The Proclamation of Jesus'. Even if one were to grant that Jeremias has reconstructed accurately the teachings of Jesus as well as Jesus' understanding of his mission, that reconstruction is precisely *not* part of the theology (and hence of the Christology) of the New Testament.

attending to the grammar of Christology and a deliberate focus on the New Testament texts, but also, in the third place, a somewhat different approach to the plurality and diversity of the Christologies in the canon. What is in view here does not 'solve' the problem of diversity by shifting into the historical mode which, as in the creation of trajectories, for example, turns generic similarities into genetic relationships; nor does it proceed theologically in order to unify the several Christologies by integrating them into a common conceptual structure as in Cullmann's Heilsgeschichte scheme, or in Herbert Braun's reduction of all Christologies to a single anthropology. Rather, what is envisioned keeps the various Christologies in a focus that is itself christological, and does so in several respects.

First, a systemic analysis indicates that there are two basic types of Christologies in the New Testament; the one works with pre-existence, and the other does not.[1] The possibilities and limitations of each deserve to be analyzed by asking christological questions of each. For example, what sort of anthropology does each entail? What is the range and depth of the human condition which each allows to become visible? What are the dangers of each type? Which type is more amenable to an adequate view of the relation between Jesus and the Old Testament? Is there any correlation between a type of Christology and the social identity and location of the people who espouse it? Here too, inquiring who first spoke of Christ's pre-existence is no substitute for trying to understand what doing so entails.

Secondly, a christological approach to the diversity of New Testament Christologies will pursue the consequences of the canon's juxtaposing precisely these Christologies. The incompleteness of these Christologies is not such that each simply complements the other, as in a jigsaw puzzle. Even if the virgin birth can be harmonized with the incarnation, at many other points the tensions are simply too great. What needs attention is the ways in which the diverse Christologies

---

1. The common distinction between two-stage and three-stage Christologies also relies on pre-existence as the key. There are, of course, other ways of classifying New Testament Christologies. For example, one can group them according to the genre in which they are found (doxological materials, terse formulae, narratives, etc.), or according to what they emphasize in the Christ-event (e.g. the character of Jesus' public mission, herald of the Kingdom, death). The advantage of using pre-existence is that it keeps in focus the shape of the event as a whole.

interact with each other. It is ironic that although historical criticism was developed largely to overcome the church's integrative interpretation by emphasizing the particularity of each text in its own historical context, the result of historical work shows in detail how New Testament texts embody a continuum of interpretation, and an interaction of traditions and texts with the communities that used them. Unless one thinks early Christians lived in isolated groups where only one Christology prevailed, one must assume that diverse Christologies interacted with each other almost from the start, even though they do not refer to each other explicitly. The point is that that juxtaposition of diverse Christologies in the canon is not an arbitrary, unfortunate imposition by ecclesiastics but a rather natural outgrowth of what had been occurring for some time. After all, the vexing problem of John and the Synoptics[1] was not created by the canon. To put the matter differently, what is true of each Gospel, where elements of diverse Christologies, logically incommensurate with each other, now interact in the overall construal of Jesus' identity and significance, is true also of the New Testament as a whole. This interaction of existing texts deserves to be explored.[2] Meaning, after all, is not limited to the moment of a text's creation or to the aims of the author. It is generated also by the contexts in which the texts exist and function, including the context of the canon.

Thirdly, a major christological issue posed by the plurality of New Testament Christologies concerns the identity of Jesus—how do we know that it is the same Jesus who is being construed?[3] Paul's accusation that his opponents in Corinth preach 'another Jesus' (2 Cor. 11.4) shows that this question is continuous with the New Testament itself. To ask whether the diverse Christologies construe the same Jesus is to seek criteria for discerning what is constitutive about his identity. At this point, the limits of christological exegesis become evident because the criteria of Jesus' identity cannot be found by exegeting one more New Testament text. Here a sustained conversation with fundamental

1. See the four essays on the subject in D. Moody Smith, *Johannine Christianity* (Columbia, SC: University of South Carolina Press, 1984), pt. 2.
2. Concern for this question is one of the themes in B.S. Childs, *The New Testament as Canon: An Introduction* (Philadelphia: Fortress Press, 1984).
3. In formulating this issue I was stimulated by the programmatic article by R. Knierim, 'The Task of an Old Testament Theology', *HBT* 6 (1984), pp. 25-57.

and systemic theology is required. Without it, New Testament study ceases to be vital and significant.

The renewal of the study of New Testament Christology will be the work of many minds, just as it will require the raising of explicitly christological issues, some of which this essay has identified and formulated, albeit in an abbreviated way.

INDEXES

INDEX OF REFERENCES

OLD TESTAMENT

APOCRYPHA

Cullman, O. 45, 51, 338

Dabeck, P. 229
Dahl, N.A. 38, 40, 60, 132, 134, 168, 323
Daniel, S. 112
Danielou, J. 84
Dauer, A. 264
Davies, G.N. 103, 126
de Boer, M.C. 127, 134, 145
de Boer, P.A.H. 73
de Jonge, M. 7-12, 21-30, 32, 33, 38-52, 55, 56, 60, 61, 63, 64, 80, 82-85, 88, 94-96, 99, 101, 102, 104, 116, 123, 129, 151, 152, 167, 168, 174, 184, 196, 202, 231, 237, 252, 261, 268, 278, 294, 308, 310
de Jonge, H.J. 7, 11, 13, 46, 127, 294
de Zwaan, J. 9
Deissmann, A. 107
Delling, G. 103
Delobel, J. 235, 243
Dibelius, M. 9, 53
Di Lella, A.A. 73
Dirkse, P.A. 108
Dodd, C.H. 95, 107, 124, 253, 254, 256, 258, 259, 261, 264, 265, 312
Dömer, M. 239, 246, 250
Doran, R. 120
Douglas, M. 305, 306
Drury, J. 229
Duling, D.C. 191
Dunn, J.D.G. 11, 103, 104, 105, 106, 130, 131, 132, 138, 141, 142, 150, 152, 153, 156, 157, 158, 159, 161, 162, 167, 168
Dupont-Sommer, A. 91, 121

Eisenman, R.H. 84
Ellis, E.E. 11, 169, 170, 171, 172
Engel, H. 114
Esler, P.F. 249
Evans, C.F. 228

Faber, R. 118
Farris, S. 217
Fee G.D. 155, 169, 171, 172
Ferch, A.J. 73

Fitzer, G. 103
Fitzmyer, J.A. 65-70, 73, 78, 80, 84, 91, 132, 135, 225, 245, 246
Flusser, D. 65, 68, 70
Ford, J.M. 91
Fortna, R.T. 266
Frei, H.W. 38
Friedrich, G. 123, 158, 331
Fuchs, E. 55
Furnish, V.P. 148, 150, 165

Gager, J. 130
Gardner-Smith, P. 253
Gaston, L. 130
Georgi, D. 130
Gibbs, J.M. 191
Godet, F. 170
Goppelt, L. 169
Goulder, M.D. 204, 209, 235
Grässer, E. 232, 233
Grayston, K. 155
Greenfield, J.C. 84, 85
Grillmeier, A. 168
Grob, F. 311, 312, 313
Grundman, W. 151
Grundmann, W. 298, 299
Gunkel, H. 110
Güttgemanns, E. 334

Haberman, J. 163, 169, 171
Hadas, M. 121
Haenchen, E. 277, 289
Hahn, F. 39, 54, 132, 151, 331
Halperin, D.J. 91
Hamm, W. 111
Hanson, A.T. 171
Hare, D.R.A. 206
Harnack, A. 179
Hartman, L.F. 73
Harvey, A.E. 151, 264
Haussleiter 139
Hay, D.M. 105, 141
Hays, R.B. 102, 105, 126, 141
Hebert, A.G. 105
Hengel, M. 69, 91, 95, 96, 149, 159-61, 168, 208, 332
Herman, Z.I. 102
Higgins, A.J.B. 254
Hill, D. 104, 107, 161, 243

JOURNAL FOR THE STUDY OF THE NEW TESTAMENT

Supplement Series